CHINESE
DIMENSIONS

THEIR ROOTS, MINDSET
AND PSYCHE

CHINESE DIMENSIONS

THEIR ROOTS, MINDSET AND PSYCHE

YOW YIT SENG

Pelanduk
Publications

Published by
Pelanduk Publications (M) Sdn Bhd
(Co. No. 113307-W)
12 Jalan SS13/3E
Subang Jaya Industrial Estate
47500 Subang Jaya
Selangor Darul Ehsan, Malaysia

Address all correspondence to
Pelanduk Publications (M) Sdn Bhd
P.O. Box 8265, 46785 Kelana Jaya
Selangor Darul Ehsan, Malaysia
Website: *www.pelanduk.com*
e-mail: *rusaone@tm.net.my*

Perpustakaan Negara Malaysia   Cataloguing-in-Publication Data

Yow, Yit Seng
    Chinese Dimensions: Their roots, Mindset and Pysche / Yow Yit
    Seng.
    Includes index
    ISBN 967-978-927-6
    1. Chinese-Social life and customs. 2. Chinese – Economic
    conditions. 3. Chinese – History. 4. Chinese – Religious life and
    customs. I. Title
    305.8951

Printed and bound in Malaysia.

Foreword

Dr. Geoff Gallop
MLA Premier of Western Australia

IT IS WITH GREAT PLEASURE that I write the foreword to Dr. Yit Seng Yow's book *The Chinese Dimensions: Their Roots, Mindset and Psyche.*

The first Chinese person to arrive in Western Australia was a carpenter called Moon Chow, who arrived in 1829, a few months after the Swan River Colony was first proclaimed. He was unique until the mid 19th Century when Chinese indentured labourers were recruited to alleviate severe farm labour shortages and then in the 1880s free Chinese settlers came to seek their fortune in the goldfields.

In more recent times many Chinese have come to Western Australia as we expanded and deepened our relations with Asia.

At times Chinese Western Australians have experienced prejudice and discrimination but that has not dented their commitment to Western Australia and its future.

Through their energy, enthusiasm and hard work our Chinese community has helped build the thriving, vibrant and multicultural State we live in and enjoy today.

Our State's cultural and linguistic diversity is arguably our most valuable asset, and I am very pleased that Dr. Yow's book adopts a bilingual approach. Language is central to culture. Through this book, the wider community will be able to learn about Chinese language, its importance to and reflection of Chinese culture, and the beauty and intricacies of Chinese culture as a whole.

Our proximity to Asia has helped enrich our State in many ways – it has expanded our economic and cultural horizons and breathed fresh life into our creative processes.

We have benefited in numerous ways from our close ties with China, and I am very pleased that we continue to strengthen this bond through initiatives such as our Sister-State relationship with China's Zhejiang Province.

Dr. Yow has long been a respected member of our State's Chinese community. Active in the Chung Wah Association, Dr. Yow has also published material dealing with the challenges minority group's face in our community. In this context, *The Chinese Dimensions: Their Roots, Mindset and Psyche* plays an important part in educating the wider community about our Chinese community's unique identity and cultural heritage. Through this sort of understanding we can continue to move forward, together, into a positive and productive future.

Dr. Geoff Gallop MLA
PREMIER

Message from Mr. Richard Tan
President, Chung Wah Association
Western Australia

DR. Y.S. YOW WAS ACTIVE in Chung Wah Association 中华会馆. He was the editor of Chung Wah news for several years, when he wrote numerous editorials and articles about the Chinese community in Western Australia. His writings reveal a deep understanding of the Chinese migrants in multi-cultural Australia, in particular their position as a minority group. His considered opinions were well received and respected.

He was also the chairperson of the Chung Wah Chinese community language schools. Through his work in the Western Australian Ethnic School council, Dr. Yow acquired a good appreciation of the teaching of the Chinese language to both Chinese and non-Chinese children in our community.

He has served as our representative in the 'Western Australian Ethnic Community Council' which collectively represents various ethnic groups in Western Australia. In this role, he gained a good insight into the contribution of ethnic communities to the development of Australia.

I understand that Dr. Yow was also the founding chairman of the 'Perth-Nanjing Friendship City' committee, initiated by the City of Perth to foster friendship between the two cities. Chung Wah Association was represented on this committee.

Dr. Yow was the author of the 'Chinese people' for the 'Living in Harmony' seminars, run by the Western Australian Chinese Chamber of Commerce to promote community understanding.

Dr. Yow's latest publication, *The Chinese Dimensions: Their Roots, Mindset, Psyche*, provides useful and valuable information on the Chinese people, their history, culture and mindset. I am confident that it would serve as a valuable source of information for both the Chinese as well as the wider Australian community, in particular the younger generation. On behalf of the Chung Wah Association I would like to congratulate Dr. Yow on yet another milestone achievement in his relentless and illustrious contribution towards the goal of building a truly multicultural Australia.

Richard W.C. Tan JP
President, Chung Wah Association
Western Australia

Message from Mr. Wilson Wu

President, Western Australia Chinese Chamber of Commerce and Industry

I HAVE KNOWN DR. YIT SENG YOW for over ten years. He is a profess-ional who has shown an interest in China, an author in Chinese culture. He is fluent in Chinese (Mandarin) and English and has a good understanding of the intricacies of Chinese thinking and business etiquette.

Dr. Yow has been contributing in many ways to the Western Australian Chinese Chamber of Commerce's numerous activities. He was the author of 'The Chinese People', based on which the Chamber organised seminars, as part of the 'Living in Harmony' program. He also sits on our 'China Desk' committee and assists in promoting trade and investment opportunities between China and Western Australia.

Our Chamber is emerging as a significant 'resource' for Western Australian businesses tapping into China's huge and rapidly growing economy. It is therefore vital that entrepreneurs dealing with China have a good understanding of Chinese culture.

I strongly recommend this book to anyone intending to do business with China or overseas Chinese in this region. I am sure you will find this a most useful and enjoyable journey!

Our heartiest congratulations to Dr. Yow on the successful launch of this book.

Wilson Wu
President, WACCC, Perth

Message from Dr. Eric Tan
A Prominent Ethnic Chinese in Australia

THIS BOOK IS A MOST useful source of information on things Chinese and should be of great interest to those seeking to understand Chinese Culture. It is highly recommended.

Congratulations and all the best.
Cheers, Dr. Eric Tan

Acknowledgement

I WOULD LIKE TO THANK everyone who has encouraged or supported me during the writing of this book. I am grateful to The Hon. Dr. Geoff Gallop, Premier of Western Australia for the Foreword; Mr. Richard Tan, President of Chung Wah Association, Western Australia; Mr. Wilson Wu, President of Western Australian Chinese Chamber of Commerce and Industry, as well as Dr. Eric Tan, a prominent West Australian Chinese, for their messages and encouragement.

I am indebted to the Hon. Tony McRae, the Member of Parliament for Riverton for his help and support, Ms Trinch Quach for the spellings of Vietnamese Chinese surnames, and Mr. Zhao Zhen for the 'coupled poem' [duilian] used as the theme of the book. I would like to express my sincere gratitude to Mr. Edward Chin, Mr. Liu Hua and Mr. A.B. Koh for proof reading some of the chapters; Ms 马碧雯 from Overseas Exchange Association of Guangdong province for proofreading the section on Guangdong. To all of them I say 诚心感谢 'chengxin ganxie' (thank you from the bottom of my heart) for their contributions.

The Australian Post is most gracious for permitting me to reproduce the Chinese zodiac stamps.

I would like to take the opportunity to thank Adam Junid for proofreading some chapters; and my sister Oi Lin for her valuable insights in writing and presentation, in addition to improving my English text. Last but not least my eternal gratitude to the person who in many ways co-contributed to the production of this book, my wife

Soi Har, who painstakingly went through every word, both in Chinese and English. Her critical comments, constructive suggestions and constant support throughout the years are crucial to the success of this book.

Contents

Chapter 9: The Pillars of Destiny: An Application of the Ancient Paradigms 338

Chapter 10: Living in a Continuously Changing World 398

Chapter 11: Conclusion: What About the Future? 442

Introduction

I think if we are to feel at home in the world ... we shall have to admit Asia to equality in our thoughts, not only politically but culturally. What changes this will bring about I do not know, but I am convinced that they will be profound and of the greatest importance.

Bertrand Russell, *History of Western Philosophy*, 1946

WRITTEN MORE THAN HALF a century ago, the foresight and philosophy of Bertrand Russell were indeed remarkable. It was written at a time when European supremacy worldwide was unchallenged and Asians were colonised or poorly understood.

True to the common Chinese saying 'Feng Shui rotates, fortunes go up and down' 风水轮流转 [*fēngshuǐ lúnliú zhuǎn*] (refer to chapter five), the relative political, economic, social and cultural equilibrium have certainly shifted.

Sixty years later, the transformation of the East Asian nations is beyond recognition. Countries in South East Asia have gained independence and emerged to various degrees as successful nations. China has emerged from the shackles of Western and Japanese domination, demonstrating vividly how 'communism' could coexist, or perhaps supplement 'market liberalism', to lead the world as an economic, political and cultural powerhouse of this millennium.

As we begin our new millennium the political and demographic landscapes have been transformed in a most interesting manner. Post war migration from Asian countries to the United States, Canada, United Kingdom, Europe, Australia and New Zealand have contributed to the ethnic diversity. In this new political climate racial tolerance and understanding need to be taken into account. The collective intelligence, strength and resilience of people from all over the world could be galvanised towards Nation building for these nations. Indeed the vigour of successful nations in the new millennium depends to a large extent on their abilities to attract and retain 'quality' people from various backgrounds.

With an impressive proportion of first or second generation migrants, the stage is set to tap into this pool of human and intellectual resources for trade, political or cultural opportunities. This is particularly so when countries such as China and India develop into massive markets, as their economies take off.

To tap these opportunities the need to understand cultural peculiarities becomes increasingly acute. An appreciation of cultural sensitivities promotes harmonious community relations, meaningful dialogues, and facilitates conflict resolution.

In these countries the Asian community is increasing in numbers, complexity and influence. To various degrees they share their hopes and aspirations with the broader community, intertwined with other citizens or residents in the workplace, churches or community associations, and adapt themselves to their adopted homelands.

Amongst the Asians the Chinese are perhaps one of the largest communities. Their background and compositions are complex; they are possibly least understood amongst all ethnic groups.

This book is dedicated to the hundreds of thousands of ethnic Chinese throughout the World, ethnic Chinese citizens or residence who would like to know more about their own heritage. The book serves as a source of information to those, through no fault of their own, were deprived of an environment to know or learn their own language or practice their own culture.

To those who seek to find out what their surname or name means, or where their dialects come from, we seek to deliver the basic background information.

Those who would like to know in simple English terms, common habits, customs, culture, historical perspectives, Chinese zodiac interpretations, philosophy and outlook will find this a valuable resource.

Last but not least the book seeks to serve as a guide for the wider community to understand the ethnic Chinese, either as neighbours, colleagues, church members, team members, classmates, partners or simply as friends. It is also useful for anyone involved in retail business, import or export trade, diplomatic missions, government agencies or departments, as long as ethnic Chinese are involved.

The title of the book *The Chinese dimensions: Their Roots, Mindset, Psyche* is self explanatory. The book seeks to provide a basic understanding of the concepts, often poorly understood in the West. The book adopts a bilingual approach, where the relevant texts are printed in Chinese, with the standard pinyin pronunciation given wherever possible, followed by translation in English.

In Chapter One, 'Crossing the Ocean', we take a general look into the situation pertaining to the ethnic Chinese community, their countries of origin, as well as touch on issues such as ethnic identity, name, religion, cultural heritage, in an attempt to profile a typical ethnic Chinese.

Chapter Two, 'Cultural Roots—Chinese Names' deals with the issue of Chinese naming system. It explains how Chinese names are structured, as well as a list of common surnames in various dialects and spellings. Some of the common names for men and women are also listed, together with their meanings.

Chapter Three 'Cultural Roots—The Chinese Language' looks at the Chinese language, its origin, development, structure, as well as salient features that make it different from any other language in the world. It looks at connections to the 'word radical', and various calligraphic styles. The Chinese pronunciation system, in particular [pinyin] is then reviewed, together with the system of intonation. Issues such as association of words with sounds or meanings, as well as how the language copes with the digital era are also discussed. The pronunciation chart of all possible word sounds in Chinese is provided, with an example of each sound.

Chapter Four, 'Cultural Roots—Land of Origin', deals with commonly spoken Chinese dialects, their distribution and origins. It also looks at the provinces and regions of origin in China where most ethnic Chinese migrated from. Various dialects spoken in Fujian, Guangdong, Hainan and Guangxi are looked into. To help people locate their region of origin, complete lists of administrative municipalities, cities and counties of these provinces are made.

Chapter Five, 'Source of Culture and Mindset—History at Play', gives a brief introduction to five thousand years of Chinese history. It goes through the various dynasties, and provides a list of key personalities (political, cultural, military, etc) over the centuries. The chapter also includes a listing of more than two hundred notable personalities in Chinese history, ranging from emperors to folk heroes. It ends with a brief outline of China's decline, the advent of European domination in the East, important landmarks in recent history, as well as current development.

Chapter Six, 'The Chinese Mindset, Collective Wisdom from Centuries of Publications', deals with thoughts and ideas behind the Chinese psyche, as reflected in Chinese literature. It begins with a list of 365 proverbs or sayings, one for each day of the week. These proverbs reflect cultural values and judgment criteria. It then looks into Chinese literature, in particular quotations or ancient texts pertaining to education, government, military, philosophy, Confucius studies, as well as some of the best known publications over the centuries. The chapter ends with a brief look at poetry, including [duilian], the 'coupled poems'.

Chapter Seven, 'Some Cultural Practice', deals with some aspects of Chinese culture. The first part looks at Taoism and Confucianism, with quotations from 'Dao De Jing' as well as various Confucius texts such as 'the Analects', 'Great Studies' and 'Doctrine of the Mean'. The second part looks into cultural norms such as family terminology, formal salutations and titles, basic social terminology and practices. The chapter also touches on taboos, family values and the position of women. It ends with words of congratulations commonly used by the Chinese.

Chapter Eight, 'In Search of Chinese Psyche—Revisiting Ancient Paradigms', looks at the basic concepts behind Chinese culture, Yin-yang and five determinant elements. These entities are described in simple terms, together with examples in terms of human personalities. The concepts of Celestial stems and Terrestrial branches, unique to Chinese computations and critical to zodiac and other analysis, are dealt with in some detail.

Chapter Nine 'The Pillars of Destiny: An Application of the Paradigms', looks at the Chinese calendar, its zodiac systems. It explains the function of the four pillars of year, month, day and hour individually. A description of each of the Chinese zodiac signs is given, together with modifications from the five determinants. The chapter touches on compatibility, clashes, as well as interaction between Celestial stems and Terrestrial branches. It ends with a look at the 'Pillar of Destiny', its basic concepts and interpretations.

Chapter Ten 'Living in a Continuously Changing World' looks at Yijing (I-Ching). It gives an introduction to the trilogy and formation of the trigrams. A short description of the eight basic trigrams, linking some of the variables is then given. The chapter looks at a few hexagrams in some detail; it then lists the sixty four hexagrams. The chapter ends with a quick look at 'divination', as examples of the applications of this fascinating topic.

We adopt the theme 'Crossing the Oceans … taking roots upon landing' 漂洋过海, 落地生根. It is a translation of two Chinese sayings; it depicts crossing the vast ocean to settle in a new land. In the process however, there is always a need to redefine one's identity, cultural heritage, as well as taking part in the overall Nation Building, based both on professional skills and cultural heritage.

Crossing the Oceans

Above: Australian stamps celebrating the year of the monkey. The issue reflects multiculturalism in practice, respecting the growing numbers of ethnic Chinese since the White Australian Policy. (This material has been reproduced with permission of the Australian Postal Corporation. The original work is held in the National Philatelic Collection).

(Throughout this book the symbols ¯, ´, ˇ, ` are commonly used to designate the four intonations. Refer to chapter three).

CROSSING THE OCEANS [漂洋过海] *piāoyáng-guòhǎi*

The ethnic Chinese originally crossed the oceans from China to settle in Southeast Asia and beyond. In Southeast Asian countries they toiled under Colonial or local rule, invariably contributed to the economic development of these countries. In the process they also laid the foundation of their economic dominance. Many became captains of

1

industries in their host countries. Resistance from local residence was muted, as most of the countries were under colonial rules.

草
草
漂
洋
过
海
无
多
他
问

In countries such as Australia and United States, resistance was much more confrontational and violent. In Australia it led directly to the White Australian policy, eventually ended by the Labour government in 1973.

Independence of Southeast Asian countries brought about new realities. Over a period of time new phases of political, economic and social equilibrium between the ethnic Chinese and the locals were reached. This is a dynamic interaction, the success of which dictates the political and economic well being of countries involved. It is determined not only by the local factors but also the emergence of China as a power house, as well as the influence of ethnic Chinese throughout the world in shaping local policies and opinions.

At the same time ethnic Chinese once again settle in substantial numbers in the North America, United Kingdom, Europe, Australia and New Zealand, most of them coming from Southeast Asia, Taiwan and Hong Kong.

The scenario could be captured by the Chinese characters printed vertically in this page 'Crossing the oceans in simple, unassuming circumstances, not asking many questions' *cǎocǎo piāoyáng guòhǎi wúduōtāwèn*. This is a special form of poetry known as 'coupled poems' [对联] *duìlián* (refer to chapter six)

(The second part of the 'coupled poems' (printed in the next page) states that 'when one has really settled down and taken roots one comes to terms with oneself.' *zhēnzhēn luòdìshēnggēn yǒuwéizìduì*.)

THE ETHNIC CHINESE

As an ethnic group the ethnic Chinese worldwide are highly visible, easily distinguished from Caucasians. They are fast emerging as a respectable group in the fields of academic, business and professional communities. The group is increasingly recognised as useful promoters for trade, cultural and political endeavours with Asia.

真
真
落
地
生
根
有
唯
自
对

Many may wonder who the ethnic Chinese are. Would it be easy to profile them? Where are their countries of origin? What makes them successful or significant even though their numbers are relatively small? How do they play a significant role in a short period when they were virtually non-visible in Australia before the seventies? What is their impact as they seek to position themselves in the fast changing global geopolitical and economic landscape?

How does the local community view them and how would they view themselves in their new homes? How would they integrate into multicultural countries or dissolve into the melting pot?

The Chinese comprise not only the 1.3 billion of Chinese living in China, but also 40 million or so overseas Chinese [华侨] *Huáqiáo*.

The overseas Chinese are more often the human face of ethnic Chinese in the Western world. They are ethnic Chinese who are citizens or residents outside China. They could be migrants from China themselves or are descendants of earlier migrants from China. This is a pool of entrepreneurial, resilient, highly adaptable and skilled work force.

They include people from dominantly Chinese places such as China, Hong Kong and Macau (both reverted to Chinese rule), Taiwan and Singapore. In countries where they are minorities, such as Cambodia, Indonesia, Laos, Malaysia, Myanmar, Pacific islands, the Philippines, Thailand and Vietnam, they are instrumental in the economic development of these countries. In addition, there is also re-migration of ethnic Chinese from one part of the world to another, for example from United Kingdom to the United States or Australia.

ETHNIC IDENTITY

It is crucial to distinguish between nationality and ethnicity. An American Chinese, Australian Chinese, British Chinese, Indonesian Chinese, Malaysian Chinese, Singaporean Chinese, Vietnamese Chinese would be an American, Australian, British, Indonesian, Malaysian, Singaporean, or Vietnamese citizen or resident of Chinese origin. However a Malaysian Chinese migrating to Australia would be statistically classified as a Malaysian but consider himself as ethnic Chinese.

PROFILING THE ETHNIC CHINESE

Contrary to common perception, it is not easy to profile a typical ethnic Chinese. It would undoubtedly be a challenge for any anthropologist as the Ethnic Chinese do not share many identifiable traits. For example:

Country of Origin: Over the centuries migrants from China have settled in South China Sea [南洋] *Nányáng*, where eighty percent of overseas Chinese reside. The picture is further complicated by migrants coming from a third country to resettle in another country.

An ethnic Chinese could come from any country or region. As these are independent countries, the country of origin, other than China, does not imply that the migrants are ethnic Chinese.

Name: Many people could be surprised to find out that ethnic Chinese from countries such as Indonesia or Thailand does not necessarily have a Chinese sounding name. Due to political needs ethnic Chinese have been discouraged from keeping their Chinese names. The issue of Chinese naming system is discussed in the next chapter.

East and Southeast Asia

North Korea

South Korea

China
Laos

Japan

Burma/ Myanmar

Taiwam

HK

The Philippines

Thailand

Vietnam

Malaysia

Brunei

Indonesia

Cambodia

Timor

Singapore

Papua New Guinea

Language: Language is certainly not a criterion to determine whether someone is an ethnic Chinese. While the first generation migrants from China or Chinese speaking families speak and write Chinese, the same cannot be said for subsequent generations. The situation varies from country to country. In Singapore Mandarin is one of the official languages, while in Malaysia parents are free to send their children to Chinese primary and secondary schools. In Indonesia however, until recently the teaching of Chinese was officially banned, signifying that most ethnic Chinese there would not speak the language. Nevertheless they might understand or perhaps speak one of the

5

dialects at home. The issue of language is discussed in Chapter Three.

The dialects most commonly spoken in Southeast Asia, where most of ethnic Chinese come from, are Cantonese [广东话] *Guǎngdōnghuà*, Hokkien [福建话] *Fújiànhuà*, Teowchew [潮洲话] *Cháozhōuhuà*, Hakka [客家话] *Kèjiāhuà*, Hainanese [海南话] *Hǎinánhuà*, Guangxi dialect [广西话] *Guǎngxīhuà*. Depending on circumstances an individual's language abilities could be confined to oral conversation, rather than reading and writing.

Religion: The Chinese community outside China does not have a dominant religion unlike the Europeans or Arabs. Depending on educational background, family heritage, etc, an ethnic Chinese could be a Buddhist, Taoist, Confucianist, Christian, Muslim, or a Bahai. There are many Christians amongst the ethnic Chinese.

Cultural Heritage: Cultural heritage is not a criterion for Chinese ethnicity. Depending on their educational background, in particular their understanding of the Chinese language and culture, the practice of culture vary tremendously, there being no typical sets of rules to be followed to the full. Some aspects of Chinese culture are discussed in Chapter 7.

Political Doctrine: Coming from such a diverse background, ethnic Chinese certainly do not subscribe to any collective political doctrine. As a whole ethnic Chinese are adaptable and pragmatic, adapting themselves quite easily from one political system to another.

Physical Features: It is true that most ethnic Chinese have broadly similar physical features such as black, relatively straight hairs, various shades of 'banana' colour skins, etc. However in terms of these features they could resemble the Japanese or Koreans.

A Chinese Profile?

It is doubtful whether a typical Chinese profile could be established, taking any of the ethnicity criteria, or a combination of them. Other than the Chinese nationals, it is increasingly difficult to typify the ethnic Chinese. This is particularly so when marriages between ethnic Chinese and other races are becoming more common.

ETHNIC CHINESE IDENTITY

It is important to note that overseas Chinese [华侨] *Huáqiáo* do not identify themselves as 中国人 *Zhōngguórén*, the term used for Chinese from China. They would call themselves 华人 *Huárén*, 汉人[1] *Hànrén* or 唐人 *Tángrén*. As you would have guessed, 人 *rén* means people.

In general terms 华 *huá* or 中华 *Zhōnghuá* refers to China or Chinese. The Chung Wah Association in Western Australia, for example, is the Cantonese version for Chinese Association 中华会馆 *Zhōnghuá huìguǎn*.

Scholars and historians of Chinese culture would be familiar with the word Táng [唐], derived from the Táng dynasty, the epoch where China achieved great political, cultural advancement more than one thousand years ago. Chinese history is discussed in Chapter 5.

To understand the diversity within the Chinese, it is relevant to look into the ethnic composition of China [中国] *Zhōngguó* the Middle Kingdom. The Hàn [汉] is the dominant race in China, comprising more than 90% of the Chinese population. The main minority races are Mǎn[2] [满], Méng [蒙] 'Mongolians', Huí [回] 'Chinese Muslims' and Zàng [藏] 'Tibetans'. Chinese minorities have their own naming systems distinct from the Hàns.

---

[1] The dominant race in China. Of course the minorities do not regard themselves as Hans.

[2] The Manchurian people are today dispersed in provinces such as Liaoning, Heilongjiang, Jilin, Hebei, Beijing, Inner Mongolia, etc.

SIMILAR YET DIFFERENT

Many a times ethnic Chinese children are sometimes described as 'bananas', yellow on the outside and white inside. These are truly locals who have grown up in a non-Chinese environment, educated with their fellow kids in the same schools, participated in the whole spectrum of activities in sports, cultural and community programs. Their command of language, knowledge of their adopted country, value judgement, perspectives in life, etc, are virtually indistinguishable from others. Yet their philosophy and thinking may seem slightly different.

Cultural Roots – Chinese Names

AS WE HAVE SEEN IN Chapter One, part of the Chinese identity and cultural roots is their names. The Chinese naming system is distinct from any other races in Southeast Asia, with the exception of the Vietnamese. In East Asia, Chinese names are distinct from the Japanese, though they could be confused with Korean names.

GETTING THE NAME RIGHT

Even today, many people in Western world are often confused with the Chinese naming system. In Southeast Asia, the same Chinese surname or name could occur in a variety of English spellings, due to their pronunciation in various dialects. (The issue of dialects is discussed in Chapter Four). In countries such as Indonesia and Thailand, ethnic Chinese may not have official Chinese-sounding names. This chapter serves to explain the Chinese naming system.

NAMES THAT TELL A STORY

The Western world would name their children from a list of established names such as Peter, François, Günther, Carlos, or Antonio. The Chinese on the other hand could create unique names by choosing meaningful words from a vast selection of vocabulary; as though you are able to create a name for your children or yourself by choosing any word from the vocabulary.

In the Chinese language there is a wide choice of words that could be coined as names, though in practice some words are used

9

more commonly than others. Other than the inherited surname, it is an art to choose suitable and meaningful words as names.

Embedded in most Chinese names are the parents' aspirations and hopes for their child. Since a person is addressed by his name throughout his life, whether he or she likes it or not, his identity, his perceived personality (until others know him well) are consciously or unconsciously implicated or associated with his name.

The character for name [名] *míng* is made up of two components, twilight [夕] *xī* and mouth [口] *kǒu*. Before the invention of electric bulbs, in twilight hours when vision is poor, one speaks out his name to be identified, hence the concept of name.

Even today, people subconsciously build up a mental picture of someone, based on his or her picture, voice and name. A good name is an excellent image maker. As we shall see later, words could be chosen to project character traits such as confidence, excellence, love and care, loyalty, peace and tranquillity, trust, etc. A list of three hundred and sixty naming words is provided in this chapter. The combination of words is enormous.

If you have a Chinese name, an understanding of what your name means not only enables you to understand what your parents hope in you, but also how others would get their 'first impression' of you, as well as a personality profile that you would be associated with, whether you like it or not.

CHINESE NAMING STRUCTURE

A typical Chinese name has two or three characters. It usually indicates that the person is of Chinese *Hàn* [汉] origin. The first character is the surname or family name [姓] *xìng*, the remaining one or two characters is the given name [名] *míng*. Let us take the following name as an example:

陈　汉　华
Chin　Hon　Fah

10

'Chin' would be the surname, 'Hon Fah' the given name. Placing the surname before the given name is consistent with the hierarchy of relationships (refer to Chapter Seven). It is an acknowledgement that the parents' and ancestors' name is more important than one's own name. Mistaking the surname as a given name, or vice-versa is often a source of confusion and embarrassment.

If one chooses to address a Chinese by his given name (usually consisting of two words), it is important to realise that both words should be used when addressing the person. The concept of a middle name, as it is known in the Western world, does not exist. It is improper to truncate one of the two words, as we do not know which of the words is common to his/her siblings, and which actually belongs to him/her.

In the example above Mr. Chin Hon Fah should be addressed as Hon Fah, rather than Hon or Fah. (The case of commonly shared characters amongst sibling is discussed later). It would be better to check with the person himself when in doubt.

The name can be written in various ways, such as

Chin Hon Fah
Chin Hon-Fah
Chin Honfah

Mr. Chin living in the Western society would probably place his surname last. His name would then become

Hon Fah Chin, or H. F. Chin

CHRISTIAN NAMES

Many people in the Southeast Asia or the Western world might know their ethnic Chinese friends by their Christian names. To make it easier for friends, ethnic Chinese would use a Christian name. In some cases they might not be Christians by faith, even though their Christian names would suggest that they are.

Should Mr. Chin adopt a Christian name, say Peter, then his name becomes

Peter Chin Hon Fah, or

Peter Chin, or

Peter H. F. Chin

SAME WORD AFTER ALL

The majority of the public may not realise that the same Chinese word is pronounced differently, sometimes very differently, in various dialects. Consider the case of Alice Khor. In Mandarin her surname is written as 许 *Xǔ*, according to the official pronunciation system, known as pīnyīn [拼音]. However the same character is pronounced as 'Khor' in Hokkien (a Chinese dialect) but 'Hii' in Hokchew dialect. (The issue of dialects is discussed in Chapter Four).

In the People's Republic of China romanised spelling of surnames are standardised, written according to pīnyīn. However, most Southeast Asian Chinese tend to write their surnames according to their dialects. As a result the same surname could be spelt and pronounced in dramatically different ways.

Back to Mr. Peter Chin. Someone familiar with Chinese dialects and naming system would know that this is most probably pronounced in the Hakka dialect. The Mandarin version would be Chen Han Hua.

Depending on which part of China the family originates from the surname Chén [陈] could be written and pronounced as

Chan (Cantonese)
Chén (Mandarin)
Chin (Hakka)
Dan (Hainan)
Tan (Hokkien, Teochew)

Tjin (Indonesian)

Tran (Vietnamese)

THE ORIGIN OF CHINESE SURNAMES

The study of Chinese surnames and their origins is fascinating. Over the centuries some surnames were bestowed by various emperors, some acquired through historical events, while others were named after particular entities. Each surname has a particular origin, typically a village or a county, from where they migrate to other parts of China and eventually overseas. Even today the majority of people of certain villages in China still share the same surname!

As an example the surname Wong [黄] *Huáng* (also pronounced as Huang, Ng, Ooi, Wee, Wong, etc, depending on their dialects) could be traced to the founding of Zhōu [周] dynasty in 1122 BC, when royal families and their descendants were each given a small kingdom to rule. One of them was given a state called Huang in Hénán [河南] province. The people of Huang then adopted the State's name as their surname[3].

Needless to say, many of the surnames would have famous personalities whom the community is proud of. They could be emperors, politicians, scholars, army generals or people of historical importance. As an example, the surname Kŏng [孔] is often associated with Confucius. Books such as the 通书 *tōngshū* Almanac, provide lists of surnames, their origins, as well as some outstanding personalities in history.

Though thousands of surnames have been collected, there are about four to five hundred common ones. Over the centuries list of top 100 surnames [百家姓] *báijiāxìng* has been compiled and updated. In practice more than 100 surnames are often listed.

---

[3] About surnames and their origins, in *Your Chinese Roots*, by Thomas Tsu-wee Tan, Times Books International, Singapore, 1986.

Due to the sheer population size and numbers, this listing would not have been too precise. It was not until recently, with the advent modern computers that it is possible to compile accurate data.

Common Chinese Surnames

Du and Yuan[4], from the Hereditary Research Institute of Chinese Academy of Sciences, compiled a list of the most common surnames from random sampling of more than half a million names obtained from the Chinese Statistics Bureau. They concluded that the top three surnames comprised 7.9%, 7.4% and 7.1% of the Hàn [汉] population (close to ninety millions each). In addition the top nineteen surnames have more than 1% of the Hàn people, the dominant race in China. The top nineteen surnames make up 55.6% of the population. The list is given in pīnyīn, followed by various spellings.

李 [Lǐ], Lee, Ly
王 [Wáng], Heng, Ong, Voung, Wong
张 [Zhāng], Chang, Cheong, Cheung, Chiang, Chong, Jung, Teo, Teoh, Truong
刘 [Liú], Lau, Lew, Liew, Low, Luu
陈 [Chén], Chan, Chang, Ch'en, Chin, Ching, Dan, Ding, Tan, Ting, Tjin, Tran
杨 [Yáng], Yeo, Yeoh, Yong, Young
赵 [Zhào], Chao, Chew, Chieu, Chiu, Trieu
黄 [Huáng], Hwang, Hyunh, Ng, Oei, Ooi, Wee, Wong
周 [Zhōu], Chau, Chew, Chiu, Chou, Chow, Joe
吴 [Wú], Eng, Ing, Goh, Ng, Ngo, Wee, Woo
徐 [Xú], Hsu, Seah, Shaw, Shu
孙 [Sūn], Soon, Suen, Ton
胡 [Hú], Ho, Hoo, Woo, Wu

---

[4] 杜若甫 and 袁义达, cited in 姓名的奥妙, by 汪爱宽, 三秦 publisher, Xi'an, China.

朱 [Zhū], Chee, Choo, Chu
高 [Gāo], Go, Kao, Ko
林 [Lín], Lam, Lim, Ling, Lum
何 [Hé], Ho
郭 [Guō], Kuo, Kuok, Kwok, Quanch, Quek
马 [Mǎ], Beh, Maa, Mah, Mar

TOP HUNDRED SURNAMES.

The top 100 surnames are tabulated in as follows; they constitute 87% of total Hàn population.

1 to 10

李 [Lǐ]　　王 [Wáng]
张 [Zhāng]　刘 [Liú]
陈 [Chén]　杨 [Yáng]
赵 [Zhào]　黄 [Huáng]
周 [Zhōu]　吴 [Wú]

11 to 20

徐 [Xú]　　孙 [Sūn]
胡 [Hú]　　朱 [Zhū]
高 [Gāo]　林 [Lín]
何 [Hé]　　郭 [Guō]
马 [Mǎ]　　罗 [Luó]

21 to 30

梁 [Liáng]　宋 [Sòng]
郑 [Zhèng]　谢 [Xiè]
韩 [Hán]　　唐 [Táng]
冯 [Féng]　于 [Yú]
董 [Dǒng]　萧 [Xiāo]

31 to 40

程 [Chéng]　曹 [Cáo]
袁 [Yuán]　邓 [Dèng]
许 [Xǔ]　　傅 [Fù]
沈 [Shěn]　曾 [Zēng]
彭 [Péng]　吕 [Lǚ]

41 to 50

苏 [Sū]　　卢 [Lú]
蒋 [Jiǎng]　蔡 [Cài]
贾 [Jiǎ]　　丁 [Dīng]
魏 [Wèi]　薛 [Xuē]
叶 [Yè]　　阎 [Yán]

51 to 60

余 [Yú]　　潘 [Pān]
杜 [Dù]　　戴 [Dài]
夏 [Xià]　钟 [Zhōng]
汪 [Wāng]　田 [Tián]
任 [Rén]　姜 [Jiāng]

61 to 70		81 to 90	
范 [Fàn]	方 [Fāng]	顾 [Gù]	侯 [Hóu]
石 [Shí]	姚 [Yáo]	邵 [Shào]	孟 [Mèng]
谭 [Tán]	廖 [Liào]	龙 [Lóng]	万 [Wàn]
邹 [Zōu]	熊 [Xióng]	段 [Duàn]	雷 [Léi]
金 [Jīn]	陆 [Lù]	钱 [Qián]	汤 [Tāng]

71 to 80		91 to 100	
郝 [Hǎo]	孔 [Kǒng]	尹 [Yǐn]	黎 [Lí]
白 [Bái]	崔 [Cuī]	易 [Yì]	常 [Cháng]
康 [Kāng]	毛 [Máo]	武 [Wǔ]	乔 [Qiáo]
丘 [Qiū]	秦 [Qín]	贺 [Hè]	赖 [Lài]
江 [Jiāng]	史 [Shǐ]	龚 [Gōng]	文 [Wén]

The family name or surname is so important that when two Chinese get together they introduce each other by (or seek to find out) the surnames, by saying 'What is your surname?' [先生贵姓] *xiānshēng guìxìng* rather than finding out their given names!

In tracing family trees some surname has a zúpǔ [族谱] — kind of a family tree book passed down from one generation to the next, whereby it is possible to tell which generation the person is from!

MEANING OF CHINESE SURNAMES

It is not surprising that many ethnic Chinese do not know what their surname or given name means, especially when their parents themselves are not certain. Surnames are after all inherited rather than chosen.

To understand the meaning of a name, it is important that the precise Chinese character be identified, as the same sound could mean more than one word in Chinese. This is particularly complicated when the words are pronounced in dialect rather than in Mandarin.

Some of the surnames are easily translated, for example:

16

白 [Bái] white
甘 [Gān] sweet, delicious
高 [Gāo] tall
古 [Gǔ] ancient
贺 [Hè] congratulate
黄 [Huáng] yellow
江 [Jiāng] river
金 [Jīn] metal, gold
雷 [Léi] thunder
林 [Lín] woods, forest
柳 [Liǔ] willow
马 [Mǎ] horse
毛 [Máo] hair
钱 [Qián] money

丘 [Qiū] hill
孙 [Sūn] grand child
田 [Tián] field
万 [Wàn] ten thousand
王 [Wáng] ruler
温 [Wēn] warm
徐 [Xú] gently
许 [Xǔ] permit
谢 [Xiè] thank
叶 [Yè] leaf
余 [Yú] surplus
钟 [Zhōng] bell
周 [Zhōu] surround, encircle

Another group of surnames are names of places, including historical sites or regions. These would be evident when we go through the history of China in Chapter Six. These include:

陈 [Chén]
梁 [Liáng]
齐 [Qí]
秦 [Qín]
宋 [Sòng]

唐 [Táng]
魏 [Wèi]
吴 [Wú]
周 [Zhōu]

Some words are used more or less exclusively as surnames, and not generally used otherwise. These include:

冯 [Féng]
郭 [Guō]
韩 [Hán]
蒋 [Jiǎng]

刘 [Liú]
潘 [Pān]
彭 [Páng]
阮 [Ruǎn]

袁 [Yuán]
赵 [Zhào]
邹 [Zōu]

However the majority of surnames do not necessarily mean anything on their own. This is commonly found amongst Chinese characters. Their interpretations and associated connotations vary when they are combined with other words. This is one of the reasons why different interpretations are given. For example:

陈 [chén]: 陈旧 *chénjiù* 'old' (object); 陈列 *chénliè* 'display'; 陈述 *chénshù* 'to relate'

程 [chéng]: 路程 *lùchéng* 'journey'; 工程 *gōngchéng* 'engineering'; 程度 *chéngdù* 'extent, standard'

董 [dǒng]: 董事 *dǒngshì* 'director'; 古董 *gǔdǒng* 'antique'

杜 [dù]: 杜鹃 *dùjuān* 'Azalea plant'; 杜绝 *dùjué* 'eradicate'

符 [fú]: 符号 *fúhào* 'symbol'; 符合 *fúhé* 'comply with'

何 [hé] 'questioning': 何必 *hébì* 'Is there a need?'; 何人 *hérén* 'who'; 何况 *hékuàng* 'let alone'

尤 [yóu]: 尤其 *yóuqí* 'particularly'

Chinese surnames in China are standardised according to pīnyīn. Outside China, however, the names are commonly written according to the dialect. In reality the spelling could actually come from the dialect of the interpreter who helps to fill up the birth certificate application, rather than the dialect of the child. The situation would be most interesting when a name has to be spelt by a non-Chinese official, often on the spot.

Surname Listing by Pīnyīn, in Alphabetical Order

Surnames according to various dialects are listed below. The pīnyīn are italicised or in [ ]. Words without meanings on their own are written as NPM (No particular meaning), as their meaning depends on combinations with other words.

To help those who learned their surnames in traditional Chinese characters, both the simplified and traditional scripts are given.

18

A

Ang: refers to 洪 *Hóng*
Auduong: refers to 欧阳 *Ōuyáng*
Auyang: refers to 欧阳 *Ōuyáng*
Auyeung: refers to 欧阳 *Ōuyáng*
Auyong: refers to 欧阳 *Ōuyáng*
Aw: refers to 欧 *Ōu*

B

Bach: refers to 白 *Bái*
[Bái] 白 (Bach, Bak Pai, Pak, Peh): white, unblemished, bright, clear, pure
Bak: refers to 白 *Bái*
Banh: refers to 彭 *Péng*
Beh: refers to 马 *Mǎ*
Boon: refers to 文 *Wén*

C

[Cài] 蔡 (Chai, Choi, Choy, Chua, Chye, Thai, Tjoa, Tsai, Ts'ai): a Chinese surname
Cam: refers to 甘 *Gān*
[Cáo] 曹 (Chao, Cho, Tow, Ts'ao, Tso, Ts'ui): a Chinese surname
Chai: refers to 蔡 *Cài*, 翟 *Zhái*
Chaim: refers to 詹 *Zhān*
Chan: refers to 陈 *Chén*, 曾 *Zēng*, 詹 *Zhān*
[Cháng] 常 (Ch'ang): frequent, common, often, constant
Chang: refers to 张 *Zhāng*, 郑 *Zhèng*, 章 *Zhāng*
Ch'ang: refers to 常 *Cháng*, 陈 *Chén*
Chao: refers to 赵 *Zhào*, 曹 *Cáo*
Chau: refers to 周 *Zhōu*
Che: refers to 谢 *Xiè*
Chee: refers to 齐 *Qí*, 朱 *Zhū*

19

[Chén] 陈, 陳 (Chan, Chang, Ch'en, Chin, Ching,
　　Dan, Ding, Tan, Tjin, Tran): NPM 陈旧
　　chénjiù 'old fashioned'; 陈列 *chénliè*
　　'display'; 陈述 *chénshù* 'to relate'

Chen: refers to 曾 *Zēng*

Ch'en: refers to 陈 *Chén*

[Chéng] 程 (Ch'eng): NPM 程度 *chéngdù* 'extent'; 程式
　　chéngshì 'formula'; 路程 *lùchéng* 'journey'; 工程
　　gōngchéng 'engineering'

Cheng: refers to 曾 *Zēng*, 郑 *Zhèng*

Ch'eng: refers to 程 *Chéng*

Cheong: refers to 张 *Zhāng*

Cheung: refers to 张 *Zhāng*

Chew: refers to 周 *Zhōu*

Chew: refers to 赵 *Zhào*

Chi: refers to 齐 *Qí*

Chia: refers to 贾 *Jiǎ*, 谢 *Xiè*

Chian: refers to 简 *Jiǎn*, 钱 *Qián*

Chiang: refers to 张 *Zhāng*, 蒋 *Jiǎng*, 江 *Jiāng*, 姜 Jiāng

Ch'iao: refers to 乔 *Qiáo*

Chiem: refers to 詹 *Zhān*

Chien: refers to 简 *Jiǎn*

Ch'ien: refers to 钱 *Qián*

Chieu: refers to 赵 *Zhào*

Chin: refers to 陈 *Chén*, 金 *Jīn*, 钱 *Qián*, 郑 *Zhèng*

Chin, Ch'in: refers to 秦 *Qín*

Ching: refers to 陈 *Chén*, 金 *Jīn*

Chiu: refers to 周 *Zhōu*, 赵 *Zhào*

Ch'iu: refers to 丘 *Qiū*

Ch'ng: refers to 曾 *Zēng*, 郑 *Zhèng*, 庄 *Zhuāng*

Cho: refers to 曹 *Cáo*

Choi: refers to 蔡 *Cài*

Chong: refers to 张 *Zhāng*

20

Choo: refers to 朱 *Zhū*

Choong: refers to 章 *Zhāng*, 钟 *Zhōng*

Chooi: refers to 崔 *Cuī*

Chou: refers to 周 *Zhōu*

Chow: refers to 周 *Zhōu*

Choy: refers to 蔡 *Cǎi*

Chu: refers to 朱 *Zhū*

Chua: refers to 蔡 *Cài*

Chuang: refers to 庄 *Zhuāng*

Chung: refers to 钟 *Zhōng*, 郑 *Zhèng*

Chuong: refers to 章 *Zhāng*

Chye: refers to 蔡 *Cài*

Co: refers to 顾 *Gù*

[Cuī] 崔 (Chooi, Thoi, Ts'ui): a Chinese surname

Cung: refers to 龚 *Gōng*

D

[Dài] 戴 (Tai): wear, put on

Dam: refers to 谭 *Tán*

Dan: refers to 陈 *Chén*

Dao: refers to 陶 *Táo*

[Dèng] 邓, 鄧 (Tang, Teng, Thean, Thian, Thien):
    a Chinese surname

Dich: refers to 易 *Yì*

Diem: refers to 阎 *Yán*

Dien: refers to 田 *Tián*

Dieu: refers to 姚 *Yáo*

[Dīng] 丁 (Dinh, Ting): the fourth element in Celestial
    Stem [天干] *tiāngān* (refer to Chapter 8)

Dinh: refers to 丁 *Dīng*

Ding: refers to 陈 *Chén*

Do: refers to 杜 *Dù*

Doan: refers to 段 *Duàn*, 尹 *Yǐn*

[Dǒng] 董 (Tong, Tung): NPM 董事 *dǒngshì* 'director';
古董 *gǔdǒng* 'antique'

Dong: refers to 童 *Tóng*

[Dù] 杜 (Do, Toh, Tu): 杜鹃 *dùjūan* 'Azalea plant'; 杜绝
dùjué 'eradicate'

Du: refers to 余 *Yú*

[Duàn] 段 (Doan, Tuan): segment, section

Duong: refers to 唐 Táng

E

Eu: refers to 余 *Yú*

Eng: refers to 吴 *Wú*

F

Farn: refers to 范 *Fàn*

[Fàn] 范, 範 (Fan, Fang, Farn, Pham): a Chinese
surname; 范围 *fàn wéi* 'range, scope'

[Fāng] 方 (Fong, Phuong): square, method,
prescription, formula

Fang: refers to 范 *Fàn*

[Féng] 冯, 馮 (Foong, Fung, Phung): a Chinese surname

Fong: refers to 方 *Fāng*

Foo: refers to 傅 *Fù*

Foong: refers to 冯 *Féng*

[Fù] 傅 (Foo, Phu): 师傅 *shīfù* 'master, expert'

Fung: refers to 冯 *Féng*

G

[Gān] 甘 (Cam, Kam, Kan): sweat, pleasant

[Gāo] 高 (Go, Kao, Ko): tall, high

Gia: refers to 贾 *Jiǎ*

Gian: refers to 简 *Jiǎn*

Giang: refers to 江 *Jiāng*

Go: refers to 高 *Gāo*

Goh: refers to 吴 *Wú*

[Gōng] 龚, 龔 (Cung, Kung): a Chinese surname

[Gù] 顾, 顧 (Co, Ku): look after, attend to

[Guān] 关, 関 (Kuan, Kwan, Quan): shut, close

[Guō] 郭 (Kuo, Kuok, Kwok, Quach, Quek): a Chinese surname

H

Ha: refers to 韩 *Hán*, 贺 *Hé*, 夏 *Xià*

[Hán] 韩, 韓 (Ha, Hon): a Chinese surname, an ancient Chinese state; Korea

[Hǎo] 郝: a Chinese surname

[Hé] 何 (Ho): questioning; 如何 *rúhé* 'how'; 何人 *hérén* 'who'; 何故 *hégù* 'why'; 何必 *hébì* 'is there a need to?'

[Hè] 贺, 賀 (Ha): congratulate

Heng: refers to 王 *Wáng*

Hew: refers to 丘 *Qiū*

Hi: refers to 许 *Xǔ*

Hii: refers to 许 *Xǔ*

Ho: refers to 何 *Hé*, 胡 *Hú*

Hoa: refers to 华 *Huà*

Hon: refers to 韩 *Hán*

[Hóng] 洪 (Ang, Hung): NPM 洪水 flood

Hong: refers to 孔 *Kǒng*

Hoo: refers to 胡 *Hú*

[Hóu] 侯 (Hau): nobleman, high official

Hsia: refers to 夏 *Xià*

Hsiao: refers to 萧 *Xiāo*

Hsieh: refers to 谢 *Xiè*

Hsiung: refers to 熊 *Xióng*

Hsu: refers to 许 *Xǔ*

Hsüeh: refers to 薛 *Xuē*

[Hú] 胡 (Ho, Hoo, Woo, Wu): a non-*Hàn* people in China; beard, reckless

[Huà] 华, 華 (Hoa): a Chinese surname

Hua: refers to 许 *Xǔ*

Hung: refers to 洪 *Hóng*, 孔 *Kǒng*, 熊 *Xióng*

[Huáng] 黄 (Hwang, Hyunh, Ng, Oei, Ooi, Wee, Wong): yellow

黄

Hui: refers to 许 *Xǔ*

Huie: refers to 许 *Xǔ*

Hwang: refers to 黄 *Huáng*

Hyunh: refers to 黄 *Huáng*

I

I: refers to 易 *Yì*

Ing: refers to 吴 *Wú*

J

Jao: refers to 饶 *Ráo*

Jee: refers to 于 *Yú*

Jen: refers to 任 *Rén*

Jeng - Refer to 曾 *Zēng*

[Jiǎ] 贾, 賈 (Chia, Gia): a Chinese surname

[Jiǎn] 简, 簡 (Chian, Chien, Gian, Kan): simple, brief

[Jiāng] 江 (Chiang, Giang, Kong): river

[Jiāng] 姜 (Chiang, Khuong): a Chinese surname

[Jiǎng] 蒋, 蔣 (Chiang, Tuong): a Chinese surname

[Jīn] 金 (Chin, Ching, Kim, King): gold, metal, money

Joe: refers to 周 *Zhōu*

Jong: refers to 张 *Zhāng*

Juan: refers to 阮 *Ruǎn*

Jung: refers to 张 *Zhāng*

K

Kam: refers to 甘 *Gān*

Kan: refers to 甘 *Gān*, 简 *Jiǎn*

Kao: refers to 高 *Gāo*

[Kāng] 康 (K'ang, Khang): health

[Kē] 柯 (Kha, Kua, Kuah): a Chinese surname

Kha: refers to 柯 *Kē*

Khang: refers to 康 *Kāng*

Khaw: refers to 许 *Xǔ*

Kho: refers to 许 *Xǔ*

Khoo: refers to 丘 *Qiū*

Khong: refers to 孔 *Kǒng*

Khor: refers to 许 *Xǔ*

Khu: refers to 丘 *Qiū*

Khun: refers to 丘 *Qiū*

Khuong: refers to 姜 *Jiāng*

Kieu: refers to 乔 *Qiáo*

Kim: refers to 金 *Jīn*

King: refers to 金 *Jīn*

Ko: refers to 高 *Gāo*

Koh: refers to 许 *Xǔ*

[Kǒng] 孔 (Hong, Hung, Khong, Kung, K'ung): orifice, hole

Kong: refers to 江 *Jiāng*

Ku: refers to 顾 *Gù*

Kua: refers to 柯 *Kē*

Kuah: refers to 柯 *Kē*

Kuan: refers to 关 *Guān*

Kung: refers to 龚 *Gōng*, 孔 *Kǒng*

Kuo: refers to 郭 *Guō*

Kuok: refers to 郭 *Guō*

Kwan: refers to 关 *Guān*

Kwok: refers to 郭 *Guō*

L

La: refers to 罗 *Luó*

[Lài] 赖, 賴: depend on, rely

Lai: refers to 黎 *Lí*

Lam: refers to 林 *Lín*

Lau: refers to 刘 *Liú*

Law: refers to 罗 *Luó*

Le: refers to 黎 *Lí*

Lee: refers to 李 *Lǐ*

[Lēi] 雷 (Loi): thunder

Lew: refers to 刘 *Liú*

Leon: refers to 梁 *Liáng*

Leong: refers to 梁 *Liáng*

Leung: refers to 梁 *Liáng*

[Lí] 黎 (Le, Lai): 黎明 *límíng* 'dawn'

[Lǐ] 李 (Lee, Ly): plum

[Liáng] 梁 (Leon, Leong, Leung, Liong, Loeung, Luong): beam

[Liào] 廖 (Lieu, Liew): a Chinese surname

Liong - Refer to 梁 *Liáng*

Lieu: refers to 廖 *Liáo*

Liew: refers to 刘 *Liú*, 廖 *Liáo*

Lim: refers to 林 *Lín*

[Lín] 林 (Lam, Lim, Lum, Ling): woods, forest

Ling: refers to 林 *Lín*

[Liú] 刘, 劉 (Lau, Lew, Liew, Low, Luu): a Chinese surname

Lo: refers to 罗 *Luó*

Loeung: refers to 梁 *Liáng*

Loh: refers to 罗 *Luó*

Loi: refers to 雷 *Léi*

Loke: refers to 陆 *Lù*

[Lóng] 龙, 龍 (Lung): Dragon, Imperial

Loo: refers to 吕 *Lǚ*

Low: refers to 刘 *Liú*

[Lú] 卢, 鲁: hut, a Chinese surname

[Lù] 陆, 陸 (Loke, Luc): land mass, shore

[Lǚ] 吕: a Chinese surname

Luc: refers to 陆 *Lù*

Lum: refers to 林 *Lín*

Lung: refers to 龙 *Lóng*

[Luó] 罗, 羅 (La, Law, Lo, Loh): trap, net, gather

Luong: refers to 梁 *Liáng*

Luu: refers to 刘 *Liú*

Ly: refers to 李 *Lǐ*

M

[Mǎ] 马, 馬 (Beh, Maa, Mah, Mar): horse, a
   common Chinese Muslim surname

Maa: refers to 马 *Mǎ*

Mah: refers to 马 *Mǎ*

Manh: refers to 孟 *Mèng*

Mar: refers to 马 *Mǎ*

[Máo] 毛: hair, fur, ten cents

[Mèng] 孟 (Manh): a Chinese surname

Mun: refers to 文 *Wén*

N

Nai: refers to 赖 *Lài*

Ng: refers to 黄 *Huáng*, 吴 *Wú*

Ngau: refers to 饶 *Ráo*

Nghiem: refers to 严 *Yán*

Ngiau: refers to 饶 *Ráo*

Ngo: refers to 吴 *Wú*

Nguy: refers to 魏 *Wèi*

Nguyen: refers to 阮 *Ruǎn*

Nhac: refers to 岳 *Yuè*

Nhan: refers to 颜 *Yán*

Nhiem: refers to 任 *Rén*

Nhieu: refers to 饶 *Ráo*

O

Oei: refers to 黄 *Huáng*

Oh: refers to 吴 *Wú*

On: refers to 温 *Wēn*

Ong: refers to 王 *Wáng*, 翁 *Wéng*

Ooi: refers to 黄 *Huáng*

[Ōu] 欧, 歐 (Au, Aw): Europe

[Ōuyáng] 欧阳, 歐陽 (Auduong, Auyang, Auyeung, Auyong, Auyoung, Ouyeung, Ouyoung, Owyang): a Chinese surname

Ouyeung: refers to 欧阳 *Ōuyáng*

Ouyoung: refers to 欧阳 *Ōuyáng*

Owyang: refers to 欧阳 *Ōuyáng*

P

[Pān] 潘 (P'an, Pham, Poon): a Chinese surname

Pai: refers to 白 *Bái*

Pang: refers to 彭 *Pēng*

Pak: refers to 白 *Bái*

Pang: refers to 彭 *Péng*

Peh: refers to 白 *Bái*

[Péng] 彭 (Banh, Pang, P'eng): a Chinese surname

Pham: refers to 范 *Fàn*

Phan: refers to 潘 *Pān*

Phung: refers to 冯 *Fáng*

Poon: refers to 潘 *Pān*

Phu: refers to 傅 *Fù*

Phuong: refers to 方 *Fāng*

28

Q

[Qí] 齐, 齊 (Chee, Chi, Ch'i, Te): orderly; even; name of
  Chinese empire

[Qián] 钱, 錢 (Chian, Ch'ien, Chin, Tien): money

[Qiáo] 乔, 喬 (Ch'iao, Kieu): a Chinese surname

[Qín] 秦 (Chin, Ch'in, Tan): an ancient Chinese empire

[Qiū] 丘 (Ch'iu, Hew, Khoo, Khun, Khu, Yeow, Yow):
  small hill, mould

Quach: refers to 郭 *Guō*

Quan: refers to 关 *Guān*

Quek: refers to 郭 *Guō*

R

[Ráo] 饶, 饒 (Jao, Ngau, Ngiau Nhieu, Yeow, Yow): 饶恕
  ráoshù 'forgive', 丰饶 *fēngráo* 'rich, plentiful'

[Rén] 任 (Jen, Nhiem, Yum): taking up a post, appoint

[Ruǎn] 阮 (Juan, Nguyen): a Chinese surname

S

Saw: refers to 苏 *Sū*

Seah: refers to 徐 *Xú*, 谢 *Xiè*

Seow: refers to 萧 *Xiāo*

[Shào] 邵 (Shaw, Thieu): a Chinese surname

Shaw: refers to 徐 *Xú*, 邵 *Shào*

She: refers to 谢 *Xiè*

Shek: refers to 石 *Shí*

[Shěn] 沈 (Sim, Sung): a Chinese surname

[Shī] 施 (Shih, Sy, Thi): grant, bestow

[Shǐ] 史 (Shi, Su): history

[Shí] 石 (Shek, Shih, Thach): rock, boulder

Shih: refers to 施 *Shi*, 石 *Shí*

Shu: refers to 徐 *Xú*

[Sīmǎ] 司马, 司馬 (Szema, Tuma): a military official

29

[Sītú] 司徒 (Szeto, Tu Do): an official of ritual ceremony

Siew: refers to 萧 *Xiāo*

Sim: refers to 沈 *Shěn*

Siu: refers to 萧 *Xiāo*

So: refers to 苏 *Sū*

Soh: refers to 苏 *Sū*

Soo: refers to 苏 *Sū*

[Sòng] 宋 (Soong, Sung, Tong): a Chinese dynasty

Soon: refers to 孙 *Sūn*

Soong: refers to 宋 *Sòng*

[Sū] 苏, 蘇 (Saw, Soo, Soh, So, To): NPM 江苏 *Jiāngsū* name of a province in China; 苏醒 *sūxing* 'revive, regain consciousness'

Su: refers to 史 *Shǐ*

Suen: refers to 孙 *Sūn*

[Sūn] 孙, 孫 (Soon, Suen, Ton): grandchild, descendant

Sung: refers to 沈 *Shěn*, 宋 *Sòng*

Sy: refers to 施 *Shī*

Szema: refers to 司马 *Sīmǎ*

Szeto: refers to 司徒 *Sītú*

T

Ta: refers to 谢 *Xiè*

Tai: refers to 戴 *Dài*

[Tán] 谭, 譚 (Dam, T'an, Tham): a Chinese surname

Tan: refers to 陈 *Chén*, 秦 [*Qín*]

[Táng] 唐 (Duong, T'ang, Tong): a Chinese dynasty

[Tāng] 汤, 湯 (T'ang, Thang): soup

Tang: refers to 邓 *Dèng*, 曾 *Zēng*

[Táo] 陶 (Dao, T'ao): ceramics

Tay: refers to 郑 *Zhèng*

Te: refers to 齐 *Qí*

Teng: refers to 邓 *Dèng*

Teo: refers to 张 *Zhāng*

Teoh: refers to 张 *Zhāng*

Thach: refers to 石 *Shí*

Thai: refers to 蔡 *Cài*

Tham: refers to 谭 *Tán*

Thang: refers to 汤 *Tāng*

Thean: refers to 邓 *Dèng*

Thi: refers to 施 *Shī*

Thian: refers to 邓 *Dèng*

Thien: refers to 邓 *Dèng*

Thieu: refers to 邵 *Shào*

Thoi: refers to 崔 *Cuī*

[Tián] 田 (Dien, T'ien, Tin): field, cultivated land

Tien: refers to 钱 *Qián*

T'ien: refers to 田 *Tián*

Tiet: refers to 薛 *Xuē*

Tieu: refers to 萧 *Xiāo*

Tin: refers to 田 *Tián*

Ting: refers to 丁 *Dīng*

Tjin: refers to 陈 *Chén*

Tjoa: refers to 蔡 *Cài*

To: refers to 苏 *Sū*

Toh: refers to 杜 *Dù*

Ton: refers to 孙 *Sūn*

[Tóng] 童 (Dong): child

Tong: refers to 董 *Dǒng*, 汤 *Tāng*, 宋 *Sòng*, 唐 *Táng*

Tow: refers to 曹 *Cáo*

Trac: refers to 翟 *Zhái*

Tran: refers to 陈 *Chén*

Trang: refers to 庄 *Zhuāng*

Trieu: refers to 赵 *Zhào*

Trinh: refers to 郑 *Zhèng*

Trou: refers to 邹 *Zōu*

Truong: refers to 张 *Zhāng*
Tsai, Ts'ai 蔡: refers to *Cài*
Tsao, Ts'ao 曹: refers to *Cáo*
Tsang: refers to 曾 *Zēng*
Tse: refers to 谢 *Xiè*
Tseng: refers to 曾 *Zēng*
Tsia: refers to 谢 *Xiè*
Tso: refers to 曹 *Cáo*
Tse: refers to 谢 *Xiè*
Tsou: refers to 邹 *Zōu*
Ts'ui: refers to 崔 *Cuī*
Tu: refers to 杜 *Dú*
Tuan: refers to 段 *Duàn*
Tu do: refers to 司徒 *Sītú*
Tue: refers to 徐 *Xú*
Tu ma: refers to 司马 *Sīmǎ*
Tung: refers to 董 *Dǒng*
Tuong: refers to 蒋 *Jiǎng*

U

U: refers to 于 *Yú*
Uong: refers to 汪 *Wāng*

V

Van: refers to 万 *Wàn*, 文 *Wén*
Vien: refers to 袁 *Yuán*
Vu: refers to 巫 *Wū*, 武 *Wǔ*
Vuong: refers to 王 *Wáng*

W

[Wàn] 万, 萬 (Van, Won): ten thousand, myriad
[Wáng] 王 (Heng, Ong, Vuong, Wong): ruler, king
[Wāng] 汪 (Uong): an expanse of water

32

Wee: refers to 黄 *Huáng*, 吴 *Wú*

[Wèi] 魏 (Nguy): an ancient Chinese kingdom

[Wēn] 温 (On): warm

[Wén] 文 (Boon, Mun, Van): culture, language, literature

[Wéng] 翁 (Ong): elderly man

Won: refers to 万 *Wàn*

Wong: refers to 黄 *Huáng*, 王 *Wáng*

Woo: refers to 胡 *Hú*, 吴 *Wú*

[Wú] 吴 (Eng, Ing, Goh, Ng, Ngo, Oh, Wee, Woo):
    ancient Chinese kingdom

[Wū] 巫 (Vu): wizard, witch

[Wǔ] 武 (Vu): martial art, fighting

Wu: refers to 胡 *Hú*

X

[Xià] 夏 (Ha, Hsia): summer; a Chinese dynasty

[Xiāo] 萧 (Hsiao, Seow, Siew, Siu, Tieu): dreary, desolate

[Xiè] 谢, 謝 (Che, Chia, Hsieh, Seah, Ta, Tsia, Tse, Tue,
    Tze): thank, decline

[Xióng] 熊 (Hsiung, Hung): bear (animal)

[Xú] 徐 (Hsu, Seah, Shaw, Shu): slowly, gently

[Xǔ] 许, 許 (Hi, Hii, Hsu, Hua, Hui, Huie, Khaw, Kho,
    Khor, Koh, Seah): permit, allow

[Xuē] 薛 (Hsueh, Tiet): a Chinese surname

Y

[Yán] 颜, 顏 (Nhan, Yen): colour

[Yán] 严, 嚴 (Nghiem, Yim): strict, severe, stern

[Yán] 阎, 閻 (Diem, Yen): king of Hell

[Yáng] 杨, 楊 (Yeo, Yeoh, Yong): the Poplar tree

[Yáo] 姚 (Dieu, Yew): a Chinese surname

Yao: refers to 尤 *Yóu*

Yee: refers to 余 *Yú*

Yen: refers to 阎, 颜 *Yán*

Yeo: refers to 杨 *Yáng*

Yeoh: refers to 杨 *Yáng*

Yeow: refers to 丘 *Qiū*, 饶 *Ráo*, 姚 *Yáo*

Yew: refers to 姚 *Yáo*, 余, 于 *Yú*

[Yì] 易 (Dich, I): easy, simple; change

Yim: refers to 严 *Yán*

[Yǐn] 尹 (Doan): ancient official title

Yip: refers to 叶 *Yè*

Yiu: refers to 姚 *Yáo*

Yong: refers to 杨 *Yáng*

Young: refers to 杨 *Yáng*

[Yóu] 尤 (Yao, Yow, Yu): exceptionally, especially

Yow: refers to 丘 *Qiū*, 尤 *Yóu*, 饶 *Ráo*, 姚 *Yáo*

[Yú] 于 (U, Yew): at

[Yú] 余 (Du, Eu, Yee): surplus

Yu: refers to 尤 *Yóu*

[Yuán] 袁 (Vien, Yuen): a Chinese surname

[Yuè] 岳 (Nhac, Yueh): wife's parent

Yueh: refers to 岳 *Yuè*

Yuen: refers to 袁 *Yuán*

Yum: refers to 任 *Rén*

Z

[Zēng] 曾 (Chen, Cheng, Chng, Jeng, Tang, Tsang, Tseng): great grandchildren or parent)

[Zhái] 翟 (Chai, Trac): a Chinese surname

[Zhān] 詹 (Chaim, Chan, Chiem): a Chinese surname

[Zhāng] 张, 張 (Chang, Cheong, Cheung, Chiang, Chong, Jung, Teo, Teoh, Truong): open, extend

[Zhāng] 章 (Chang, Chuong): chapter; 文章 *wénzhāng* 'article'; 印章 *yìnzhāng* 'seal'

[Zhào] 赵, 趙 (Chao, Chew, Chieu, Chiu, Trieu):
   a Chinese surname
[Zhèng] 郑, 鄭 (Chan, Cheng, Chng, Chung, Trinh): NPM
   郑重 *zhèngzhòng* 'serious, solemn'
[Zhōng] 钟, 锺 (Chung): clock, bell
[Zhōu] 周 (Chau, Chew, Chiu, Chou, Chow, Joe): week
[Zhū] 朱 (Chee, Choo, Chu): scarlet
[Zhuāng] 庄, 莊 (Ch'ng, Chuang, Trang): village
[Zōu] 邹, 鄒 (Trau, Tsou): a Chinese surname

In the above list, only three surnames have two Characters. They are 欧阳 *Ōuyáng*, 司马 *Sīmǎ* and 司徒 *Sītú*.

ENGLISH SPELLINGS

English spellings of Chinese names are derived from the sounds of Chinese words. In pīnyīn it is not a problem, as the pronunciation is standardised. The situation is however not too clear-cut in dialects.

If a Mr. Chen would like to marry Ms Chen, they should check their surnames in Chinese. If their Chinese surnames are different, for example Mr. Chen, 陈 *Chén* in Chinese, and Miss Chen, 曾 *Zēng* in Chinese, there is absolutely no problem. As a rule Chinese people strongly discourage marriage between persons of the same surnames, so as to avoid inbreeding.

Websites: Numerous websites of interests pertaining to Chinese surnames are available on the Internet. However most of the good websites require Chinese reading software, as pīnyīn itself is insufficient to identify a particular word, even if intonation is known. The following sites are worth viewing:

'The hundred family surnames':
   www.geocities.com/Tokyo/ 3919/hundred.html
'In Search of your Asian Roots: Genealogical Research on Chinese Surnames':

www.geocities.com/Tokyo/3919/asianroots.html
'Chinese surnames':
www. zhongwen.com/xingshi.htm

GIVEN NAMES

Typically there are two characters for the given name, though in some cases a single word is used. An example of a single character name would be the former prime minister of China, Mr. Lǐ Péng [李鹏]. As some surnames could be made up of two characters, a Chinese name could range from two to four characters.

SIBBLINGS

It is a tradition that brothers or sisters in the family (as well as cousin brothers or sisters) share one of the two characters. For example three brothers in the family (or amongst cousins sharing the same surname) could be named

Chan Weng-Hoong
Chan Weng-Loong
Chan Weng-Ming

In the example above the first word 'Chan' would be the surname, the second word 'Weng' is common to all brothers, and the last word is the name dedicated to the particular individual. The common word 'Weng' indicates the generation that he belongs to, known as 'beì' [辈].

None of the children is allowed to use the generation word that belongs to his father's generation. As such the issue of father and son sharing the same name, distinguished only by Sr. or Jr. does not arise.

Since names are made of commonly used words, a wide range of words could be used. Words are carefully chosen to denote certain personalities or properties. Characters used in surnames are also acceptable as given names. Whether the person is male or female is often indicated by the choice of names. Though some of the names are obviously male or female, quite a number of words could be used in either sex.

As explained in Chapter Eight, some of the words are selected in an attempt to supplement inherent deficiencies according to the yīn-yáng, five elements theory'. Sometimes the Chinese zodiac, based on the year of birth (refer to Chapter Nine), is also taken into consideration.

THREE HUNDRED AND SIXTY-SIX COMMON GIVEN NAMES

Some of the more commonly used characters (not necessarily the most important) are given below. The symbols (F) and (M) indicate that these names are more commonly used for females and males respectively. Both the simplified as well as traditional Chinese characters are given, in addition to their meaning in English.

The names are spelt according to pīnyīn. As we have seen in the surnames, the same word would be spelt differently in a dialect. Consult someone who knows, to confirm the correct word and its meaning.

A

蔼, 靄 [ǎi] friendly, amicable

爱, 愛 [ài] (F) love, to be fond of, to like

艾, 哎 [ài] (F) name of a herb (*Artemisia vulgaris*, Chinese mugwort)

安 [ān] peace, tranquil, secure, content, calm, still, quiet, pacify.

昂 [áng] (M) holding high, raise (head), soar, lift.

B

白 [bái] white, unblemished, empty, blank, bright, clear, pure.

邦 [bāng] (M) nation, state, country

苞 [bāo] (F) bud, calyx

37

保 [bǎo] protect, defend, insure, guarantee, maintain, hold, keep, guard

宝, 寶 [bǎo] treasure, precious

备, 備 [bèi] equip, prepare, get ready, provide.

本 [běn] (M) basis, foundation, origin, source, root, fundamental, the current item, this.

碧 (F) [bì] green, blue, bluish-green jade

标, 標 [biāo] (M) sign, mark, label, indication, prize, award

彬 [bīn] courteous, refined, urbane

冰 [bīng] ice

兵 [bīng] soldier, army, military

炳 [bǐng] brilliant, bright, luminous

伯 [bó] (M) father's elder brother, respectful form of address to a man, senior

C

才 [cái] talent, ability, endowment, gift, expert

财, 財 [cái] wealth, riches, valuables, money

彩 [cǎi] (F) colour, colourful, variety, lottery prize, variegated

操 [cāo] manage, operate, exercise, act.

婵, 嬋 [chán] (F) lovely, beautiful, graceful

昌 [chāng] flourish, prosperous

嫦 [cháng] (F) the legendary goddess of the moon

常 [cháng] frequent, always, often, common, general, constant

畅, 暢 [chàng] uninhibited, fluent, smooth

超 [chāo] (M) exceed, overtake, surpass, transcend, super, ultra.

辰 [chén] 5th Terrestrial Branch, dragon

成 [chéng] achieved, developed, finish, complete, accomplish, succeed.

诚, 誠 [chéng] sincere, honest

程 [chéng] (M) rule, regulation, formula, journey, procedure, sequence; Chinese surname

骋, 騁 [chěng] (M) gallop

崇 [chóng] lofty, esteemed, dignified, honoured, highly regarded

楚 [chǔ] (M) an ancient Chinese kingdom; 清楚 [qīng chǔ] clear-cut, easily understood, distinct

春 [chūn] spring time, joy, youth

传, 傳 [chuán] convey, transmit, pass on, transfer, spread, disseminate.

创, 創 [chuàng] (M) initiate, inaugurate, begin, start, create.

慈 [cí] compassionate, kind, humane, merciful.

聪, 聰 [cōng] intelligent, intellect, bright, clever, wise.

翠 [cuì] (F) a type of jade, jadeite.

D

达, 達 [dà] reach, attain, achieve, realise, convey

大 [dà] big, grand, huge, large, massive, major, great, eldest

德 [dé] virtue, moral, ethics, character.

涤, 滌 [dí] clean, cleanse

丁 [dīng] (M) an able bodied man, 4th Celestial Stem; Chinese surname.

东, 東 [dōng] (M) east

栋, 棟 [dòng] (M) pillar

斗 [dǒu] volume measure, funnel

端 [duān] proper, appropriate.

敦 [dūn] honest, sincere

E

娥 [è] (F) pretty lady

恩 [ēn] kindness or benefits bestowed, grace, favour

儿, 兒 [ér] child, son

F

发，發 [fā] (M) send out, emit, issue, develop
法 [fǎ] (M) law, method, way
繁 [fán] numerous, manifold
范，範 [fàn] pattern, model, example; Chinese surname
芳 [fāng] (F) fragrant
方 [fāng] square
飞，飛 [fēi] fly
芬 [fēn] (F) fragrance
凤，鳳 [fèng] (F) phoenix
枫，楓 [fēng] maple
丰，豐 [fēng] abundant, plentiful
锋，鋒 [fēng] (M) sharp edge of a knife or tool
峰 [fēng] (M) pinnacle, mountain top, peak, summit
烽 [fēng] (M) beacon fire, flame
夫 [fū] (M) husband, man
福 [fú] blessed, good fortune
富 [fù] wealthy, rich

G

敢 [gǎn] (M) bold, daring, courageous
刚，剛 [gāng] (M) just, exact; tough, firm, hard, strong, exactly
钢，鋼 [gāng] (M) steel
高 [gāo] tall, high.
耿 [gěng] dedicated, loyal, devoted, just
姑 [gū] (F) aunt (father's sister)
菇 [gū] (F) mushroom
冠 [guān] crown, crest, hat, cap
光 [guāng] bright, light
广，廣 [guǎng] vast, extensive
贵，貴 [guì] expensive, precious, noble, respectful word for 'your'

国, 國 [guó] country, nation, state

H

海 [hǎi] ocean, sea
汉, 漢 [hàn] (M) Chinese; man, fellow, name of a dynasty
豪 [háo] (M) an outstanding person, grand, heroic
皓 [hào] (F) luminous, bright, white
浩 [hào] (M) vast, grand, great
和 [hé] harmony, peace, and, together, with, union
荷 [hé] (F) lotus
亨 [hēng] smooth going, prosperous
恒 [héng] perseverance, endurance, permanent, eternal
衡 [héng] measure, weight, judge
宏 [hóng] magnificent, grand, great, immense
洪 [hóng] flood
鸿, 鴻 [hóng] (M) swan, grand, great
弘 [hóng] (M) grand, great, magnificent, Expand, enlarge
红 [hóng] red, popular, revolutionary, bonus
虹 [hóng] (F) rainbow
虎 [hǔ] (M) tiger
花 [huā] (F) flower, blossom, pattern, spend
华, 華 [huá] China, Chinese, splendid, magnificent, flourish
欢, 歡 [huān] happy, exalting, joy, pleased
焕 [huàn] (M) shine, glow, brilliant, illustrious
辉, 煇 [huī] brilliant, glorious
慧 [huì] (F) intelligence
惠 [huì] benefit, kindness, kind deeds
蕙 [huì] (F) orchid species

J

吉 [jí] auspicious
济, 濟 [jì] relieve, help, benefit, aid
家 [jiā] family, home; specialist

41

加 [jiā] add, plus
佳 [jiā] excellent, fine
嘉 [jiā] excellent, fine
稼 [jiā] sowing

建 [jiàn] build, establish, construct, set up
健 [jiàn] healthy
剑, 劍 [jiàn] sword
箭 [jiàn] arrow
江 [jiāng] river
教 [jiāo] educate, religion
姣 [jiāo] (F) beautiful looking
娇, 嬌 [jiāo] (F) lovable, charming, pampered, tender
    loving, delicate
杰, 傑 [jié] outstanding, prominent, illustrious
金 [jīn] gold, metal, money
锦 [jǐn] brocade, glorious, embroidered work, bright
景 [jǐng] scenery, view
精 [jīng] refined, essence, excellent
晶 [jīng] crystal
静 [jìng] tranquil, quiet, still, calm
敬 [jìng] respect, venerate, salute, offer
靖 [jìng] peace, tranquilly
菊 [jú] (F) chrysanthemum
巨 [jù] (M) huge, giant, enormous, tremendous
聚 [jù] accumulate, assemble, gather
军, 軍 [jūn] (M) military, army
俊 [jùn] (M) handsome
骏, 駿 [jùn] (M) fine horse
君 [jūn] (M) gentleman, lord, monarch, sovereign
娟 [juān] (F) grace, beauty
鹃 [juān] (F): 杜鹃 [dùjuān] Azalea plant

K

开, 開 [kāi] open, initiate

克 [kè] overcome, subdue, restrain; gram weight

坤 [kūn] one of the trigrams/hexagrams [yìjīng], female, earth

宽, 寬 [kuān] (M) broad, wide, lenient

L

来 [lái] come, arrive

兰, 蘭 [lán] (F) orchid

劳 [láo] (M) labour, work, toil

乐, 樂 [lè] happy, cheerful, Chinese surname

雷 [léi] (M) thunder, Chinese surname

蕾 [lěi] (F) flower bud

礼, 禮 [lǐ] etiquette, manners, social custom, rite, propriety; gift

利 [lì] advantage, favourable, benefit, profit, sharp

莉 [lì] (F): 茉莉 [mòli] Jasmine

丽, 麗 [lì] (F) pretty, beautiful

俐 [lì] (F): 伶俐 [línglì] witty, clever, intelligent, bright

理 [lǐ] logic, reason, principles; science

立 [lì] setup; upright, stand

力 [lì] power, force, strength

励, 勵 [lì] encourage, exhort

莲, 蓮 [lián] (F) lotus

良 [liáng] (M) good, fine, very

樑 [liáng] (M) beam

林 [lín] forest, woods

琳 [lin] (F) beautiful jade, gem

玲 [líng] (F): 玲珑 [línglóng] dainty, exquisite

凌 [líng] soaring, rising high

铃, 鈴 [líng] bell

伶 [líng] (F) actor or actress

龙, 龍 [lóng] (M) dragon, imperial; Chinese surname

43

隆 [lóng] (M) thriving, prosperous, grand

璐 [lù] (F) pretty jade

露 [lù] (F) dew

律 [lǜ] regulation, law

M

满 [mǎn] full, filled, packed; Manchuria

曼 [màn] (F) graceful

茂 [mào] luxuriant, flourish

梅 [méi] (F) plum blossom

玫 [méi] (F) rose

眉 [méi] (F) eyebrow, features

美 [měi] (F) beautiful, pretty

妹 [mèi] (F) younger sister

媚 [mèi] (F) cute, lovely, charming

蜜 [mi] (F) honey

勉 [miǎn] urge, encourage, exhort

苗 [miáo] sprout

敏 [mǐn] quick, nimble, sensitive, keen

民 [mín] (M) people, civilian, race, nationality, citizen

铭, 銘 [míng] inscription, engrave

明 [míng] bright, clear; understand; next

茉 [mò] (F) 茉莉 [mòli] Jasmine

慕 [mù] admire, yearn for

N

耐 [nài] endure, tolerate

南 [nán] south

宁, 寧 [níng] peace, tranquil

妞 [niū] (F) little girl

暖 [nuǎn] (F) warmth

女 [nǚ] (F) female, woman

44

P

庞, 龐 [páng] (M) huge, tremendous, Chinese surname

培 [péi] cultivate

佩 [pèi] (F) wear (at the waist)

沛 [pèi] (M) abundant

澎 [péng] splash, surge, sound of waves

朋 [péng] friend

鹏, 鵬 [péng] legendary, huge bird

琵 [pí] a Chinese musical instrument

平 [píng] even, level, flat; calm, peaceful

萍 [píng] (F) duckweed

苹, 蘋 [píng] apple

璞 [pǔ] uncut jade, simple, down to earth

Q

齐, 齊 [qí] orderly, even; name of a Chinese empire

琦 [qí] (F) fine jade; outstanding

琪 [qí] (F) fine jade

奇 [qí] strange, queer; wonderful!

谦, 謙 [qiān] humble, modest

千 [qiān] thousand

茜 [qiàn] name of a plant, *Rubia cordiolia*

强 [qiáng] (M) strength, powerful

巧 [qiǎo] ingenious, skilful

俏 [qiào] (F) pretty, attractive

勤 [qín] diligent, hard-working

琴 [qín] (F) a type of musical instrument

钦, 欽 [qīn] admire, esteem, respected; imperial

庆, 慶 [qìng] celebrate

情 [qíng] (F) sentiment, feeling, emotion, passion

清 [qīng] clear, pure

青 [qīng] green, blue-green

琼 [qióng] (F) fine jade, refined; Hainan

秋　[qiū] autumn
泉　[quán] (M) spring, source, fountain

R

容　[róng] contain, allow, hold; appearance, look
融　[róng] harmonious, compatible
荣, 榮　[róng] pride, honour, glory
蓉　[róng] (F): 芙蓉 cotton rose hibiscus
柔　[róu] (F) tender, soft, gentle
如　[rú] resemble, such as
瑞　[ruì] auspicious, propitious
蕊　[ruǐ] (F) stamen or pistil
锐, 銳　[ruì] (M) sharp, acute
润, 潤　[rùn] moist, lubricate

S

珊　[shān] (F) coral
韶　[sháo] (F) splendid, elegant
绅, 紳　[shēn] (M) gentleman
慎　[shèn] cautious
升　[shēng] ascend, arise, raise, promote
生　[shēng] life, live, produce, born, grow
胜, 勝　[shèng] victory, win
圣, 聖　[shèng] sage, holy, spiritual, sacred, saint
诗, 詩　[shī] poetry, poetic
狮　[shī] (M) lion
实, 實　[shí] solid, substantial, true, real, solid; honest
史　[shǐ] history, historical
世　[shì] world, era; life, generation
水　[shuǐ] water
淑　[shū] (F) kind and gentle
丝, 絲　[sī] (F) silk, thread, trace
思　[sī] thoughts, think

松 [sōng] (M) pine
宋 [sòng] name of a dynasty, Chinese surname
颂, 頌 [sòng] praise, song
苏, 蘇 [sū] revive
肃, 肅 [sù] (M) solemn, serious
素 [sù] (F) vegetarian, simple, plain

T

涛, 濤 [tāo] big waves
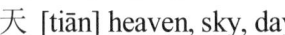
天 [tiān] heaven, sky, day
添 [tiān] (M) add on, replenish, increase
甜 [tián] (F) sweet
铁, 鐵 [tiě] (M) iron, steel
婷 [tíng] (F) graceful, elegant
桐 [tóng] (M) tung tree, Paulownia tree
通 [tōng] unimpeded, connect, communicate, through
统, 統 [tǒng] unify, unite, rule

W

婉 [wǎn] (F) gracious, tactful
万, 萬 [wàn] (M) ten thousand; myriad, Chinese surname
玮, 瑋 [wěi] (F) name of a jade, rare, precious
伟, 偉 [wěi] (M) great
温 [wēn] warm
文 [wén] culture, language, writing
武 [wǔ] (M) martial art
务, 務 [wù] affair, business, matters
悟 [wǔ] awakening, realisation, aware

X

西 [xī] west, occidental
希 [xī] hope, wish; rare, uncommon
惜 [xī] cherish, value, treasure

霞 [xiá] (F) morning/evening rosy clouds
娴, 嫻 [xián] (F) refined, gentle
贤, 賢 [xián] virtuous, noble
显, 顯 [xiǎn] prominent, conspicuous
香 [xiāng] fragrance, scented; savoury; popular
祥 [xiáng] auspicious, propitious
翔 [xiáng] soar, hovering in the air
享 [xiǎng] enjoy
晓, 曉 [xiǎo] dawn; know
小 [xiǎo] little, small; young
心 [xīn] heart, mind
欣 [xīn] joyous, happy
新 [xīn] new
兴, 興 [xìng] prosper, flourish
雄 [xióng] (M) masculine, heroic, powerful
修 [xiū] cultivate; study
秀 [xiù] elegant
绪, 緒 [xù] beginnings, clues, mood
旭 [xù] rising sun, dawn
宣 [xuān] declare, announce
璇 [xuán] (F) beautiful jade
玄 [xuán] mysterious
学, 學 [xué] study, learn, knowledge
雪 [xuě] snow
训, 訓 [xùn] teach, lecture, coach, instruct

Y

雅 [yǎ] elegant
亚, 亞 [yà] runner-up; 亚洲 [yàzhōu]: Asia
炎 [yán] (M) heat, flame
妍 [yán] (F) beautiful, delicate, dainty
艳, 艷 [yàn] (F) colourful, gorgeous, glamorous
燕 [yàn] (F) sparrow

阳, 陽 [yáng] (M) masculine, sun
杨, 楊 [yáng] (M) Poplar tree
扬, 揚 [yáng] raise up, propagate
耀 [yào] (M) brilliant, glorious

晔, 曄 [yè] bright, light
怡 [yí] composed, pleasant
忆, 憶 [yì] recollect, remembrance
逸 [yì] peace, tranquillity, leisure
艺, 藝 [yì] artistic
益 [yì] benefits
义, 義 [yì] righteousness
亿, 億 [yì] one hundred millions
毅 [yì] perseverance
瑛 [yīng] (F) pretty jade, lustre of jade
樱 [yīng] (F) cherry
鹰, 鷹 [yīng] (M) hawk, eagle, falcon
英 [yīng] illustrious, heroic
颖, 穎 [yíng] clever, gifted
盈 [yíng] surplus, profit, filled
永 [yǒng] always, perpetual, forever
勇 [yǒng] (M) courageous, brave
优, 優 [yōu] merit, strong point, excel, outstanding
有 [yǒu] have, possess, own
裕 [yù] plentiful, affluent, abundant
玉 [yù] jade
豫 [yù] happy, joyous
源 [yuán] source, origin, roots
月 [yuè] noon
岳 [yuè] Chinese surname, 岳父母 wife's parent
云, 雲 [yún] cloud

Z

泽, 澤 [zé] wetland

哲 [zhé] philosophy

珍 [zhēn] (F) treasure, precious

贞, 貞 [zhēn] (F) faithful, loyal, chaste

震 [zhèn] vibrate, shock, a trigram, hexagram

征 [zhēng] expedition, journey, conquer

正 [zhèng] proper, right, correct, principled

志 [zhì] resolve, will, aspiration

治 [zhì] govern, rule, manage, control

致 [zhì] present, deliver

智 [zhì] intelligence, intellect, wisdom

中 [zhōng] central, middle

钟, 鍾 [zhōng] clock

忠 [zhōng] loyal

重 [zhòng] heavy, emphasis, major, important

宙 [zhòu] universe, cosmos

珠 [zhū] (F) pearl, jewellery

资, 資 [zī] resource, capital, qualification

子 [zǐ] child

宗 [zōng] ancestor, clan

祖 [zǔ] ancestor, founder

Naming Word Combinations

In addition to words listed above, there is a huge pool of meaningful words to choose from. However it is the suitable combination of characters, rather than each individual character, that makes a name meaningful. Some of the suitable combinations include:

For Male

光耀 [Guāng Yào], 光明 [Guāng Míng]

丰昌 [Fēng Chāng], 丰顺 [Fēng Shùn]

建国 [Jiàn Guó], 建丰 [Jiàn Fēng]

俊良 [Jùn Liáng], 俊挺 [Jùn Tíng]

世昌 [Shì Chāng], 世豪 [Shì Háo]

颂义 [Sòng Yì], 颂德 [Sòng Dé]
文杰 [Wén Jié], 文彬 [Wén Bīn]
泽民 [Zé Mín], 泽华 [Zé Huá]
志豪 [Zhì Háo], 志伟 [Zhì Wěi]
子平 [Zǐ Píng], 子文 [Zǐ Wén]
有本 [Yǒu Běn], 豪本 [Háo Běn]
荣烈 [Róng Liè], 兴烈 [Xìng Liè]
希明 [Xī Míng], 维明 [Wéi Míng]
志启 [Zhì Qǐ], 敬启 [Jìng Qǐ]
思恕 [Sī Shù], 允恕 [Yǔn Shù]
天祥 [Tián Xiáng], 兆祥 [Zhào Xiáng]
知训 [Zhī Xùn], 文训 [Wén Xùn]
紫阳 [Zǐ Yáng], 耀阳 [Yào Yáng]
修义 [Xiū Yì], 民义 [Mín Yì]
吉汉 [Jí Hàn], 卓汉 [Zhuó Hàn]

For Female

慧颖 [Huì Yíng], 慧情 [Huì Qíng]
嘉惠 [Jiā Huì], 嘉玲 [Jiā Líng]
静仪 [Jìng Yí], 静芬 [Jìng Fēn]
丽梅 [Lì Méi], 丽琴 [Lì Qín]
美华 [Měi Huá], 美娟 [Měi Juān]
媚曼 [Mèi Màn], 媚英 [Mèi Yīng]
琴韵 [Qín Yùn], 琴美 [Qín Měi]
淑芬 [Shū Fen], 淑贤 [Shū Xián]
怡洁 [Yí Jié], 怡敏 [Yí Mǐn]
雅玲 [Yǎ Líng], 雅婷 [Yǎ Tíng]
翠嫦 [Cuì Cháng], 碧嫦 [Bì Cháng]
娟惠 [Juān Huì], 巧惠 [Qiǎo Huì]
香兰 [Xiāng Lán], 幽兰 [Yōu Lán]
宝莲 [Bǎo Lián], 敏莲 [Mǐn Lián]
容姗 [Róng Shān], 少姗 [Shào Shān]
黛玉 [Dài Yù], 慧玉 [Huì Yù]

豫婉 [Yù Wǎn], 素婉 [Sù Wǎn]
喜艳 [Xǐ Yàn], 冰艳 [Bīng Yàn]
艳樱 [Yàn Yīng], 春樱 [Chūn Yīng]
彩姿 [Cǎi Zī], 玉姿 [Yù Zī]

Refer to the lists above for individual meanings. As a matter of interest the first combination 光耀 *Guāng Yào* 'brilliance', is the given name of the former prime minister of Singapore, Mr. Lee Kuan Yew.

(In China, the two characters could have their pīnyīn combined, for example Guāngyào. In Southeast Asia, they would be separated, for example Guāng Yào.)

Needless to say, there are many other good combinations, too many to be listed. An interesting website pertaining to the frequency counts of Chinese names and surnames, available at *www.geocities. com/hao510/namefreq/*

It is important to note that though the individual word or words might sound good, their meanings would be drastically different when combined. As an example the characters 名望 *míngwàng* meaning 'good reputation', would be an excellent choice to combine with most surnames. However it would be unsuitable for people with the surname 吴 *Wú*, as this surname sounds similar to the character 无 *wú* which means 'without', and with a name like 'Wu Ming Wang' it could only mean 'without any reputation'.

INTERPRETING CHINESE NAMES

It is important to note the following:

Ethnic Chinese from countries such as Indonesia and Thailand do not necessarily have Chinese names.

Muslim converts of Chinese origin have Muslim names, for example Mustapha Abdullah.

Chinese ladies using a combination of Christian names and the surname of her non-Chinese husband could be indistinguishable from any other Christian names. How would you know whether Esther Pritchard is an ethnic Chinese?

ADOPTING A CHINESE NAME

Some Caucasians, in particular businessmen who deal frequently with the Chinese, might like to adopt a Chinese name. These names could be translated phonetically from English or else a Chinese name could be coined.

It is important that the appropriate words corresponding to the source be chosen, because the same sound could have different meanings depending on the different Chinese characters. It is also important to choose the characters that have good meanings. For example the name 'Julian' could be translated as 猪脸 'pig face', 祖念 'in memory of ancestors' or a three-word Chinese sounding name 朱利安 *Zhū Lì'ān.*

Increasingly ethnic Chinese, in particular those familiar with both languages, coin Chinese names that are not only meaningful but easily translated into English.

The meanings of Chinese words could be found in dictionaries, or certain websites such as:

'Chinese characters and culture': *zhongwen.com/*

'Chinese character dictionary':

    www.chinalanguage.com/CCDICT/

Some websites enable you to get a list of Chinese name from a name in English. (For example *zhongwen.com/qianming.htm*). Some websites enable you to get a name from both given name as well as surnames, mainly through phonetics. (For example *www.mandarin tools.com/chinesename.html*), which also give you explanations of the words chosen. As we have seen in the case of 'pig face' versus 'in memory of ancestors', it is important to have the meanings checked out.

The issue of formal addresses is discussed in Chapter Seven, under Social Etiquette.

Cultural Roots – The Chinese Language

CENTRAL TO THE UNDERSTANDING OF any culture is the language itself. Outside China, not all Chinese families speak Mandarin, though most families would speak a dialect at home. Some attend Chinese schools, while others could be totally illiterate in the language of their ancestors. Cultural heritage such as names stem from the language; a basic understanding of the fascinating Chinese language would be necessary to understand the Chinese mindset and psyche.

This chapter looks into various aspects of the Chinese language, its origin, development, the written components and pronunciation. It ends with looking at how the language deals with the creation of vocabulary or conceptual word combinations, as well as evolution towards the digital era.

A SNAPSHOT OF THE CHINESE LANGUAGE

In reality the Chinese language is fascinating, though it can be a difficult language to speak or write.

It is fascinating when one realises that this is the only major language written without any alphabet, where each character needs to be learned, practised and remembered individually.

It is fascinating when one realises that each character is derived from pictures, whether the words convey objects, verbs, adjectives or some highly imaginary concepts. Each character originated as a pictogram.

It is fascinating when one is told that it is one of the oldest languages, passed down from generation to generation throughout the centuries, and is still used, developed and expanded.

It is fascinating to note that in spite of the complexity of the language; more than 1.3 billion Chinese use it as the primary language of every day use, more than any other language in the world. It is also the second most used language on the Internet after English.

Chinese characters are also used in the Japanese language as 'Kanji' 漢字. In Korea it is known as 'Hanja', 한자.

WORDS FROM PICTURES

Chinese characters originate from pictures, for example:

The character for water 水 *shuǐ* is derived from the picture.

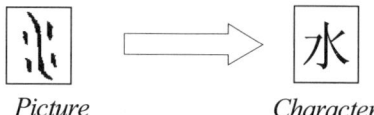

Picture　　　　　　*Character*

Numerous Chinese characters including river, stream, flow, gush, soup, tear, incorporates 'water' as a component, known as word radical. This could be written as 水 *shuǐ* or 'Three doted water' radical [氵] 三点水 *sāndiǎnshuǐ*. This is elaborated later on.

The Chinese character for 'heart' *xīn*, is depicted as:

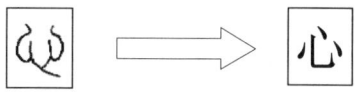

Characters pertaining to sentiments or emotions normally have heart as a radical, such as angry, bored, forget, loyal, tolerance, fear, feeling, love, sad, thought, etc. The heart character component 心 can be written in another form 忄. The Characters having the heart radical in this form include emotion, fear, hate, memory, panic, respect, understand and worry.

The character for 'door' 門 *mén* is depicted below.

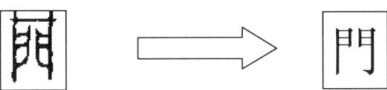

The character is now simplified as 门. It appears as a component in other characters including 'open' 開, 'close' 関, now simplified as 开, 关

The word 'fish' 魚 *yú* requires little explanation.

The resemblance to a fish is remarkable. Originally the characters were in all shapes, but they are now presented to fit into square format.

The challenge comes when one needs to express concepts or abstract ideas such as emotions. Let us look at a few examples.

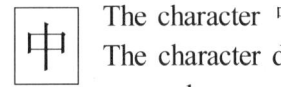

The character 中 *zhōng* refers to middle, central or centre. The character depicts a line drawn right in the centre of a rectangle.

When the words 'central' and 'heart' are combined we get the scenario whereby the heart remains central, not swayed by circumstances, giving rise to the character 忠 *zhōng* meaning loyalty.

Let us look at the word 'love' *ài*

Note that there is the character 心 *xīn* 'heart' at the centre, representing emotion, feeling or sentiment. The closest character that lies beneath the heart that makes any sense would be 友 *you* 'friend', indicating that there is emotion between friends. The sentiment and emotion is capped by ⌐⌐ (see enclosure above the heart), indicating that the sentiment or relationship is exclusive, not open to any body else. Finally there is the claw component 爪 *zhǎo* on top, implying a powerful grip, emotional or physical, on the people concerned. Such is the power and emotions involved in love.

 In the process of simplifying the characters, the 心 *xīn* 'heart' component was left out. The present character for love is one without the heart, though the component for friend is more defined. Does this reflect modern times, whereby the heart is not necessary for love?

 Let us look at the character 國 *guó* 'nation or country'. First of all there is a well defined boundary or territory, as shown by the outer shell 囗. Within the territory a straight line at the bottom '_' depicts land, on which people represented by 口 *kǒu* 'mouth' resides. Within the framework there is the 戈 *gē* 'spear', signifying defence of the territory, its land, its people and all the associated assets and values.

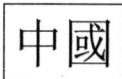 China, the Middle Kingdom, is written as two characters, the Middle Kingdom.

Several websites feature origin and development of Chinese characters. They include:

Chinese characters – Origin of Chinese characters –
www.euroasiasoftware.com/english/chinese/characters/ursprungeng.html
Origin of the Chinese script:
www.chinavista.com/experience/hanzi/hanzi.html
Origin of Chinese characters
chineseculture.about.com/library/weekly/aa101699.htm

EVOLUTION OF CHARACTERS

Today not all characters could be easily explained or analysed, due to evolution. The first Chinese dictionary 说文解字 *shuōwénjiězì*, compiled around 100 AD, attributed six categories [六书] *liùshū* of evolution. They are:

1. **Pictographs** [象形] *xiàngxíng* modified sketches or drawings representing the object.
2. **Indicatives** [指示] *zhǐshì*. Pointing to an idea, for example 上 *shàng* 'up', 下 *xià* 'down'.
3. **Semantic-phonetic** [形声] *xíngshēng*. A component gives the sound, while another indicates the application. For example the character 河 *hé* 'river' is made up of 氵 *shuǐ* 'water' and a component providing a similar sound 可 *kě*.
4. **Associated understanding** [会意] *huìyì*. For example the character 信 *xìn* 'credibility' is composed from 亻 *rén* 'man' standing by his 言 *yán* 'words'.
5. **Extended or evolved meaning** [转注] *zhuǎnzhù*. The meanings of some characters could have been extended and eventually evolved to become another character after some time. The commonly given example is for the characters 老 *lǎo* 'old' and 考 *kǎo* 'seasoned, tested'. Both characters not only look similar but have closely associated meanings. One is thought to have evolved from another.
6. **Pretend to loan** [假借] *jiǎjiè*. This is the most difficult category, whereby a character is coined from other words, usually phonetically. An example is the character 祥 *xiáng* 'good omen', borrowing the sound from the character 羊 *yáng* 'goat' and adding another component 礻 *yī* 'indicate'.

CHARACTER FORMS

Over the centuries Chinese characters have undergone numerous revisions and changes.

One of the earliest Chinese characters were found on ceramics, known as 陶文 *táowén*. Records of Chinese writing were found on animal bones and tortoise shells, known as 'shell and bone characters' [甲骨文] *jiǎgúwén* dating from the Shāng 商 dynasty (15th century BC) (refer to p. 128).

The next development was the 篆书 *zhuàn shū*, used even today in official seals. After Shi Huang Ti [秦始皇] *Qín Shǐhuàng* (p. 166) unified China in 221 BC, he introduced a standardised system of writing the 小篆 *xiǎozhuàn* for the whole of China, replacing various forms of characters then existing (refer to p. 133).

The various font types are illustrated towards the end of this chapter.

FURTHER DEVELOPMENT

Before the advent of pen, characters were written using ink brushes, which brought elegance to the writings. The brushes make it possible to vary the breadth of any stroke from thick to thin and vice-versa. As the mixture of thick and thin strokes needs to be properly structured and balanced in appearance, the shapes of Characters became more regular and squarer.

Indeed Chinese writing is known as 'writing in square blocks' [方块字] *fāngkuàizì*. Throughout the years different forms such as the 楷书 *kǎishū* 行书 *xíngshū*, 草书 *cǎoshū* and 隶书 *lìshū* were developed. These provide flexibility and introduce elegance and calligraphy into the writings.

STRUCTURE OF CHINESE CHARACTERS

As we know the English words are composed of 26 alphabets, arranged from left to right. The Chinese characters, on the other hand, are made up of combinations of about a dozen or so strokes[5] [笔画] *bǐhuà*, comprising

⌐ [héng] 横 horizontal stroke

丨 [shù] 竖 vertical stroke

丿 [piě] 撇 downward stroke to the left

乀 [nà] 捺 downward stroke to the right

丶 [diǎn] 点 dot

⌐ [zhé] 折 right angle stroke

[gōu] 勾 hook, written downwards with a quick tap of the brush. In practice five types of hooks are available

⌐ [tí] 提 upward stroke to the right

L [piědiǎn] 撇点

〈 [shùzhé] 竖折

SEQUENCE OF STROKES
Because the Chinese characters were originally written with a brush, rules have been developed as to how the characters are written. The

---

[5] Stroke is used in a very general manner. It could be a stroke, a hook, an angle, etc.

rules are based on the ease with which the brush could move. Children are taught from a very young age that each character has to be written in a definite sequence called 笔顺 *bǐshùn*.

In general the following rules are observed:

- ❖ Write a stroke from top to bottom, not from bottom to top
- ❖ Write from left to right, not right to left
- ❖ Horizontal strokes are written before vertical strokes
- ❖ If a word is contained within an enclosure, write the left vertical stroke first, then the right angle stroke. Then put in the content, finally seal the enclosure with a horizontal stroke at the bottom. For example in writing the character 因*yīn*, write the left vertical stroke of the shell, ' | ', then the top and right as a stroke 冂. The inner component 大 is then written in, and the bottom of the outer shell joined, completing the character 因.
- ❖ Write the middle stroke first before strokes on the right and left

EXAMPLE OF A STROKE SEQUENCE
The surname character 张 *zhāng* is written as follows

丿 乛 𡿨 弓 弓' 弖 张 张

An average student of Chinese language needs to practise, normally by repeatingly writing the words until he remembers. Software is now available that illustrates the sequence of strokes for each word. With the development of computers and Chinese software it is perhaps more important to know how to recognise and type in Chinese characters on a word processor, rather than memorise each character and its sequence of strokes!

TOP TO BOTTOM, RIGHT TO LEFT

Traditionally Chinese characters are written from top to bottom, from right to left, as shown below. This is still practised in some Chinese paintings or calligraphy.

The abridged 'coupled poem' of our book 'Crossing the Oceans, Taking roots' in Chinese scripts, written from top to bottom, illustrated on the left.

Today the Chinese scripts are written horizontally from left to right. Chinese word processors could easily transform left-to-right texts to top-to-bottom settings.

SIMPLIFICATION OF CHARACTERS

In 1956 the Chinese undertook to simplify the written Chinese, reducing the number of strokes, resulting in characters that are easier to learn and use. This was a bold move to promote basic education, in particular the reading and writing abilities. In the past too many people only spoke the language (at least a dialect) without the ability to read or write.

The first word within the box has been simplified from 13 strokes to the one on the bottom with 3 strokes. Both words mean vast, pronounced as *guǎng*.

In general it is easier for a person familiar with the traditional text to understand or guess simplified character than the other way round.

The simplified version, known as 简体字 *jiǎntǐzì*, is used in China, and is the version taught in Australian schools and universities. The traditional version, known as 繁體字 *fántǐzì*, is used in Taiwan, United States, etc. Increasingly the trend is moving towards simplified Chinese.

Examples of simplified and traditional Chinese characters can be found in the section on Chinese surnames and names, where both scripts are written. The 繁體字 *fántǐzì* is also used in Chapter Seven for the writing of congratulatory words on plaques and newspaper advertisements. The rest of the book is based on simplified Chinese.

CALLIGRAPHY

Various styles of writing the character longevity 壽 *shòu,*
engraved on wooden strips, joined together to make a fan.

Writing with an ink brush produces the elegance not otherwise achievable. Chinese calligraphy is an art, and is regarded as such.

An excellent example of Chinese calligraphy found in a stamp celebrating the year of the dragon [龍] *lóng*. The calligraphy looks superb in traditional characters. The simplified characters is written as 龙.

There are numerous websites on Chinese calligraphy. They provide examples over a broad range of calligraphic styles. These include

Art of Chinese Calligraphy: *www.chinapage.com/callig1.html*
Appreciation of Chinese Calligraphy:
  www.chinapage.com/calligraphy.html
Chinese Calligraphy (Brush calligraphy):
  www.asiawind.com/art/callig/Default.htm

CHINESE CHARACTER RADICALS

A 'Chinese character radical' [部首] *bùshǒu* is a component that associates the meaning or core ideas to the character. For example, most metals and minerals would have the metal radical 钅 *jīn*. The word 铜 *tóng* 'copper' is made up of the metal radical 钅 *jīn* together with the character 同 *tóng*, which gives it the sound. Though the recognition of word radical indicates the nature of the character, it bears no relationship to the phonetics of the character.

Other word radicals include food [饣] *shí* radical used in words pertaining to eating or food, water [氵] *shuǐ* radical, for things that relate to water; word [讠] *yán* radical, associated with speech, etc.

Some of the word radicals exist only as components of words, and do not mean anything themselves. For example the radical 纟 *sī* does not mean anything, though it implies something relating to textile. Similarly the radical 亻 *rén* is not a word in its own right though it is used for words relating to people or human.

Most words today are derived from a combination of radicals and an appropriate component which satisfy the phonetical requirement for the word, or has an appropriate meaning.

The importance of word radicals cannot be over estimated. It forms an essential part of written Chinese. Until the development of phonetics it was the main method of word search in Chinese dictionaries.

Interestingly many people do not know how the radicals are pronounced, even though they are used to search for words. The Language Research Institute of the Chinese Academy of Social Science (CASS) [中国社会科学院语言研究所] *Zhōngguó shèhuì kēxuéyuàn yǔyán yánjiusuǒ*, presented the dictionary 'Modern Chinese dictionary' [现代汉语词典] *xiàndài hànyǔcídiǎn*, which gives the most authoritative ordering of characters by radicals, as well as naming of these radicals.

The first eighty of the one hundred and eighty-nine radicals are listed below, with three examples for each radical. They are arranged according to their complexity (the number of strokes). The radical is followed by the way it is called, together with its pīnyīn.

One stroke

1. Dot [丶] 一点 *yīdiǎn*. Found in the characters 义 *yì* 'righteous'; 丸 *wán* 'pills'; 头 *tóu* 'head'.
2. Horizontal stroke [一] 一横 *yīhéng*. Found in the characters 上 *shàng* 'above'; 下 *xià* 'below'; 三 *sān* 'three'.
3. Vertical stroke [丨] 一竖 *yīshù*. Found in the characters 丰 *fēng* 'plentiful'; 中 *zhōng* 'middle'; 串 *chuàn* 'string together'.
4. Left downward stroke [丿] 一撇 *yīpiě*. Found in the characters 九 *jiǔ* 'nine'; 千 *qiān* 'thousand'; 升 *shēng* 'rise'.
5. Horizontal stroke with double bend hook [乙] 横折折勾 *héngzhézhégōu*. Found in the characters 乙 *yǐ* 'second Celestial Stem'; 乞 *qì* 'beg'; 飞 *fēi* 'fly'.

Two Strokes

6. Top of the character 'six' 六 [亠] 六字头 *liùzìtóu*. Found in 六 *liù* 'six'; 市 *shì* 'city'; 交 *jiāo* 'exchange'.
7. Two doted water [冫] 两点水 *liǎngdiǎnshuǐ*. Found in 冰 *bīng* 'ice'; 冯 *féng* 'a surname'; 次 *cì* 'times'
8. Bald cap of the character 宝 *bǎo* [冖] 秃宝盖 *tūbǎogài*. Found in 写 *xiě* 'write'; 冠 *guān* 'crown'; 军 *jūn* 'military'.

9. Speech [讠] 言字旁 *yánzìpáng*. Found in 话 *huà* 'speech'; 记 *jì* 'remember'; 许 *xǔ* 'permit'.

10. Two [二] 二字部 *èrzìbù*. Found in 元 *yuán* 'dollar'; 干 *gān* 'branch'; 云 *yún* 'clouds'.

11. Ten [十] 十部 *shíbù*. Found in 克 *kè* 'overcome'; 古 *gǔ* 'ancient'; 支 *zhī* 'branch'.

12. Factory [厂] 偏厂部 *piānchǎngbù*. Found in 厅 *tīng* 'hall'; 压 *yā* 'press'; 历 *lì* 'history'.

13. Three sided frame [匚] 三筐栏 *sānkuānglán*. Found in 区 *qū* 'district'; 巨 *jù* 'giant'; 医 *yī* 'medical'.

14. Divination [卜] 卜字部 *bǔzìbù*. Found in 外 *wài* 'outer'; 桌 *zhuō* 'table'; 卧 *wò* 'sleep'.

15. Upright knife [刂] 立刀旁 *lìdāopáng*. Found in 刊 *kān* 'magazine'; 刘 *liú* 'a Chinese surname'; 刻 *kè* 'engrave'.

16. Frame of the character 同 [冂] 同字筐 *tóngzìkuāng*. Found in 肉 *ròu* 'meat'; 周 *zhōu* 'week'; 网 *wǎng* 'net'.

17. Eight [八] 八字部 *bāzìbù*. Found in 公 *gōng* 'public'; 分 *fēn* 'distribute'; 兴 *xìng* 'pleasure'.

18. People [人] 人字头 *rénzìtóu*. Found in 个 *gè* 'individual'; 仓 *cāng* 'storehouse'; 命 *mìng* 'life'.

19. Single person [亻] 单人旁 *dānrénpáng*. Found in 任 *rèn* 'appoint'; 何 *hé* 'how'; 你 *nǐ* 'you'.

20. Wrap [勹] 包子头 *bāozǐtóu*. Found in 句 *jù* 'sentence'; 勾 *gōu* 'tick off'; 包 *bāo* 'wrap'.

21. Child [儿] 儿字部 *érzìbù*. Found in 元 *yuán* 'dollar'; 兄 *xiōng* 'elder brother'; 允 *yǔn* 'permit'.

22. Small table [几] 几字部 *jīzìbù*. Found in 凡 *fán* 'ordinary'; 风 *fēng* 'wind'; 充 *chōng* 'fill up'.

23. Private [厶] 私字部 *sīzìbù*. Found in 去 *qù* 'go'; 县 *xiàn* 'county'; 参 *cān* 'take part'.

24. Again [又] 又字部 *yòuzìbù*. Found in 友 *yǒu* 'friend'; 双 *shuāng* 'pair'; 对 *duì* 'correct'.

25. Build [廴] 建之旁 *jiànzhīpáng*. Found in 建 *jiàn* 'build up';

延 *yán* 'prolong'; 廷 *tíng* 'Imperial court'.

26. Single ear [卩] 单耳旁 *dan'ěrpáng*. Found in 印 *yìn* 'print'; 即 *ji* 'immediate'; 卫 *wèi* 'health'.

27. Left ear [阝] 左耳刀 *zuǒ'ěrdāo*. Found in 队 *duì* 'troop'; 防 *fáng* 'prevent'; 阻 *zǔ* 'impede'.

28. Right ear [阝] 右耳刀 *yòu'ěrdāo*. Found in 邪 *xié* 'evil'; 邮 *yǒu* 'postal'; 邻 *lín* 'neighbour'.

29. Holding cup [凵] 三道筐 *sāndàokuāng*. Found in 凶 *xiōng* 'fierce'; 出 *chū* 'out'; 函 *hán* 'document'.

30. Knife [刀] 刀字部 *dāozìbù*. Found in 切 *qiè* 'cut'; 分 *fēn* 'distribute'; 争 *zhēng* 'fight for'.

31. Strength [力] 力字旁 *lìzìpáng*. Found in 加 *jiā* 'add'; 劝 *quàn* 'advice'; 功 *gōng* 'work'.

Three Strokes

32. Three doted water [氵] 三点水 *sāndiǎnshuǐ*. Found in 满 *mǎn* 'full'; 江 *jiāng* 'river'; 汤 *tāng* 'soup'.

33. Upright heart [忄] 竖心旁 *shùxīnpáng*. Found in 忆 *yì* 'remembrance'; 忙 *máng* 'busy'; 忧 *yōu* 'worry'.

34. Cover of character 宝' [宀] 宝盖部 *bǎogàibù*. Found in 它 *tā* 'it'; 家 *jiā* 'family'; 客 *kè* 'guest'.

35. The side of the character 将 [爿] 将字旁 *jiàngzìpáng*. Found in 将; 将 *jiàng* 'imminent'; 壮 *zhuàng* 'powerful'; 妆 *zhuāng* 'dowry'.

36. Broad [广] 广字旁 *guǎngzìpáng*. Found in the Chinese 唐 *táng* 'dynasty'; 庄 zhuāng 'village'; 床 *chuáng* 'bed'.

37. Door [门] 门字筐 *ménzìkuāng*. Found in 闭 *bì* 'close'; 问 *wèn* 'ask'; 闽 *mǐn* 'Fujian'.

38. Movement [辶] 走之部 *zǒuzhībù*. Found in 过 *guò* 'passing by'; 达 *dā* 'reach'; 这 *zhè* 'this'.

39. Work [工] 工字部 *gōngzìbù*. Found in 功 *gōng* 'effort'; 巫 *wū* 'witch'; 左 *zuǒ* 'left'.

40. Earth [土] 土字部 *tǔzìbù*. Found in 去 *qù* 'go'; 在 *zài* 'at';

场 *chǎng* 'venue'.

41. Scholar [士] 士字头 *shìzìtóu*. Found in 吉 *jí* 'good omen'; 声 *shēng* 'noise'; 壳 *kè* 'shell'.

42. Grass [艹] 草字头 *cǎozìtóu*. Found in 草 *cǎo* 'grass'; 花 *huā* 'flower'; 蔡 *cài* 'a surname'.

43. Big [大] 大字部 *dàzìbù*. Found in 太 *tài* 'excess'; 夺 *duó* 'rob'; 奇 *qí* 'strange'.

44. Bottom of the character 弄 radical [廾] 弄字底 *nòngzìdǐ*. Found in 异 *yì* 'different'; 卉 *huì* 'grass'; 弄 *nòng* 'play with, manipulate'.

45. Particularly [尤] 尤字旁 *yóuzìpáng*. Found in 尤 *yóu* 'particularly'; 尴 *gān* 'awkward'; 尬 *gà* 'embarrassing'.

46. Inch [寸] 寸字部 *cùnzìbù*. Found in 对 *duì* 'correct'; 寺 *sì* 'temple'; 寻 *xún* 'search'.

47. Arrow with attached string [弋] 弋字旁 *yìzìpáng*. Found in 式 *shì* 'style'; 贰 *èr* 'two'; 弋 *yì* 'arrow with attached string'.

48. Hand [扌] 提手旁 *tíshǒupáng*. Found in 打 *dǎ* 'hit'; 找 *zhǎo* 'search'; 折 *zhé* 'bend'.

49. Small [小] 小字部 *xiǎozìbù*. Found in 少 *shǎo* 'few'; 尖 *jiān* 'sharp'; 光 *guāng* 'light'.

50. Mouth [口] 口字部 *kǒuzìbù*. Found in 古 *gǔ* 'ancient'; 叫 *jiào* 'call'; 鸣 *míng* 'animal cry'.

51. Square frame [囗] 方筐 *fāngkuāng*. Found in 囚 *qiú* 'prison'; 国 *guó* 'country'; 回 *huí* 'return'.

52. Napkin [巾] 巾字底 *jīnzìdǐ*. Found in 币 *bì* 'currency'; 帅 *shuài* 'marshall'; 帐 *zhàng* 'tent'.

53. Mountain [山] 山字部 *shānzìbù*. Found in 岁 *suì* 'age'; 峰 *fēng* 'peak'; 崩 *bēng* 'collapse'.

54. Double persons [彳] 双人旁 *shuāngrénpáng*. Found in 行 *xíng* 'walk'; 很 *hěn* 'very'; 往 *wǎng* 'towards'.

55. Three downward left strokes [彡] 三撇 *sānpiē*. Found in 形 *xíng* 'shape'; 参 *cān* 'take part'; 须 *xū* 'need to'.

56. Sunset [夕] 夕字头 *xīzìtóu*. Found in 名 *míng* 'name'; 岁 *suì*

'age'; 多 *duō* 'many'.

57. Top of the character 冬 [夂] 冬字头 *dōngzìtóu*. Found in 冬 *dōng* 'winter'; 各 *gè* 'every'; 夏 *xià* 'summer'.

58. Dog [犭] 反犬旁 *fǎnquǎnpáng*. Found in 猪 *zhū* 'pig'; 狗 *gǒu* 'dog'; 狐 *hú* 'fox'.

59. Food [饣] 食字旁 *shízìpáng*. Found in 饥 *jī* 'hungry'; 饮 *yǐn* 'drink'; 饭 *fàn* 'rice'.

60. Pig's head [彐] 彐字部 *jìzìbù*. Found in 归 *guī* 'return'; 寻 *xún* 'search'; 慧 *huì* 'intelligence'.

61. Corpse [尸] 尸字头 *shīzìtóu*. Found in 尺 *chǐ* 'foot (length)'; 尾 *wěi* 'tail'; 居 *jū* 'reside'.

62. Self [己] 己字部 *jǐzìbù*. Found in 包 *bāo* 'wrap'; 导 *dǎo* 'guide'; 异 *yì* 'different'.

63. Bow [弓] 弓字旁 *gōngzìpáng*. Found in 引 *yǐn* 'draw in'; 张 *zhāng* 'extend'; 弱 *ruò* 'weak'.

64. Sprout [屮] 屮字头 *chūzìtóu*. Found in 艸 *cǎo* 'plant type'; 蚩 *chī* 'idiotic'; 芻 *chú* 'fodder'.

65. Female [女] 女字旁 *nǚzìpáng*. *Found in* 妈 *mǎ* 'mother'; 姐 *jiě* 'elder sister'; 妹 *mèi* 'younger sister'.

66. One [幺] 幺字旁 *yāozìpáng*. Found in 幺 *yāo* 'one'; 乡 *xiāng* 'village'; 幼 *yòu* 'tender, young'.

67. Child [子] 子字部 *zǐzìbù*. Found in 孔 *kǒng* 'hole'; 孙 *sūn* 'grandchild'; 学 *xué* 'learn'.

68. Silk [纟] 绞丝旁 *jiǎosīpáng*. Found in 丝 *sī* 'silk'; 纸 *zhǐ* 'paper'; 绑 *bǎng* 'tie up'.

69. Horse [马] 马字部 *mǎzìbù*. Found in 驾 *jià* 'drive'; 骄 *jiāo* 'proud'; 驯 *xùn* 'tame'.

70. Three bends [巛] 三拐部 *sānguǎibù*. *Found in* 巢 *chāo* 'nest'; 甾 *zāi* 'an organic compound'; 灾 *zāi* 'disaster'.

Four Strokes

71. Four dotted fire [灬] 四点火 *sìdiǎnhuǒ*. Found in 点 *diǎn* 'dots'; 燕 *yàn* 'sparrow'; 热 *rè* 'hot'.

72. Funnel [斗] 斗字部 *dǒuzìbù*. Found in 斗 *dǒu* 'funnel'; 料 *liào* 'material'; 斜 *xié* 'incline'.
73. Script [文] 文字部 *wénzìbù*. Found in 刘 *liú* 'a Chinese surname'; 齐 *qí* 'orderly'; 文 *wén* 'arts'.
74. Square [方] 方字部 *fāngzìbù*. Found in 房 *fáng* 'room'; 方 *fāng* 'square'; 放 *fàng* 'release'.
75. Fire [火] 火字部 *huǒzìzìbù*. Found in 炼 *liàn* 'heat treatment'; 炎 *yán* 'heat'; 烟 *yān* 'cigarette, smoke'.
76. Heart [心] 心字底 *xīnzìdǐ*. Found in 思 *sī* 'thoughts'; 忍 *rěn* 'tolerate'; 忠 *zhōng* 'loyal'.
77. Household [户] 户字部 *hùzìbù*. Found in 房 *fáng* 'room'; 肩 *jiān* 'shoulder'; 扁 *biǎn* 'thin' (*vs.* thick).
78. Clothing [衤] 衣字旁 *yīzìpáng*. Found in 礼 *lǐ* 'manners'; 祖 *zǔ* 'ancestors'; 社 *shè* 'society'.
79. King [王] 王字旁 *wángzìpáng*. Found in 玉 *yù* 'jade'; 全 *quán* 'total'; 主 *zhǔ* 'chief'.
80. A Chinese surname 韦 [韦] 韦字旁 *wéizìpáng*. Found in 韩 *hán* 'a Chinese surname'; 韦 *wéi* 'another Chinese surname'; 韧 *rèn* 'resilient'.

There are character radicals with twelve or more strokes, an example of which is 黑 *hēi* black. Altogether one hundred and eighty nine word radicals are listed in the dictionary.

MOST COMMON WORD RADICALS
According to *ABC Chinese-English dictionary* by John DeFrancis, the 25 most commonly used radicals are:

1. Horizontal stroke radical [一] 一横 *yīhéng*
2. Speech radical [讠] 言字旁 *yánzìpáng*
3. Single person radical [亻] 单人字旁 *dānrénzìpáng*
4. Three doted water radical [氵] 三点水 *sāndiǎnshuǐ*
5. Upright heart radical [忄] 竖心旁 *shùxīnpáng*

71

6. Movement radical [辶] 走之部 *zǒuzhībù*
7. Earth radical [土] 土字部 *tǔzìbù*
8. Grass radical [艹] 草字头 *cǎozìtóu*
9. Hand radical [扌] 提手旁 *tíshǒupáng*
10. Mouth radical [口] 口字部 *kǒuzìbù*
11. Female radical [女] 女字旁 *nǚzìpáng*
12. Silk radical [纟] 绞丝旁 *jiǎosīpáng*
13. Fire radical [火] 火字部 *huǒzìbù*
14. Heart radical [心] 心字底 *xīnzìdǐ*
15. King radical [王] 王字旁 *wángzìpáng*
16. Wood radical [木] 木字旁 *mùzìpáng*
17. Sun radical [日] 日字部 *rìzìbù*
18. Moon radical [月] 月字旁 *yuèzìpáng*
19. Sick radical [疒] 病字旁 *bìngzìpáng*
20. Stone radical [石] 石字旁 *shízìpáng*
21. Eye radical [目] 目字旁 *mùzìpáng*
22. Metal radical [钅] 金字旁 *jīnzìpáng*
23. Worm radical [虫] 虫字旁 *chóngzìpáng*
24. Bamboo radical [⺮] 竹字头 *zhúzìtóu*
25. Leg radical [足] 足字部 *zúzìbù*

WORD RADICAL IN EVERYDAY USE

In European languages we have a fair idea of where the words could be found once we are familiar with the basic phonetics. In Chinese there is little correlation between the pronunciation and the way it is written. Even an experienced user is occasionally frustrated by the difficulty in searching a word using a Chinese dictionary.

Given the fact that Chinese characters are not based on alphabets and that they come from a wide range of pictures, presenting the characters in a format easy to be searched is in itself a huge task.

The use of word radicals was the most common method of finding a word in a Chinese dictionary. The Word radical search engine provides an effective way of searching according to the 'root' concept.

Once the radical is identified, the words are searched in the order of their complexity, i.e., the number of strokes, there is no other way! The two hundred or so radicals are themselves organised by the number of strokes.

However not all Chinese characters could be so conveniently organised. There would be words that could have more than one radical.

Words in modern dictionaries are now listed according to their sound pattern, the pīnyīn. For those who are familiar this offers a convenient method of searching for the right word, provided you know how the word is pronounced in Mandarin. Once the pīnyīn is identified, it is a matter of going to the correct intonation and search for the word from a series of words having the same intonation. There are normally four intonations, with the exception of a fifth tone used for repeating words, for example 哥哥 *gēge* 'elder brother', rather than *gēgē*.

OTHER APPLICATIONS

Very often in oral conversation when one is not sure of a word from a given sound, the word radical is used to specify a word from others. For example the Chinese surname 陈 *chén* 'Chen' is often described as ěrdōng-Chén, indicating that the word is made up of 阝 *ěr* 'ear radical' and 东 *dōng* 'east'. Another surname is 胡 *hú* 'Hu', often described as gǔyuè-Hú [古月-胡], made up of the components 古 *gǔ* 'old' and word radical 月 *yuè* 'moon'. The surname 李 *lǐ* 'Lee' is often described as mǔzǐ-Lǐ [木子-李], implying that the word is composed of 木 *mù* 'wood' and 子 *zǐ* 'son'.

RADICAL ARRANGEMENT

The character radical and other components can be built up in several ways.

The first combination is placing them side by side, as in 陈 'Chen', made up of 阝 *ěr* and 东 *dōng*.

The second combination is placing them up and down, as in 李 *Lǐ*, made up of 木 *mù* and 子 *zǐ*.

The third combination is outer and inner arrangement, for example in the character 圆 *yuán* 'round', composed of a square frame radical 囗 [方筐] *fāngkuāng* on the outside and 员 *yuán* 'member' on the inside, which gives it the sound.

Websites dedicated to word radicals include
What are radicals: *www.lightcc.com/main.html*
Chinese radicals:
    www.euroasiasoftware.com/english/chinese/learn/grundstrecken g.html#Radikaler
The 214 radicals: *www.chinaknowledge.de/Literature/radicals.htm*

COMPLEXITY OF CHARACTERS

In European languages we measure the length of words by the number of alphabets. In Chinese, complexity is measured by the number of strokes. The following examples indicate the increasing number of strokes for some commonly used Chinese characters.

1. One stroke: 一 *yī* 'one'
2. Two strokes 十 *shí* 'ten', 人 *rén* 'people'
3. Three strokes 女 *nǚ* 'female', 口 *kǒu* 'mouth'
4. Four strokes 木 *mù* 'wood', 火 *huǒ* 'fire'
5. Five strokes 可 *kě* 'permit', 头 *tóu* 'head'
6. Six strokes 回 *huí* 'return', 在 *zài* 'at'
7. Seven strokes 你 *nǐ* 'you', 花 *huā* 'flower'
8. Eight strokes 学 *xué* 'learn', 林 *lín* 'forest'
9. Nine strokes 说 *shuō* 'speak', 南 *nán* 'south'
10. Ten strokes 爱 *ài* 'love', 通 *tōng* 'through'
11. Eleven strokes 教 *jiāo* 'teach', 黄 *huáng* 'yellow'

12. Twelve strokes: 答 *dá* 'reply', 黑 *hēi* 'black'
13. Thirteen strokes 意 *yì* 'meaning', 简 *jiǎn* 'simple'
14. Fourteen strokes 歌 *gē* 'song', 算 *suàn* 'calculate'
15. Fifteen strokes 颜 *yán* 'colour', 靠 *kào* 'rely'
16. Sixteen strokes 整 *zhéng* 'whole', 澳 *ào* 'Australia'

Thanks to the simplification of Chinese characters, there are relatively few words with more than twenty strokes.

COMPUTER FONTS

The use of Chinese word processing software enables a wide range of computer fonts to be used. As Chinese characters are two-dimensional, rather than linear entities, the font varieties are impressive.

As examples the phrase 'crossing the ocean' [漂洋过海] is printed using several fonts as follows:

漂洋过海　　文鼎中行书简 font

漂洋過海　　經典魏碑繁 font

漂洋过海　　长城行楷体 font

漂洋過海　　華康古印體(P) font

漂洋過海　　華康楷書體W3 font

漂洋過海　　華康彩帶體(P) font

漂洋過海　　華康勘亭流 font

漂洋過海　　華康少女文字W3(P) font

漂洋過海　　新宋体 font

漂洋過海　　經典爨寶子繁 font

漂洋过海 经典中圆简 font
漂洋過海 经典繁毛楷 font

CHINESE PRONUNCIATION

It is important to distinguish between Chinese dialects such as Cantonese or Hokkien from Mandarin, the official language. The dialects are discussed in the next chapter.

Unlike European languages, the number of possible syllables is actually limited in Chinese. The Chinese language is spoken as a series of distinct, single syllables.

Pīnyīn

Pīnyīn is a phonetic system using alphabets to represent Chinese syllabus. In the West the pīnyīn system replaces Wade-Giles, the pronunciation system used in the West before pīnyīn was adopted.

In China pīnyīn replaces the traditional Chinese phonetic system, the 注音 *zhùyīn*. However the traditional zhùyīn phonetic system is still used in Taiwan today. A comparison of pīnyīn and zhùyīn is given later in the chapter.

The simplification of Chinese characters from traditional to simplified characters does not in any way change the way words are pronounced.

PRONUNCIATION SYSTEM

A syllable is obtained by combining a consonant with a vowel.

CONSONANTS

There are 21 consonants, namely:

b, p, m, f, d, t, n, l, g, k, h,
j, q, x, zh, ch, sh, r, z, c, s.

Note that the Chinese consonants are not arranged according to Western alphabetical order.

They are classified in groups, each with a distinct sound type, as follows:

	Represented by	pīnyīn	zy*	WG	Sound type
b	玻	bō	ㄅ	p	labial
p	坡	pō	ㄆ	p'	labial
m	摸	mō	ㄇ	m	labial
f	佛	fō	ㄈ	f	labial
d	得	dé	ㄉ	T	dental
t	特	tè	ㄊ	t'	dental
n	讷	nè	ㄋ	n	dental
l	勒	lè	ㄌ	l	dental
g	哥	gē	ㄍ	k	velar
k	科	kē	ㄎ	k'	velar
h	喝	hē	ㄏ	h	velar
j	基	jī	ㄐ	ch	palatal
q	欺	qī	ㄑ	ch'	palatal
x	希	Xī	ㄒ	hs	palatal
zh	知	zhī	ㄓ	ch	vs
ch	蚩	chī	ㄔ	ch'	vs
sh	诗	shī	ㄕ	sh	vs
r	日	rì	ㄖ	j	uc
z	资	zī	ㄗ	ts	sibilant
c	雌	cí	ㄘ	ts'	sibilant
s	思	sī	ㄙ	s	sibilant

zy refers zhùyīn 注音.
WG refers to Wade-Giles.
The various sound types are as follows:
labial: *a sound produced by movement of the lips*
dental: *a sound produced with the aid of the teeth*

77

velar: *a sound produced with the back of the tongue touching or near the soft palate, as in g for gun.*

palatal: *a semivowel produced with the tongue near the palate*

vs: *a variant of sibilant form.*

uc: *unclassified, as the pronunciation is unique in Chinese, not found in other systems.*

sibilant: *a consonant characterised by a hissing sound (like s or sh)*

The labials, dentals, velars and palatals are relatively easy to pronounce. Sounds that could give problems are slight differences between sibilant and their variant, as well as the sound 'r', which is not at all retroflex (rolling of the tongue).

VOWELS AND THEIR COMBINATIONS

There are 33 vowels, compound vowels or combinations:

a, o, e, ai, ei, ao, ou, an, en, ang, eng, ong, i, ia, ie, iao, iou, ian, in, iang, ing, iong, u, ua, uo, uai, uei, uan, uen, uang, ueng, ü, üan, ün.

The basic vowels are:

	said as	pīnyīn	ZY	WG
a	啊	ā	ㄚ	a
e	鹅	ē	ㄜ	è
i	衣	yī	ㄧ	i
o	喔	ō	ㄛ	o
u	乌	wū	ㄨ	u
ü	迂	yü	ㄩ	ü

In Chinese vowel endings include *n* or *ng* are added to some vowels. With that in mind the list of vowel endings is as follows:

	named as	pīnyīn	ZY	WG
ai	哀	āi	ㄞ	ai
an	安	ān	ㄢ	an
ang	昂	áng	ㄤ	ang
ao	熬	āo	ㄠ	ao
ei	欸	ǎi	ㄟ	ei
en	恩	ēn	ㄣ	èn
eng		ēng	ㄥ	èng
ia	呀	yā	ㄧㄚ	ia
ian	烟	yān	ㄧㄣ	ien
iang	央	yāng	ㄧㄤ	iang
iao	腰	yāo	ㄧㄠ	iao
ie	耶	yē	ㄧㄝ	ieh
in	因	yīn	ㄧㄣ	in
ing	英	yīng	ㄧㄥ	ing
iong	雍	yōng	ㄩㄥ	iung
iou	优	yōu	ㄧㄡ	iou
ong		ōng	ㄨㄥ	ung
ou	欧	ōu	ㄡ	ou
ua	蛙	wā	ㄨㄚ	ua
uai	歪	wāi	ㄨㄞ	uai
uan	弯	wān	ㄨㄢ	uan
uang	汪	wāng	ㄨㄤ	uang
uei	威	wēi	ㄨㄟ	wei
uen	温	wēn	ㄨㄣ	ucn
ueng	翁	wēng	ㄨㄥ	ueng
uo	窝	wō	ㄨㄛ	uo
üan	冤	yuān	ㄩㄢ	üan
ün	晕	yún	ㄩㄣ	ün

There is generally little problem in pronouncing the vowels or vowel endings.

All Chinese words can be spoken by combining one of the consonants with one of the vowels. However not all combinations of the 23 consonants and 33 vowels produce words.

Taking the example with the vowel *ao* the following words can be produced.

bāo [包]	– wrap	qao	– no known word
pǎo [跑]	– to run	xao	– no known word
máo [毛]	– hair	zhǎo [找]	– search
fao	– no known word	chāo [超]	– exceed
dāo [刀]	– knife	shào [少]	– few
táo [逃]	– escape	ráo[6] [饶]	– forgive
nǎo [脑]	– brain	zǎo [早]	– morning
lǎo [老]	– old	cǎo [草]	– grass
gāo [高]	– tall	sǎo [嫂]	– elder brothers' wife
kǎo [考]	– test	wao	– no known word
hǎo [好]	– good	yào [要]	–want
jao	– no known word		

Note that there exist no words with the sounds *fao, jao, qao, xao* or *wao*.

In reality there could be more than one word that could be produced from one of the consonant-vowel combinations above. As an example there are 23 words with the pronunciation of *bao*[7] of different meaning.

Based on the consonant *b* the following words can be found.

bā	[八] – eight	bó	[伯] – father's elder brother
be	– no word listed	bǎi	[百] – hundred
běi	[北] – north	bāo	[包] – wrap

---

6 There is no English equivalent of the sound depicted by *r* in Chinese.

7 *Concise English-Chinese Dictionary*, Oxford University Press, 1999.

bou	– no word listed	bàn [半] – half	
běn [本] – basis, origin		bāng [帮] – help	
bēng [崩] – collapse		bong	– no word listed
bì [币] – currency		bia	– no word listed
bié [别] – another		biǎo [表] – surface	
biou	– no word listed	biān [边] – side	
bīn [彬] – courteous		biang	– no word listed
bīng [兵] – soldier		biong	– no word listed
bù [不] – not		bua	– no word listed
buo	– no word listed	buai	– no word listed
buei	– no word listed	buan	– no word listed
buen	– no word listed	buang	– no word listed
bueng	– no word listed	bü	– no word listed
büan	– no word listed	bün	– no word listed

Chinese pronunciation is difficult for the uninitiated. The key to proper pronunciation lies with an ability to listen and distinguish between tones, as well as willingness to produce sounds that might sound odd or strange to the speaker initially.

Some of the sounds are inherently confusing and difficult to distinguish, in particular *z* and *zh*, *c* and *ch*, as well as *s* and *sh*. Deciding whether a word ends in *in* or *ing* could be quite tricky.

INTONATION

Another complication is the four intonations of sounds. Consider the following sounds, all pronounced as *ma*.

When listened carefully these words are pronounced in four rather distinct intonations, each with a totally different meaning.

First intonation: mā [妈] mother
Second intonation: má [麻] hemp
Third intonation: mǎ [马] horse
Fourth intonation: mà [骂] scold

The symbols ˉ, ´, ˇ, ` are commonly used to designate the four intonations. Once again listen carefully, distinguish the intonations and nuances, be willing to produce sounds that might sound strange and you are on your way to success.

Intonations are important in spoken Mandarin. You could give different meanings or impressions depending on intonations. However when spoken in sentences very often listeners are able to guess the meanings even though intonations may not be accurate. Intonations are unimportant in word processing.

Not all the intonations of a given sound produce words. The sound *neng* only produces one word in the second intonation 'able' 能 *néng*, there is no word in the other three intonations.

COMPARISON OF PĪNYĪN AND ZHÙYĪN

It is interesting to compare the 'coupled poem' of our book 'Crossing the oceans, taking roots' in pīnyīn and zhùyīn.

	漂	洋	过	海	,	落	地	生	根
pīnyīn	piāo	yang	guò	hǎi		luò	dì	shēng	gēn
zhùyīn	ㄆㄧㄠ	ㄧㄤ	ㄍㄨ	ㄛㄏㄞ		ㄌㄨㄛ	ㄌㄧ	ㄕㄥ	ㄍㄣ

Both systems produce accurate pronunciation. For people familiar with alphabets used in European languages the pīnyīn is easier to learn.

A grasp of pīnyīn would enable you to pronounce names and places in China. With pīnyīn you are able to 'write' Chinese without knowing the number of strokes and its sequence, through the use of Chinese software.

Once you could recognise Chinese characters you should be able to search any word in the Chinese dictionary, provided you know how the word is pronounced in pīnyīn. It certainly enables you to pronounce the words more accurately, as there are well-defined guidelines.

PĪNYĪN PRONUNCIATION CHART

The consonants and vowels are arranged in Chinese sequence, not Western, alphabetical order. Not all combinations of consonants and vowels produce valid sounds in Chinese pronunciation. As far as possible characters having the first intonation are selected.

		b	p	m	f	d	t	n	l	g	k
a	ā 阿	bā 爸	pà 怕	mā 妈	fā 发	dā 搭	tā 他	nà 那	lā 拉	--	kā 咖
o	ō 噢	bō 玻	pō 颇	mō 摸	fó 佛	--	--	--	--	--	--
e	è 恶	--	--	me 么	--	dé 德	tè 特	ne 呢	le 了	gē 哥	kē 柯
er	èr 二	--	--	--	--	--	--	--	--	--	--
ai	āi 哀	bái 白	pài 派	mǎi 买	--	dāi 呆	tāi 胎	nǎi 奶	lài 赖	gāi 该	kāi 开
ei		bēi 杯	pèi 佩	méi 梅	fēi 飞	--	--	nèi 内	léi 雷	gěi 给	--
ao	āo 凹	bāo 包	pāo 抛	māo 猫	--	dāo 刀	tāo 涛	nǎo 脑	lǎo 老	gāo 高	kǎo 考
ou	ōu 欧	--	--	mǒu 某	fǒu 否	dòu 豆	tōu 偷	--	lóu 楼	gōu 勾	kòu 扣
an	ān 安	bān 班	pān 潘	màn 慢	fàn 范	dān 单	tān 贪	nán 男	lán 兰	gān 甘	kān 刊
en	ēn 恩	bēn 奔	pén 盆	mèn 闷	fēn 芬	--	--	nèn 嫩	--	gēn 跟	kěn 肯
ang	áng 昂	bāng 帮	páng 旁	máng 忙	fāng 方	dāng 当	tāng 汤	náng 囊	láng 郎	gǎng 港	kāng 康
eng	--	bēng 崩	péng 彭	mèng 孟	féng 冯	dēng 灯	téng 疼	néng 能	lěng 冷	gēng 庚	Kēng 坑
ong	--	--	--	--	--	dōng 东	tōng 通	nóng 农	lóng 龙	gōng 公	kōng 空
i	yī 医	bǐ 比	pī 批	mī 眯	--	dī 底	tī 梯	nǐ 你	lǐ 李	--	--
ia	yā 压	--	--	--	--	--	--	--	--	--	--
iao	yāo 腰	biǎo 表	piāo 漂	miào 妙	--	diāo 雕	tiāo 挑	niǎo 鸟	liào 寥	--	--

83

ie	yè 叶	bié 别	piē 撇	miè 灭	--	diē 跌	tiē 铁	niè 孽	liè 列	--	--
iu	yóu 尤	--	--	--	--	diū 丢	--	niú 牛	liú 刘	--	--
ian	yān 阉	biān 边	piān 偏	miàn 面	--	diān 颠	tiān 天	niān 拈	lián 莲	--	--
in	yīn 因	bīn 宾	pīn 拼	mín 民	--	--	--	nín 您	lín 林	--	--
iang	yáng 杨	--	--	--	--	--	--	Niáng 娘	liáng 梁	--	--
ing	yīng 英	bīng 兵	píng 平	míng 明	--	dīng 丁	tīng 听	níng 宁	líng 玲	--	--
iong	yōng 庸	--	--	--	--	--	--	--	--	--	--
u	wú 吴	bù 不	pǔ 普	mù 木	fù 傅	dū 都	tǔ 土	nǔ 努	lù 陆	gū 姑	kū 哭
ua	wā 挖	--	--	--	--	--	--	--	--	guā 瓜	--
uo	wō 窝	--	--	--	--	duō 多	tuō 托	nuò 诺	luó 罗	guō 郭	--
uai	wāi 歪	--	--	--	--	--	--	--	--	guāi 乖	--
ui	--	--	--	--	--	duī 堆	tuī 推	--	--	guī 归	--
uan	wān 弯	--	--	--	--	duàn 段	tuán 团	nuǎn 暖	luàn 乱	guǎn 管	--
un	--	--	--	--	--	dùn 顿	tūn 吞	--	lùn 论	gǔn 滚	kūn 坤
uang	wáng 王	--	--	--	--	--	--	--	--	guāng 光	--
ueng	wēng 翁	--	--	--	--	--	--	--	--	--	--
ü	yǚ 于	--	--	--	--	--	--	nǚ 女	lǚ 吕	--	--
üe	yuè 月	--	--	--	--	--	--	nüe 虐	lüe 略	--	--
üan	yuán 袁	--	--	--	--	--	--	--	--	--	--
ün	yún 云	--	--	--	--	--	--	--	--	--	--

Pīnyīn Guidelines

The guidelines on pīnyīn according to China National standards GB/T 16159—1996 include:

- Individual words serve as the basis for spelling.
- Words are written together to express an integral meaning. For example *Zhōngguó* 中国 'China', rather than *Zhōng guó*. Another example is *tāmen* 他们 'they, them', rather than *tā men*.
- Words written together for emphasis are written as one word, for example *kànkan* 看看 'to look around', rather than *kàn kàn*.
- Nouns with suffixes or prefixes are written as one word, for example *háizimen* 孩子们 'children'; *fùjiàoshòu* 副教授 'associate professor'.
- Chinese names are written as two words, with the family name first, followed by the given name as one word, both words begin with capital letters, for example *Dèng Xiǎopíng* 邓小平, the late paramount ruler of China.
- Salutations are written as one word after the surname, for example *Wáng xiānshēng* 王先生 'Mr. Wang', or *Lǐ lǎoshī* 李老师 'Teacher Li'.
- Position words after nouns are written separately, for example *hé lǐ*, 'in the river' not *hélǐ*. The same goes for *tiān shàng* 'in the sky'.
- Numbers from 1 to 99 are written as one word, for example, *bāshíliù* '86'.
- Number prefix 第 *dì* is separated by a hyphen, for example *dì- bāshíliù* 'No. 86 or 86th'.

ASSOCIATED SOUNDS OR MEANINGS?

Unlike European languages, the Chinese pronunciation or meaning cannot be based on the word structure.

While the word radicals give an indication of the associated meaning of a word, there is no correlation on how the word should be pronounced. Consider the following:

呵 [hē] from 口 [kǒu] and 可 [kě], 'exhale'
诃 [hē] from 讠 [yán] and 可 [kě], 'scold'
何 [hé] from 亻 [rén] and 可 [kě], an interrogative word
河 [hé] from 氵 [shuǐ] and 可 [kě], 'river'
荷 [hé] from 艹 [cāo], 亻 [rén] and 可 [kě], 'lotus'.

The pronunciation pattern contrasts sharply with the following:

陈 [Chén] from 阝 [ēr] and 东 [dōng], 'a Chinese surname'
冻 [dòng] from 氵 [bīng] and 东 [dōng], 'freezing'
拣 [jiǎn] from 扌 [shǒu] and 东 [dōng], 'select'
炼 [liàn] from 火 [huǒ] and 东 [dōng], 'heat treatment'

ONE WORD, TWO MEANINGS

A small number of Chinese characters are pronounced differently, depending on the situation. Generally they are regarded as different words. In dictionaries based on pīnyīn they have two or more listings. They are known as 同字异意 *tóngzìyìyì* 'same word, different meanings'.

Examples are as follows:

长 could be *cháng* 'long' or *zhǎng* 'grow'
朝 could be *cháo* 'dynasty' or *zhāo* 'morning'
传 could be *chuán* 'convey' or *zhuàn* 'bibliography'
斗 could be *dǒu* 'volume measure' or *dòu* 'compete'
行 could be *háng* 'profession' or *xíng* 'walk'
好 could be *hǎo* 'good' or *hào* 'favourite, like'
会 could be *huì* 'meet, assemble' or *kuài* 'accounting'
教 could be *jiāo* 'teach' or *jiào* 'religion'

乐 could be *lè* 'happy' or *yuè* 'music'
少 could be *shǎo* 'few' or *shào* 'youth'
中 could be *zhōng* 'centre' or *zhòng* 'hit the target'
种 could be *zhǒng* 'kind, type' or *zhòng* 'planting'

Care should be taken to pronounce the same words differently according to the circumstances. For example,

便 is pronounced as *biàn* 'convenient'; it is pronounced *pián* as in *piányi* 便宜 'cheap'

漂 is spoken as *piāo* 'float', *piǎo* 'bleach' and *piào* 'pretty'

华 is pronounced as *huā* 'flower', *huá* China, Chinese, or *huà* 'a surname'

正 is pronounced as *zhèng* 'just, right', but *zhēng* when applied to the words such as *zhēngyuè* 正月 'January'

CHINESE GRAMMAR
Compared to the difficulties in character recognition and phonetics, Chinese grammar is relatively simple to master, especially when compared to European languages.

❖ There is no tense in verbs. The same verb is used for present tense, past tense, present continuous tense, future tense, etc. No provision is provided for conditional or subjunctive tenses. The same set of words is usually used to denote time, for example,

我写 *wǒ xiě* 'I write'
我已经写了 *wǒ yǐjīng xiě le* 'I have written'
我正在写 *wǒ zhèngzài xiě* 'I am writing'
我将会写 *wǒ jiānghuì xiě* 'I will write'

There is no change to the verb. These 'time words' are simply added every time when the situation demands.

❖ There is no gender issue, whereby a noun, a verb or an adverb is identified as masculine, feminine, or neutral in languages such as French or German.
❖ There is no difference between singular or plural nouns.
❖ There are no singular or plural verbs. The same verb applies to all situations.
❖ There is no distinction in verbs associated with first person, second person or third person.
❖ There are no comparative or superlative words. All that is required is the word 更 *gèng* 'more' and 最 *zuì* 'most' in front of the relevant verb. This is evident from the following examples:

好 *hǎo* 'good'; 更好 *gèng hǎo* 'better'; 最好 *zuì hǎo* 'best'
高 *gāo* 'tall'; 更高 *gèng gāo* 'taller'; 最高 *zuì gāo* 'tallest'

CREATING NEW VOCABULARY

New words and compound words need to be created from time to time when circumstances demand. This is particularly so in an era of fast changing technology when concepts unheard of are constantly being created.

More often than not, new products and concepts are represented by compound words, joining two or three words together.

The word computer, for example, is written either as 计算机 *jìsuànjī* 'a computing machine', or 电脑 *diànnǎo* 'an electronic brain'. A whole spectrum of words for the IT industry has been coined.

The system has the impact of minimising the amount of words used. From the character 鸡 *jī* 'chicken', a whole range of compound words have been created, using words that are already in use.

蛋鸡 *dànjī* 'chicken for laying eggs - layers'
公鸡 *gōngjī* 'male chicken – rooster'
母鸡 *mǔjī* 'female chicken – hen'
肉鸡 *ròujī* 'chicken raised for the meat – broiler'
小鸡 *xiǎojī* 'young chicken – chicks'
野鸡 *yějī* 'wild chicken – pheasant'

The Chinese reader is hence used to the association of ideas relating to various combinations, rather than memorising words of narrow, well defined meanings. This implies that the average reader is not bogged down by having to memorise thousands and thousands of words. The Chinese vocabulary is exceptionally stable (very few new Chinese characters were created), relatively small in numbers compared to European languages, as it relies on compound words rather than new words. It also trains the reader to correlate or network ideas and concepts, and find solutions from existing wealth of information.

ADOPTING NEW CONCEPTS

Very often new ideas from the West are incorporated into Chinese thoughts. In translating concepts of Western origin, efforts are made to choose words that are meaningful. For example the word 'gene' is translated as 基因 *jīyīn*, 基 *jī* implies fundamental, root or basic, while 因 *yīn* could be explained as basis or source of.

If nothing comparable could be identified, the concept is translated phonetically in its entirety. An example would be 'clone', written as 克隆 *kèlóng*.

CREATING NEW WORDS

In exceptional circumstances, new words could be created. An example would be 镭 *léi* 'Radium' (a radioactive metal). The character was created by 'word radical' 金 *jīn* 'metal', together with the sound 雷 *léi* 'thunder'. This is very rare. As a matter of fact the vocabulary in Chinese is stable, and there has not been much change in recent years. There is no need to create new words, though some software has the provision to do so.

A combination of the three measures above, especially conjugating new compound words and borrowing words from the West has enriched vocabulary used in academic, professional or any other area. Use of Chinese as a language for any technical or social study is altogether possible.

PRINTING IN CHINESE

Long ago, most Chinese texts were handwritten. Books needed to be copied word for word by hand!

Typing Chinese characters used to be a complicated, time consuming and laborious undertaking. Imagine a keyboard with a few thousand keys! The keys are kept in trays, a few hundred to each tray. The keyboard operator needed months of training to choose a correct word from the correct tray! If she needs to print characters in two sizes, she needs two sets of characters. If she needs two fonts, she needs two entirely different sets. For that reason ancient Chinese books were normally hand written rather than typed.

The invention of Chinese software brought printing to offices and households. The software searches for every word based on several input methods such as pīnyīn or zhùyīn.

DIGITAL ERA OF CHINESE LANGUAGE

Just twenty years ago the Chinese were concerned that their language would not be usable on computers. Today we can input Chinese characters in several ways, including pīnyīn, zhùyīn, Cāng Jiē [仓颉] (p. 153), five strokes, etc.

Most advanced software allows access through typing just the first alphabets of compound words. For example the characters 朋友 *péngyǒu* 'friends' could be input through typing 'py', from which a limited list of words such as 朋友 *péngyǒu*, etc would be selected.

Other features include auto-generated word suggestions for commonly used additions. For example once the character 电 *diàn* (electricity) has been typed in, a series of choices include Chinese words with *diàn* in front, such as phone, telex, cable, electronics, etc are displayed.

More advanced software enables input through equivalent English words in meaning. A list of Chinese characters matching the input is then displayed, from which the appropriate word is chosen.

With these and other features, Chinese character input can be done at a rate equal to or even faster than typing in English.

To type the word 'address' in English would require 7 keystrokes. It can be done in Chinese with 2 or 3 keystrokes, (*d*, *z*) or (*d*, *zh*) plus one more to select. The word 'telephone' requires 9 keystrokes in English; it can be done with 2 keystrokes, (*d*, and *h*) plus one more to select. Some software automatically moves the most commonly used words to the front of the list.

It is obvious that the Chinese language is in no way disadvantaged in the age of information technology, enabling Chinese characters to be digitised. At present Chinese is probably the second most commonly used language on the Internet. A search of Google news (newspapers, journals, TV, radio, etc) in English provides 4,500 sites. Next comes Chinese with 1,000 sites, followed by Spanish (700 sites) and French (500 sites).

LEARNING CHINESE

Not every ethnic Chinese writes or speaks fluent Chinese.

❖ The first generation ethnic Chinese, in particular those from Chinese speaking countries or backgrounds, reads and writes in Chinese, to various degrees of competence. They insist that their children be bilingual, mastering both English and Chinese. As far as possible they communicate with their children in Mandarin or one of the dialects.

❖ Those without a strong Chinese background themselves and who are not in a position to evaluate or coach their own children just want their children to have a 'general' knowledge or understanding of the language.

❖ There are of course others who do not see any need, and is indifferent whether their children learn Japanese or Indonesian.

In general most people see the need to communicate, emphasise mainly spoken, rather than written language. Depending on the learning environment at home and at school, facilities such as language laboratory and interactive software, teaching method, as well as the enthusiasm and background knowledge of students, the realisable objectives differ.

Some of the most important factors leading towards success or failure are:

❖ The inherent background of the Chinese language learning environment. This ranges from legal or social constraints, to the opportunity of learning Chinese at school or at home.

❖ The language environment at home. Circumstantial evidence indicate that kids learn best when the parents could not communicate with them other than in Chinese! Under these circumstances, the kids have no choice but to pick up a Chinese language, notably one of the dialects.

❖ In some countries, there is less opportunity to practise the language. Though Chinese programmes are sometimes available on the television, in general they require a certain level of Chinese studies to understand or appreciate.

For most people there is no real need to memorise characters, their stroke sequences, as long as you recognise the appropriate character. The key lies in the ability to speak and master pīnyīn, as

Chinese software enables you to pick up a suitable word from a list. However at the end of the day you definitely benefit if you could listen, read and write the characters correctly.

In addition to speaking, listening and speaking abilities can be enhanced through songs (including *Karaoke*), watching movies, listening to news broadcast, etc.

The process of learning Chinese could be perceived in several phases.

❖ 'You could only speak correctly if you could comprehend what is being spoken to' [听得懂才讲得出] *tīngdedǒng cái jiǎngde chū* — In the first phase seek to cultivate listening ability, distinguish the nuances, intonations, etc. Understand what is being spoken, how the sounds are formed, so as to be able to repeat the sounds, and speak accurately.

❖ 'You could only understand after you could read the text' [讲得出才看得明白] *jiǎngdechū cái kānde mīngbǎi* — Once you are able to distinguish spoken words and be able to repeat them, you will be able to understand what you read, ie associating sounds with written words.

❖ 'You could only write correctly after you could read the text' [看得明白才写得对] *kānde mīngbǎi cái xiěde duì* — After you are able to recognise the characters you can then seek to write the characters accurately. There is little point of writing the character a hundred times if you cannot recognise it, understand its word radical and components.

The question of how many characters there are in the Chinese vocabulary is a subject of interest. The first Chinese dictionary 说文解字 *shuōwénjiězì* compiled around 100 AD, collected 9,353 characters. The most comprehensive dictionary 康熙字典 *kāngxizìdiǎn* 'Kangxi Dictionary' lists about 40,000 characters. One reason for large number of characters is that they include all of the different characters in the different variations of Chinese. It is estimated that about 3,000 characters are needed to read a Chinese newspaper, and 4,000 to 5,000 constitute a decent education.[8]

---

[8] *www.en2.wikipedia.org/wiki/Chinese_character*

Cultural Roots – Land of Origin

ANOTHER ASPECT OF CULTURAL ROOTS involves a basic knowledge of the land of origin. For ethnic Chinese this could be the countries where they were born or come from, in particular Southern China or parts of Southeast Asia.

The other cultural dimension lies with the dialect spoken at home or in the community, which is substantially different from Mandarin. This is in itself a fascinating topic, given the fact that dialects differ substantially from one another.

This chapter looks into the dialects spoken in China, in particular those spoken by overseas Chinese. It also surveys briefly the geography of southern provinces of China, from which most overseas Chinese originate. The names of various districts and counties, of which their ancestors come from, are listed.

Historically where Chinese settled overseas, the family link, or more commonly the village of origin provided the platform for migration, welfare as well as other support in the strange, new land. The surnames could foster powerful bonds, especially when they are written the same way in Chinese and spelt the same way in English, indicating that they probably speak the same dialect, and share common regional ancestry.

It is not surprising then that community associations are formed on the basis of regions of migration, for example the Hokkien Association or Hakka Association. Associations could also be based on district or county level, for example the Eng Choon Association, whose members come from Yǒngchūn county [永春县], which belongs to Quánzhōu municipality [泉州], in the province of Fújiàn [福建].

CHINESE DIALECTS

The hundreds of dialects throughout China could be grouped into the following categories:[9]

Northern dialects [北方话] *běifānghuà*. Several sub-categories are included. These dialects, including Mandarin, are used by about 70% of total Hàn population.

Wú [吴] dialect, used in Jiāngsū [江苏] and Zhèjiāng [浙江] provinces, by 8% of total Hàn population.

Xiāng [湘] dialect, used in Húnán [湖南] province, by 5% of total Hàn population.

Gàn [赣] dialect, used in Jiāngxī [江西] province and eastern corner of Húběi [湖北] province, by 2% of total Hàn population.

Kèjiāhuà [客家话], the Hakkas, used in several provinces, mainly in the south, by 4% of total Hàn population.

Yuèyǔ [粤语], Cantonese, or more commonly known as Guǎngdōnghuà [广东话], used in Guangdong, Hong Kong, Macau, by 5% of total Hàn population.

Mǐnyǔ [闽语], Hokkien, used in Fujian, Taiwan, South Zhejiang, as well as part of Guangdong, by 4% of total Hàn population.

Most of the earlier migrants that migrated to 'South China Seas' [南洋] *Nányáng* countries (Southeast Asia) come from coastal provinces of Southern China. They bring with them their own dialects, often not understood by settlers from another province.

---

[9] 简明不列颠百科全书, Chinese Encyclopaedia Publishers, Beijing, 1986.

Historically dialects were the only language earlier migrants knew, and were the languages spoken at homes. They were also the *lingua franca* in communities where majority of settlers speak the language. Even when Mandarin, English, or the local language is used as the official language or media of instruction in schools, dialects are still very often spoken at home.

Note that the dialect spoken at home does not necessarily reflect the origin of the family. It simply reflects to the dialects that the parents themselves know, or agree to speak to. A couple who speak Cantonese at home could well be Hakka in origin.

OVERSEAS CHINESE DIALECTS

In addition to Mandarin, hundreds of local dialects are spoken throughout China. These do not include minority languages such as Tibetan and Mongolian, which uses their own alphabets or scripts. Dialects are written in the same way as Mandarin, using the same word radicals, components and identical sequence of strokes. Words are pronounced differently in each dialect, though their written characters and meanings are exactly the same.

The main dialect groups amongst overseas Chinese, (80% of which are in Southeast Asia), are Hokkien, Teochew, Cantonese, Hainanese, Hakka, as well as dialects from Guangxi.

In most Chinese families dialects are important for the parents, more importantly the grand-parents who could not communicate with their children or grand-children in English or the language in which the child or grandchild is educated. Of course the practice inevitably ends when parents or children are not too fluent in their dialects.

Amongst the Overseas Chinese, the regions of origin of their dialects are rather well defined, with the exception of the Hakkas.

A GLIMPSE OF WHERE THE OVERSEAS CHINESE COME FROM

With the exception of migrants from China, most ethnic Chinese, in particular those living in Western countries know very little about their dialect background. Few have visited China themselves. Those who have been to China would probably visit tourist sites such as Beijing and Shanghai, rather than their home province or regions.

Some ethnic Chinese are aware, for example, that they are Hakka, even though have no clue which Hakka group they belong to. Others learn that they are from Fujian Yongchun, without any idea of what it means or where it is. Some Teochews [潮洲] *Cháozhōu* people do not realise that their ancestors are actually from Guangdong province, even though their dialect are closer to Hokkien [福建] *Fújiàn*. It is therefore necessary to have a quick glimpse of the provinces where the dialects originate, to understand the situation.

Four provinces, Fujian, Guangdong, Hainan and Guangxi, from which most overseas Chinese originate, would be looked at. These provinces are located at the Southern coast of China, as shown in the map below.

FÚJIÀN PROVINCE [福建省]

Known as 闽 *Mǐn* in short, or Hokkien in the dialect. The Province is located in China's southeast coastal region, bordering Zhejiang Province to the north, Jiangxi Province to the west and Guangdong Province to the south; it is separated from Taiwan by the Taiwan Straits.

A map of Fujian administrative region.

It is estimated that there are over ten million overseas Chinese who originated from Fujian province, nearly one-third of its population of 34.71 millions (March 2001). In addition to those in Southeast Asia, about 1 million are in Hong Kong and over 80% of Taiwanese are descendants from Fujian, just across the Straits.

Fujian has nine administrative municipalities, with the capital city of Fúzhōu [福州].

The administrative municipalities are:

福州 Fúzhōu
泉州 Quánzhōu
莆田 Pútián
厦门 Xiàmén, (Amoy)
漳州 Zhāngzhōu
南平 Nánpíng
三明 Sānmíng
龙岩 Lóngyán

Dialects spoken in Fujian province depend largely on geographical location.

Southern Fujian [闽南] *Mǐnnán*

This is the region where Hokkien is the dominant dialect, spoken by more than six and a half million people.[10] It is the dialect that is spoken along the southern regions of Fujian, such as Xiàmén [厦门], Quánzhōu [泉州] and Zhāngzhōu [漳州]. Due to the fact that Xiàmén [厦门] (also known as Amoy) became an important regional export centre, the Xiàmén dialect has developed to be representative of Mǐnnán [闽南].[11]

The Mǐnnán dialect is also common in other Southern districts of Fujian, parts of Guangdong, Hainan and pockets in other provinces. In addition the language is used widely in Taiwan. In Southeast Asia the Hokkiens are the most numerous Chinese ethnic groups. They predominate in countries, such as the Indonesia, Philippines Singapore, and Malaysia (in areas such as Penang and Johore).

---

[10] Official website of Fujian Government, *www.fujian.gov.cn/*
[11] Ibid.

According to *Ethnologue*,[12] the Mĭnnán [闽南] dialect is spoken by about 45 millions people worldwide. They include 25,725,000 in mainland China (1984), 2.5% of the population, inclusive of 1,000,000 Xiàmén [厦门]] dialect (1988 census), 6,000,000 Quán-zhōu [泉州] dialect. Outside China, the Mĭnnán dialect is spoken by:

- 10,000 in Brunei (1979).
- 700,000 speakers in Indonesia (1982).
- 1,946,698 in Malaysia, including 1,824,741 in Peninsular Malaysia.
- 493,500 to 592,200 in the Philippines (1982).
- 736,000 in Singapore (1985)
- 15,000,000 in Taiwan (1997)
- 17,640 in Thailand (1984)

Northern Fujian [闽北] *Mĭnbĕi*
This is the region where 'Hokchia' is spoken, centering around the city of Fúqīng [福清市], in the municipality of Fúzhōu [福州], the capital city. According to *Ethnologue*, the Mĭnbĕi [闽北] dialect is spoken by 10,290,000 1.2% of the population (1984). It is also spoken by 4,000 speakers in Singapore.

Eastern Fujian 闽东 *Mĭndōng*
This is the region where the Hokchew [福州] *Fúzhōu* dialect dominates. Within Fujian province it is predominant in two areas, the mountainous areas of the North, centering around Fú'ān [福安], as well as areas in the south, centering Fúzhōu, the capital city.

According to 'ethnologue', the Mĭndōng [闽东] dialect is spoken by about 247,000 worldwide.

Outside China it is spoken by:

---

[12] http://www.ethnologue.com/show_language.asp?code=CFR

- 6,000 in Brunei (1979).
- 20,000 in Indonesia (1982).
- 206,013 in Malaysia, including 85,368 in Peninsular Malaysia, 120,645 in Sarawak (1979)
- 15,000 speakers of Foochow out of 31,391 in ethnic group in Singapore (1985).

Outside China, Sibu in the State of Sarawak (East Malaysia) is a city where Hokchew is the dominant Chinese dialect. Particular mention should be made of Mr. Wong Nai Siong. Having leased a piece of land from Raja Brooke of Sarawak, Mr. Wong gathered his fellow Fúzhōu [福州] people to build a pioneer colony in Sarawak. This colony is today's Sibu, known also as New Fuzhou to many Chinese.[13]

Central Fujian [闽中] *Mǐnzhōng*

This is a less known dialect amongst overseas Chinese, centering around Púxiān [莆仙], where 'Henghua' dialect is spoken. It is common among the central areas of Fujian, in particular Chéngxiāng district [城厢区], Xiùyǔ district [秀屿区], and Hánjiāng district [涵江区].

Western Fujian: The Hakkas

Fujian is also the home of one of the Hakka dialect group, distributed along the Western region of Fujian (bordering the province of Guangdong, notably Lóngyán [龙岩] municipality, such as Chángtīng [长汀], Liánchéng [连城], Shànghàng [上杭].

As the Hakkas also come from other provinces, a description of it is found towards the end of this chapter.

---

[13] Thomas Tsu-wee Tan, *Your Chinese Roots*. Times Books International, Singapore, 1986.

Fujian Geography: As a reference for those who would like to trace their ancestral places, the districts [区] *qū*, cities [市] *shì* or counties [县] *xiàn* under the administrative municipalities are as follows:

Fúzhōu [福州] Municipality

    Districts: Gǔlóu district [鼓楼区], Táijiāng district [台江区], Cāngshān district [仓山区], Mǎwěi district [马尾区], Jìn'ān district [晋安区].

    Cities: Fúqīng city [福清市], Chánglè city [长乐市].

    Counties: Mǐnhóu county [闽侯县], Mǐnqīng county [闽清县], Yǒngtài county [永泰县], Liánjiāng county [连江县], Luóyuán county [罗源县], Píngtán county [平潭县].

Xiàmén [厦门] Municipality

    Districts: Jíměi district [集美区], Hǎicāng district [海沧区], Sīmíng district [思明区], Húlǐ district [湖里区], Tóng'ān district [同安区], Xiáng'ān district [翔安区].

Sānmíng [三明] Municipality

    Districts: Méiliè district [梅列区], Sānyuán district [三元区].

    City: Yǒng'ān city [永安市].

    Counties: Míngxī county [明溪县], Jiānglè county [将乐县], Dàtián county [大田县], Nínghuà county [宁化县], Jiànníng county [建宁县], Shā county [沙县], Yóuxī county [尤溪县], Qīngliú county [清流县], Tàiníng county [泰宁县].

Pútián [莆田] Municipality

    Districts: Chéngxiāng district [城厢区], Hánjiāng district [涵江区], Lìchéng district [荔城区], Xiùyǔ district [秀屿区].

    Counties: Xiānyóu county [仙游县].

Quánzhōu [泉州] Municipality

Districts: Lǐchéng district [鲤城区], Fēngzé district [丰泽区],
Luòjiāng district [洛江区], Quángǎng district [泉港区],
Qīngméng district [清濛区].

Cities: Shíshī city [石师市], Jìnjiāng city [晋江市], Nán'ān city
[南安市].

Counties: Huì'ān county [惠安县], Yǒngchūn county [永春县],
Ānxī county [安溪县], Déhuà county [德化县], Jīnmén
county [金门县].

Zhāngzhōu [漳州] Municipality

Districts: Xiāngchéng district [芗城区], Lóngwén district [龙文区].

Cities: Lónghǎi city [龙海市].

Counties: Pínghé county [平和县], Nánjìng county [南靖县],
Zhǎo'ān county [诏安县], Zhāngpǔ county [漳浦县],
Huá'ān county [华安县], Dōngshān county [东山县],
Chángtài county [长泰县], Yúnxiāo county [云霄县].

Nánpíng [南平] Municipality

Districts: Yánpíng district [延平区]

Cities: Jiàn'ōu city [建瓯市], Shàowǔ city [邵武市], Wǔyishān
city [武夷山市], Jiànyáng city [建阳市].

Counties: Sōngxī county [松溪县], Guāngzè county [光泽县],
Shùnchāng county [顺昌县], Pǔchéng county [浦城县],
Zhènghé county [政和县].

Lóngyán [龙岩] Municipality

District: Xīnluó district [新罗区].

City: Zhāngpíng city [漳平市].

County: Chángtīng county [长汀县], Wǔpíng county [武平县],
Shànghàng county [上杭县], Yǒngdìng county 永定县,
Liánchéng county [连城县].

Níngdé [宁德] Municipality
    District: Jiāochéng district [蕉城区].
    Cities: Fú'ān city [福安市], Fúdǐng city [福鼎市].
    Counties: Shòuníng county [寿宁县], Xiápǔ county [霞浦县],
        Zhèróng county [柘荣县], Píngnán county [屏南县], Gǔtián
        county [古田县], Zhōuníng county [周宁县].

Fujian dialect is the dominant dialect in Singapore, the only nation in Southeast Asia with an ethnic Chinese majority. Nevertheless the Singaporean government encourages the use of Mandarin, rather than dialects, in Singapore.

Websites pertaining to Fujian province include:

中国福建 (Official Fujian Provincial Government website):
    www.fujian.gov.cn/
People's daily on-line: Fujian Province:
    www.english.peopledaily.com.cn/data/province/fujian.html
Wikipedia – Fujian:
    www.en.wikipedia.org/wiki/Fujian

GUĀNGDŌNG PROVINCE [广东省]

The other province where huge numbers of ethnic Chinese come from is Guangdong. Known as 粤 *yuè* in short, the Province is located in China's southeast coastal region, bordering Fujian Province to the East, Guangxi Province to the west and connected to Hong Kong to the south.

Guangdong is a populous province with a population of some 86 millions. Guangdong is the home of Pearl River delta [珠江三角洲] *Zhūjiāng sānjiǎozhōu*, one of the earliest and economically most developed regions in China. Its is linked by road, rail and ship to Hong Kong, the gateway for overseas Chinese into China in the earlier days.

A map of Guangdong administrative regions is shown below:

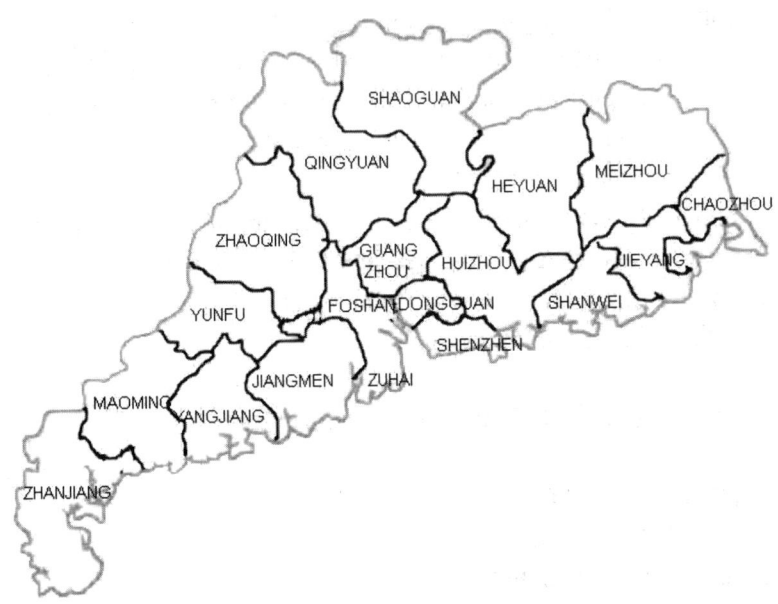

The administrative municipalities of Guangdong are:

广州 Guāngzhōu   东莞 Dōngguǎn
中山 Zhōngshān   佛山 Fóshān
江门 Jiāngmén   阳江 Yángjiāng
深圳 Shēnzhèn   湛江 Zhànjiāng
珠海 Zhūhǎi   茂名 Màomíng
汕头 Shàntóu   肇庆 Zhàoqìng
韶关 Sháoguǎn   清远 Qīngyuǎn
河源 Héyuán   潮州 Cháozhōu
梅州 Méizhōu   揭阳 Jiēyáng
惠州 Huìzhōu   云浮 Yúnfú
汕尾 Shànwěi

In terms of dialect Guangdong is the home to three distinct dialects groups amongst overseas Chinese, the Cantonese, Teochew and some Hakkas.

Cantonese [广东话] *Guǎngdōnghuà*
The term Cantonese[14] comes from the city of Canton, officially known as Guāngzhōu [广州]. It is spoken by the people of the Pearl River delta, centering on Guangzhou, the Capital City.

According to *Ethnologue*, Cantonese is spoken by about 71 million people world wide, including 52 millions in mainland China, 4.5% of Chinese population (1984). Outside China, Cantonese is spoken widely. According to *Ethnologue*, it is spoken by:

- 3,500 in Brunei (1979)
- 4,500 in Costa Rica (1981)
- 180,000 in Indonesia (1982)
- 748,010 in Malaysia, including 704,286 in Peninsular Malaysia, 24,640 in Sarawak, 19,184 in Sabah (1980)
- 6,000 to 7,200 in the Philippines (1982)
- 314,000 in Singapore (1985)
- 29,400 in Thailand (1984)
- 900,000 in Vietnam (1993)

Cantonese is an important Chinese dialect in Vietnam, where the majority of Chinese in Vietnam are from nearby Guangdong province.

In European, North American and Australian cities Cantonese is often the dominant dialect where ethnic Chinese congregate. It is also the preferred dialect (after Mandarin) for radio media or language schools. Indeed Cantonese is so important amongst overseas Chinese

---

[14] The word 'Cantonese' does not exist in the vocabulary of Mandarin or dialects in other Provinces, though it is used to represent *Guangdong hua* in the Western world.

that to work in a Chinese restaurant one needs to be conversant in Cantonese. There are also numerous websites dedicated to the learning of Cantonese. Recent massive migration of Hong Kong residents to Canada makes it the lingua franca among the ethnic Chinese there.

Teochew Dialect [潮州话] *Cháozhōuhuà*
On the North-Eastern region of Guangdong Province, next to Fujian Province is Cháozhōu [潮州] Municipality, where the Teochew[15] speaking people originates. Cháozhōu dialect is also spoken in parts of Fujian province.

The 'eight towns of Cháozhōu' [潮州八邑] *Cháozhōubāyì*, often used in the names of Teochew Associations are:

From Cháozhōu [潮州] Municipality: Ráopíng [饶平], Cháo'ān [潮安]
From Shàntóu [汕头] Municipality: Nán'ào [南澳], Dènghǎi [澄海], Cháoyáng [潮阳]
From Jiēyáng [揭阳] Municipality: Pǔníng [普宁], Huìlái [惠来], Jiēyáng [揭阳].

Some of these towns are now classified as counties, cities or even municipality.

The Teochews constitute the second largest Chinese dialect group in Southeast Asia.[16]

In Singapore, Malaysia, Indonesia, and Vietnam, Teochews formed the second major Chinese dialect group.[17]

According to *Ethnologue*, there are:

- 360,000 speakers of Teochew (1985) in Singapore (1993)
- 1,058,400 Teochew speakers in Thailand (18%)

---

[15] Known as Chew Zhow in Cantonese.
[16] *The Encyclopaedia of the Chinese Overseas* edited by Lynn Pan. Published by the Chinese Heritage Centre, Singapore.
[17] Ibid.

The Hakka Dialect [客家话] *Kèjiāhuà*
Also on the North-Eastern region of Guangdong, next to Fujian Province are three groups of Hakkas

- From Méizhōu [梅州] Municipality, in particular Méi county [梅县], Dàpǔ county [大埔县], and to a smaller extent Fēngshùn county [丰顺县]
- From Huìzhōu [惠州] Municipality further south. (Please note that this sounds rather close to, but certainly distinctly different from 非洲 [fēizhōu] Africa)
- From Jiēyáng [揭阳] Municipality, where the Hépó Hakkas [河婆客] come from.

As the Hakkas also come from Fujian or other provinces, the distribution of the Hakkas is discussed towards the end of this chapter.

The 'Four Towns' [四邑] *sìyì* **Dialect**
Better known as 'Szeyap', this dialect is spoken in a region surrounded by four towns in Jiāngmén [江门] Municipality of Guangdong. The towns are Ēnpíng city [恩平市], Tāishān city [台山市], Xīnhuì city [新会市] and Kāipíng city [开平市]. Some of them are now classified as counties or cities. The 'Szeyap' dialect is distinct from Cantonese.

Guangdong Geography: As a reference for those who would like to trace their ancestral places, the districts 区 *qū*, cities 市 *shì* or counties 县 *xiàn* under the administrative municipalities are as follows:

Guǎngzhōu [广州] Municipality
　　Districts: Yuèxiù district [越秀区], Dōngshān district [东山区],
　　　　　　Hǎizhū district [海珠区], Lìwān district [荔湾区], Tiānhé

district [天河区], Báiyún district [白云区], Huángpǔ district [黄埔区], Fāngcūn district [芳村区], Huādū district [花都区], Pānyú district [番禺区].
Cities: Cónghùa city [从化市], Zēngchéng city [增城市].

Shēnzhèn [深圳] Municipality
District: Fútián district [福田区], Luóhú district [罗湖区], Nánshān district [南山区], Bǎo'ān district [宝安区], Lónggāng district [龙岗区], Yántián district [盐田区].

Zhūhǎi [珠海] Municipality
Districts: Xiāngzhōu district [香洲区], Dǒumén district [斗门区], Jīnwān district [金湾区].

Shàntóu [汕头] Municipality
District: Cháoyáng district [潮阳区], Cháonán district [潮南区], Dènghǎi district [澄海区], Háojiāng district [濠江区], Jīnpíng district [金平区], Lónghú district [龙湖区].
County: Nán'àoxiàn [南澳县].

Sháoguān [韶关] Municipality
Districts: Běijiāng district [北江区], Zhēnjiāng district [浈江区], Wǔjiāng district [武江区].
Cities: Lèchāng city [乐昌市], Nánxióng] city南雄市.
Counties: Rénhuà county [仁化县], Shǐxìng county [始兴县], Wēngyuán county [翁源县], Qǔjiāng county [曲江县], Xīnfēng county [新丰县], Rǔyuán Yao People Autonomous County [乳源瑶族自治县].

Hēyuán [河源] Municipality
District: Yuánchéng district [源城区].

Counties: Hépíng county [和平县], Lóngchuān county [龙川县], Zǐjīn county [紫金县], Liánpíng county [连平县], Dōngyuán county [东源县].

Méizhōu [梅州] Municipality
District: Méijiāng district [梅江区].
City: Xìngníng city [兴宁市].
Counties: Méi county [梅县], Jiāolǐng county [蕉岭县], Dàpǔ county [大埔县], Fēngshùn county [丰顺县], Wǔhuá county [五华县], Píngyuǎn county [平远县].

Huìzhōu [惠州] Municipality
District: Huìchéng district [惠城区]
City: Huìyáng city [惠阳市]
Counties: Huìdōng county [惠东县], Bóluó county [博罗县], Lóngmén county [龙门县].

Shànwěi [汕尾] Municipality
District: Chéng district [城区].
City: Lùfēng city [陆丰市].
County: Hǎifēng county [海丰县], Lùhé county [陆河县].

Dōngguǎn [东莞] Municipality

Zhōngshān [中山] Municipality

Jiāngmén [江门] Municipality
Districts: Jiānghǎi district [江海区], Péngjiāng district [蓬江区], Xīnhuì district [新会区].
Cities: Tāishān city [台山市], Kāipíng city [开平市], Hèshān city [鹤山市], Ēnpíng city [恩平市].

Fóshān [佛山] Municipality
  District: Shùndé district [顺德区], Nánhǎi district [南海区],
    Sānshuǐ district [三水区], Gāomíng district [高明区],
    Chánchéng district [禅城区].

Yángjiāng [阳江] Municipality
  District: Jiāngchéng district [江城区].
  City: Yángchūn city [阳春市].
  Counties: Yángxī county [阳西县], Yángdōng county [阳东县].

Zhànjiāng [湛江] Municipality
  District: Chìkān district [赤坎区], Xiáshān district [霞山区], Pōtóu
    district [坡头区], Mázhāng district [麻章区].
  Cities: Liánjiāng city [廉江市], Léizhōu city [雷州市], Wúchuān
    city [吴川市].
  Counties: Xúwén county [徐闻县], Suìxī county [遂溪县].

Màomíng [茂名] Municipality
  Districts: Màonán district [茂南区], Màogǎng district [茂港区].
  Cities: Gāozhōu city [高州市], Huàzhōu city [化州市], Xìnyí
    city [信宜市].
  County: Diànbái county [电白县].

Zhàoqìng [肇庆] Municipality
  District: Duānzhōu district [端州区], Dǐnghú district [鼎湖区].
  Cities: Gāoyàoshì [高要市], Sìhuì city [四会市].
  Counties: Guǎngníng county [广宁县], Déqìng county [德庆县],
    Fēngkāi county [封开县], Huáijí county [怀集县].

Qīngyuǎn [清远] Municipality
  District: Qīngchéng district [清城区].
  Cities: Yīngdé city [英德市], Liánzhōu city [连州市].

Counties: Fógāng county [佛冈县], Yángshān county [阳山县], Qīngxīn county [清新县], Liánshān Zhuang and Yao People autonomous county [连山壮族瑶族自治县], Liánnán Yao People autonomous county [连南瑶族自治县].

Cháozhōu [潮州] Municipality
District: Xiāngqiáo district [湘桥区].
Counties: Cháo'ān county [潮安县], Ráopíng county [饶平县].

Jiēyáng [揭阳] Municipality
District: Róngchéng district [榕城区].
City: Pǔníng city [普宁市].
Counties: Jiēdōng county [揭东县], Jiēxī county [揭西县], Huìlái county [惠来县].

Yúnfú [云浮] Municipality
District: Yúnchéng district [云城区].
City: Luódìng city [罗定市].
Counties: Yún'ān county [云安县], Xīnxìng county [新兴县], Yùnán county [郁南县].

Websites
广东省人民政府 (The peoples' Government of Guangdong Province): *www.gd.gov.cn/*
广东省行政区划 (Guangdong Administration Regions):
www.china.org.cn/ch-quhua/guangdong.htm
Guangdong Province (People's Daily on-line):
www.english.peopledaily.com.cn/data/province/guangdong.html

HAINAN ISLAND [海南岛] [Hǎinándao]
Another source of migrants is the province of Hainan, known as Qióng [琼] for short. The island lies at the southernmost tip of China, facing Guangdong province to the north across the Qiongzhou Strait,

Vietnam in the west across the Gulf of Tonkin and Taiwan in the east across the South China Sea. It is the special administrative region for 16 counties that contain South China Sea islands.

Hainan has a population of 8 million and is the home to some 36 ethnic groups.

South China Sea is rich in oil and gas. Gas reserves are estimated at 13 trillion cubic metres; oil reserves at 10.2 billion tons. Oil and gas reserves are concentrated in the offshore waters around Hainan Island.[18]

A map of Hainan administrative regions is shown below:

Note that Hokkien is also spoken in parts of Hainan. According to *Ethnologue*, Hainanese is spoken by

---

[18] China offshore oil and gas industry:
www.users.qwest.net/~kryopak/ChinaOffshoreO&G.htm

74,000 in Singapore (1985)

5,880 in Thailand (1985)

Hainan Geography. As a reference for those who would like to trace their ancestral places, the districts, cities or counties under the administrative municipalities are as follows:

Two municipalities [地级市] *dìjìshì*: Hǎikǒu municipality [海口市] and Sānyà municipality [三亚市].

Seven county level cities [县级市] *xiànjìshì*: Dānzhōu city [儋州市], Dōngfāng city [东方市], Qiónghǎi city [琼海市], Wànníng city [万宁市], Wénchāng city [文昌市], Wǔzhǐshān city [五指山市].

Four counties [县] *xiàn*: Chéngmài county [澄迈县], Túnchāng county [屯昌县], Dìng'ān county [定安县], Língāo county [临高县].

Six autonomous counties [自治县] *zìzhìxiàn*: Báishā Lí People autonomous county [白沙黎族自治县], Bǎodīng Lí People autonomous county [保定黎族自治县], Chāngjiāng Lí People autonomous county [昌江族自治县], Lèdōng Lí People autonomous county [乐东黎族自治县], Língshuǐ Lí People autonomous county [陵水黎族自治县], Qióngzhōng Lí People Miáo People autonomous county [琼中黎族苗族自治县].

In addition there is the office of West, South, and Central Sha Archipelagos 西, 南, 中沙群岛办事处, which covers the South China Sea islands.

Websites:

海南省人民政府 (Hainan Province People's Government):
www.hainan.gov.cn/style1/
www.english.peopledaily.com.cn/data/province/hainan.html
Illuminating China's Provinces, Municipalities and Autonomous
Regions: *www.china.org.cn/english/features/43578.htm*

GUĂNGXĪ PROVINCE [广西省]

According to the statistics of 1990, overseas Chinese of Guangxi amounted to more than 2.6 million, just less than those of Guangdong and Fujian provinces. Guangxi Zhuang Autonomous Region is one of the main overseas Chinese hometowns of China.[19]

Unlike migrants from Guangdong, Fujian and Hainan, who mainly travel to Southeast Asia by sea, people of Guangxi went abroad by both sea and land.

The main channels include 'Silk Road on the sea' with Hépŭ [合浦] as the gate to sea; the freshwater channel from Wúzhōu [梧州] to Guangzhou along Western River with Hong Kong as the gateway; the southern border channel from Fángchéng port [防城港], Dōngxìng [东兴], Jiaohua River to Indochina; the southwestern mountainous channel from Zhennan Barrier, Shuikou, Pinger, Pingmeng, Aidian to Vietnam[20].

A map of Guangxi administrative regions is shown as follow:

---

[19] Guangxi People's Government,
www.gxi.gov.cn/English/overseas%20Chinese/survey%20index.htm
[20] Ibid.

There are 12 nationalities in Guangxi, the Zhuàng people [壮族], the Hàn people [汉族], the Yáo people [瑶族], the Miáo people [苗族], the Dòng people [侗族], the Mùlǎo people [仫佬族], the Máonán people [毛南族], the Jīng people [京族], the Huí people [回族], the Shuǐ people [水族], the Yí people [彝族] and the Gēlāo people [仡佬族]. There are also 25 smaller ethnic groups in the region. Guangxi has a population of 46.33 million, of whom 15.18 million are the Zhuang people [壮族], the largest of China's 55 ethnic groups. Each ethnic group has its own language, and their customs, food, housing and traditional costumes vary greatly. A wide range of dialects are spoken in Guangxi[21].

Guǎngxī Geography

As a reference for whose who would like to trace their ancestral places, the districts [区] *qū*, cities [市] *shì* or counties [县] *xiàn* under the administrative municipalities are as follows:

Nánníng [南宁] Municipality
>District: Xīnchéng district [新城区], Xìngníng district [兴宁区], Yǒngxīn district [永新区], Chéngběi district [城北区], Jiāngnán district [江南区].
>Counties: Yōngníng county [邕宁县], Wǔmíng county [武鸣县], Lóng'ān county [隆安县], Mǎshān county [马山县], Shànglín county [上林县], Bīnyáng county [宾阳县], Héng county [横县].

Liǔzhōu [柳州] Municipality
>District: Chéngzhōng district [城中区], Yúfēng district [鱼峰区], Liǔběi district [柳北区], Liǔnán district [柳南区], Shíjiāo district [市郊区].

---

21 Ibid.

Counties: Liǔjiāng county [柳江县], Liǔchéng county [柳城县], Róngshuǐ Miáo People autonomous county [融水苗族自治县], Lùsài county [鹿寨县], Róng'ān county [融安县], Sānjiāng Tóng People autonomous county [三江侗族自治县].

Guìlín [桂林] Municipality

District: Xiùfēng district [秀峰区], Diécǎi district [叠彩区], Xiàngshān district [象山区], [Qīxīng] district [七星区], Yànshān district [雁山区].

Counties: Yángshuò county [阳朔县], Línguì county [临桂县], Língchuān county [灵川县], Quánzhōu county [全州县], Pínglè county [平乐县], Xìng'ān county [兴安县], Guànyáng county [灌阳县], Lìpǔ county [荔浦县], Zīyuán county [资源县], Yǒngfú county [永福县], Lóngshèng various people autonomous county [龙胜各族自治县], Gōngchéng Yáo People autonomous county [恭城瑶族自治县].

Wúzhōu [梧州] Municipality

District: Wànxiù district [万秀区] district, Diéshān district [蝶山区], Shìjiāo district [市郊区].

City: Cénxī city [岑溪市].

Counties: Cāngwú county [苍梧县], Téng county [藤县], Méngshān county [蒙山县].

Běihǎi [北海] Municipality

District: Hǎichéng district [海城区], Yínhǎi district [银海区], Tiěshāngǎng district [铁山港区].

Counties: Hépǔ county [合浦县].

Fángchénggǎng [防城港] Municipality
District: Gǎngkǒu district [港口区], Fángchéng district [防城区].
City: Dōngxìng city [东兴市].
Counties: Shàngsī county [上思县].

Qīnzhōu [钦州] Municipality
District: Qīnnán district [钦南区], Qīnběi district [钦北区].
Counties: Língshān county [灵山县], Pǔběi county [浦北县].

Guìgǎng [贵港] Municipality
District: Gǎngběi district [港北区], Gāngnán district [港南区].
City: Guìpíngshì city [桂平市].
Counties: Píngnán county [平南县].

Yùlín [玉林] Municipality
District: Yùzhōu district [玉州区].
City: Běiliú city [北流市].
Counties: Róng county [容县], Lùchuān county [陆川县], Bóbái
county [博白县], Xīngyà county [兴业县].

Chóngzuǒ [崇左] Municipality
District: Jiāngzhōu district [江洲区].
Counties: Níngmíng county [宁明县], Fúsuí county [扶绥县],
Lóngzhōu county [龙州县], Dàxīn county [大新县],
Tiānděng county [天等县].

Láibīng [来宾] Municipality
District: Xīngbīng district [兴宾区].
City: Héshān city [合山市].
Counties: Xiàngzhōu county [象州县], Wǔxuān county [武宣县],
Xīnchéng county [忻城县], Jīnxiù Yáo People
autonomous county [金秀瑶自治县].

Hèzhōu dìqū [贺州地区] Municipality
  City: Hèzhōu city [贺州市].
  Counties: Zhōngshān county [钟山县], Zhāopíng county [昭平县], Fùchuān Yáo People autonomous county [富川瑶族自治县].

Báisè [百色] Municipality
  Counties: Língyún county [凌云县], Píngguǒ county [平果县], Xīlín county [西林县], Lèyè county [乐业县], Débǎo county [德保县], Tiánlín county [田林县], Tiányáng county [田阳县], Jìngxī county [靖西县], Tiándōng county [田东县], Nàpō county [那坡县], Lónglín Various People autonomous county [隆林各族自治县].

Héchídì [河池地区] Municipality
  Cities: Héchí city [河池市], Yízhōushì city [宜州市].
  Counties: Tiān'é county [天峨县], Fèngshān county [凤山县], Nándān county [南丹县], Dōnglán county [东兰县], Dū'ān Yáo People autonomous county [都安瑶族自治县], Luóchéng Gēlǎo People autonomous county [罗城仫佬族自治县], Bāmǎ Yáo People autonomous county [巴马瑶族自治县], Huánjiāng Máonán People autonomous county [环江毛南族自治县], Dàhuà Yáo People autonomous county [大化瑶族自治县].

Websites dedicated to Guangxi include:
广西壮族自治区 Guangxi Zhuang People Autonomous Regional Government: *www.gxi.gov.cn/english/*
Guangxi Zhuang Autonomous Region – People's Daily online.
  www.english.peopledaily.com.cn/data/province/guangxi.html
Western China – Guangxi:
  www.china.org.cn/e-xibu/2JI/3JI/guanxi/guangxi-ban.htm

A NOTE ON THE HAKKAS

The term 客人 *Kèrén* means guests or visitors. The term 客家人 *Kèjiārén* refer to the Hakkas, an important dialect group who were migrants from the central or northern parts of China to the south. This historical reality is reflected in the close resemblance of the Hakka dialects to northern languages such as Mandarin, rather than local dialects in the south such as Cantonese, Hokkien or Hainanese. Known as nomads of China, their migration to Southeast Asia and elsewhere was a continuation of earlier southward movement. It is not surprising then to find that the Hakka (as Kèjiā is pronounced in their own dialect) is found in pockets of concentration in several places over several locations, rather than in one place.

In addition to Guangdong, Fujian, and Taiwan, Hakkas are also found in Jiangxi and in pockets of Sichuan, Hunan, Guangxi, Yunnan and Hainan Island. The Hakkas of Fujian and Guangdong migrated to southern China in two separate waves: during the tenth century and between the twelfth and thirteen centuries.

According to *Ethnologue*, there are 33 million Hakka speakers worldwide, 25,725,000 in mainland China, 2.5% of the population (1984). Population total in all countries amount to 33,000,000 (1999).

Today, the Hakkas formed the fourth largest Chinese dialect group in Southeast Asia. Outside China there are:

- 3,000 in Brunei (1979)
- 5,000 in French Guiana (1987)
- 19,200 in French Polynesia (1987)
- 985,635 in Malaysia, including 786,097 in Peninsular Malaysia, 109,060 in Sarawak, 90,478 in Sabah (1980).
- 6,000 in Panama (1981)
- 69,000 in Singapore (1980)
- 6,000 in Surinam
- 2,366,000 in Taiwan (1993)
- 58,800 in Thailand (1984)

It is interesting to note that several prominent politicians are of Hakka descent. They include Sun Yat-Sen (father of modern China), Deng Xiaoping (the post-Mao Chinese leader who modernised China), Ye Jianying (Chinese military and political stewart), Lee Kuan Yew (prime minister of Singapore from 1965-1991) as well as Lee Teng Hui (the former Taiwanese President).

In Malaysia Yap Ah Loy, another Hakka was considered to be the founder of Kuala Lumpur, though the Hakkas were subsequently outnumbered by Cantonese.

MULTIDIALECTAL CHINESE

Learning dialects come naturally due to environmental factors. In Malaysia, for example, Cantonese is spoken in most cities, in particular Kuala Lumpur (the capital city of Malaysia).

The situation for multidialectal Chinese develops as follows. For example Cantonese is widely spoken amongst the Chinese in Kuala Lumpur; a person could very well speak his own dialects (such as Hakka, Hainanese, and Teochew) at home. If his friends, playmates speak another dialect, then he could also pick up a third dialect. This accounts for why many ethnic Chinese speak several dialects.

FUTURE TREND

Modern migrations of ethnic Chinese from China or Southeast Asian countries are based on individual criteria rather than clan or family ties. Migrants to U.S., Europe or Australia/New Zealand are based on business acumen or professional considerations. With migrants coming from virtually all provinces of China, over a long period of time the dominance of dialects from Southern provinces would diminish, and the relative importance of Cantonese as a migrant lingua franca overseas would be relatively unimportant. However in exceptional circumstance, such as the massive migrants from Hong Kong to Canada to create a 'Cantonese speaking enclave' could not be ruled out.

DIALECTS OF LOVE

We would like to end this chapter with the phrase 'I love you', spoken in several dialects. The written character 我爱你 is exactly the same.

Mandarin:	*wǒ ài nǐ*
Cantonese:	*ngo oi nei*
Hakka:	*ngai oi ngee*
Hokkien:	*wa ai lu*
Teochew:	*gao ai li*

Source of Culture and Mindset:
History at Play

AN IMPORTANT SOURCE OF CULTURAL roots and mindset is derived from history. Invariably events in the past shape the present thinking and outlook. On a macro scale historical events shape the demographic and socio-political landscape of nations.

The migration of Chinese within China and out of China is largely shaped by history. This is evident when we consider the case of Chinese settlement in Southeast Asia, as well as re-migration to countries such as Europe, North America and Australia.

Thanks to the early development of written language, the invention of printing and paper, China has a long continuous record of quite detailed history. The study of Chinese history is indeed fascinating. Salient features pertaining to Chinese history and its impact include:

❖ For thousands of years Chinese historians dutifully compiled and recorded detailed events and circumstances of their times. Some of the records were centred round the emperor, the emperor's courts, army generals and battles, heroes and bandits. Some of these memorable characters form part of the folklore, affecting the psyche of modern kids. Some of them are listed in the 'notable personalities' in this chapter. They are also mentioned in relevant chapters throughout this book.

❖ Since a lot of the writings involve events and judgement of history through the dynasties, Chinese history serves as benchmark on ethics, value system, wisdom and morality. It provides a valuable insight into the cultural values, wisdom, as well as philosophical thoughts.

❖ A study of Chinese history, coupled with an understanding of the cultural and circumstantial events at the time provide valuable insight into the thinking of contemporary Chinese people.

❖ Chinese history has profound influence on its neighbours, ranging from Japan, Korea, Mongolia in the North, as well as Southeast Asia in the South.

❖ Migration to countries outside China in the past few hundred years created the overseas Chinese, to whom this book is dedicated.

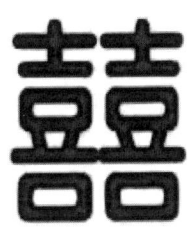

Double Happiness: a symbol often seen at weddings. Wedding between 松赞干布 *Sōngzàn Gānbù* the Tibetan ruler and 文成公主 *Wénchéng gōngzhǔ* the Chinese princess forms part of Chinese history. Even today, inter-racial marriages between ethnic Chinese and other Asians or Caucasians are not uncommon in Western countries.

A BRIEF TOUR TO 5,000 YEARS OF HISTORY

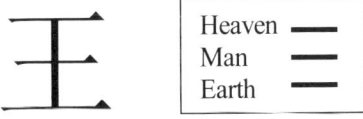

Chinese history relates how emperors and kings created empires and kingdoms. The King is represented simply as 王 *wáng*, which is also a common Chinese surname. It consists of three horizontal strokes, linked together by a vertical stroke. The top stroke represents Heaven, the bottom stroke Earth. Mankind is located between heaven and earth, represented by the middle stroke. The king is the person who successfully unifies or harmonises the heaven, the earth and mankind.

The Chinese history is often discussed in terms of kingdoms and dynasties, some ruled by members of the same family for generations. (For example the Shāng [商] dynasty (p. 128) lasted 640 years, ruled by 17 generations and 31 emperors. The Táng [唐] dynasty was ruled by 20 emperors, lasting 290 years (p. 141).

The dynasty concept leave such impressions that we speak of the Táng dynasty noted for poetry [诗], the Sòng dynasty noted for prose [词], Míng dynasty noted for porcelain [瓷], and so on.

The most comprehensive records of early history would be the 史记 *Shǐjì* 'Historical Records', written in early Hàn (206-220 BC) by Sīmǎ Qiān [司马迁] (p. 168). It provides accounts of earlier periods from legendary times to Xià (p. 128), Shāng (p. 128), Zhōu dynasties, through the Spring and Autumn period (p. 129), the Warring States (p. 131) to Qín dynasty (p. 132) and early Hàn (p. 133) (refer to the Chronology of Chinese history). One could even draw on earlier texts such as 左传[22] *Zuǒzhuàn*, 世本 *Shìběn*, etc, a monumental work of 130 volumes, covering 12 volumes of 本记 *Běnjì*, 10 volumes of 表 *Biǎo*, 8 volumes of 书 *Shū*, 30 volumes of 世家 *Shìjiā*, as well as 70 volumes of 列传 *Lièzhuàn*. It gave vivid accounts of events during these times, from Emperors to commoners (p. 249).

The next major work would be 资治通鉴 *Zīzhì Tōngjiàn*, written by Sīmǎ Guāng [司马光] (p. 168). The 294 volumes collection

---

[22] Written around 3rd century BC, the oldest record of Chinese narrative history. It portrays a chronicle of the feudal kingdoms between 722 and 468 BC. Little is known about the author.

provided a comprehensive historical record of some 1,362 years from 403 BC to 959 AD.

Though there were numerous historical writings through the periods, the next historian of importance was Zēng Xiānzhī [曾先之] (p. 175), who lived towards end of Sòng and beginning of Yuán dynasty (towards the end of 13th century. (Little is known about the author as he lived at a time of war, a transition from one empire to another. His work 十八史略 *shíbāshǐlüè* 'The eighteen historical notes', gives a general introduction to events from the 史记 *Shǐjì* 'Historical Records' to the Sòng dynasty.

CHRONOLOGY OF CHINESE HISTORY

A very brief description of Chinese history could be summarised as follows. Some of the dates might overlap, indicating that different events are happening in different parts of China. Some of the personalities are listed towards the end of this chapter (refer to the relevant chapters for personalities or events mentioned).

Chinese worldwide call themselves descendants of 'Yán-Huáng zǐsūn' [炎黄子孙]. They refer to two tribal rulers, Emperor Huángdì [黄帝] (p. 158) and Emperor Yándì [炎帝] (p. 174), who lived at about four thousand years ago along the Yellow River, the cradle of Chinese civilisation. Together they defeated another tribe, the 蚩尤 *chīyōu*.

During this period Cāng Jiē [仓颉] (p. 153), attributed with the 'invention' of Chinese characters, was one of the officials of Huángdì [黄帝] (p. 158).

(Legendary) Emperors Yáo [尧], Shùn [舜] about 3rd Millennium BC

Emperor Yáo [尧] (died 2258 BC) was the earliest legendary emperor. Rather than appointing his son 丹朱 *Dānzhū* as the next emperor, he passed his throne to the highly capable and popular Shùn [舜].

Xià [夏] Dynasty About 2205-1752 BC

Civilisation evolved around water supplies. Rivers provided water but also brought about floods. During the reign of Emperor Yáo [尧], the emperor appointed 鲧 *Gǔn* to tackle the massive flood problem. His approach of building more embankment resulted in failure. His son Yú [禹] spent thirteen years to solve the flood problems, using a combination of embankment and drainage techniques. The emperor was so impressed by his ability that he abdicated in favour of Yú. When Yú passed away, his son was appointed, forming the first dynasty in Chinese history Xià [夏]. It was ruled by 16 emperors through 13 generations.

> The story of Great Yú [大禹] (p. 154) forms part of Chinese psyche. Rather than treating flood as a punishment of God to be feared or avoided, the Chinese view flood as a natural phenomena to be dealt with. The spirit of 'men overcoming nature' was established very early in Chinese history. What is required is hard work, sacrifice, in addition to leadership. Even today the Chinese are planning to divert water from the South to the North in a massive scale.
>
> This was also the beginning of Bronze Age in China. The use of bronze in household, agricultural tools and military equipment brought about a new level of technology and sophistication. It was also used to cast ornaments, musical instruments and other symbols of status or authority.

Shāng [商] (Yīn) (殷) Dynasty 1751-1112 BC

Shāng [商] was the second dynasty in China, founded by Tāng [汤]. The capital was relocated to a place called Yīn [殷]. Shāng [商] dynasty, also known as Yīn [殷] dynasty, was ruled by 17 genera-tions and 31 emperors. Commerce and agriculture prospered.

A huge amount of archaeological artefacts indicated that language, known as 'shell and bone characters' [甲骨文] *jiǎgúwén* were developed during this period (refer to p. 60). In addition the practice of divination (refer to p. 424) was already quite common.

Zhōu [周] Dynasty 1027-249 BC

Zhōu Wǔwáng 周武王 destroyed the Shāng [商] dynasty, and established the Zhōu [周] dynasty. The first part of the dynasty was known as Western Zhōu, with the capital in Gàojīn [镐京]. In 771 BC the capital was moved to Luòyì [洛邑], on the Eastern part.

Western Zhou [西周[*xī zhōu* 1066-771 BC
Eastern Zhou [东周[*dōng zhōu* 771-221 BC

Zhōu Wénwáng [周文王] (p. 178) wrote the authoritative book on 'I-Ching' *yījīng* while in prison. Zhōuyì [周易] evolved as a sophisticated method for decision making (refer to Chapter ten).

Imperial courts at this time had song and dance. Numerous poems from this period was collected, then compiled as 诗经 *Shījīng* 'The Book of Poetry'. The 305 collections were classified into 3 categories, 风 *fēng*, dedicated to music and poetry from the general population, 雅 *yǎ*, pertaining to Imperial court and its surroundings, as well as 颂 *sòng*, words of praise in religious ceremonies. This was the first poetry book in China. It reflected a highly developed language, high literacy standards, cultural richness and sophistication at this time.

Spring and Autumn [春秋] *chūnqiū* 722-481 BC

The collapse of Zhōu [周] dynasty resulted in numerous states, each ruled by local warlords, each trying to annex each other. Power was decentralised, assimilation of weaker states were typical.

Key states during the period include Qí [齐], Lǔ [鲁], Chǔ [楚], Sòng [宋], Jìn [晋], Qín [秦], Chén [陈], Cài [蔡], Zhèng [郑], Xǔ [许] and Wú [吴].

The five outstanding statesmen during this period, collectively known as 'the five strongmen of chūnqiū [春秋 五霸] were Qí Hénggōng [齐桓公], Jìn Wéngōng [晋文公], Sòng Rànggōng [宋襄公], Qín Mùgōng [秦穆公] and Chǔ Zhuàngwáng [楚庄王].

During this period, the steady erosion of nobility brought about widespread literacy, which further developed into expressions of thought and technology. Several scholars and philosophers emerged during the Spring-Autumn and Warring States period (p. 131).

Lǎo Zǐ [老子] (p. 160), philosopher and founder of Dàoism, came from the kingdom of Chǔ [楚]. His *Dàodéjīng* [道德经] provided a rigorous, provocative and intellectual analysis of nature as well as human behaviour. It challenges emotional and intellectual values of people throughout the centuries, guiding people away from the purely superstitious or 'blind' understanding of nature. His concept of duality, flexibility and humility is still valued today (refer to p. 267)

Confucius Kǒngzǐ [孔子] (p. 159) was born in the Kingdom of Lǔ [鲁]. He was probably the person in Chinese history best known to the Western world. Highly regarded as an intellectual, philosopher and educationist, he travelled to various states to preach his messages of benevolence, mutual respect and humanity. His philosophy was not accepted during a period of war. He developed a school of thought, incorporating righteousness based on the concepts of 'benevolence' [仁] *rén* and 'social etiquettes' [礼] *lǐ*. The philosophy could be applied to self cultivation, management of families and nations, as well as ethical, moral, social and political standards. In his late years he edited several important Chinese classics (refer to p. 275).

Sūn Wǔ [孙武] (p. 170), military strategist to the Kingdom of Wú [吴], declined an Imperial post, and wrote his famous book, 'the art of war'. The concepts embedded in the 'Art of war' are widely used in military, business, politics and management practices (refer to p. 239).

Important episodes during this period include the King of Yuè Gōujiàn [勾践] savouring the bitter taste of gall bladder while sleeping on a pile of firewood [卧薪尝胆], to remind himself of the bitterness of defeat. He eventually regained his kingdom. Another interesting episode was a beauty, Xī Shī [西施] (p. 173), who was offered to Emperor Fū Chāi [夫差] as a diplomatic and military tool. Bewitched by her beauty Fū Chāi soon slacked in his state affairs and killed his best advisor Wǔ Zǐxù [伍子胥], leading to his own downfall.

Warring States [战国] zhànguó 480-222 BC

This was the period when different parts of China were controlled by local powerful warlords, who clashed with one another to gain more territories. Eventually 'Seven Great Powers' 战国七雄 zhànguó qīxióng, emerged, comprising Qí [齐], Chǔ [楚], Yàn [燕], Hán [韩], Zhào [赵], Wèi [魏] and Qín [秦].

Mèngzǐ [孟子] (p. 164), the great Confucian philosopher, was born during this period. He believed that human nature is inherently good, or at least capable of being good. Human nature could be improved through self-cultivation.

Mòzǐ [墨子] (p. 165), a philosopher, also lived during this period. He denounced warfare and extravagance, favoured simplicity and frugality.

Zhuāngzǐ [庄子] (p. 179), another philosopher, made significant contribution to Dàoism. He used parables, anecdotes and paradoxes, to express his ideas of nature and non-materialistic life.

An interesting person who lived in this era was a craftsman Lǔ Bān [鲁班] (p. 164), widely acknowledged as the 'father of carpentry or craftsmanship' in China. He designed mobile assault ladders to scale towers. Another book on military strategy, 孙膑兵法 *Sūnbīn bīngfǎ* was written during this period by Sūnbīn [孙膑].

Qū Yuán [屈原] (p. 166), the patriotic poet from the kingdom of Chǔ [楚], wrote numerous poems based on nationalism, nature, religion, etc. He committed suicide in a river, when his advice was not heeded.

Other important works during this period include 吕氏春秋 *Lǚshì chūnqiū* (p. 164). Notable philosophers include Xúnzǐ [荀子] (p. 174) and the philosopher and political thinker Hán Fēizǐ [韩非子] (p. 157), who proposed a combination of legal techniques and morals, rather than just relying on the ruler's authority, as the basis of governance

Qín [秦] Empire 221-206 BC

All six powers were defeated by Qín rulers, resulting in the earliest unification of China under Qín Shǐ Huáng [秦始皇] (p. 166). He wanted to be known as 'Emperor' Huángdì [皇帝], rather than 'king' [王] *wáng*. He proclaimed himself to be the 'founder emperor' [始皇帝] *shǐ huáng dì*. Indeed he is known in the West as 'Shi Huang Ti'. The Qín dynasty was translated as 'Ch'in', which gave rise to the name 'China'.

Together with Lǐ Sī [李斯] (p. 161), the prime minister, a series of reforms were carried out. Rather than appointing feudal rulers, he adopted a system of centralised bureaucracy, dividing the country into 36 administrative divisions, with officials directly controlled by the Emperor.

He also introduced the unified Chinese transport system, standard measuring units, currency, the legal system, and more importantly a uniform written Chinese language, the 'Seal character' [小篆] *xiǎozhuàn* (refer to p. 60).

To prevent nomadic attacks from the North, he joined various sections of fortresses to become a long, continuous wall, the 'Great Wall of China'. Till date this is the only man-made structure visible from space. The Great wall served as border defence. It separates high levels of civilisation and agriculture within the wall, from grassland, deserts and nomadic tribes without. Even today the 'Great Wall' has considerable impact on the psyche of Chinese citizens, as it is embedded in the National Anthem of People's Republic of China.

Draconian actions were taken against scholars who do not agree with his policies and projects. Books were burned, and Confucius scholars were buried alive.

An idea of the civilisation during this period could be seen from the Museum of Qín Terra Cotta Warriors and Horses in Shaanxi Province. This is probably the biggest art and military museum of the Ancient World, incorporating some seven thousand life size terracotta figures of warriors, horses and chariots arranged in battle formations.

Hàn [汉] Dynasty 202 BC-220 AD

Western Hàn [西汉] *xī hàn* 206 BC-23 AD

Hundreds of thousands of people were mobilised to build the Great Wall of China, the palace, as well as development in the south. More resources were diverted to build his massive mausoleum, which housed the terracotta soldiers. This led to popular uprising, first by

Chén Shèng [陈胜] (p. 154): Chén Shèng and Wú Guǎng [吴广], who led the first, large-scale popular peasant uprising in Chinese history in 209 BC.

Later on Liú Bāng [刘邦] (p. 162) together with the 'three heroes of early Hàn' [汉初三杰] *hànchū sānjié*, Xiāo Hé [萧何], Zhāng Liáng [张良] and Hán Xìn [韩信] (p. 157), defeated Xiàng Yǔ [项羽] to become the first emperor of Hàn dynasty.

An outstanding ruler was Liú Chè [刘彻] (p. 163), who ruled as Hàn Wǔdì [汉武帝], 5th emperor of Western Hàn. He brought about renewal of Chinese scholarship, destroyed during Shi Huang Di. He promoted the study of culture and collection of books, and established Confucianism as the official doctrine of the state.

He also commissioned two of his generals, Wèi Qīng [卫青] and Huò Qùbìng [霍去病] to bring the nomadic tribes under control. He also brought Hainan island under Chinese control.

The Hàn dynasty brought about a period of peace, prosperity and stability. For the first time the Chinese contacted the outside world. Hàn Wǔdì [汉武帝] despatched an adventurer and diplomat Zhāng Qiān [张骞] (p. 175) to liaise with desert countries to the West. These trips eventually led to the 'silk route', linking the East and West.

To bring about peace with the nomadic Xiongnu kingdom, Wáng Zhāojūn [王昭君] (p. 171), one of the four beauties in Chinese history, volunteered to marry into Xiongnu kingdom. Her life became the story of 昭君出塞 'Zhāojūn leaves for the frontier'.

The notable historian Sīmǎ Qiān [司马迁] (p. 168) wrote the 史记 *shǐjì* 'Historical Records' while in prison. It vividly described Chinese history from legendary times to Xià

[夏], Shāng [商] and Zhōu [周] dynasties, through the 'Spring and Autumn' (p. 129) as well as 'Warring States' (p. 131), to Qín dynasty and early Hàn.

An insight into the civilisation of the Hàn period could be seen from the Mǎ Wáng Duī [马王堆] tomb in Hunan Province. About 3000 relics were found including a well preserved cadaver and complete text of I-Ching written on silk. Amongst the paintings is one which depicts 'Celestial realm', 'Human realm' and 'sub-terrestrial realm'.

During the Hàn period, 'performance arts' [百戏] *bǎixì* were highly developed. In addition to songs, cultural dances, acrobatics, martial arts and weaponry demonstrations, various musical instruments were used.

Xīn [新] 9-23 AD

This is a short period of 15 years when Wáng Mǎng 王莽 took power.

Eastern Hàn [东汉] *dōng hàn* 25-220 AD

Liú Xiù [刘秀] (p. 163), also known as Hàn Guāngwǔdì [汉光武帝] established the capital at Luòyáng [洛阳]. This is known in history as Eastern Hàn [东汉] *dōng hàn* or later Hàn [后汉] *hòu hàn*.

Liú Zhuāng [刘庄] (p. 164) ruled as Hàn Míngdì [汉明帝], the second emperor of Eastern Hàn. He dreamt of a person with a bright halo, rising to the sky, moving towards the west. He then despatched officials to seek Buddhism from the west. They came back with two eminent monks —Shè Móténg [摄摩腾] and Zhú Fǎlán [竺法兰] and a white horse carried the sutra and the figure of Buddha. To acknowledge the white horse's contribution, the Emperor ordered the construction of the temple and named it White Horse Temple [白马寺] *báimǎsì* near the city of Luòyáng [洛阳].

135

Entrance to the 'White Horse Temple.'

A famous scientist Zhāng Héng [张衡] (p. 175) lived during this period. A mathematician, astronomer and geographer, he became chief astrologer and minister. In the year 132 he invented the first seismoscope.

Cài Lún [蔡伦] (p. 153) invented paper, one of the four great Chinese inventions. Prior to this writings were either engraved on stones, bronze ware or carved onto bamboos. Invention of paper facilitated communications and cultural dissemination, in the days long before audio devices were invented.

Xǔ Shèn [许慎] (p. 173) compiled the first Chinese dictionary 说文解字 *shuōwénjiězì*. The dictionary was composed of 15 chapters and collected 9,353 characters.

Engraving characters on stones were developed into a fine art. In the year 175 a project called 熹平石经 *xīpíng shíjīng* 'Xīpíng classics on stone' were undertaken, whereby seven complete Confucius texts were engraved on stones!

A historian, Bān Gù [班固] (p. 152) compiled an important historical document, the 汉书 'History of Hàn period'. He also wrote an interesting book 白虎通德論 *báihǔ tōngdélún* 'Discussion about Virtue at White Tiger Hall'. This was a theoretical discussion between theology, superstition, the relationship between heaven and men. The yīn-yáng and five determinant elements (refer to p. 314) became more stable as a basis for understanding of natural social sciences, as well as human relationships.

Three Kingdoms [三国] *sānguó*

China then entered a period of Three Kingdoms, during which three kingdoms fought against each other.

Wèi [魏]: 220-265
Shǔ [蜀]: 221-263
Wú [吴]: 222-280

Well known personalities in this period were Cáo Cāo [曹操] (p. 153), Cáo Pī [曹丕] (p. 154) and Cáo Zhí [曹植] (p. 154) for the Kingdom of Wèi [魏].

Liú Bèi [刘备] (p. 162) was the key figure in the Kingdom of Shǔ [蜀]. To enlist the service of Zhūgé Liàng [诸葛亮] (p. 178), Liú Bèi visited his hut three times, to express his sincerity. This episode is known as 三顾茅庐 'three visits to thatched hut'. His able generals were Guān Yǔ [关羽] (p. 156) and Zhāng Fēi [张飞] (p. 175).

Sūn Quán [孙权] (p. 169) and Zhōu Yú [周瑜] (p. 178) were the key figures of the Kingdom of Wú [吴].

An important novel written by Luó Guanzhōng [罗贯中] (p. 164) known as 三国演义 *sānguóyǎnyì* 'The Romance of the Three Kingdoms' vividly describes this period (refer to p. 249).

A well-known battle fought over this period was the 赤 壁之战 *chìbì zhī zàn* 'Battle of Chìbì', where Zhōu Yú [周 瑜] (p. 178) used fire to destroy a mighty army, commanded by Cáo Cāo [曹操] (p. 153).

A notable military victory through diplomatic strategy was achieved by Zhūgé Liàng [诸葛亮] (p. 178), in wining over the loyalty of Mèng Huò [孟获], an influential but rebellious tribal leader. Mèng Huò was captured and released (rather than killed) six times. On his seventh capture, he was convinced that he could not win in battle, was grateful for his life, and from then on swore his allegiance to Zhūgé Liàng, ending a period of unrest and military expenses to keep the peace.

Other well known figures were two medical doctors, Huà Túo [华陀] (p. 158), the legendary physician, and Zhāng Zhòngjǐng [张仲景] (p. 176), author of medical text books 伤寒论 *Shānghánlùn* and 金匮要略 *Jīnkuìyàolùe*.

In literature, Cài Wénjī [蔡文姬] (p. 153) wrote various poems including 胡笳十八拍 *hú jiā shíbā pāi* (p. 263) as well as 悲愤诗 *bēi fèn shī*. Others include 后出师表 *hòuchūshībiǎo* by Zhūgé Liàng [诸葛亮] as well as poems from Cáo Cāo [曹操] and Cáo Zhí [曹植].

Jìn [晋] 265-420 AD

Sīmǎ Yán [司马炎] (p. 168) established the Jìn kingdom. The period 265-316 is known as Western Jìn, with the Capital at Luòyáng [洛阳]. The empire collapsed but was rebuilt by Sīmǎ Yán [司马睿] in 317, known as Eastern Jìn, with the capital at Jiànkāng [建康].

Well-known personalities in this period include Sīmǎ Yán [司马炎] (p. 168), the founder of Jìn dynasty. However decadence during his rule leads to mass discontent. Upon his death his two sons were too incapable to provide effective rule.

This period of social unrest saw the rise of Buddhism. Notable monks include Zhī Dùn [支遁] (p. 177), Dào Ān [道安] (p. 154), Huì Yuǎn [慧远] (p. 158), Jiūmóluóshén [鸠摩罗什] (p. 159) and Dào Shēng [道生] (p. 155). Jiūmóluóshén translated important Buddhist scriptures into Chinese.

An outstanding Chinese calligrapher, Wáng Xīzhī [王羲之] (p. 171) lived in this period. Táo Yuānmíng [陶渊明] wrote 桃花源记 *Táohuāyuānjì*, describing his vision of paradise land, where people lived in peaceful environment free of worries (p. 170).

The next phase was the Southern and Northern dynasties [南北朝] *nánběicháo*, whereby two dynasties developed.

Southern Dynasties [南朝] *náncháo* (420-589 AD), comprised four dynasties:

Sòng	[宋]	420-479
Qí	[齐]	479-502
Liáng	[梁]	502-557
Chén	[陈]	557-589

Northern Dynasties [北朝] *běicháo* (439-589 AD), comprised four dynasties:

Northern Wèi	[北魏]	389-534
Eastern Wèi	[东魏]	534-550
Northern Qí	[北齐]	550-577
Northern Zhōu	[北周]	557-581

An eminent mathematician and astronomer Zǔ Chōngzhī [祖冲之] (p. 179) compiled the 大明曆 'Dàmíng calendar', working out the time required for the moon to move one round to within one second accuracy. He also worked out the value of 'π' to seven decimal places.

Buddhism became popular during this period. The Emperor Liáng Wǔdì [梁武帝] (born as Xiāo Yán) [萧衍] (p. 173) even became a monk for four days.

An important Buddhism site built during this period is the Yūngāng caves [云冈石窟] (Shanxi province), where forty five caves, containing more than 51,000 stone carvings big and small, could still be seen today. Built at a time of war, it became a refuge of peace.

Another important stone cave is the Lóngmén grottoes [龙门石窟] near the city of Luòyáng [洛阳], whose construction continued for another 400 years. It contains more than 10,000 statues of various sizes with beautiful decorations.

Suí [隋] Dynasty 581-618 AD

Suí Yángdì [隋炀帝], born as Yáng Guāng [杨广] (p. 174) unified China, to establish a relatively short dynasty of 28 years. Landmark features of Chinese civilisation such as the establishment of Imperial examination system for civil service [科举] kējū, which enlisted scholars to serve as government officials. This provided a pathway for anyone to achieve positions of power through their intelligence and hard work. From this time on, civil servants became China's most envied elite, replacing the hereditary nobles and landlords.

The construction of Grand Canal linking north and south China, a distance of 1,747 kilometres, was also carried out. The Grand Canal subsequently facilitated commerce and cultural exchange.

Táng [唐] Dynasty 618-907 AD

Lǐ Yuān [李渊] (p. 162) established the Táng dynasty in 618. His son Lǐ Shìmín [李世民] (p. 161), who ruled as Táng Tàizōng [唐太宗], was the most outstanding, second emperor of the Táng dynasty. He gave power to educated civil servants rather than aristocrats or military officers. The emperor reigned over a period of peace and prosperity, extended the Silk Road to Central Asia.

This was one of the most prosperous dynasties in China. Even today Chinese call themselves the Táng people [唐人] *tángrén*. Effective central and local government were established. Buddhism came to China. The arts flourished, with literature, music, etc. Numerous poets composed their poetry during this period. Till today the Táng poetry [唐诗] *táng shī* is well known to any Chinese scholar, and popular amongst students. Gunpowder and printing were invented. The dynasty had 20 emperors, lasting 290 years.

Xuán Zhuāng [玄奘] (p. 173) a Buddhist monk went across the desert to India, where he learned Buddhism for five years before bringing home the scriptures. His travels were recorded in his book 大唐西域记 *Dàtáng xīchéngjì*.

Along the silk route, at the edge of Gobi desert, are about five hundred Dūnhuáng [敦煌] cave temples built during this period. It contains highly decorated, vivid, colourful paintings of Buddhist personalities. In total more than 25,000 square metres wall paintings and more than 3,000 painted sculptures are well preserved, making it a unique Buddhist art collection in the World. This is an important site for the study of medieval Chinese civilisation.

Jiān Zhēn [鉴真] (p. 159), a monk from the Daming temple in Yangzhou, spread Buddhism to Japan. At 66, he finally reached Japan on his sixth attempt. Another monk, Fǎ Zàng [法藏] (p. 155) made great contribution to the development and consolidation of the Huàyán [华严] sect.

Wénchéng gōngzhǔ [文成公主] (p. 172), a Chinese princess was arranged to marry the Tibetan ruler Sōngzàn Gānbù [松赞干布] (p. 169). This brought about important cultural and economic exchange between the two parties.

Yáng Guìfēi [杨贵妃] (p. 174), one of the four beauties in Chinese history, became the concubine of Emperor Táng Xuánzōng [唐玄宗], and contributed to the Emperor's downfall.

Lǐ Chúnfēng [李淳风] (p. 160) and Yuán Tiāngāng [袁天罡] (p. 175), astrological advisers to the Emperor, authored the earliest book on prediction 推背图 *tuī bèi tú* 'Diagrams of Rubbing the Back', several centuries before Nostradamus (refer to p. 252).

Táng dynasty was noted for poets. They included Lǐ Bái [李白] (p. 160), Dù Fǔ [杜甫] (p. 155), Bái Jūyì [白居易], Hán Yù [韩愈] (p. 157), Liú Yúxī [刘禹锡], Liǔ Zōngyuán [柳宗元] (p. 164), Mèng Hàorán [孟浩然] (p. 164), Wáng Hàn [王翰], Wáng Jiàn [王建] (p. 171), Wáng Wéi [王维] (p. 171) and Wáng Zhīhuàn [王之涣] (p. 172).

The famous calligrapher Liǔ Gōngquán [柳公权] (p. 164) lived during this period.

142

Through a series of manipulations, Wǔ Zétiān [武则天] (p. 173) came to the throne, and became the only Empress in Chinese history.

Five Dynasties [五代] *wǔdài* **907-979 AD**
This period is known as 五代十国 *wǔdài shíguó* 'five dynasties and 10 kingdoms'.
In the Central and North of China five dynasties were established, namely

Later Liáng	[后梁]	907-923
Later Táng	[后唐]	923-936
Later Jìn	[后晋]	936-947
Later Hàn	[后汉]	947-950
Later Zhōu	[后周]	951-960

In the south ten kingdoms were established namely Wú [吴], Nán Táng [南唐], Wú Yuè [吴越], Chǔ [楚], Mǐn [闽], Nán Hàn [南汉], Qián Shǔ [前蜀], Hòu Shǔ [后蜀], Xingnán [荆南] and Běi Hàn [北汉].

Xú Zǐpíng [徐子平] (p. 173) developed the 命理学 *mìnglǐxué* 'The Study of Life Destiny' (p. 380), during the five dynasties/Sòng period.

Sòng [宋] Dynasty 960-1279 AD
Sòng Dynasty could be divided into two periods: Northern Sòng [北宋] when the capital was in the city of Kāifēng [开封] in Hénán [河南] province from 960 to 1127. This period was ruled by 9 emperors, lasting 167 years. Southern Sòng [南宋] with the capital in Hángzhōu [杭州] in Zhèjiāng [浙江] province from 1127 to 1279. It lasted 153 years, also ruled by 9 emperors.

Zhào Kuāngyìn [赵匡胤] (p. 176) who ruled as Sòng Tàizǔ [宋太祖] founded the Sòng dynasty. To prevent military coups he established a professional army under strict control of the central government.

Sòng Dynasty ranks along the Táng and Hàn in importance. China enjoyed impressive economic growth coupled with great artistic and intellectual achievement. Famous personalities in the literary world include Fàn Zhòngyān [范仲淹] (p. 155), Lù Yóu [陆遊], Ōuyáng Xiū [欧阳修] (p. 165), Zēng Gǒng [曾巩] (p. 175), Wáng Ānshí [王安石] (p. 171), Sū Xùn [苏洵] (p. 169), Sū Shì [苏轼] (p. 169), Sū Zhé [苏辙] (p. 169) and Zhū Xī [朱熹] (p. 179). Another outstanding person is a female poet Lǐ Qīngzhào [李清照] (p. 161), famous for her nostalgic poetry.

Fàn Zhòngyān [范仲淹] (p. 155) and Wáng Ānshí [王安石] (p. 171) were also statesmen and reformers. Other important characters include Bāo Zhěng [包拯], better known as Bāo Gōng [包公], an incorruptible judge known for his fearlessness and impartiality (p. 153).

In the field of science and technology, Shěn Kuò [沈括] (p. 167), a noted scientist, left behind notes and research findings in the fields of geography, geology, astronomy and mathematics. He also identified petroleum, and predicted that it would have a myriad of applications. Bì Shēng [毕升] (p. 153) invented printing by carving individual characters on squares of clay, baked to make printing blocks.

Towards the end of Sòng dynasty, a military hero Yuè Fēi [岳飞] (p. 175), who won brilliant victories was betrayed at Imperial court by Qín Kuǎi [秦桧]. Yuè Fēi's poem 满江红 mǎnjiānghóng 'The Whole River is Red' is still popular today (p. 263).

Dā Mó [达摩] Bodhidharma (p. 154), the legendary Indian Monk who went to China, established the chán [禅]

Buddhism in China. He was also credited with the setting up of Shàolin temple [少林寺] *shào lín shi*.

An interesting piece of painting is the 清明上河图 *Qīngmíng shànghé tú* by Imperial court painter Zhāng Zéduān [张择端] (p. 176). This is a lengthy five-metre scroll that depicts in realistic artistic style with historical detail, life in the Sòng period. The painting is kept at the Palace Museum in Beijing.

Yuán [元] Dynasty 1279-1368 AD

The Yuán dynasty was started with conquest by Genghis Khan (p. 156), the Mongolian warrior. When Genghis Khan died in 1227, he had just finished conquering the city of Beijing. By 1241, the Mongols had conquered all of northern China. In 1260, Kublai Khan, a grandson of Genghis Khan, became the Great Khan. He relocated his capital from Mongolia to Beijing and in 1271 he established the Yuán dynasty. The Chinese eventually culturally assimilated the Mongolians. Marco Polo visited China during this time, and Chinese inventions such as gunpowder and printing were brought to Europe.

The Yuán rulers retained some Hàn advisers and experts, amongst whom was Guō Shǒujìng [郭守敬] (p. 156), mathematician and astronomer who helped develop the astronomical observatory in Beijing in 1280. They worked out the duration of a year, accurate to 26 seconds. Guo was also an expert in irrigation.

During this period Marco Polo, the explorer from Venice, visited China in 1275, and was very impressed by its culture and civilisation. He stayed in China for 17 years, and brought back items such as gunpower, printing and compass to Europe.

The Yuán rulers classified the population into four ethnic groups, each receiving different treatment. Top of the list were the Mongols, next were other minorities in the north, followed by the Hàns, then the people in the south. Needless to say these discrimination lead to widespread discontent.

Outstanding painters included Huáng Gōngwàng [黄公望] (p. 158), Ní Zàn [倪瓒] (p. 165), Rèn Rénfǎ [任仁发] (p. 167), Wáng Méng [王蒙] (p. 171) and Wú Zhèn [吴镇].

Míng [明] Dynasty 1368-1644 AD

Founded by Zhū Yuánzhāng [朱元璋] (p. 179). The dynasty lasted 277 years, ruled by 17 Emperors.

The prime minister during the beginning of Míng dynasty was Liú Bówēn [刘伯温] (p. 163), famous for 烧饼歌 *shāobǐnggē* which predicted events into the future, very much like Nostradamus.

Emperor Yǒng Lè [永乐] born as Zhū Dì [朱棣] (p. 178) commissioned Admiral Cheng Ho [郑和] *Zhèng Hé* (p. 177) to seven naval missions, reaching Southeast Asia, Africa, Indian sub-continent, Persian Gulf, Arab states and the Red Sea. His sea crew of some 27,800 included not only sailors but also craftsmen, navigators and medical personnel. The naval force was well beyond European capabilities. This maritime achievement, long forgotten in the West, is etched in Chinese naval psyche. These expeditions were not sent to colonise territories, they were diplomatic or fact finding missions. The Yǒng Lè encyclopaedia of 22,877 volumes was compiled (p. 178).

Literary works in this period were impressive. Luó Guan Zhōng [罗贯中] (p. 164) wrote 三国演义 *sānguóyǎnyì* 'The Romance of the Three Kingdoms' (p. 249); Shī Nài'ān [施耐庵] (p. 167) authored the 水浒传 *shuǐhǔzhuàn* 'Tale of the Water Margin' (p. 250) and Wú Chéng'ēn [吴承恩]

(p. 172) wrote 西遊记 *xīyóujì* 'Journey to the West' (p. 254).

One of the best-known medical doctors, Lǐ Shízhēn [李时珍] (p. 161), was from this period. He spent 27 years to compile 本草纲目 *běncǎo gāngmù* 'Compendium of Chinese Herbs', with about 2000 entries and 1,100 illustrated diagrams. Also included were 10,000 herbal recipes.

Painters during this period include Xú Wěi [徐渭], Chén Dàofù [陈道复] and Chén Hóngshòu [陈洪绶]; Four painters from Suzhou: Shěn Zhōu [沈周] (p. 167), Táng Yǐn [唐寅] (p. 170), Wēn Zhēngmíng [文徵明] (p. 172) and Chóu Yīng [仇英] (p. 154) were outstanding.

Xú Xiákè [徐霞客], an adventurer and geographer, made significant contribution to the study of the mountains and caves. His travels were detailed in his book 徐霞客游记 *Xú Xiákè yóujì* 'The Travels of Xú Xiákè'.

During the second half of the Míng Dynasty, European expansion began. Early in the 16th century Portuguese traders arrived and leased Macao as their trading post. Matteo Ricci, an Italian Jesuit, arrived in Macao. Because of his knowledge of science, mathematics, astronomy, his willingness to learn Chinese and adapt to Chinese life, he was accepted and became the first foreigner allowed to live in Peking permanently. Other Jesuits followed him and served emperors as mapmakers, calendar reformers, and astronomers. Sino-Western relationship was cultural, mutually respectful. One of the earliest to learn from the West was Xú Guāngqǐ [徐光启] (p. 173), who translated texts on mathematics, hydraulics and geography into Chinese, including Euclid's elements. He was also the author of 农政全书 *nōngzhèng quánshū* 'Agricultural Compendium', a 500,000 words guide to agriculture.

Towards the end of the dynasty a succession of weak emperors encouraged incompetence and corruption.

Qīng [清] Dynasty 1644-1911 AD

This was the last dynasty in China, ruled by the Manchu. Unlike the Mongols the Manchu adopted Chinese culture and were more acceptable to the Chinese. By appointing Chinese scholars in government and promoting Confucianism, the Manchu rulers established themselves as Confucian rulers in China. Historians divide the Qīng dynasty into two periods.

The earlier Qīng (1644-1840) referred to the time when the Chinese had rather prosperous feudal rule, under Kāng Xī [康熙] (p. 151), the longest serving emperor (61 years) in Chinese history. He was a Confucius scholar in his own right, credited with the completion the dictionary 康熙字典 *Kāngxī zìdiǎn* (p. 93). Other emperors included Yǒng Zhèng [雍正] (p. 152) and Qián Lóng [乾隆] (p. 151).

The later period (1840 to 1911) was critical, when western influence began to be quite dominant in China, forcing the Chinese to concede in several parts of China to the West, leading to the opium war. The Qīng dynasty witnessed 11 emperors, lasting 276 years.

The Empress Dowager Cí Xǐ [慈禧] (p. 154) wielded real power towards the end of Qìng dynasty when China was faced with infringement from the West. Pǔ Yí [溥仪] (p. 165) was the last emperor of the Qīng dynasty.

By 1800s, China was economically subjugated by the West, culminating in a series of humiliating territorial concessions.

In 1840 Lín Zéxú [林则徐] (p. 162) emerged as a hero when he challenged the British during the opium war. He confiscated and destroyed around 20,000 cases of opium from the British and American merchants in 1839. The Chinese demanded to end the drug trafficking was protested by the British, in the pretext of 'Violation of Free Trade'. To protect this lucrative 'Free Trade' British declared war and sent gunboats to Canton.

In 1842, this gun boat diplomacy ended with the treaty of Nanking, which forced open the enormous Chinese market, created new ports for trade, allowed Britain to demand a cash indemnity of $21 million, as well as the ceding of Hong Kong to Britain.

In 1984-85 the first Sino-Japanese War, fought in the year of jiǎwǔ [甲午战争] *jiǎwǔ zhànzhēng* resulted in quick, repeated defeat for China. An 'unequal' treaty was signed, resulting in massive war compensation (equivalent to seven times Japan's annual income). The massive financial windfall contributed to subsequent Japanese military prowess. The defeat of China at the hands of Japan increased calls for accelerated modernisation and reform. The reformers Kāng Yǒuwéi [康有为] (p. 159) and Liáng Qǐchāo [梁启超] (p. 162) made a submission requesting rejection of the Treaty. But the statement failed to reach the Emperor. They formed 学会 *xuéhuì* 'study societies' to organise political reforms to save the country.

Important personalities during this period include the author and revolutionary Lǔ Xùn [鲁迅] (p. 164), as well as educator and reformer Cài Yuánpéi [蔡元陪] (p. 153).

At a time of upheaval there were people who sought refuge in monasteries. Four monks emerged as painters during this period. They included Hóng Rén [弘仁], Kūn Cán [髡残], Zhū Dā [朱耷] and Shí Tāo [石涛]. Another prominent group came from Yangzhou, the 'eight eccentrics of Yangzhou' *Yāngzhōu báguài*. They had strong individualities and features. They were Li Shàn [李鱓], Wàng Shì

Shèn [汪士慎], Jīn Nóng [金農], Huáng Shèn [黄慎], Gāo Xiáng [高翔], Zhèng Xiè [郑燮], Lǐ Fāngyīng [李方膺] and Luó Pìn [罗聘]. In addition there were other painters of various styles.

An interesting painter was Giuseppe Castiglione, born in Italy but went to China in 1714 at the age of 26 and became an Imperial court painter. He served three emperors and was well liked by them. He introduced European techniques such as oil painting and copperplate etching. He also combined Chinese and Western styles in his paintings.

Republic of China [中华民国] *Zhōnghuámínguó* Established in 1911
People's Republic of China [中华人民共和国] *Zhōnghuá Rénmín gònghéguó* Established in 1949

Website dedicated to the history of China include:
The National Museum of China: *www.nmch.gov.cn/gb/index.asp*
Chinese History: *www.nmch.gov.cn/gb/index.asp*
Chinese cultural studies—Political history of China:
academic.brooklyn.cuny.edu/core9/phalsall/texts/chinhist.html

Notable Personalities in Chinese History

名人

Famous people are known as 名人 *míngrén*. The character 名 *míng* means name and the character 人 rén people, denoting people who make a name for himself.

'Circumstances create heroes' [时势造英雄] *shìshì zhào yīngxióng* is a common saying in Chinese. In Chinese history heroes would emerge to end tyrannical rule. Without an unpopular regime, there is simply no platform for such a hero.

Another facet of Chinese history would be the key personalities in history, some of them still have an impact on contemporary Chinese. The names of emperors deserve special attention. Most Chinese know the emperors by the calendar name of the years of which they were proclaimed, known as 年号 *niánhào* in Chinese. For example a well-known emperor was Qián Lóng [乾隆], popularly known as such. Few people know him as Qīng Gāozōng [清高宗], least of all as Aixīnjuéluó.hónglì [爱新觉罗.宏历], his name at birth.

We have selected more than two hundred personalities (arranged according to pīnyīn alphabetical order), some of whom have considerable impact on the Chinese psyche.

1. Aiyùlíbálìbādá [爱育黎拔力八达] (1285-1320): Ruled as Yuán Rénzōng [元仁宗]: Emperor of Yuán dynasty

2. Aixīnjuéluó.Fúlín [爱新觉罗.福临] (1638-1661): Ruled as Qīng Shìzhǔ [清世主], first emperor of Qīng dynasty. His years of rule were proclaimed as 顺治 *Shùn Zhì*.

3. Aixīnjuéluó.hónglì [爱新觉罗.宏历] (1710-1799): Ruled as Qīng Gāozōng [清高宗]. His years of rule were proclaimed as 乾隆 *Qián Lóng* (p. 148). Reigned over a period of peace and cultural development. Ruled for 60 years before abdicating in favour of his son.

4. Aixīnjuéluó.Mínníng [爱新觉罗.旻宁] (1782-1850): Ruled as Qīng Xuānzōng [清宣宗], 6th emperor of Qīng dynasty. His years of rule were proclaimed as 道光 *Dào Guāng*.

5. Aixīnjuéluó. Xuányè [爱新觉罗.玄烨] (1654-1722): Ruled as Qīng Shèngzǔ [清圣祖]. His years of rule were proclaimed as 康熙 *Kāng Xī*. Second emperor of Qīng dynasty. Confucius scholar, during his time the dictionary 康熙字典 *Kāngxī zìdiǎn* was compiled (refer to p. 93).

6. Aixīnjuéluó.Yìnzhēn [爱新觉罗.胤祯] (1678-1735): Ruled as Qīng Shìzōng [清世宗], third emperor of Qīng dynasty, ruled from 1722 to 1735. His years of rule were proclaimed as 雍正 *Yōng Zhèng*.

7. Aixīnjuéluó.Yìzhū [爱新觉罗.弈詝] (1831-1861): Ruled as Qīng Wénzōng [清文宗], 7th emperor of Qīng dynasty. His years of rule were proclaimed as 咸丰 *Xián Fēng*.

8. Aixīnjuéluó.Yóngyān [爱新觉罗.颙琰] (1760-1820): Ruled as Qīng Rénzōng [清仁宗], 5th emperor of Qīng dynasty. His years of rule were proclaimed 嘉庆 *Jiā Qíng*.

9. Aixīnjuéluó.Zàitián [爱新觉罗. 载湉] (1871-1908): Ruled as Qīng Dézōng [清德宗], 9th emperor of Qīng dynasty, Came to the throne at the age of 5, but the power lied in the hands of Empress Dowager. His years of rule were proclaimed as 光绪 *Guāng Xù*.

10. Aixīnjuéluó.Zàizhūn [爱新觉罗.载淳] (1856-1875): Ruled as Qīng Mùzōng [清穆宗], 8th emperor of Qīng dynasty. His years of rule were proclaimed as 同治 *Tóng Zhì*.

11. Bā Jīn [巴金] (1904-) A contemporary author and playwright. Amongst his works include 爱情的三部曲 *àiqíng de sānbùqǔ* 'Three Episodes of Love'; 雾, 雨, 电 'Fog, Rain, Lightning'; 激流三部曲 *jíliú sānbùqū* 'Three Episodes in Rapid Succession' and 家, 春, 秋 *jiā, chūn, qiū* 'Family, Spring, Autumn'.

12. Bái Jūyì [白居易] (772-846): Poet from the Táng dynasty. Amongst his most popular ones are 忆江南 *yìjiāngnán* 'Memories of South of the River' (p. 264); 长恨歌 *chánghèngé* 'Song of Everlasting Sorrow' and 鸟 *niǎo* 'Bird' (p. 257). His poems such as 新乐府 *xīnlèfǔ* and 琵琶行 *pípáxíng* reflect realities arising from corrupt officials.

13. Bān Gù [班固] (32-92 AD): Historian of the Eastern Hàn dynasty, credited for the book 白虎通德论 *báihǔ tōngdélún* 'Discussion about Virtue at White Tiger Hall' (58 AD), a theoretical discussion between Heaven and Men (p. 137).

14. Bāo Zhěng [包拯]: An incorruptible judge from the Sòng dynasty, known for his fearlessness, impartiality and willingness to stand up to pressure groups. He is better known as Bāo Gōng [包公] (p. 144).

15. Bì Shēng [毕升] (1041-1048): Invented printing by carving individual characters on squares of sticky clay, baked to make printing blocks in 1040s (p. 144).

16. Cài Yuánpéi [蔡元陪] (1868-1940): The President of Beijing University, founder and first president of the Academia Sinica, China's highest national research institute. Advocated educational and political reforms, when China was subjugated by Japan and the West (p. 149).

17. Cài Lún [蔡伦] (? -121): Invented paper, one of the four great Chinese inventions, during the Hàn period (p. 136).

18. Cài Wénjī [蔡文姬]: A celebrated Chinese woman. Captured by Hú [胡] troops, she spent years in captivity. She was then redeemed by Cáo Cāo. Poet, author of the famous 胡笳十八拍 *hú jiā shíbā pāi* (p. 263). The poem reflects her mixed sentiments when she had to leave her children behind in Hú territory, to return to the place she originated from and loved. Her sentiments were also reflected in the 悲愤诗 *bēi fèn shī* 'Poem of Sorrow and Resentment' (p. 262).

19. Cāng Jié [仓颉] (about 2,700 BC): The legendary statesman attributed with the 'invention' of Chinese characters. He sketched objects into simplified pictures, while capturing their essence of reality. These were then engraved onto bones and shells (refer to p. 127).

20. Cáo Cāo [曹操] (155-220): Emperor of Wei empire, one of the three kingdoms (p. 137). He was also a poet, credited with poem such as 短歌行 *duǎngēxíng* (p. 262). The Cáo Cāo [曹操] family was important in jian'an [建安] literature, reflecting war-time scenarios.

21. Cáo Pī [曹丕]: Second son and successor of Cáo Cāo [曹操]. He forced his brother, Cáo Zhí [曹植], to write the 七步诗 *qībùshī* 'A Poem in Seven Paces' (p. 260). He plays an important role in jian'an [建安] literature.

22. Cáo Xuěqín [曹雪芹] (1715-1763): Author of 红楼梦 *Hónglóu Mèng* 'A Dream of Red Mansions', one of the popular novels (refer to p. 248).

23. Cáo Zhí [曹植] (192-232): Son of Cáo Cāo, better known for his contributions in literature. Author of the famous 七步诗 *qībùshī* 'A Poem in Seven Paces' (p. 260). He plays an important role in jian'an [建安] literature.

24. Chén Shèng [陈胜]: Chén Shèng and Wú Guǎng [吴广] were the leaders in the first, large-scale popular peasant uprising in Chinese history in 209 BC (p. 134).

25. Chéng Guān [澄观] (737-838): The fourth patriarch of Huàyán Buddhism.

26. Chóu Yīng [仇英]: One of the four famous painters from Suzhou during the Míng dynasty. His specialty was figure (especially women) painting; however he was also good at landscapes as well as 'flowers and birds' (p. 147).

27. Cí Xǐ [慈禧] (1835-1908): Empress Dowager. Wields real power towards the end of Qìng dynasty, when China was faced with infringement from the West (p. 148).

28. Dà Yú [大禹] (2140 BC?): The legendary leader of Xià [夏] dynasty credited with solving massive floods problems (p. 128).

29. Dā Mó [达摩]: Bodhidharma, the legendary Indian Monk who went to China during the Southern Sòng dynasty. Acknowledged as the founder of chán [禅] Buddhism in China. Credited with setting up the Shàolin temple [少林寺] *Shào lín shi*. He is also known by the title of 圆觉大师 *yuánjué dàshī* (p. 145).

30. Dào Ān [道安] (312-385): Buddhist scholar during the Jin period. Made contributions to early Buddhist scriptures (p. 139).

31. Dào Shēng [道生] (355-434): An eminent Buddhist scholar during the Jin period (p. 139).

32. Dèng Xiǎopíng [邓小平] (1904-1997): Paramount ruler of China after the reign of Máo Zédōng [毛泽东] (p. 164). Credited with bringing China into the modern era.

33. Diāo Chán [貂蝉]: A legendary Chinese beauty, appeared in the *Romance of the Three Kingdoms* (refer to p. 249).

34. Dù Fǔ [杜甫] (712-770): Outstanding poet who lived towards the decline of the Táng dynasty. His poetry depicts human sufferings during the time of war, such as separation between couples and family break-ups (refer to pp. 262-263).

35. Dù Shùn [杜顺] (557-640): The first patriarchs of Huáyán [华严] Buddhism.

36. Dēng Xī [登析] (500 BC): A minister of the state of Zhèng, introduced a penal code system.

37. Fǎ Zàng [法藏] (643-712): A Táng dynasty scholar-monk, who made great contribution to the development and consolidation of the Huàyán [华严] sect, considered to be the third patriarch of Huàyán Buddhism (p. 142).

38. Fàn Zhēn [范缜] (About 450-515): Atheist, who disputes the concept of 'infinite soul'. Author of 神灭论 *Shénmièlùn*

39. Fàn Zhòngyān [范仲淹] (989-1052): Politician and scholar of Northern Sòng dynasty (p. 144). He tried to carry out reform, but could not proceed without the Emperor's backing. Author of 范义正公集 *Fànwénzhèng gōng jí*. In 岳阳楼记 *Yuèyáng-lóují*, his famous saying 'To worry and be concerned before the event occurs; so as to be happy and enjoy after the event has occurred.' 先天下之忧而忧, 后天下之乐而乐 is still often quoted today.

40. Fú Xī [伏羲] (Around 2953-2838 BC): Legendary emperor of China. Credited with the invention of the lunar calendar. After observing the sky, the earth and natural phenomena, the cause

and effect relationship, he invented the trigrams and hexagrams used in 'I-ching' [易经] *yìjīng* (refer to p. 398).

 *The yīn-yáng diagram depicts complementary nature and mutual acceptability of yīn and yáng.*

41. Gé Hóng [葛洪]: A 4th century Dàoist practitioner, author of 抱朴子 *bàopūzǐ* 'The Master Embracing Simplicity'. It delved into the topics such as transcendence, immortality, alchemy health cultivation [养生] *yǎngshēng*, circulation of bio-energy [行气] *xíngqì*, sexual practices [房中术] *fángzhōngshù*, herbs taking [服药] *fúyào* and talismanic charms [神符] *shénfú*.

42. Genghis Khan [成吉思汗]: Ruled as Yuán Tàizǔ [元太祖] (1162-1227). Elected Genghis Khan or 'Universal Ruler' in 1206. One of the most impressive military campaigners. Led his army south into China and west into Central Asia and even Europe. When he died, the Mongol armies were poised to conquer Hungary (refer to p. 145).

43. Gù Dònggāo [顾栋高] (1679-1759): Historian from the Qīng dynasty, author of 春秋大事表 *Chūnqiū dàshìbiǎo*.

44. Guān Yǔ [关羽]: Also known as Guān Gōng [关公], deified as Guān Dì [关帝]. The outstanding general who fought with Liu Bei during the Three Kingdoms period (refer to p. 137).

45. Guǎn Zhòng [管仲] (d. 645 BC): A minister of the state of Qí, he introduced a system of rewards and punishments to make the officials a well functioning instrument of the ruler.

46. Guǐ Gǔzi [鬼谷子]: Lived in the 'Spring and Autumn' Period (p. 129). An early legendary expert on I-Ching and divination.

47. Guō Shǒujìng [郭守敬] (1231-1316): Mathematician and astronomer who helped develop the astronomical observatory in Beijing in 1280. Calculated the length of the year to within the accuracy of 26 seconds; developed an extremely reliable calendar (refer to p. 145).

48. Hán Fēizǐ [韩非子] (280-233 BC): Thinker and political philosopher during the end of Warring States (p. 131). He proposed a combination of legal techniques and morality, rather than just the ruler's moral authority (p. 132).

49. Hán Xìn [韩信] (?-196 BC): Military strategist during the Hàn-Qín period (refer to p. 134). Author of the book *Military Techniques* [兵法] *bīngfǎ*.

50. Hán Yù [韩愈] (768-827): Well-known philosopher, Confucianist and poet from the Táng dynasty. One of the eight literary greats from Táng-Sòng dynasties. Proposed revival of 'proper, ancient language' [古文运动] *gǔwén yùndòng*, together with Liǔ Zōngyuán [柳宗元] (p. 164).

> Hàn Aidì [汉哀帝]: Refer to Liú Xīn [刘欣]
> Hàn Gāozǔ [汉高祖]: Refer to Liú Bāng [刘邦]
> Hàn Guāngwǔdì [汉光武帝]: Refer to Liú Xiù [刘秀]
> Hàn Hédì [汉和帝]: Refer to Liú Zhào [刘肇]
> Hàn Jǐngdì [汉景帝]: Refer to Liú Qǐ [刘启]
> Hàn Míngdì [汉明帝]: Refer to Liú Zhuāng [刘庄]
> Hàn Píngdi [汉平帝]: Refer to Liú Kàn [刘衎]
> Hàn Wéndì [汉文帝]: Refer to LiúHéng [刘恒]
> Hàn Wǔdì [汉武帝]: Refer to Liú Chè [刘彻]
> Hàn Xiàndì [汉献帝]: Refer to Liú Xié [刘协]
> Hàn Xuāndì [汉宣帝]: Refer to Liú Xún [刘询]
> Hàn Yuándì [汉元帝]: Refer to Liú Shuǎng [刘奭]
> Hàn Zhāngdì [汉章帝]: Refer to Liú Dá [刘炟]
> Hàn Zhāodì [汉昭帝]: Refer to Liú Fúlíng [刘弗陵]

51. Hóng Yìngmíng [洪应明]: Scholar from the 17th century, author of the book on self cultivation 菜根谭 *Càigéntán* (p. 246).

52. Hóng Xiùquán [洪秀全] (1812-1864): Leader of Taiping Rebellion, established the 'Heavenly Kingdom of Taiping' [太

平天国] *tàipíng tiānguó*. The 'kingdom' only lasted as long as the rebellion did.

Hū Bìliè [忽必列]: Refer to Kublai Khan (p. 160).

53. Huā Mùlán [花木兰]: A legendary heroine famous for disguising herself as a man to replace her aging father for conscription.

54. Huà Túo [华陀] (?-208): The legendary doctor from the Three Kingdoms period (p. 138). An authority in the use of herbs, acupuncture, surgery as well as qi-gong exercise.

55. Huáng Dàopó [黄道婆]: a legendary woman who contributed to innovate as well as popularising the weaving and spinning techniques in the 13th century.

56. Huángdì [黄帝] (2698-2598 BC): The legendary emperor of China. Famous for a range of innovations in agriculture, medicine, etc (refer to p. 127). 黄帝内经 *Huángdìnèijīng* 'The Huángdì's book of Internal Medicine', used by traditional Chinese medical practitioners today, was compiled. Ethnic Chinese worldwide consider themselves as 'Descendants of Yán-Huáng' emperors [炎黄子孙] *yánhuáng zǐsūn*.

57. Huáng Gōngwàng [黄公望] (1269-1354): One of the four outstanding Yuán dynasty painters, specialising on painting nature in ink brush, in a category that known as 'mountain and water paintings' [山水画] *shānshuǐhuà* (p. 146).

58. Huì Yuǎn [慧远] (334-416): An eminent disciple of Dào Ān [道安] (p. 154). He preached in Lúshán [庐山] for more than thirty years. Founder of Pureland Buddhism in China (p. 139).

59. Huāng Zōngxī [黄宗羲]: An authoritative analyst on yìjīng, with emphasis on the numerical and symbolic aspects, author of 易学象数論 *Yìxué xiǎngshùlùn*.

60. Huì Dòng [惠栋] (1697-1758): Yìjīng and Confucianism expert from the Qīng dynasty. His various works on Yìjīng include 周

易述*Zhōuyìshù*,易汉学*Yìhànxué*,专宗汉易*Zhuānzōnghànyì* and 古文尚书考 *Gǔwén shàngshūkǎo* (refer to p. 399).

61. Jiā Cái [迦才] (562-645): Author of Buddhist text 'Pure Land Treatise' [净土论] *jìngtǔlùn*.

62. Jiān Zhēn [鉴真] (688-763): The monk from Táng dynasty who spread Buddhism to Japan. In 753, at the age of 66 he succeeded, at his sixth attempt to reach Japan (p. 142).

63. Jiǎng Jièshí [蒋介石] (1887-1975): Chiang Kai Shek. Trusted ally of Sun Yat Sen, Fought together with the Communists against the Japanese during Second World War, but embroiled in a bitter struggle with the Communist after the war. Retreated to Taiwan in 1949.

64. Jiūmóluóshén [鸠摩罗什] (343-413): Born as Kumarajiva in Xinjiang, bordering China and India. He was one of the most important translators of Buddhist scripture into Chinese, including 大品般若經 *Dàpǐnbānruòjīng*, 維摩詰經 *Wéimójiéjīng*, 妙法蓮華經 *Miàofǎliánhuájīng*, 金剛經 *Jīngāngjīng* and 大智度论 *Dàzhìdùlùn* (p. 139).

Jìn Wǔdì [晋武帝]: Refer to Sīmǎ Yán [司马炎].

65. Kāng Yǒuwéi [康有为] (1858-1927): A prominent Confucian scholar-official and reformer during the time when China was threatened by military might of the West. Developed an idealistic vision of modernising China within its Confucianist structure (p. 149).

66. Kǒngzǐ [孔子] (551-479 BC): Confucius. Probably the person in Chinese history best known in the world. He was born as Kong Qiu in the Kingdom of Lǔ [鲁] during the Spring and Autumn period (p. 129). He travelled to various states, but his philosophy was not accepted during a period of war. In his late years he contributed to Chinese culture, editing classics such as 诗经 *Shījīng*, 尚书 *Shàngshū* and 春秋 *Chūnqiū*. He also made

significant contribution to the study of yìjīng (I-Ching refer to Chapter ten). Confucianism is respected and practised to various degrees not only in China but also in countries such as Japan and Korea (refer to pp. 130, 275).

67. Kublai Khan [忽必列] (1215-1294): First emperor of Yuán dynasty. The grandson of Genghis Khan (p. 156). The founder of Yuán dynasty in 1279, the first dynasty ruled by a foreign power. In power for 35 years.

68. Lǎo Shè [老舍] (1899-966): Modern Chinese novelist and playwright.

69. Lǎo Zǐ [老子]: Philosopher, Founder of Dàoism, from the kingdom of Chǔ [楚] during Spring and Autumn period (refer to pp. 130, 267).

70. Lí Yuánhóng [黎元洪] (1864-1928): President of the Republic of China in 1916.

71. Lǐ Ǎng [李昂] (809-840): Ruled as Táng Wénzōng [唐文宗], 14th emperor of Táng dynasty.

72. Lǐ Bái [李白] (701-762): One of the most famous poets from the Táng dynasty. The collection of some 900 poems is still much appreciated today. His famous poems include 静夜思 *Jìngyèshī* (p. 259), 下江陵 *Xiàjiānglíng* (p. 264) and 早发白帝城 *Zǎo fā bái dì chéng* (p. 264). Lǐ Bái and Dù Fǔ [杜甫] (p. 155) are known as two of the best poets in China.

73. Lǐ Chún [李纯] (778-820): Ruled as Táng Xiànzōng [唐宪宗], 11th emperor of Táng dynasty

74. Lǐ Chúnfēng [李淳风]: Co-authored with Yuán Tiāngāng [袁天罡] (p. 175) the earliest book on prediction 推背图 *tuī bèi tú* 'Diagrams of Rubbing the Back' (refer to p. 252).

75. Lǐ Dàn [李旦] (662-716): Ruled as Táng Ruìzōng [唐睿宗], 5th emperor of Táng dynasty.

76. Lǐ Dǐngzhà [李鼎诈]: An authority on I-Ching, (refer to Chapter 10) from the Suí-Táng period, author of the book 周易集解 *Zhōuyìjíjiě* (refer to p. 399).

77. Lǐ Hēng [李亨] (711-762): Ruled as Táng Sùzòng [唐肃宗], 7th emperor of Táng dynasty.

78. Lǐ Lóngjī [李隆基] (685-762): Ruled as Táng Xuánzōng [唐玄宗], 6th emperor of Táng dynasty.

79. Lǐ Qīngzhào [李清照] (1083-1149): Female poet of Sòng dynasty, famous for her nostalgic poetry. Her works include 声声慢 *Shēng shēng màn* (p. 264).

80. Lǐ Shì [李适] (742-805): Ruled as Táng Dézōng [唐德宗], ninth emperor of Táng dynasty.

81. Lǐ Shízhēn [李时珍] (1518-1593): A well known medical doctors from the Míng dynasty. He spent 27 years to compile 本草纲目 *běncǎo gāngmù* 'Compendium of Chinese Herbs', with about 2000 entries and 1,100 illustrated diagrams. Also included were about 10,000 herbal recipes (p. 147).

82. Lǐ Shìmín [李世民] (599-649): Ruled as Táng Tàizōng [唐太宗], the most outstanding, second emperor of the Táng dynasty. Gave power to educated civil servants rather than aristocrats or military officers. Reigned over a period of peace and prosperity, extended the Silk Road to Central Asia. His rule was recorded in the book 贞观政要 'Zhēnguān Governance' (refer to p. 255), Zhēnguān [贞观] is the name proclaimed to his years of rule (refer to p. 141).

83. Lǐ Sī [李斯] (? 208 BC): Prime minister during Qín Shǐ Huáng's reign [秦始皇]. Amongst other things, responsible for standard-isation of written characters in China (p. 132).

84. Lǐ Sòng [李诵] (761-806): Ruled as Táng Shùnzōng [唐顺宗], 10th emperor of Táng dynasty.

85. Lǐ Tōngxuān [李通玄] (635–730 BC): An eminent Buddhist scholar in the Táng dynasty, contributed to the development and popularisation of Huáyán [华严] Buddhist sect.

86. Lǐ Xiǎn [李显] (656-710): Ruled as Táng Zhōngzōng [唐中宗], 4th emperor of Táng dynasty.

87. Lǐ Yǎn [李儼] (862-888): Ruled as Táng Xīzōng [唐僖宗], 18th emperor of Táng dynasty.

88. Lǐ Yuān [李渊] (566-635): Ruled as Táng Gāozǔ [唐高祖], first emperor of Táng dynasty. Overthrew the unpopular Suí dynasty (p. 141). Redistributed land among the people. Ruled from 618-626 in an environment of peace and unity (p. 141).

89. Lǐ Yuánhào [李元昊] (1003-1048): First emperor of Western Xià [西夏] dynasty.

90. Lǐ Zhì [李治] (628-683): Ruled as Táng Gāozōng [唐高宗], 3rd emperor of Táng dynasty.

91. Lǐ Zìchéng [李自成] (1606-1645): A Chinese hero who organised a popular uprising, eventually ended up in failure due to poor management and other factors.

92. Liáng Qǐchāo [梁启超] (1873-1929): Educationist, political activist and author (refer to p. 149).

   Liáng Wǔdì [梁武帝]: Refer to [萧衍] Xiāo Yán.

93. Lièzǐ [列子]: Famous scholar and thinker of the early 'Warring States' period (p. 131).

94. Lín Yǔtáng [林语堂] (1895-1976): Modern scholar, linguist and author who studied in the United States and Germany. Written numerous books in Chinese and English. Translated numerous works into English.

95. Lín Zéxú [林则徐] (1785-1850): Qīng official who challenged the British during the opium war. Confiscated and destroyed about 20,000 cases of opium from the British and American merchants in 1839 (refer to pp. 148, 183).

96. Liú Bāng [刘邦] (256-195 BC): Ruled as Hàn Gāozǔ [汉高祖], founder emperor of Western Hàn dynasty (p. 134).

97. Liú Bèi [刘备] (161-223): The Founder of Shǔ [蜀] Kingdom during Three Kingdoms period. Benefited from military strategist Zhūgé Liàng [褚葛亮] (refer to p. 137).

98. Liú Bówēn [刘伯温]: Prime minister during the beginning of Míng dynasty. He was famous for 烧饼歌 *shāobǐnggē* which predicted events into the future, very much like Nostradamus. He was the author of an authoritative book on 'life destiny analysis' 滴天髓 *dītiānsuǐ* (See pp. 146, 252).

99. Liú Chè [刘彻] (156-87 BC): Ruled as Hàn Wǔdì [汉武帝], 5th emperor of Western Hàn (refer to p. 134).

100. Liú Dá [刘炟] (58-88): Ruled as Hàn Zhángdì [汉章帝], 3rd emperor of Eastern Hàn.

101. Liú Fúlíng [刘弗陵] (94-74 BC): Ruled as Hàn Zhāodì [汉昭帝], 6th emperor of Western Hàn.

102. Liú Héng [刘恒] (202-157 BC): Ruled as Hàn Wéndì [汉文帝], 3rd emperor of Western Hàn.

103. Liú Kàn [刘衎] (9 BC to 5 AD): Ruled as Hàn Píngdi [汉平帝], 11th emperor of Western Hàn dynasty.

104. Liú Qǐ [刘启] (188-141 BC): Ruled as Hàn Jǐngdì [汉景帝], 4th emperor of Western Hàn.

105. Liú Shuǎng [刘爽] (76-33 BC): Ruled as Hàn Yuándì [汉元帝], 8th emperor of Western Hàn.

106. Liú Xié [刘协] (181-234): Ruled as Hàn Xiandì [汉献帝], last emperor of Eastern Hàn.

107. Liú Xié [刘勰]: From the Nánběicháo period (p. 139). Literary critic, author of 文心雕龙 *Wén xīn diǎo lóng*.

108. Liú Xīn [刘欣] (25-1 BC) ruled as Hàn Aidì [汉哀帝], 10th emperor of Western Hàn.

109. Liú Xiù [刘秀] (6 BC to 57 AD): Ruled as Hàn Guāngwǔdì [汉光武帝], founder of Eastern Hàn dynasty (p. 135).

110. Liú Xún [刘询] (91-49 BC): Ruled as Hàn Xuāndì [汉宣帝], 7th emperor of Western Hàn.

111. Liú Zhào [刘肇] (79-105): Ruled as Hàn Hédì [汉和帝], 4th emperor of Eastern Hàn dynasty.

112. Liú Zhuāng [刘庄] (27-75): Ruled as Hàn Míngdì [汉明帝], 2nd emperor of Eastern Hàn (p. 135). He dreamt of a person with a

bright halo rising to the sky, moving towards the West. He then despatched officials to seek Buddhism from the 'West'.

113. Liǔ Gōngquán [柳公权] (778-865): Chinese calligrapher. His works include 金刚经 and 神策军碑 (p. 142).

114. Liǔ Zōngyuán [柳宗元] (773~819) One of the eight literary greats from Táng-Sòng dynasties. His writings involved a wide range of topics. His works have been compiled into a thirty-volume collection, named 柳子厚集 *Liǔzǐ hòují*. Active in 'revival of ancient language' 古文运动 *gǔwén yùndòng*, together with Hán Yù [韩愈] (pp. 143, 157).

115. Lǔ Bān 鲁班 (507-444 BC). Lived during the 'Warring States Period' (p. 131). He is widely acknowledged as the 'father of craftsmanship, carpentry and building' in China. He designed mobile assault ladders to scale towers (p. 132).

116. Lǔ Xùn [鲁迅] (1881-1936): Modern Chinese thinker, revolutionary, political activist, reformist and most outspoken essayist. Wrote satirical novels such as 阿Q正传 'The true story of Ah Q' (p. 246), attacking the legacy of Confucian practice. Famous for 自嘲 *zì cháo* 'Mocking at Myself' (p. 264).

117. Lǔ Bùwéi [吕不韦] (?-235 BC): Statesman during the end of 'Warring States' (p. 131), credited with the book 吕氏春秋 *Lǔshì chūnqiū*.

118. Luó Guànzhōng [罗贯中]: Novelist who wrote 三国演义 *sānguóyǎnyì* 'The Romance of the Three Kingdoms' (p. 138).

119. Máo Zédōng [毛泽东] (1893-1976): Chairman Máo, founder of People's Republic of China in 1949. Revolutionary and military leader. In later life his 'Great Leap Forward' and 'Cultural Revolution' plunged China into chaos.

120. Mèng Hàorán [孟浩然] (689-740): A famous Táng dynasty poet. Famous for 春眠 *chūnmián* 'Asleep in Spring' (p. 262).

121. Mèngzǐ [孟子] (372-289 BC): Philosopher, author, political commentator during Warring States period (p. 131). Mèngzǐ is considered the second greatest Confucian philosopher, he and

Confucius are often regarded as the pillars of Confucianism. Wrote 孟子 'The Book of Mèngzǐ'. Believed that human nature is inherently good, though it could be perfected through self-cultivation (refer to p. 286).

Míng Chéngzū [明成祖]: Refer to Zhū Dì [朱棣]
Míng Shénzōng [明神宗]: Refer to Zhū Yìjūn [朱翊钧]
Míng Shìzōng [明世宗]: Refer to Zhū Hòuzòng [朱厚熜]
Míng Sīzōng [明思宗]: Refer to Zhū Yóujiǎn [朱由检]
Míng Tàizǔ [明太祖]: Refer to Zhū Yuánzhāng [朱元璋]
Míng Wǔzōng [明武宗]: Refer to Zhū Hòuzhào [朱厚照]
Míng Xiànzōng [明宪宗]: Refer to Zhū Jiànshēn [朱见深]
Míng Xīzōng [明熹宗]: Refer to Zhū Yóuxiào [朱由校]

122. Mòzǐ [墨子] (470-391 BC): Ancient philosopher. Initially a disciple of Confucius (p. 159). A moralist, he denounced warfare and extravagance. He favoured simplicity and frugality, advocated a system of rewards and punishment. He developed his school of thought, based on his book Mòzǐ (p. 132).

123. Ní Zàn [倪瓒] (1301-1374): One of the four outstanding Yuán dynasty painters, specialising on nature, known as 'mountain and water paintings' [山水画] shānshuǐhuà (p. 146).

124. Nurhachi [奴尔哈赤] (1559-1626): Manchurian, Founder of Qīng dynasty.

125. Ōuyáng Xiū [欧阳修] (1007-1072): Leading literary figure and historian from the Northern Sòng dynasty. One of the eight literary greats from Táng-Sòng dynasties. Wrote poems, lyrics, prose. Some of his works include 醉翁亭记 Zuìwēng tīngjì, 朋党论 Péngdǎnglùn, 五代史伶官传序 Wǔdàishǐ língguān zhuànxù (refer to p. 144).

126. Pǔ Yí [溥仪] (1906-1967): Last emperor of Qīng dynasty. In 1911 he ended 267 years of Qīng dynasty and more than 2,000 years of rule by emperors (refer to p. 148).

127. Qín Shǐ Huáng [秦始皇] (259-210 BC): Known in the West as Shi Huang Ti. First emperor to unify China. Credited with standardisation of Chinese characters, building of 'Great Wall of China'; also responsible for destruction of books and scholars (refer to p. 132).

> Qīng Dézōng [清德宗]: Refer to Aixīnjuéluó.Zàitián [爱新觉罗.载湉].
>
> Qīng Gāozōng [清高宗]: Refer to Aixīnjuéluó.hónglì [爱新觉罗.宏历].
>
> Qīng Mùzōng [清穆宗]: Refer to Aixīnjuéluó. Zàizhūn [爱新觉罗.载淳]
>
> Qīng Rénzōng [清仁宗]: Refer to Aixīnjuéluó.Yóngyān [爱新觉罗颙琰]
>
> Qīng Shèngzū [清圣祖]: Refer to Aixīnjuéluó. Xuányè [爱新觉罗.玄烨]
>
> Qīng Shìzhǔ [清世主]: Refer to Aixīnjuéluó. Fúlín [爱新觉罗.福临]
>
> Qīng Shìzōng [清世宗]: Refer to Aixīnjuéluó.Yìnzhēn [爱新觉罗.胤禛]
>
> Qīng Wénzōng [清文宗]: Refer to Aixīnjuéluó.Yìzhǔ [爱新觉罗.弈詝]
>
> Qīng Xuǎnzōng [清宣宗]: Refer to Aixīnjuéluó. Mínníng [爱新觉罗.旻宁]

128. Qū Yuán [屈原] (340-277 BC): The earliest famous poet, from the kingdom of Chǔ [楚]. Wrote numerous poems based on nationalism, nature, religion, etc. The righteous patriot committed suicide when his good advice was not heeded by the emperor. He left behind numerous poems, the most famous of which is 'The lament' [离骚] lísāo (p. 263), where he expressed anger at traitors of the country. The festival of 5th May on Chinese calendar is dedicated to the memory of this poet.

Glutinous rice dumplings called zòng [粽] are thrown into the river, with the hope that fish would eat the dumpling rather than his body.

129. Rèn Rénfǎ [任仁发] (1254-1310): The painter and hydrographer in the Yuán Dynasty (p. 146). He was good at calligraphy, flower-and-bird as well as human figure paintings. He was famous for his painting of horses, especially the satirical 二马图 èr mǎ tú 'Two Horses Painting' (refer to p. 146).

130. Shào Kángjié [邵康节] (1011-1077): The Sòng dynasty I-Ching [易经] yìjīng expert who developed the art of intuitive divination called 'plum flower divination' [梅花易数] méihuāyìshù. Author of the 'futuristic' book 皇极经世书 Huáng jíjīng shìshū (refer to p. 339).

Shén Nóng [神农]: Refer to Yándì [炎帝]

131. Shěn Kuò [沈括] (1031-1095): Scientist, geologist, cartographer, compiled the first comprehensive map of China [天下郡国图]. He was a noted scientist, who left behind a great store of notes and research findings in the fields of geography, geology, astronomy and mathematics. His work 梦溪笔谈 'Dream Stream Essays' contains early discussions of the compass and printing technology. This book is of great value for the study of the history of science. He also identified petroleum, and predicted that it would have a myriad of applications (p. 144).

132. Shěn Zhōu [沈周] (1427-1509): One of the four famous painters from Suzhou during the Míng dynasty. He was an accomplished poet, calligrapher and painter. Most of his work depicted the life of scholars (refer to p. 147).

133. Shī Nài'ān [施耐庵]: author of the novel 水浒传 shuǐhǔzhuàn 'Tale of the Water Margin' (refer to p. 250).

134. Sīmǎ Guāng [司马光] (1019-1086): Historian and politician from Northern Sòng dynasty, spent 19 years to compile a com-

prehensive historical record 资治通鉴 *zīzhì tōngjiàn*, over a period of some 1362 years from 403 BC to 959 AD. This was written to help the Emperor running the country (p. 126).

135. Sīmǎ Qiān [司马迁] (206-220 BC): Served as an Imperial historian during Hàn dynasty. Author of 史记 *Shǐjì* 'Historical Records' while in prison. This was a major historical document on early China, with accounts of earlier periods from legendary times to Xià [夏], Shāng [商], Zhōu [周] dynasties, through the 'Spring and Autumn' (p. 130), 'Warring States' (p. 131), to Qín dynasty and early Hàn (refer to p. 126).

136. Sīmǎ Yán [司马炎]: Ruled as Jìn Wǔdì [晋武帝]. Founder of Western Jìn [西晋] dynasty. However decadence during his rule lead to mass discontent (refer to p. 139).

Sòng Gāozōng [宋高宗]: Refer to Zhào Gòu [赵构]
Sòng Guāngzōng [宋光宗]: Refer to Zhào Dūn [赵惇]
Sòng Huīzōng [宋徽宗]: Refer to Zhào Jí [赵佶]
Sòng Lǐzōng [宋理宗]: Refer to Zhào Yún [赵昀]

137. Sòng Měi Líng [宋美龄] (1901-2003): Wife of Chiang Kai Shek. Addressed the U.S. congress in 1943 to seek support against Japanese invasion (Refer to Chiang Kai Shek) (p. 159).

Sòng Níngzōng [宋宁宗]: Refer to Zhào Kuò [赵扩]
Sòng Qīnzōng [宋钦宗]: Refer to Zhào Huán [赵桓]

138. Sòng Qìng Líng [宋庆龄] (1893-1981): Sister of Sòng Měi Líng. Wife of Sun Yat Sen, the founder of Republic of China.

Sòng Rénzōng [宋仁宗]: Refer to Zhào Zhēn [赵祯]
Sòng Shénzōng [宋神宗]: Refer to Zhào Xū [赵顼]
Sòng Tàizōng [宋太宗]: Refer to Zhào Líng [赵灵]
Sòng Tàizǔ [宋太祖]: Refer to Zhào Kuāngyìn [赵匡胤]

Sòng Xiàozōng [宋孝宗]: Refer to Zhào Shèn [赵慎]

139. Sòng Yīngxīng [宋应星]: Compiled 天工开物 tiāngōng kāiwù 'Exploitation of the Works of Nature'. It contained the cream of traditional Chinese science and technology.

140. Sōngzàn Gānbù [松赞干布] (617-650): The Tibetan ruler who married the Chinese princess Wénchéng gōngzhǔ [文成公主].

Sòng Zhézōng [宋哲宗]: Refer to Zhào Xī [赵熙]

Sòng Zhēnzōng [宋真宗]: Refer to Zhào Héng [赵恒]

Sū Dōngpō [苏东坡]: Refer to Sū Shì [苏轼]

141. Sū Shì [苏轼] (1037-1101): Better known as Sū Dōngpō [苏东坡]. One of the eight literary greats from Táng-Sòng dynasties. Famous literary figure, painter, calligrapher and poet. His father Sū Xùn [苏洵] and brother Sū Zhé [苏辙] were also famous in the literary world, known together as the 'Three Su'. His works include 念奴娇 niàn nú jiāo (p. 263) and 水调歌头 shuǐdiàogētóu (p. 260).

142. Sū Xùn [苏洵] (1009-1066): One of the eight literary greats from Táng-Sòng dynasties. Some of his works include 六国论 liùguólùn and 心術 xīnshù (p. 144).

143. Sū Zhé [苏辙] One of the eight literary greats from Táng-Sòng dynasties. His works include 栾城集 luánchéngjí

Suí Wéndì [隋文帝]: Refer to Yáng Jiān [杨坚]

Suí Yángdì [隋炀帝]: Refer to Yáng Guǎng [杨广].

144. Sūn Quán [孙权] (182-252): Founder of Wu dynasty during the three kingdom period. Also known as Wú Dàdì [吴大帝]. Appointed Zhōu Yú [周瑜] (p. 178) to defeat Cáo Cāo [曹操] in the famous Battle of Chìbì [赤壁] (refer to p. 138).

145. Sūn Wǔ [孙武]: Military strategist in 'Spring and Autumn' period. Wrote 孙子兵法 *Sūnzǐ bīngfǎ* 'The Art of War' (p. 239).

146. Sūn Zhōngshān [孙中山] (1866-1925): Also known as Sun Yat Sen [孙逸仙]. Father of China in both Communist China and Taiwan. Overthrew Qīng dynasty in 1911. His three principles of nationalism, populism and socialism is still practised in Taiwan today.

    Táng Dézōng [唐德宗]: Refer to Lǐ Shì [李适]
    Táng Gāozōng [唐高宗]: Refer to [李治] Lǐ Zhì
    Táng Gāozǔ [唐高祖]: Refer to [李渊] Lǐ Yuán
    Táng Ruìzōng [唐睿宗]: Refer to [李旦] Lǐ Dàn
    Táng Shùnzōng [唐顺宗]: Refer to [李诵] Lǐ Sòng
    Táng Sùzōng [唐肃宗]: Refer to [李亨] Lǐ Hēng
    Tāng Tàizōng [唐太宗]: Refer to [李世民] Lǐ Shìmín
    Táng Wénzōng [唐文宗]: Refer to [李昂] Lǐ Ǎng
    Táng Xīzōng [唐僖宗]: Refer to [李俨] Lǐ Yǎn
    Táng Xiànzōng [唐宪宗]: Refer to [李纯] Lǐ Chún
    Táng Xuānzōng [唐玄宗]: Refer to Lǐ Lóngjī [李隆基]
    Táng Zhōngzōng [唐中宗]: Refer to Lǐ Xiǎn [李显]

147. Táng Yǐn [唐寅] (1470-1523): One of the four painters from Suzhou during the Míng dynasty. He painted a variety of paintings, landscape, figures and flower-birds (p. 147).

148. Táo Yuānmíng [陶渊明] (365-427): He composed poems based on the rural life and farms. He is considered to be a 'pastoral' poet. He also wrote an interesting article entitled 桃花源记 *táohuāyuānjì*, describing a fisherman who came across a paradise land, where people lived in peaceful environment free of worries. Though this is a fictional dreamland, the article is popular (refer to p. 139).

149. Tiě Mù'er [铁木耳] (1265-1307): Temur Khan, ruled as Yuán Chéngzōng [元成宗], emperor of Yuán dynasty for 14 years.

150. Wáng Ānshí [王安石] (1021-1086): A prominent adviser to emperor Sòng Shénzōng. A pragmatic reformer based on Confucius doctrines. He was also one of the eight literary greats from Táng-Sòng dynasties. His works cover writings in politics, poetry, short articles, etc. They include 临川集 *línchuānjí* and 周官新义 *zhōuguānxīnyì* (refer to p. 144).

151. Wáng Bì [王弼] (226-249): Philosopher in the Wei kingdom during Three Kingdoms period.

152. Wáng Mēng [王蒙] (1308-1385): One of the four outstanding Yuán dynasty painters, specialising on nature, known as 'mountain and water paintings' [山水画] *shānshuǐhuà* (p. 146).

153. Wáng Jiàn [王建] Táng dynasty poet, famous for his poem 新嫁娘 *xīnjiàniáng* (refer to p. 264).

154. Wáng Wei [王维] (701-761): A poet, painter, calligrapher and musician during the Táng period. He was the pioneer of 'scholar-painter', incorporated painting, poetry, calligraphy, philosophy and a touch of music in his masterpieces (refer to p. 143).

155. Wáng Xīzhī [王羲之] (303-361): Chinese calligrapher. His works include 乐毅论 *Lèyìlùn*, 黄庭经 *Huáng tíng jīng*, written in (kǎi) style. His influence on 行书 *xíngshū* and 草书 *cǎoshū* styles is significant (refer to p. 139).

156. Wáng Xiànzhī [王献之] (344-386): Chinese calligrapher. Works on a wide range of styles. His work includes 洛神赋十三行 *luòshénfù shísān xīng* written in kǎi style, 鸭头九帖 *yātóu jiǔ tiè* in xíng style and 中秋帖 *zhōngqiūtiè* in cǎo style. He was the seventh son of Wáng Xīzhī [王羲之].

157. Wáng Zhāojūn [王昭君]: One of the four beauties in Chinese history. Volunteered to marry into Xiongnu kingdom, considered as less civilised. Her life became the story 昭君出塞 'Zhāojūn leaves for the frontier' (refer to p. 134).

158. Wáng Zhèngjūn [王政君] (70 BC-13 AD) Empress of Western Hàn.

159. Wáng Zhīhuàn [王之涣] (688-742) A famous poet from the Táng dynasty. Noted for his poem 登鹳雀楼 *dēngguànquèlóu* (refer to p. 262).

160. Wèi Bóyáng [魏伯阳]: Dàoist, yìjīing expert from Eastern Hàn period, author of famous book on yìjīing, 周易参同契 *zhōuyì cāntóngqì*.

161. Wénchéng gōngzhǔ [文成公主]: The Chinese princess who was arranged to marry the Tibetan ruler Sōngzàn Gānbù [松赞干布] (p. 169).

162. Wén Tiānxiáng [文天祥] (1236--1283), Nationalist and poet, wrote the famous 正气歌 *Zhèngqìgē*.

163. Wēn Zhēngmíng [文徵明] (1470-1559): One of the four famous painters from Suzhou during the Míng dynasty. One of his best known paintings depicted two beautiful women, entitled 'Two Hunan Ladies' (refer to p. 147).

164. Wú Chéng'ēn [吴承恩] (1506-1582): Author of the highly popular 西遊记 *xīyóujì* 'Journey to the West' (p. 254), a fiction, highly imaginative story of the adventures of the monk Táng Sánzàng [唐三藏], and his three disciples, the monkey-god Sūn Wùkōng [孙悟空], Zhū Bājiè [猪八戒] and Shā Zēng [沙憎] on his way to India in search of Buddhist scripts. The real Táng Sánzàng [唐三藏] was a very determined man who went to India without the help of any 'monkey-god'.

165. Wú Jìng [吴兢] Táng dynasty: The historian who wrote 贞观政要 'Zhēnguān Governance', a narrative history covering the rule of Emperor Táng Tàizōng [唐太宗], born as Lǐ Shìmín [李世民], the most outstanding emperor of the Táng dynasty (refer to p. 161).

166. Wú Sānguì [吴三桂] (1612-1678): Conspired to bring in Qīng dynasty through Sanhaiguan. The infamous traitor in Chinese history.

167. Wǔ Zétiān [武则天] (624-705): The only ruling empress in the history of China. Ruled for 50 years in prosperity (p. 143).

168. Xī Shī [西施]: One of the beauties in the 'Spring and Autumn' period (p. 129). Offered to Emperor Fū Chāi [夫差] as a diplomatic and military strategy. Bewitched by her beauty Fū Chāi soon slacked in his state affairs and killed his best advisor Wǔ Zǐxù [伍子胥] (refer to p. 131).

169. Xiāo Yán [萧衍] (464-549): Ruled as Liáng Wǔdì [梁武帝]. Founder of Liang dynasty (Southern dynasty). Scholar in his own right, he wrote books on Confucianism and Buddhism. Promoted the Buddhist practice of vegetarian diet (p. 140).

170. Xú Guāngqǐ [徐光启] (1562-1633): Author of 农政全书 *nóngzhèng quánshū* 'Agricultural Compendium'. This was in sixty volumes, 500,000 words guide to agriculture. Topics covered included agriculture, irrigation, machinery, animal husbandry, silk worm, land management. He also translated 6 volumes of Euclid's Elements into Chinese (p. 147).

171. Xǔ Shèn [许慎] (About 147 AD). Credited with compiling the first Chinese dictionary 说文解字 *shuōwénjiězì*. The dictionary was composed of 15 chapters and collected 9,353 characters (refer to p. 136). He was also the author of 五经异义 *wǔjīngyìyì*.

172. Xú Zǐpíng [徐子平] from the five dynasties/Sòng period. Developed 命理学 *mìnglǐxué* 'The Study of Life Destiny'. Life reading analysis is largely unknown in the Western World (refer to p. 380).

173. Xuán Zhuāng [玄奘] (605-664): Born as Chén Huī [陈祎]. Also known as Sānzàng fǎshī [三藏法师] (Sānzàng [三藏] is the name given to Buddhist scriptures). He was a highly resolute and strong willed monk, who went across the desert, going through hardships to reach India. He studied Buddhism for five years before bringing more than six-hundred Buddhist scriptures home. His travels were recorded in his book 大唐西域记

dàtáng xīchéngjì, which became an important book on the customs and geography of that region (p. 141).

174. Xúnzǐ [荀子] (313-238 BC): Philosopher and educator at the end of Warring States (p. 132). Considered the third greatest Confucian thinker after Confucius and Mèngzǐ. Famous students included Hán Fēizǐ [韩非子] (p. 157) as well as Lǐ Sī [李斯] (p. 161). Authored the book of 荀子 *Xúnzǐ* (refer to p. 132).

175. Yándì [炎帝] The legendary emperor of China, who lived about four thousand years ago. Ethnic Chinese worldwide consider themselves as 'Descendants of Yán-Huáng' emperors [炎黄子孙] *yánhuáng zǐsūn* (refer to p. 127).

176. Yán Zhēnqīng [颜真卿] (709-785): Chinese calligrapher. Important works include 东方朔画赞 *dōngfáng shuòhuà zàn*. Also noted for his poetry such as 劝学 *qùan xué* (refer to p. 263).

177. Yáng Guāng [杨广] (569-618): Ruled as Suí Yángdì [隋炀帝], 2nd emperor of Suí dynasty. Conscripted 3 million people over six years to construct the grand-canal linking Beijing to Hangzhou, a distance of about 1,747 km. However overtaxing the people into poverty led to his downfall (p. 140).

178. Yáng Guìfēi [杨贵妃] (719-756): One of the four beauties in Chinese history. Concubine of Emperor Táng Xuánzōng [唐玄宗]. Blamed for the rebellion, forcing Táng Xuánzōng to order her execution (p. 142) Bái Jūyì [白居易] (p. 152), a poet, recounted the tragic love story of Yáng Guìfēi in his poem 长恨歌 *chánghèngē* 'Song of Everlasting Sorrow'.

179. Yáng Jiān [杨坚] (541-604): Ruled as Suí Wéndì [隋文帝], first emperor of Suí dynasty.

Yuán Chéngzōng [元成宗]: Refer to [铁木耳] Tiě Mù'er
Yuán Rénzōng [元仁宗]: Refer to Aiyùlíbálìbādá [爱育黎拔力八达]

180. Yuán Shìkǎi [袁世凯]: (1859-1916): Became President of the Republic of China in 1912, Attempted to become 'emperor' of China.

Yuǎn Tàizǔ [元太祖]: Refer to Genghis Khan 成吉思汗.

181. Yuán Tiāngāng [袁天罡]: Co-author with Lǐ Chúnfēng [李淳风] (p. 160), the earliest book on prediction 推背图 *tuī bèi tú* 'Diagrams of Rubbing the Back' (refer to p. 252).

182. Yuè Fēi [岳飞] (1103-1142): General from Southern Sòng period. A national hero who won brilliant victories and recovered most territory from the Jin tribes. However the real power at Imperial court was wielded by [秦桧] Qín Kuǎi. Qín Kuǎi collaborated with the enemy, and betrayed Yuè Fēi, fabricating false accusations, sending the General to prison and had him executed. Yuè Fēi's poem 满江红 *mǎnjiānghóng* 'The Whole River is Red' is still popular today (p. 263).

183. Zēng Gǒng [曾巩] (1019-1083): Scholar and historian of the Sòng dynasty (p. 144). A follower of Ōuyáng Xiū [欧阳修] (p. 165), he produced some four hundred poems.

184. Zēng Xiānzhī [曾先知]: Historian of Yuán/Sòng dynasty, who compiled the important work on history 十八史列 *shíbā shǐliè* (p. 127).

185. Zhāng Fēi [张飞]: One of the Generals in the Romance of Three Kingdoms (refer to pp. 137, 249).

186. Zhāng Héng [张衡] (78-139): Astronomer from the Eastern Hàn period. A mathematician, astronomer and geographer, he became chief astrologer and minister. In the year 132 he invented the first seismoscope (refer to p. 136).

187. Zhāng Qiān [张骞] (?-114 BC): The first explorer sent to liaise with desert countries to the west. Trips like his contributed to the 'silk route', linking the east and west (p. 134).

188. Zhāng Xù [张旭]: Famous Táng dynasty Chinese calligrapher. He was also a poet, famous for his poem 山中留客 *shānzhōng líukè* (p. 264).

189. Zhāng Zài [张载] (1020-1077): Sòng dynasty metaphysics philosopher, postulating that 'Qi' is the source of all things.

190. Zhāng Zéduān [张择端]: Imperial court painter from Sòng dynasty. Famous for the 清明上河图 *Qīngmíng shànghé tú*, a five-metre scroll that depicts in realistic artistic style and historical detail, life in the Sòng period. This is an 'encyclopaedia', depicting streets, river, bridges, boats, carriages, city walls, houses, riverside scenes, horses, camels and people in pursuits such as trading, drinking tea,. The painting is kept at the Palace Museum in Beijing (p. 145).

191. Zhāng Zhòngjǐng [张仲景] (150-219): Authored text books on Chinese medicine such as 伤寒论 *shānghánlùn* and 金匮要略 *jīnkuìyàolùe* (refer to p. 138).

192. Zhào Dūn [赵惇] (1147-1200): Ruled as Sòng Guāngzōng [宋光宗], 12th emperor of the Southern Sòng dynasty.

193. Zhào Gòu [赵构] (1107-1187): Ruled as Sòng Gāozōng [宋高宗], 10th Emperor of the Southern Sòng dynasty.

194. Zhào Héng [赵恒] (958-1022): Ruled as Sòng Zhēnzōng [宋真宗], 3rd emperor of Sòng dynasty.

195. Zhào Huán [赵桓] (1100-1156): Ruled as Sòng Qīnzōng [宋钦宗], 9th emperor of Sòng dynasty.

196. Zhào Jí [赵佶] (1082-1135): Ruled as Sòng Huīzōng [宋徽宗], 8th emperor of Sòng dynasty. As an emperor he was rather inept, he was better known for his painting and writing achievements.

197. Zhào Kuāngyìn [赵匡胤] (927-976): Ruled as Sòng Tàizǔ [宋太祖]. Founder of Sòng dynasty. To prevent military coups he established a professional army under strict control of the central government (refer to p. 144).

198. Zhào Kuò [赵扩] (1168-1224): Ruled as Sòng Níngzōng [宋宁宗], 13th emperor of Sòng dynasty.

199. Zhào Líng [赵灵] (939-997): Ruled as Sòng Tàizōng [宋太宗], second emperor of Sòng dynasty, brother of Sòng Tàizǔ [宋太祖].

200. Zhào Mèngfǔ [赵孟頫] (1254-1322): An important 'scholar-painter' and calligrapher of the Yuán dynasty. Scholar-painters 'express' their feelings and thoughts through art, poems and calligraphy.

201. Zhào Shèn [赵慎] (1127-1194): Ruled as Sòng Xiàozōng [宋孝宗], 11th emperor of Sòng dynasty.

202. Zhào Xī [赵熙] (1077-1100): Ruled as Sòng Zhézōng [宋哲宗], 7th Emperor of Sòng dynasty.

203. Zhào Xū [赵顼] (1048-1085): Ruled as Sòng Shénzōng [宋神宗], 6th emperor of Sòng dynasty.

204. Zhào Yún [赵昀] (1205-1264): Ruled as Sòng Lǐzōng [宋理宗], 14th Emperor of Sòng dynasty.

205. Zhào Zhēn [赵祯] (1010-1063): Ruled as Sòng Rénzōng [宋仁宗], 4th emperor of Sòng dynasty, in power for 41 years.

206. Zhèng Chénggōng [郑成功] (1624-1662): Nationalist and military leader. Reclaimed Taiwan from the Dutch in 1662.

207. Zhèng Hé [郑和] (1371-1435): Admiral Cheng Ho, navigator and diplomat. Led 7 missions to Southeast Asia, Indian subcontinent, Persian Gulf, Arab states, the Red Sea and parts of Africa. Visited more than 30 countries over 28 years (p. 146).

208. Zhī Dùn [支遁] (314-366): Famous Buddhist scholar during the Jin period. Made significant contributions to 般若经 *bānruò-jīng* (refer to p. 139).

209. Zhī Yán [智俨] (600-668): The second patriarch of Huàyán Buddhism.

210. Zhī Yǐ [智顗] (538-597): Master of Tīantái Buddhism.

211. Zhōu Ēnlái [周恩来] (1898-1976): First premier of China from 1949 to 1976. Revolutionary, politician, diplomat, military strategist.

212. Zhōu Wénwáng [周文王]: Emperor of Zhōu 周 dynasty (1066-256 BC). Developed yījīng into a sophisticated method for decision making based on natural, political and humanitarian considerations (refer to p. 399).

213. Zhōu Yú [周瑜]: A hero during the three kingdom period. Credited with the 'Battle of Chìbì' [赤壁之战] *chìbì zhī zàn* (p. 138), where he used fire to destroy a mighty army, commanded by Cáo Cāo [曹操] (p. 153).

214. Zhū Dì [朱棣] (1360-1424): Ruled as Míng Chéngzǔ [明成祖], third Emperor of the Míng dynasty. His years of rule were proclaimed as 永乐 *Yǒng Lè*. Commissioned Admiral Cheng Ho [郑和] *Zhèng Hé* (p. 177) to sail to Southeast Asia and Africa (p. 146). Also credited with production of the encyclopaedia 永乐大典 *Yǒnglè dàdiǎn*, of some 22,877 volumes, compiled by about 3,000 people, totalling some 380 million words (refer to p. 228).

215. Zhūgé Liàng [诸葛亮] (181-234): Also known as Kōng Míng [孔明]. Military strategist during the 'Three Kingdoms period' with Liú Bèi [刘备] (p. 162). Author of 后出师表 *hòuchū-shībiǎo*, advise to his young emperor (son of Liú Bèi) on how to rule his kingdom wisely (p. 138).

216. Zhū Hòuzhào [朱厚照] (1491-1521): Ruled as Míng Wǔzōng [明武宗], 10th emperor of Míng dynasty. His years of rule were proclaimed as [正德] Zhèng Dé.

217. Zhū Hòuzōng [朱厚熜] (1507-1566): Ruled as Míng Shìzōng [明世宗], the eleventh Emperor of the Míng dynasty. His years of rule were proclaimed as 嘉靖 *Jiā Jìng*.

218. Zhū Jiànshēn [朱见深] (1447-1487): Ruled as Míng Xiànzōng [明宪宗], the eighth emperor of Míng Dynasty. His years of rule were proclaimed as 成化 *Chéng Huà.*

219. Zhū Xī [朱熹] (1130-1200): Great literary figure in Sòng dynasty, philosopher, educator. Leading intellectual of Neo-Confucian movement and influential thinker of Chinese imperial era. Major contributor to yìjīng, Confucianism and philosophy. Author of books on Confucianist 'four classics' [四书章句集注] *sìshū zhāngjù jízhù,* I-Ching [周易本义] *zhōuyì běn yì,* etc (refer to pp. 144, 276, 399).

220. Zhū Yìjūn [朱翊钧] (1563-1620): Ruled as Míng Shénzōng [明神宗], 13th emperor of the Míng Dynasty. His years of rule were proclaimed as 万历 *Wàn Lì.*

221. Zhū Yóujiǎn [朱由检] (1611-1644): Ruled as Míng Sīzōng [明思宗], the last emperor of Míng dynasty. His years of rule were proclaimed as 崇祯 *Cóng Zhēn.*

222. Zhū Yóuxiào [朱由校] (1605-1627): Ruled as Míng Xīzōng [明熹宗], the 15th Emperor of Míng dynasty. His years of rule were proclaimed as 天启 *Tiān Qǐ.*

223. Zhū Yóuyē [朱由榔] (1623-1662): Emperor of Southern Míng. His years of rule were proclaimed as 永历 *Yǒng Lì.*

224. Zhū Yuánzhāng [朱元璋] (1328-1398): Ruled as Míng Tàizǔ [明太祖]. He was orphaned at an early age, sought refuge in a temple and became a monk. He consolidated the power of emperor, ending 97 years of Yuán rule. He then abolished position of premier (refer to p. 146).

225. Zhuāngzǐ [庄子] (369-286 BC): Philosopher during Warring States (p. 131). Author of 庄子 *Zhuāngzǐ* (p. 255).

226. Zǔ Chōngzhī [祖冲之] (429-501): Mathematician and astronomer, who compiled 大明曆 'Dàmíng calendar', named after the reign of Sòng Xiàowǔdì [宋孝武帝]. He also worked out the value of 'π' (the ratio of circumference and diameter, accurate to

7 decimal points. This was done centuries before calculators were available (refer to p. 140).

ECONOMIC AND TECHNOLOGY IMPERATIVES

风水轮流转 'Fēng shuǐ rotates, taking turns', is a common Chinese saying, meaning that fortunes go up and down for everyone. Some Chinese believe that if their fortunes had been poor for the past couple of centuries, and it would be on the way up, because fortune goes in cycles.

Throughout the centuries empires come and go. During periods of stability a culture of prosperity, economic and cultural development led to China being the 'Middle Kingdom' in the region, surrounded by smaller or weaker vassal states.

Chinese history should perhaps be analysed in economic, technology, military, rather than political terms.

The Middle Kingdom was doing pretty well politically and economically, culminating in the stable dynasties of Táng and Sòng. Agriculture, the arts, trade and industry prospered.

One of the reasons for stability would be an efficient civil service, brought about by a system of Imperial Examination [科举] *kējǔ*.

Introduced in the year 587 by Emperor Suí Wéndì [隋文帝], in the Suí dynasty, the Imperial examinations to recruit officials for civil service were organised once in three years at various levels. Many famous statesmen in Chinese history began their careers after passing the Imperial examinations.

A candidate starts from the village, to qualify as a 'local scholar' [秀才] *xiùcái*. They then sit for examinations to quality as 举人 *jǔrén*. Successful jǔrén then sit for examinations in the capital cities to compete for the positions of [贡士] *gòngshì*. The bright and brilliant gòngshì then sat for the Imperial examination. Successful scholars from Imperial examinations qualified as 进士 *jìngshì*. They were listed in three groups. The first group was bestowed the title of 进士及第 *jìngshìjídì*, the second group were bestowed 进士出身

jìngshìchūshēn, the third group were bestowed 同 进 士 出 身 *tóngjìngshìchūshēn*. There were only three on the first group, the best of whom is known as 状元 *zhuàngyuán*; the second 榜眼 *bǎngyǎn* and the third 探花 *tànhuā*. At various levels, appropriate civil service positions are bestowed. The system was abolished in 1905 in favour of schools, colleges and universities.

The Imperial examination brought together intellectuals, scholars, and people with judgement to rule the country. It contributed to the maintenance of cultural values, stability and social order throughout the centuries. It ensured that people who administered the country were educated and reasonable.

Politically, China was buffered by the Himalayas in the West, the China Sea to the East and South. Emperor Qín Shǐ Huáng joined up the Great Wall to prevent invasion from the North[23]. Any instability usually came from in-fighting leading to geo-political fragmentation.

More importantly China was ahead of her neighbours in terms of politics, agriculture, economy, technology, military and culture.

Politically China was immense, compared to countries in the South. Permanent agriculture, rather than shifting agriculture, started in the Zhōu dynasty (7th Century BC). In years of peace the economy would be strong, as farmers had one of the most fertile and good climatic conditions for agriculture. Her technology was impressive, with inventions ranging from gunpowder to printing. Her military was good, backed by centuries of internal war strategies, economy and technology. Finally Chinese culture was so deep-rooted that it eventually assimilated the Mongolian invaders from Yuán dynasty.

---

[23] The strategy worked until a combination of circumstances, the rise of Genghis and Kublai Khan, as well as conspiracy from Wu San Gui, the gate-keeper, who let the Mongols in.

THE TECHNOLOGY DECLINE

In the final analysis the Chinese downfall was a result of relative decline in technology, with the associated impact on economy. After Yuán Dynasty (ended in 1368), China struggled to maintain its economic advantages. Though there were economic gains significant technological impetus which marked earlier epochs was lost.

Interestingly enough, part of the reason for the technology decline was due to the Imperial Examination for Civil Service. The examination syllabus had too much emphasis on philosophy and the humanities, while totally ignoring science and technology. This became an obvious defect and liability when China faced the West as well as Japan.

Subsequently Europe started the Industrial Revolution, which provided the Europeans with the technological, then economic and military edge. In Asia, Japan after Emperor Meiji acquired technology from the West to become the regional power in the East.

The other factor would be the lack of communication with the rest of the world, in particular advances in Europe. The Chinese were too contented with their political system and cultural heritage, oblivious to the threat from the West.

By 1800s, China was economically subjugated by the West, culminating in a series of humiliating territorial concessions.

Colonisation, culminating in the ceding of Hong Kong to Britain, is perhaps one of the most important events affecting the Chinese psyche, until Hong Kong was returned to China. It is of such fundamental importance to the Chinese (in particular those from China) that a brief description of their perspective is warranted.

In the 18th century the Portuguese discovered that huge profits could be made by selling opium from India to China, a relatively rich country. In 1750 the British colonised India through the East India Company (EIC). In 1773 the EIC obtained the exclusive trading agency in China and in 1797 the monopoly to purify opium from India.

The trade grew exponentially. In a period of 20 years (by 1800) the same silver bullion that had been shipped to China to purchase tea had been shipped back to Britain. Subsequently trade significantly drained the Chinese treasury. By 1839 opium became the largest export from India.

The Chinese demanded to end the 'legal' drug trafficking was protested by the British, in the pretext of 'A Violation of Free Trade'. To protect this lucrative 'Free Trade' British declared war and sent gunboats to Canton in 1840. This gun boat diplomacy forced open the enormous Chinese market, created new ports for trade, allowed Britain to demand a cash indemnity of $21 millions, as well as the ceding of Hong Kong to Britain.

Hong Kong: Reverted to China in 1997.

OTHER IMPORTANT EVENTS

Events that shaped the ethos of ethnic Chinese included colonisation, war against the Japanese, the Communist-Kuoming Tang rivalry, as well as how Chinese migrants were treated in Southeast Asian countries. These include:

1839-1842: Opium War in China
1894-1895: First Sino-Japanese War.

1901:   Passing of 'Immigration Restriction Act', marking the start of White Australian Policy.

1937-1945: Sino-Japanese War, also known as War of Resistance against the Japanese. Though the war has ended, Japan has yet to apologise for War crimes and atrocities.

1953:   End of Korean War

1957:   Independence of Malaya from Britain, with a Malay-Chinese-Indian coalition.

1959:   The Dalai Lama escaped from China.

1962:   Sino-Indian War.

1963:   Formation of Malaysia incorporating Malaya, Singapore, Sabah and Sarawak.

1964:   The first Chinese Atomic Bomb test

1965:   Indonesia, massacre of about half a million people, the ethnic Chinese bore the brunt of the attack.

1965:   Independence of Singapore from Malaysia

1966:   First Chinese guided missile.

1966:   First Chinese thermonuclear fusion device

1966:   Beginning of Cultural Revolution.

1969:   Racial riots in Malaysia after the dominant Malay party suffered losses in elections. The ethnic Chinese were the main target of blood letting.

1969:   End of Cultural Revolution.

1970:   Launch of first Chinese satellite.

1971:   Admission of China to the United Nation.

1973:   Removal of White Australian policy by Whitlam Labor Government.

1973:   Recognition of China by Australia (Whitlam Labour Government).

1976:   Death of Mao Zedong, followed by the rise of Deng Xiaoping. Through a series of reforms Deng brought China to the modern era.

1979:   Sino-Vietnam War
1980s and 90s: Beginning of ethnic Chinese migrants into
            Australia.
1989:   Tian An Men incident in China.
1997:   Return of Hong Kong to China, making the end of
            the last important Western colony outpost in Asia.
1998:   Indonesia, massacre and rape of Chinese residents
            after the fall of President Suharto.
1999:   Return of Macau to China. Every inch of Asian soil
            now governed by Asians.
2003:   First Chinese spaceman launched and returned.

Quand la Chine S'evillera, le Monde tremblera.
(When China wakes up, the World will tremble)
                                    NAPOLEON BONAPARTE

The emergence of China as a regional and world power would be an important chapter for future Historians. The quotation from Napoleon Bonaparte, at one time the most powerful man in Europe is most refreshing.

The Chinese Mindset, Collective Wisdom from Centuries of Publications

HISTORICAL EVENTS AND PERSONALITIES, as described in Chapter 5, certainly contributed to the Chinese mindset. Over the centuries, thousands of sayings, proverbs, poetry and books collectively form part of the Chinese psyche. These 'cultivated values' are passed on from one generation to the next, practised in one way or another, and remain relevant and important today.

This chapter surveys the Chinese literature, to bring out sayings that are somehow embedded in the 'subconscious'. These include proverbs as well as quotable quotes from various texts over the centuries. They are listed according to topics such as education, government and military. Taoism and Confucianism are discussed in the next chapter.

WORDS OF WISDOM

There are probably more quotable quotes from ancient classics in Chinese than in any other language. This could be attributed to the fact that the language was developed very early, which gave them a head start. The invention of printing preserved many of these records, and the invention of paper enabled records to be kept in large quantities. In addition the large population and political stability in periods of Chinese history promoted huge quantities of works.

There are thousands of literary works and quotable quotes, dating back to centuries ago. Though circumstances have changed due to technological advancement and new discoveries, the basic human nature and inter-personal relationship remains the same. Most of these quotes are still valid today.

In reality it is more relevant to be able to use the quotations in specific applications, rather than understanding in detail the exact translation or the original Chinese text. We will deal with proverbs, as well as quotable quotes from the literature.

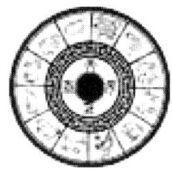

Chinese zodiac signs arranged in chronological order in a cycle. This is often seen in books, calendars, feng shui objects and so on.

PROVERBS

There is a huge range of Chinese proverbs and common sayings, often spoken and used without thoughts by teachers and parents. This is part of the reasons why communication is sometimes difficult because one party is so used to it while the other wonders what it is all about. While the speaker feels that he or she has expressed fully, the listener sort of half understood, without wanting to interrupt or demand a full explanation.

Furthermore, some of the proverbs are hard to translate, or even worse, difficult to be explained without going back to the relevant Chinese cultural matters.

Some of the proverbs are used in greeting cards, banners, or plaques in offices and homes. They are normally used whenever the situation, or something similar, arises.

Indeed proverbs reflect cultural value, judgment criteria, as well as underlying thoughts. We are after all moulded through education, including expressions and proverbs. An understanding of the proverbs provides useful insight into the reasoning, mentality, psyche as well as cultural sensitivities of any race.

Mastery of Chinese proverbs could be difficult, their usage often reflect the command of the Chinese language itself.

Three Hundred and Sixty-Five Commonly Used Proverbs

The way we think is reflected in the language used. A review of the proverbs and common sayings gives a good indication of our thinking process, value judgment, as well as things that consciously or subconsciously shape our thoughts and speeches. We list herewith three hundred and sixty five commonly used proverbs, bearing in mind that the translation is done to the best of our ability. Listing is done alphabetically according to pīnyīn, the literal translation is then given, followed by our interpretation of the phrase. The 36 stratagems refer to military strategies, described later (refer to p. 234).

1. 'Would love to help but is unable to' [爱莫能助] *àimònéngzhù*. Willing at heart, but unable to assist.

2. 'An affair or happening in the dark' [暧昧之事] *àimèizhīshì*. Referring normally to illicit affairs.

3. 'Not forgetting danger even when there is peace' [安不忘危] *ānbù wàngwéi*. Reminding people to be constantly on the alert.

4. 'Keep within one's place and exercise self-restraint' [安分守己] *ānfēn-shǒujǐ*. To mind one's business; inferring that the priority goes to looking after oneself, not infringing on others.

5. 'As stable as the Tai Mountain' [安如泰山] *ānrútàishān*. Tàishān is one of the tallest mountains in China. Refers to something rock solid and safe.

6. 'Hold on to the troops, not making a move' [按兵不动] *ànbīng-bùdòng*. Waiting for the right time or opportunity to strike.

7. 'Proceed according to prescribed way' [按部就班] *ànbù-jiùbān*. Progress in an orderly manner.

8. 'Difficult to defend oneself from an arrow fired in the dark' [暗箭难防] *ànjiàn-nánfáng*. A covert attack, where the enemy is invisible or not exposed, is difficult to defend against.

9. 'Killing with a hidden arrow' [暗箭杀人] *ànjiàn-shārén*. Stabbing somebody in the back.

10. 'No end to unfathomable complexities' [奥妙无穷] *àomiào-wúqióng*. Extremely subtle and fascinating.

11. 'Draw up the sword to help someone in need' [拔刀相助] *bádāo- xiāngzhù*. Referring to someone helping to render justice.

12. 'Seeing the real thing is better than listening a hundred times' [百闻不如一见] *bǎiwén bùrú yījiàn*.

13. 'Having attained the height of a hundred feet pole, you can progress even further' [百尺竿头，更进一步] *bǎichǐ gāntóu gèng jìnyībù*. Used to encourage people to advance even further.

14. 'A hundred flowers blooming together' [百花齐放] *bǎihuāqífàng*. Referring to richness or variety of things.

15. 'A happy union of a hundred years' [百年好合] *báinián-hǎohé*. A common congratulatory phrase for weddings (refer to p. 306).

16. 'Building an empire with bare hands' [白手起家] *báishǒuqǐjiā*. Referring to self made man, who establishes himself or accumulate wealth through his own efforts.

17. 'The heart is not afraid when someone knocks at the door at midnight' [半夜敲门心不惊] *bànyè qiāomén xīn bùjīng*. Comes from the saying 'Keep your conscience clear, the heart is not afraid when someone knocks at the door in the middle of the night' [为人莫作亏心事，半夜敲门心不惊].

18. 'Inclusive of ten thousand items' [包罗万象] *bāoluó-wànxiàng*. Containing a wide variety of things, all inclusive.

19. 'We come from the same roots, why are we in such a haste to fry each other?' [本是同根生, 相煎何太急] *běn shì tóng gèn shēng, xiāng jiān hé tài jí*. After the death of Emperor Cáo Cāo [曹操] (p. 153), his second son Cáo Pī [曹丕] succeeded him as emperor. Cáo Pī wanted to remove his brother Cāo Zhí [曹植] as a potential threat to his throne. He forced him to compose a poem in seven paces, to state why he should not be executed. Cáo Zhí composed the famous poem, which is still commonly cited today. The citation is used whenever in-fighting amongst siblings occurs. It is also commonly cited in the China-Taiwan issue. The original poem is as follows: 'bean stalks burn to cook beans from the same plant; the beans in the pot cry out: 'We come from the same roots, why are we in such a hurry to fry each other?' [煮豆燃豆萁, 豆在釜中泣. 本是同根生, 相煎何太急] (refer to p. 260).

20. 'There is another motive' [别有用心] *biéyǒu yòngxīn*. There exists an ulterior motive, not always obvious.

21. 'A layer of ice three feet deep does not come from a single day of cold weather' [冰封三尺, 绝非一日之寒] *bīngfēng sānchǐ, juéfēi yīrìzhīhán*. Things do not happen overnight, a situation takes time to develop.

22. 'Diseases get in through the mouth' [病从口入] *bìngcóng-kǒurù*. A lot of medical problems originate from the food we eat, ranging from poor quality food, impulsive eating to unbalanced diet, etc. Often quoted together with 'Trouble getting out from the mouth' [祸从口出] *huòcóngkǒuchū* (Proverb No. 99).

23. 'Be humble enough to seek advice, do not feel embarrassed about it' [不耻下问] *bùchǐ xiàwèn*. Never be ashamed to ask (no one knows everything)!

24. 'Does not win people's heart' [不得人心] *bùdérénxīn*. Someone unpopular.

25. 'Parted in unhappy circumstances' [不欢而散] *bùhuān-érsàn.*

26. 'Not moving forward amounts to actually going backwards' [不进则退] *bùjìnzétuì.* In a competitive world, if one does not advance, one is relatively in retreat, as others advance. Comes from the proverb 'A boat going against the current, goes backward if it does not go forward' [逆水行舟, 不进则退].

27. 'Cannot withstand a single blow' [不堪一击] *bùkānyījī.* Someone weak and easily defeated.

28. 'Beyond imagination' [不可思议] *bùkě-sīyi.* Something beyond imagination, inconceivable or mysterious.

29. 'Obtaining it without making any effort' [不劳而获] *bùláo'érhuò.* Something easily achieved.

30. 'Does not bend back, does not flinch' [不屈不挠] *bùqū-bùnáo.* A firm, unyielding attitude.

31. 'How do you get a cub without entering the tiger's den?' [不入虎穴, 焉得虎子] *bùrù hǔxué, yāndé hǔzǐ.* This highlights the need to take calculated risks in order to succeed.

32. 'Without any feeling, unaware of human activities' [不省人事] *bù shěngrénshì.* Referring to people in a state of unconsciousness.

33. 'Nothing unusual or extra-ordinary' [不足为奇] *bùzú-wéiqí.* Referring to things that are not unusual or outstanding, nothing surprising.

34. 'A grain in the ocean' [沧海一粟] *cānghǎi yīsù.* Equivalent to 'a drop in the ocean'.

35. 'In the Yangtze waves from the back pushes waves in front; In the world new people replace old faces' [长江后浪推前浪, 世上新人换旧人] *chángjiāng hòulàng tuī qiánlàng, shìshàng xīnrén huàn jiùrén.* There are always fresh bloods to replace existing people.

36. 'When there is a fire it is the right time to raid' [趁火打劫] *chènhuǒ-dǎjié*. Usually used to describe opportunism, strike when the target or enemy is in disarray – one of the 36 stratagems (refer to p. 235).

37. 'Not good enough to make something a success, but more than sufficient to ruin it' [成事不足, 败事有余] *chéngshìbùzú, bàishìyǒuyú*. Describe someone who fails more than succeeds.

38. 'As you eat till an old age you learn till an old age' [吃到老学到老] *chīdàolǎo-xuédàolǎo*. There is always something to learn no matter how old you are

39. 'Stuff the ear, refuse to listen' [充耳不闻] *chōng' ěrbùwén*. Referring to people not willing to listen, or selectively deaf.

40. 'Move when one is least expected to' [出其不意] *chūqíbùyì*. The element of 'surprise' is important in military and business. This proverb is normally used to launch something totally unexpected by the enemy or competitor, catching them off-guard. This proverb is commonly used together with 'Attack when the enemy is not prepared' [攻其不备] *gōngqí bùbèi* (Proverb No. 75).

41. 'Totally unexpected' [出人意料之外] *chūrén yìliàozhīwài*.

42. 'Head above others' [出人头地] *chūréntóudì*. Referring to someone who has achieved his goal, towering above the others

43. 'Stooping, feeling deflated' [垂头丧气] *chuítóu sàngqì*. A sense of dejection and hopelessness.

44. 'Not in time to save by the hand' [措手不及] *cuòshǒubùjí*. Caught unprepared.

45. 'To fight against injustice' [打抱不平] *dǎbàobùpíng*.

46. 'Beating the grass would scare the snake' [打草惊蛇] *dǎcǎo jīngshé*. Beating the grass, the natural environment of the snake, has two meanings. It is important not to let the enemy know that we are probing their hide-outs, so as not to

heighten their alertness. It could also refer to tactical moves to disturb the environment, 'beat the grass' so as to bring out the snake, in cases where their exact location is not clear—one of the 36 stratagems (refer to p. 236).

47. 'Reduce a big problem into a small one; reduce a small problem to no problem at all' [大事化小, 小事化无] *dàshì-huàxiǎo, xiǎoshìhuàwú*. A common advice to minimise or nullify problems.

48. 'The deciding factors are no longer in favour' [大势已去] *dàshì-yǐqù*. The situation is no longer under control.

49. 'Huge courtyard, large crowd' [大庭广众] *dàtíng-guǎngzhòng*. Referring to public premises, where anything done could be watched by anyone.

50. 'The players are unable to 'see' clearly' [当局者迷] *dāngjúzhěmí*. Very often those involved could not see or think clearly, they just react impulsively, they lack objectivity. Contrast with another proverb 'Observers understands clearly' [旁观者清] *pángguānzhěqīng* (Proverb No. 171).

51. 'Whenever you can forgive someone do forgive him' [得饶人处且饶人] *dé ráorén chù qiě ráorén*. A common saying to reduce unnecessary problems for oneself in the future, as well as reducing bad karmic effects.

52. 'Ascend the summit and attained the extreme' [登峰造极] *dēngfēng-zàojí*. Referring to someone breaking record, or achieving a high standard of excellence.

53. 'To take the right as wrong, the wrong as right' [颠倒是非] *diāndǎo shìfēi*. Intentionally distorting the truth.

54. 'To turn stone into gold' [点石成金] *diǎnshíchéngjīn*. Turning something cheap and simple to something extremely valuable.

55. 'Head reaching the sky and feet on the ground' [顶天立地] *dǐngtiān-lìdì*. Someone with gigantic stature.

56. 'Rushing to the east and running to the west' [东奔西跑] *dōngbēn-xīpǎo*. Extremely busy.

57. 'Arise again from the Eastern Mountain' [东山再起] *dōngshānzàiqǐ*. Historically Xiè Ān [谢安] took refuge in the Eastern mountain [东山] *dōngshān* for 23 years, before launching a comeback as ruler. This proverb refers to a comeback after initial failure.

58. 'Looking at the East and West' [东张西望] *dōngzhāng-xīwàng*. Looking aimlessly at all directions.

59. 'Answer like water flow' [对答如流] *duìdá-rúliú*. Answering fluently.

60. 'Prescribing medicine according to the illness' [对症下药] *duìzhèng-xiàyào*. Identify the root cause and deal with it.

61. 'The evil person will eventually suffer at the hand of an evil person' [恶人终受恶人磨] *èrén zhōng shòu èrén mó*. Comes from the saying 'There is always someone who is much stronger, the evil person will eventually suffer at the hand of an evil person' [强中更有强中手, 恶人终受恶人磨].

62. 'Flip and flop without any constant pattern' [反复无常] *fǎnfùwúcháng*. Inconsistent, fickle minded.

63. 'Be on guard, though it is almost impossible to guard against all eventualities' [防不胜防] *fángbùshèngfáng*. Impossible to put up a fool-proof guard against attack.

64. 'A heart on the alert is indispensable' [防人之心不可无] *fángrénzhīxīn bùkěwú*. In reality one needs to be constantly on the alert, as a natural self protection mechanism. This phrase is used in conjunction with 'A heart that harms others is not permissible' [害人之心不可有] *hàirénzhīxīn bùkěyǒu* (Proverb No. 86) (refer to p. 247).

65. 'Put down the butcher's knife' [放下屠刀] *fàngxià túdāo*. Describing a desire to abandon evil deeds, to repent and reform.

66. 'Calm sea without any wind' [风平浪静] *fēngpíng làngjìng*. All quiet and peaceful.

67. 'Fortune goes in cycles' [风水轮流转] *fēngshuǐlúnliú zhuàn*. This is part of the Chinese psyche, that there are ups and downs in life. When you are down, do not give up, wait for better times. Refer to 'Luck has changed from bad to good' [时来运到] *shílái yùndào* (Proverb No. 215).

68. 'When you meet someone it is good enough to tell him thirty percent, do not throw your heart at him yet' [逢人且说三分话，未可全抛一片心] *fēngrén qiě shuō sānfēnhuà, wèikě quán pāo yīpiànxīn*. Beware of strangers; do not divulge all that you know.

69. 'Bearing a thick thorn at the back to beg for forgiveness' [负荆请罪] *fùjīng qǐngzuì*. The incidence was recorded in the 'Historical Records' *Shǐjì*, when Kang Po literally born a thick thorn on his back to apologise—Make a humble and unconditional apology.

70. 'Going through hot soup and walking through fire' [赴汤蹈火] *fùtāng- dǎohuǒ*. Do whatever it takes.

71. 'Pull out the firewood from under the cauldron' [釜底抽薪] *fǔdǐ chōuxīn*. When the enemy is strong, weaken it by weathering off its support, to prevent him from succeeding—one of the 36 stratagems (refer to p. 237).

72. 'High above the rest' [高高在上] *gāogāo-zàishàng*. Remote from the masses.

73. 'Seats filled with honoured guests' [高朋满座] *gāopéng mǎnzuò*. Used in plaques or advertisement to congratulate opening of restaurants.

74. 'The grandfather has the grandfather's logic, the grandmother has the grandmother's reasons' [公有公理，婆有婆

理] *gōngyǒugōnglǐ- póyǒu pólǐ*. In any dispute each party has its own reasons. It is important to hear from both sides.

75. 'Attack when the enemy is not prepared' [攻其不备] *gōngqíbùbèi*. In warfare maximum impact is achieved when the enemy is least prepared for the assault. This proverb is commonly used together with 'Appearing when one is least expected to' [出其不意] *chūqíbùyì* (Proverb No. 40). Both phrases taken from 'The Art of War' (refer to p. 241).

76. 'When the job is done it is time to withdraw' [功成身退] *gōngchéng-shēntuì*. A relevant reminder to those who like to cling on to power) (refer to p. 270).

77. 'Supply cannot cope with demand' [供不应求] *gòngbùyīngqiú*. Often used in marketing.

78. 'Purposely make it mysterious and complicated' [故弄玄虚] *gùnòng-xuánxū*. Things are sometimes rather simple, but made to sound complicated or difficult. Often seen in marketing and politics.

79. 'A lone person cannot fight a whole crowd' [寡不敌众] *guǎbùdízhòng*. Hopelessly outnumbered.

80. ''Hanging up the goat head for sale while actually selling dog meat' [挂羊头卖狗肉] *guàyángtóu màigǒuròu*. Used to describe someone who does not practise what is preached.

81. 'Keep rolling in' [滚滚而来] *gǔngǔn'érlái*. Referring to the situation where, once it is set up, the returns are continuous.

82. 'Crossed the bridge, then pull it down' [过河拆桥] *guòhé chāiqiáo*. Referring to someone extremely ungrateful and selfish, towards his/her saviour.

83. 'Scooping for a needle from under the sea' [海底捞针] *hǎidǐ-láozhēn*. Similar to 'A needle in the haystack'.

84. 'Wide sea and open sky' [海阔天空] *hǎikuò tiānkōng*. Often used to depict wide and open scenarios, boundless as the ocean and sky.

85. 'The horse that brings down the whole herd' [害群之马] *hàiqúnzhīmǎ*. The black sheep, bad apple of the community.

86. 'A heart that harms others is not permissible' [害人之心不可有] *hàirénzhīxīn bùkěyǒu*. Harming others would only result in retribution. Refer to 'Do not have a heart not on the alert' [防人之心不可无] *fángrénzhīxīn bùkěwú* (Proverb No. 64) (p. 247).

87. 'News of good deeds does not get out of the door, news of bad deeds spreads around for a thousand miles' [好事不出门, 恶事传千里] *hǎoshì bùchūmén, èshì chuánqiānlǐ*.

88. 'Not tired of learning' [好学不倦] *hàoxué-bùjuàn*. Referring to people who like studying or learning.

89. 'Why wouldn't you be happy to do it?' [何乐不为] *hélèbùwéi*. When you could do something that is beneficial, why not?

90. 'A tree with wide girdle grows from a tiny seed' [合抱之木生於毫末] *hébào zhī mù shēngyúháowèi*. However big the project is, it started off as something tiny. Success is not built overnight, it takes time to nurture (refer to p. 273).

91. 'The crane standing amongst a flock of chicken' [鹤立鸡群] *hèlìjīqún*. Referring to someone outstanding.

92. 'Moving around without any concern or fear' [横行无忌] *héngxíng wújì*. Referring to outrageously inconsiderate conduct.

93. 'An excellent new blood with huge potential' [后起之秀] *hòuqǐzhīxiù*.

94. 'Strike late and you will be in disaster' [后下手遭殃] *hòu xiàshǒu zāoyāng*. Emphasises on the importance of early intervention, before events get out of control (Normally used together with 'Strike first to gain the upper hand' [先下手为强] *xiān xiàshǒu wéiqiáng* (refer to Proverb 273).

95. 'Flowery speech and cunning words' [花言巧语] *huāyán qiǎoyǔ*. Cunning, deceiving statements.

96. 'Flowers in the sky and wine on earth' [花天酒地] *huātiānjiǔdì*. Equivalent to wine, women and song—a decadent lifestyle.

97. 'Flower and branches display to attract attention' [花枝招展] *huāzhīzhāozhǎn*. Used to describe female with elaborate costumes or makeup to attract.

98. 'There is always the shore when you turn back' [回头是岸] *huítóushì'àn*. Phrase often used to encourage turning over a new leaf, it is never too late.

99. 'Trouble getting out from the mouth' [祸从口出] *huòcōngkǒuchū*. Referring to people who speak without thinking, hence creating enemies and troubles for themselves. Often used to warn people to be careful about what they speak. Used in conjunction with 'Diseases getting in through the mouth' *bìngcóngkǒurù* 病从口入 (Proverb No. 22).

100. 'Groping fish in troubled waters' [混水摸鱼] *hùnshuǐ-mōyú*. This is a classic situation, create 'turbidity' in the enemy's camp; attack where there is confusion in the enemy territory —one of the 36 stratagems (refer to p. 237).

101. 'Changing the soup without changing the medicine' [换汤不换药] *huàntāng bùhuànyào*. Chinese medicine can be served with a variety of ingredients making up the soup; the efficacy however comes from the core herbs, not soup ingredients. This normally refer to superficial or apparent changes, the content remains the same.

102. 'As dangerous as being on a high mountain peak' [岌岌可危] *jíjí-kěwéi*. Description of perilous situation

103. 'To live under some one else's fence' [寄人篱下] *jìrénlíxià*. To be dependent on others.

104. 'Do not do unto others what you do not want to be done unto you' [己所不欲，勿施于人] *jǐsuǒbùyù wùshīyúrén*. This is an often quoted phrase by Confucius (p. 159).

105. 'An ordinary home cooked meal' [家常便饭] *jiācháng-biànfàn*. Frequently used to describe a home-cooked meal in a humble manner.

106. 'Ugly aspects of the family are not to be broadcasted' [家丑不能外扬] *jiāchǒu bùnéng wàiyáng*. Dirty linen is not laundered in public.

107. 'There is a difficult script to be cited in each household' [家家有本难念的经] *jiājiā yǒu běn nánniàn de jīng*. In every family, however good it looks from the surface, often there is something unpleasant that the family does not want it to be told.

108. 'Hard to prevent family thieves' [家贼难防] *jiā zéinánfáng*. In a family or a corporation, it is often difficult to prevent pilferage or sabotage from within. Very often it occurs unsuspected or undetected.

109. 'Act silly but not insane' [假痴不颠] *jiǎchībùdiān*. Very often there is little point to disclose one's true strength. This is part of psychological warfare, to put the enemy off-guard —one of the 36 stratagems (refer to p. 238).

110. 'Setting foot on firm ground' [脚踏实地] *jiǎotā-shídì*. Be practical and realistic.

111. 'It is easy to change the rivers and mountains (referring to the State), it is hard to change one's fundamental nature' [江山易改, 本性难移] *jiāngshānyìgǎi, běnxìng nányí*. It is extremely difficult to change one's nature—a leopard does not change its spots.

112. 'A capable general with a non-interfering king wins' [将能而君不御者胜] *jiàng néng ér jūn bù yù zhě shèng*. In terms of operation the chief executive or general needs to be given the flexibility to act without interference (p. 243).

113. 'Killing a person using some one else's knife' [借刀杀人] *jièdāoshārén*. This is a classic strategy to destroy an enemy

using someone else, often without his knowing—one of the 36 stratagems (p. 235).

114. 'Using the wine to drown away sorrow' [借酒浇愁] *jièjiǔjiāochóu*. Used to describe someone in a state of disappointment and heartache, trying to drown his sorrow. The original poem states that 'using wine to drown sorrow generates more sorrow' [举杯消愁, 愁更愁].

115. 'Borrow a corpse to bring back life' [借尸还魂] *jièshī-huánhún*. In this context 'corps' refer to a "useless" individual, but when craftily used could boost one's position or influence. A classic example is to use the name of a descendant of a deceased popular leader as a front line leader. As long as the descendant is not powerful in its own right this fits the criteria—one of the 36 stratagems (p. 236).

116. 'To make use of a topic to express himself' [借题发挥] *jièti-fāhuī*. Referring to people who would like to grasp the opportunity or opportune time to give his point of view.

117. 'A branch sprouting from outside the joint' [节外生枝] *jiéwài-shēngzhī*. Referring to unexpected event or complications. Too often events do not happen according to plans.

118. 'Difficult to escape from destiny' [劫数难逃] *jiéshùnántáo*. Describes the inevitability of an unfortunate event. Quite often this is attributed by some to fate.

119. 'The golden cicada shedding off its shell' [金蝉脱壳] *jīnchán-tūoké*. Disappearing from the scene, leaving an empty shell, without the enemy aware of the disappearance —one of the 36 stratagems (refer to p. 237).

120. 'Measuring and comparing every jin' [斤斤计较] *jīnjin jìjiào*. Jīn is a weight measure. This proverb refers to someone extremely calculating.

121. 'When one is close to red, one tends to turn red, when one is close to black ink, one tends to turn black' [近朱者赤, 近

墨者黑] *jìnzhūzhéchì jìnmòzhéhēi*. This refers to the ease of influence from peers.

122. 'Expertly executed, finely calculated' [精打细算] *jīngdǎ xìsuàn*. Refer to well thought through and carefully worked out approaches.

123. 'Startle the heaven and move the earth' [惊天动地] *jīngtiān dòngdì*. Something extraordinary, an astounding event.

124. 'Respect him but keep a distance' [敬而远之] *jìng'ér-yuǎnzhī*. Used to describe someone powerful, whom you do not wish to offend or get close to. (Comes from 'Respect the spirits and deities, but keep away from them' [敬鬼神而远之] by Confucius).

125. 'Nine dead and one alive' [九死一生] *jiǔsǐyīshēng*. Only one out of ten chances that he would survive; extremely risky or dangerous venture.

126. 'Replay the old tune' [旧调重弹] *jiùdiàochóngtán*. Nothing original.

127. 'To reject someone a thousand miles away' [拒于千里之外] *jùyú qiānlǐ zhīwài*. Referring to someone extremely unfriendly.

128. 'Roll up the earth and return' [卷土重来] *juǎntǔ chónglái*. Recover lost ground and make a big come back.

129. 'Drawn into the spiral of complications' [卷入旋涡] *juánrù-xuánwō*. Getting embroiled in a bad situation or scenario.

130. 'Worthy of praise and tears' [可歌可泣] *kěgē-kěqì*. To be moved to tears, usually referring to heroic acts.

131. 'To overcome difficulties and endure hardship' [刻苦耐劳] *kèkǔnàiláo*. Hardworking spirit, a much promoted virtue.

132. 'Castle in the air' [空中楼阁] *kōngzōnglóugé*. Normally referring to something fanciful, impractical.

133. 'To whip an already fast horse' [快马加鞭] *kuàimǎjiābiān*. To accelerate, putting more efforts.

134. 'The old horse would know the way' [老马识途] *lǎomǎ-shítú*. An experienced person knows the ins and outs.

135. 'Endless shame leads to anger' [老羞成怒] *lǎoxiū-chéngnù*. Referring to someone turning from shame to rage upon repeated insults.

136. 'Exhaust his energy, dim his fighting spirit' [累其气力, 消其斗志] *lèiqíqìlì, xiāoqídòuzhì*. This comes from one of the 36 stratagems. If the energy was exhausted and its fighting spirit dimmed, the final battle would be easier, with fewer casualties (refer to p. 237).

137. 'Extreme joy begets sorrow' [乐极生悲] *lèjí-shēngbēi*.

138. 'Sacrifice a pear to get a plum' [李代桃僵] *lǐdàitáojiāng*. In any operations there are bound to be casualties, the strategy then is to sacrifice one person or resource for another—one of the 36 stratagems (p. 236).

139. 'Conflict of interest' [厉害冲突] *lìhài-chōngtū*.

140. 'Every grain comes with great difficulties' [粒粒皆辛苦] *lìlìjiēxīnkǔ*. Taken from a poem by Lǐ Shēn [李绅]: 'At noon the hoe digs on the soil, drops of sweat blends onto the soil. Who knows that every grain on the plate, comes with much sweat and toil' [鋤禾日当午, 汗粒禾下土. 谁知盘中餐, 粒粒皆辛苦]. Often used to remind people that food does not come easy. A lot of effort has been put in to produce them (refer to p. 258).

141. 'Digging a well only when one feels thirsty' [临渴掘井] *línkējuéjǐng*. Before piped water, well was the only source of water, unless one lived near a river. Digging for a well when you are thirsty is obviously too late.

142. 'Good medicine taste bitter' [良药苦口] *liángyào-kǔkǒu*. Good advice grates the ears.

143. 'Both parties are loosing and injured' [两败俱伤] *liǎngbài-jùshāng*. There is no winner, both sides suffered.

144. 'Sparse, not even a few' [寥寥无几] *liáoliáo wújǐ*. Something scarce and limited.

145. 'As familiar as our fingers and palms' [了如指掌] *liǎorúzhǐzhǎng*. Something thoroughly familiar and understood.

146. 'To withdraw or retreat just before going into battle' [临阵退缩] *línzhèn-tuìsuō*. To back down before the actual confrontation.

147. 'Beautiful fragrance that diffuses for centuries' [流芳百世] *liúfāngbǎishì*. Excellent reputation that becomes a legend.

148. 'Struggle between the dragon and tiger' [龙争虎斗] *lóngzhēng-hǔdòu*. A fierce struggle between two powerful competitors.

149. 'When the horse arrives, it signals success' [马到成功] *mǎdào-chénggōng*. Normally referring to something successfully achieved. Used to wish someone well on a mission.

150. 'Deceive the Heaven to cross the ocean' [瞒天过海] *mántiān-guòhǎi*. This involves operations under cover—one of the 36 stratagems (refer to p. 235).

151. 'Return with a full load' [满载而归] *mānzài-érguī*. Normally referring to successful outcome from a mission.

152. 'To steal a moment of leisure' [忙里偷闲] *mánglǐ-tōuxián*. Getting some time off from a busy schedule.

153. 'Possible to trap birds in front of the door' [门可罗雀] *ménkěluòquè*. Birds are normally afraid of human presence, there would not be any if customers come in and out of the shop—normally referring to shops whose business are not good, with too few customers.

154. 'The skilful hand brings back Spring' [妙手回春] *miàoshǒu-huíchūn*. Used mainly on plaques to congratulate or praise skilled medical practitioners.

155. 'The reputation is not spread around incorrectly' [名不虚传] *míngbùxūchuán*. Living up to one's good reputation.

156. 'The reputation corresponds to actual facts' [名副其实] *míngfùqíshí.*

157. 'Listed after Sūn Shān' [名落孙山] *míngluò-Sūnshán.* Sūn Shān was last on the success list in the Imperial examination. This refers to someone who has failed his examinations.

158. 'The name reverberates across the four seas' [名扬四海] *míngyáng-sìhǎi.* Describing someone well known, someone globally famous.

159. 'Pre-destined in life' [命中注定] *mìngzhōng-zhùdìng.* Describe inevitability of event, or fate.

160. 'Does not understand at all' [莫名其妙] *mòmíngqímiào.* Baffled by something inexplicable.

161. 'The man puts in the efforts, but the Heaven makes it a success.' [谋事在人, 成事在天] *móushìzàirén, chéng shìzàitiān.* An often quoted statement, implying that though one could try their best, the final outcome could be very circumstantial.

162. 'The wood has already become a boat' [木已成舟] *mùyǐchéngzhōu.* Something fait accompli, irreversible.

163. 'I would rather that others disappoint me, not I disappointing others' [宁可人负我, 切莫我负人] *níngkě rénfùwǒ, qiēmò wǒfùrén.*

164. 'Provoke him if he gets angry easily' [怒而挠之] *nù'érnáozhī.* While some people could remain calm, others loose their cool when provoked. These are the people who could be provoked to loose their 'clear head' (refer to p. 241).

165. 'The angry hair 'pushing up' the cap' [怒发冲冠] *nùfà-chōngguān.* Referring to someone extremely furious. (Originated from a famous poem, 'The Whole River is Red' [满江红] (p. 263) *mǎnjiānghóng*, by Yuè Fēi [岳飞] (p. 175).

166. 'Trying to be clever but ends up clumsily' [弄巧反拙] *nòngqiǎo-fǎnzhuō*. Try to do something smart but results turn out badly.

167. 'Even though the lotus roots are broken the fibres are still linked' [藕断丝连] *ǒuduànsīlián*. Normally referring to sentiments lingering between couples even after separation.

168. 'Seven ups and eight downs' [七上八下] *qīshàng-bāxià*. Confused, total disarray.

169. 'Bang the table and cry out bravo' [拍案叫绝] *pāi'ànjiàojué*. An expression of approval and joy.

170. 'Moving mountains and emptying seas' [排山倒海] *pāishān-dǎohǎi*. Going all out, doing something with all his might.

171. 'Observers understands clearly' [旁观者清] *pángguānzhěqīng*. Very often the observers see both sides of the argument objectively and have a clear idea of the overall scenario. Contrasts with 'The players are confused' [当局者迷] *dāngjúzhěmí* (Proverb No. 50).

172. 'As if there is no one around' [旁若无人] *pángruò-wúrén*. Referring to arrogant, inconsiderate acts, ignoring those around him.

173. 'Pacing up and down, incapable of making any decision' [彷徨无主] *pánghuáng-wúzhǔ*. Referring to people who are unsettled or having perturbed minds.

174. 'The skin smiles, the flesh does not' [皮笑肉不笑] *píxiàoròubùxiào*. Referring to a hypocritical or superficial smile, not one from the heart.

175. 'Throw a brick to attract a gem' [抛砖引玉] *pāozhuānyǐnyù*. Give away something of small value to attract something substantial, a tactic used in business or military—one of the 36 stratagems (refer to p. 237).

176. 'The poor who lives in a busy city does not have any visitor, the rich who lives in the deep jungle has distant relatives'

[贫居闹市无人问, 富在深山有远亲] *pín jū nàoshì wúrén wèn, fù zài shēnshān yǒu yuǎnqīn*. When you are poor no one bothers about you, but when you are rich, lots of people wanted to know you, claiming to be distant relatives.

177. 'Break loose his mouth, scolding ferociously' [破口大骂] *pókǒu-dàmà*. Shouting abuse.

178. 'The chess player meets an opponent' [棋逢对手] *qíféng-duìshǒu*. Normally referring to a worthy competitor or situations of strong competition.

179. 'Difficult to get off the tiger's back while riding on it' [骑虎难下] *qíhǔ-nánxià*. Used to describe a difficult situation which is hard to back out from. Also used as a warning not to get entangled in situations beyond one's means.

180. 'A person from the 'Qi' country worrying that the sky might fall down' [杞人忧天] *qǐrényōutiān*. Needless and unnecessary worries.

181. 'A journey of a thousand miles begins with the first step' [千里之行始于足下] *qiānlǐ zhī xíng shǐ yú zúxià*. This highlights the importance of taking the first step. Taken from Dàodéjīng [道德经] (refer to p. 273).

182. 'Thousand methods and hundred plans' [千方百计] *qiānfāng-bǎijì*. A commonly used phrase in business and politics, referring to trying out all sorts of ways and means.

183. 'Warning from the vehicle in front' [前车之鉴] *qiánché-zhījiàn*. In the battlefield an overturned cart warns of imminent danger. This proverb refers to learning from other's mistakes.

184. 'One generation planted trees, future generations enjoy the shades' [前人种树后人乘凉] *qiánrén zhòngshù hòurén chéngliáng*. Used often to describe how future generations benefit from the hard work or foresight from an earlier generation.

185. 'Create division if his forces are united' [亲而离之] *qīnérlízhī*. The 'divide and rule' strategy (refer to p. 241).

186. 'To catch the thieves, arrest the chief' [擒贼擒王] *qínzéi qínwáng*. Deal with the leader rather than rank and file —one of the 36 stratagems (refer to p. 237).

187. 'It is easy to invite a deity but difficult to send away one' [请神容易送神难] *qǐng shén róngyì sòng shén nán*. It is easy to invite a powerful figure as a partner or ally, but very difficult to get rid of him, when he is still powerful.

188. 'Seeking help from others is not as good as doing it oneself' [求人不如求己] *qiú rén bùrú qiú jǐ*. Better to rely on oneself than relying on others. Comes from the saying 'using the mouth is not as good as moving yourself, seeking help from others is not as good as seeking help from oneself' [使口不如自走, 求人不如求己].

189. 'If people don't offend me, I don't offend them. If people offend me, I will certainly offend them' [人不犯我, 我不犯人; 人若犯我, 我必犯人] *rénbùfànwǒ-wǒbùfànrén, rénruòfànwǒ-wǒbìfànrén*.

190. 'Do not judge a person by his appearance' [人不可貌像] *rénbùkě màoxiàng*. Do not judge a book by its cover. Unless one is trained in the art of physiogamy, it is dangerous to judge a person by his appearance. However for those familiar with the art, a lot can be deciphered by how a person looks. This ranges from personality analysis, his state of mind, to cycles of ups and downs in life.

191. 'Human sentiment/relationship is like paper, every sheet is thin' [人情似纸张张薄] *rénqíng shìzhǐ zhāngzhang bó*. This refers to 'giving' or 'taking' favour in human relationship. In times of need human relationship could be 'paper thin'.

192. 'The person has gone and the house empty' [人去楼空] *rénqùlóukōng*. Normally referring to someone disappearing without a trace.

193. 'A man has his fortune changing from morning to evening' [人有旦夕祸福] *rén yǒu dànxì huófú*. This emphasise the uncertainty and unpredictable fortunes. Often used with 'There is unpredictable wind and clouds in the sky' [天有不测风云] *tiān yǒu bù cè fēngyún* (Proverb No. 242).

194. 'When one operates in the field, the body does not follow the mind' [人在江湖. 身不由己] *rén zài jiānghú shēn bù yóu jǐ*. In real life, many factors such as cultural practice and circumstantial events are beyond the control of individuals. This saying is often used to describe factors beyond control.

195. 'Benevolence and righteousness are worth a thousand pieces of gold' [仁义值千金] *rényì zhí qiānjīn*. Comes from the saying 'Money and properties are like faeces and soil. Benevolence and righteousness are worth a thousand pieces of gold' [钱财如粪土, 仁义值千金]. This highlights the importance of benevolence and righteousness in traditional Chinese psyche.

196. 'To shoulder the responsibility and take the blames' [任劳任怨] *rènláo-rènyuàn*. A common phrase of praise for volunteers, elected officials, as well as parents.

197. 'Building up by the day and by the month' [日积月累] *rìzhí-yuèlěi*. Accumulating slowly.

198. 'The sun is already at a height of three poles' [日上三竿] *rìshàng sāngān*. It is getting late in the morning.

199. 'There is firmness within something soft' [柔中有刚] *róuzhōng-yǒugāng*. Gentle but firm. This highlights the yīn-yáng concepts, common in Chinese psyche.

200. 'As if there is no such thing' [若无其事] *ruòwúqíshì*. Ignoring what is happening or has happened.

201. 'If you do not want others to know, do not do it yourself' [若要人不知除非己莫为] *ruòyàorén bùzhī chúfēi jǐmòwéi.* Whatever one does, inevitably someone gets to know it.

202. 'Like a tiger added with wings' [如虎添翼] *rúhǔtiānyì.* Adding strength to something already powerful.

203. 'Applying both the soft and hard tactics' [软硬兼施] *ruǎnyìng-jiānshī.* A very common practice, using a combination of stick and carrot.

204. 'Think thrice before acting' [三思而行] *sānsīerxíng.* Comes from 'Think thrice before acting, think again if possible' [三思而行, 再思可矣]. Refer to 'A word spoken cannot be retrieved by the fast horse' [一言既出, 驷马难追] *yīyán jícchū, sìmǎ nánzhuī* (Proverb No. 316).

205. 'Three hearts (thoughts) and two ideas' [三心两意] *sānxīn-liǎngyì.* Fickle minded, undecided.

206. 'Eventually the good and the evil will be repaid, the only issue is whether it comes early or late' [善恶到头终有报, 只争来早与来迟] *shàn'è dàotóu zhōgyǒubào, zhǐzhēng láizǎo yú láichí.* The inevitability of karmic effect is obvious.

207. 'Kind deeds are repaid with kindness' [善有善报] *shànyǒu-shànbào.* A much cherished Buddhist value.

208. 'When the upper beam is not straight, the lower beam is crooked' [上樑不正下樑歪] *shàngliángbùzhèng xiàliángwāi.* When the conduct of parents, elders or leaders is improper, the children or subordinates tend to follow.

209. 'The team with rank and file sharing the same wish wins' [上下同欲者胜] *shàngxià tóng yù zhě shèng.* A team with a common purpose is a winner! (refer to p. 243).

210. 'A situation seldom seen is thought to be strange' [少见多怪] *shǎojiàn-duōguài.* Used to describe inexperienced or unfamiliar situations.

211. 'If one does not work hard when one is young, it would be useless to feel miserable when one is old' [少壮不努力, 老大徒伤悲] *shàozhuàng bù nǔlì, lǎodà tú bēishāng*. This is often used by the elders to advise the young ones not to waste their youth away.

212. 'The winner becomes the King, the loser the Bandit' [胜者为王, 败者为寇] *shèngzhěwéiwáng, bàizhěwéikòu*. At the end of the day the winner takes all.

213. Create noise in the East to attack the West' [声东击西] *shēngdōng-jīxī*. A tactic designed to distract attention prior to attack. The strategy works as long as the enemy's intelligence does not discover it—one of the 36 stratagems (p. 235).

214. 'Deities appearing and ghosts disappearing' [神出鬼没] *shénchū-guǐmò*. Used to describe a situation that is totally baffling and mysterious.

215. 'The time has come and good luck arrived' [时来运到] *shílái yùndào*. Chinese believe that fortune goes up and down. When you are down be conservative, cautious. When you are up, you could afford to take more risks. The up and down cycles can be mapped. Refer to 'Fortune goes in cycles' [风水轮流转] *fēngshuǐlúnliú zhuàn* (refer to proverb No. 67).

216. 'Ambushed on ten sides' [十面埋伏] *shímiàn-máifú*. Totally surrounded, ambushed

217. 'The reality wins over vigorous argument' [事实胜于雄辩] *shìshí shèngyú xióngbiàn*. Actions speak louder than words.

218. 'Over a long period we know a person's heart' [事久见人心] *shìjiǔjiànrénxīn*. Comes from the saying 'Over a long distance we know a horse's stamina, over a long period we know a person's heart' [路遥知马力, 事久见人心]. The test of time reveal a person's inner desires.

219. 'In this world there exists no task that is difficult, the only concern is whether there are determined people' [世上无难事，只怕有心人] *shìshàng wúnánshì-zhǐpà yǒuxīnrén*. When there is a will there is a way.

220. 'Leave some sentiments with your hands' [手下留情] *shǒuxiàliúqíng*. To have mercy.

221. 'Wait for the rabbit under a tree' [守株待兔] *shǒuzhū-dàitù*. A farmer once caught a rabbit without any effort; that was when the rabbit killed itself by bashing onto a tree accidentally while running. Since then the farmer waited for the next rabbit to 'commit suicide'. The proverb highlights the futility of waiting naïvely for something to happen.

222. 'May you live as long as Mount Nan' [寿比南山] *shòubǐ-nánshān*. A common wish to elderly celebrating his birthday. (Used in speeches or advertisement to congratulate birthdays of elderly people. Refer to p. 305).

223. 'Both pipes going down simultaneously' [双管齐下] *shuāngguǎnqíxià*. Accelerating the process by operating with more than one means, used often in business or politics.

224. 'When the water recedes, the rock is exposed' [水落石出] *shuǐluò-shíchū*. The reality becomes evident when the masks are removed.

225. 'Trickling water eventually creates a hole in a hard rock' [水滴石穿] *shuǐdīshíchuān*. Highlighting the importance of small but persistent forces.

226. 'When the water level rises, the boat goes up' [水涨船高] *shuǐzhàng-chuángāo*. Things improve accordingly when the general situation improves.

227. 'Scooping out the moon from (its reflection) the water' [水中捞月] *shuǐzhōnglāoyuè*. Used to describe a totally naïve or unrealistic idea.

228. 'Conveniently lead away the goat' [顺手牵羊] *shùnshǒu-qiānyáng*. Normally refer to stealthily taking away certain items. In military strategy it involves exploitation of the enemy's imperfection to gain advantage. The benefits might not be material gain; it could be intelligence, loyalty or an overall improvement of strategic position or strength. This is normally done by stealth, without anyone noticing – one of the 36 stratagems (refer to p. 236).

229. 'To escape from the jaws of death' [死里逃生] *sǐlǐtáoshēng*.

230. 'Divided into four and split into five' [四分五裂] *sìfēn-wǔliè*. Usually referring to totally fragmented or divided group of people or opinion—hopelessly disunited.

231. 'To change according to time and circumstances' [随机应变] *sujī-yīngbiàn*. Flexibility, adaptability.

232. 'To harm others so as to benefit oneself' [损人利己] *sǔnrén-lìjǐ*. To benefit oneself at the expense of others.

233. 'How easy it is to talk in theory' [谈何容易] *tánhéróngyì*. Normally referring to things that are not easily achieved in practice.

234. 'The colour changes when the tiger is mentioned' [谈虎色变] *tánhǔsèbiàn*. Referring normally to something threatening or terrifying.

235. 'A transient appearance of the flower, "tánhuā"' [昙花一现] *tánhuāyīxiàn*. This plant only flowers once in a blue moon, and for only a few hours, referring to something that comes rarely and goes away quickly.

236. 'Lift the heart and suspend the gall bladder' [提心吊胆] *tíxīndiàodǎn*. Extremely nervous and scared.

237. 'Enduring as long as the sky and last as long as the earth' [天长地久] *tiāncháng-dìjiǔ*. Used to describe enduring or everlasting event, or everlasting love.

238. 'Flowers from Heaven falling all over the place' [天花乱坠] *tiānhuā luǎnzhuì*. Description of exaggerated and highly improbable events, amounting to 'bull-shitting'.

239. 'The talents endowed to me by Heaven must be useful' [天生我才必有用] *tiān shēng wǒ cái bìyǒu yòng*. A common phrase used to highlight the fact that everyone is useful in society.

240. 'God does not provide any road leading to a dead end' [天无绝人之路] *tiān wú juérén zhī lù*. A common phrase used to urge people not to give up. Rather than being fatalistic, be positive, as there is always a way out.

241. 'All the crows in this world are equally black' [天下乌鸦一样黑] *tiānxià wūyā yīyàng hēi*. Normally refer to negative impressions of association with crooks or undesirable elements.

242. 'There is unpredictable wind and clouds in the sky' [天有不测风云] *tiān yǒu bùcè fēngyún*. This is commonly used to highlight unpredictability of events in life, and the need to accept and prepare for this reality. This saying is often used together with 'A man has his fortune changing from morning to evening' [人有旦夕祸福] *rén yǒu dànxì huòfú* (refer to proverb No. 193).

243. 'God's favourite child' [天之骄子] *tiānzhījiāozǐ*. Referring to someone born with a silver spoon.

244. 'Lure the tiger to leave the mountain' [调虎离山] *tiāohǔlíshān*. Tiger refers to a strong enemy, while mountain refers to his natural habitat or environment favourable to him. The mission is to get the tiger out of his natural habitat. This can be done by diversion, seduction or other tactics—one of the 36 stratagems (refer to p. 237).

245. 'Iron face with no private deals' [铁面无私] *tiěmiànwúsī*. Someone totally impartial and incorruptible.

246. 'Hearing but not listening' [听而不闻] *tīng'érbùwén*.

247. 'Suffering from the same illness, having sympathy for each other' [同病相怜] *tóngbìng xiānglián*. Mutual feelings and sympathy.

248. 'Sharing both the sweetness as well as bitterness' [同甘共苦] *tónggān-gòngkǔ*. For better or for worse.

249. 'Coming to an end together' [同归于尽] *tóngguīyújìn*. Perish together, destruction for all.

250. 'Living together, dying together' [同生共死] *tóngshēng-gòngsǐ*. This refers to the spirit of comradeship, for better or for worse.

251. 'Stealing on work and short changed on material' [偷工减料] *tōugōng-jiǎnliào*. Cheat on product quality, cut corners.

252. 'Steal the beam and change the column' [偷梁换柱] *tōuliánghuànzhù*. The beam and the column remains the main thrust of a house. Altering them however does not change the outward appearance. Refers to structural change without creating suspicion—one of the 36 stratagems (p. 238).

253. 'Get rid of the old, out with something new' [推陈出新] *tuichén-chūxīn*. Fresh product, new idea or people.

254. 'Dragging through mud and water' [拖泥带水] *tūonidàishuǐ*. Not clear-cut, indecisive.

255. 'To repair the gate only after the sheep is lost' [亡羊补牢] *wángyáng-bǔláo*. Referring to action taken after the event, when it is too late.

256. 'Besiege the state of Wei to rescue the state of Zhao' [围魏救赵] *wéiwèi-jiùzhào*. Diverting the enemy's resources by forcing it to defend another place under siege—one of the 36 stratagems (refer to p. 235).

257. 'Danger lies between morning and evening hours' [危在旦夕] *wéizàidànxī*. Imminent danger; could collapse any moment.

258. 'To know the end results before being forecasted' [未卜先知] *wèibu- xiānzhī*. As anticipated.

259. 'Wishing the son to be a dragon' [望子成龙] *wàngzǐchénglóng* Hoping that the son be outstanding or successful.

260. 'To patch up the roof before it rains' [未雨绸缪] *wèiyǔ-chóumóu*. Be prepared.

261. 'Listen to one, could deduce ten' [闻一知十] *wényī-zhīshí*. Able to understand from little information gathered.

262. 'Does not feel ashamed when he asks his heart' [问心无愧] *wènxīnwúkuì*. Have a totally clear conscience. A phrase commonly used by people who wish to state that they are honest to themselves and to their conscience.

263. 'I move, I operate in my own ways' [我行我素] *wǒxíngwǒsù*. Usually refer to people who stick to their own ways of doing things.

264. 'There could be no waves without wind blowing' [无风不起浪] *wúfēngbùqǐlàng*. An idiom which indicates that there is always a reason for things to be in a certain situation. Things do not happen on their own.

265. 'There being no opening which it cannot get into' [无孔不入] *wúkǒng-bùrù*. Something that permeates everywhere.

266. 'No crevice to penetrate in' [无隙可乘] *wúxi-kěchèng*. No loophole to exploit.

267. 'Did not intend to plant the willow trees but the trees have grown to provide shade' [无心插柳柳成荫] *wúxīn chāliǔ liǔchéngyīn*. Comes from the saying 'Intended to plant flowers but the flowers did not blossom, did not intend to plant willow trees but the trees have grown to provide shade' [有意栽花花不发, 无心插柳柳成荫]. This is often quoted when the intended outcome is not as expected or planned.

268. 'No shadow or trace' [无影无踪] *wúyǐng-wúzōng*. Used to describe a person or event that vanishes or disappears without a trace.

269. 'Fabricating something out of nothing' [无中生有] *wúzhōng-shēngyǒu*. Creating credible illusions, false images or rumours; also used as a military or political strategy —one of the 36 stratagems (refer to p. 235).

270. 'Those at fifty steps away laughing at those at a hundred steps' [五十步笑百步] *wǔshíbù xiào bǎi bù*. When the troop is retreating, those at fifty steps are basically in the same position as those at hundred steps, all retreating—Pot is calling the kettle black.

271. 'Becoming natural through habits' [习惯成自然] *xíguàn-chéngzìrán*. Once a habit is formed it comes naturally.

272. 'Respect the silk garment first, then respect the person' [先敬羅衣后敬人] *xiānjìngluóyī hòujìngrén*. When a person is not known, others tend to judge him by his attire and appearance, before they get to know him better. This highlights the importance of the first impression and presentation.

273. 'Strike first to gain the upper hand' [先下手为强] *xiānxià-shǒuwéiqiáng*. Emphasise on the importance of controlling the situation early, before things get out of hand. (Usually followed by 'Strike late and you will be in disaster' [后下手遭殃] *hòu xiàshǒu zāoyāng* (refer to proverb 94).

274. 'Compliment each other' [相辅相成] *xiāngfu-xiāngchéng*. Refer to people or situations that support each other.

275. 'Lots of people know me, but how many are in a position to know my heart' [相识满天下, 知心能几人] *xiāngshì mǎntiānxià, zhīxīn néng jǐrén*.

276. 'When small funds do not go out, big fortunes do not in' [小财不出, 大财不进] *xiǎocái bùchū dàcái bùjìn*. This is a common phrase amongst businessmen. Small funds are

required to cultivate network, before big funds could be acquired.

277. 'With care one can steer a ship for ten thousand years' [小心驶得万年船] *xiǎoxīn shǐde wànnián chuán*. This is a commonly used phrase to advise people to be careful, be constantly on the alert, and strive for long term benefits rather than immediate gains.

278. 'Hidden knife behind a smiling face' [笑里藏刀] *xiàolǐcángdāo*. Used to describe an apparently friendly but treacherous person—one of the 36 stratagems. This highlights the need to be alert for confidence tricksters, as well as a whole range of people who win over the confidence of customers' while hiding their dangerous intentions (refer to p. 236).

279. 'Cleanse the ears to listen attentively' [洗耳恭听] *xǐ'ěrgōngtīng*. Referring to someone listening attentively.

280. 'The heart is convinced, so is the mouth' [心服口服] *xīnfú-kǒufú*. Totally convinced.

281. 'Willing in heart and spirit' [心甘情愿] *xīngān-qíngyuàn*. Referring to someone acting on his own free will, rather than being coerced.

282. 'The heart is cruel and the hands ruthless' [心狠手辣] *xīnhènshǒulà*. Depicting someone heartless, cruel and ruthless.

283. 'The heart is panicky and the mind confused [心慌意乱] *xīnhuāngyìluàn*. Panicked and confused.

284. 'The heart is dispirited and the mind lazy' [心灰意懒] *xīnhuīyìlǎn*. Referring to someone utterly disappointed and has given up.

285. 'As if a knife is piercing through his heart' [心如刀割] *xīnrúdāogē*. An extremely painful sensation or emotion, a heartfelt painful event.

286. 'The heart is entangled like hemp' [心乱如麻] *xīnluǎn-rúmá.* Extremely unsettled state of mind.

287. 'The heart is like dead ashes' [心如死灰] *xīnrú-sǐhuī.* Usually refer to one's emotion, being totally dispirited and emotionally 'dead'.

288. 'Two hearts reflecting or impressing on each other' [心心相印] *xīnxīn-xiāngyìn.* Common phrase used to congratulate newly wed couples (refer to p. 306).

289. 'Create the impression of weakness when you are weak, create doubts where it is already doubtful' [虚者虚之, 疑中生疑] *xūzhěxūzhī yízhōngshēngyí.* When the defence of a city is poor and the surrounding enemy is strong, try to deceive the enemy by opening the door wide, give the impression that the enemy could be ambushed if they go in. Refer to 'Creating an illusion of an unguarded, vacated city' [空城计] *kōngchéngjì,* one of the 36 stratagems (p. 239).

290. 'There is no limit to learning' [学无止境] *xuéwú-zhǐjìng.* A common phrase, used in a wide range of situations.

291. 'Delivering charcoal in the thick of snow' [雪中送炭] *xuězhōng-sòngtàn.* Helping others in difficult circumstances or hardship.

292. 'A little spark could start a fire that burns the entire bushland' [星星之火可以燎原] *xīngxingzhīhuǒ kěyǐ liáoyuán.* Do not underestimate the potential destruction that a seemingly petty problem can cause.

293. 'High spirit and happy' [兴高采烈] *xìnggāo-cǎiliè.* Reflecting a sense of happiness and joy.

294. 'Hollow sentiments, false intentions' [虚情假意] *xūqíng-jiǎyì.* Describing someone totally insincere.

295. 'Pulling the seedlings to help it grow' [揠苗助长] *yàmiáo-zhùzhǎng.* Doing something without understanding why. Stupidity and ridiculous efforts

296. 'The speaker may not mean it, but the listener takes it to heart' [言者无意, 听者有心] *yánzhěwúyì, tīngzhěyǒuxīn*. A saying to warn people not to speak without much thought, especially when words can be misinterpreted.

297. 'Sharp eyes and quick hands' [眼明手快] *yǎnmíng-shǒukuài*. Someone alert, sharp and fast reacting.

298. 'Fallen leaves return to their roots' [叶落归根] *yèluòguīgēn*. Referring to things or people returning to their original source or place.

299. 'Maintain the army for a thousand days, though they may be deployed for a short critical time' [养兵千日, 用兵一时] *yǎngbīng qiānrì, yòngbīng yīshí*. This highlights the importance of maintaining the military, and the need to be ready and prepared for any eventuality.

300. 'An inch of time, an inch of gold; it is hard to buy the inch of time with the inch of gold' [一寸光阴一寸金, 寸金难买寸光阴] *yī cùn guāngyīn yīcùnjīn, cǔnjīn nánmǎi cùnguāngyīn*. Highlights the value of time.

301. 'Ticked off with the stroke of a brush' [一笔勾销] *yībǐ-gōuxiāo*. Normally referring to forget what has happened, let bygone be bygone.

302. 'One sings and the other harmonises' [一唱一和] *yīchàng-yīhé*. Referring to two people cooperating or acting in unison.

303. 'Untainted by a spec of dust' [一尘不染] *yīchenbùrǎn*. Pure and clean, uncontaminated.

304. 'Smooth sailing' [一帆风顺] *yīfānfēngshùn*. Used often when sending someone off, wishing him a safe journey.

305. 'Killing two birds with one arrow' [一箭双雕] *yījiàn-shuāngdiāo*. Killing two birds with one stone.

306. 'A horse coming to the fore' [一马当先] *yīmǎ-dāngxiān*. To lead or being the first to thrust forward.

307. 'Not willing to pull out one hair' [一毛不拔] *yīmáo-bùbá*. Referring to a miser, not willing to spend one cent.

308. 'A single cry that startles and impresses everyone' [一鸣惊人] *yīmíng-jīngrén*. Instant success, leading to immediate fame.

309. 'A year's plan starts in spring' [一年之计在于春] *yīnián zhījì zàiyú chūn*. It is important to plan out the year's activity early in spring time (refer to proverb No. 311).

310. 'As poor as being thoroughly 'cleaned out' [一贫如洗] *yīpín-rúxǐ*. Totally broke.

311. 'Planning for the day starts in the morning' [一日之计在于晨] *yīrì zhījì zàiyú chén*. Highlights the importance of planning for the day early in the morning (Proverb No. 309).

312. 'A promise is worth a thousand pieces of gold' [一诺千金] *yīnuòqiānjīn*. The value of credibility.

313. 'Be equally kind to everyone seen' [一视同仁] *yīshì-tóngrén*. Treat everyone equally, without any special favour.

314. 'Capturing everything with one scoop' [一网打尽] *yīwǎng-dǎjìn*. Netting everything, nothing escapes. Capture the whole group.

315. 'With deep feelings always' [一往情深] *yīwǎng-qíngshēn*. Referring to deep affection.

316. 'A word spoken cannot be retrieved by the fast horse' [一言既出, 驷马难追] *yīyán jíchū, sìmǎ nánzhuī*. These points to the importance of thinking carefully before speaking. Once a word is spoken intentionally or unintentionally, it is hard to be recalled. Refer to 'Think thrice before acting' [三思而行] *sānsīhòuérxíng*.

317. 'Once verbally agreed, it is confirmed' [一言为定] *yīyán-wéidìng*. In dealing with the Chinese, 'Gentlemen's agreement' or words of honour are important. Sometimes verbal agreement based on good faith forms the basis of solid development. Nevertheless it is still important to have legal documents signed nowadays.

318. 'Unwilling to leave, wanting to hang on' [依依不舍] *yīyi-bùshě*. Usually referring to unwilling to bid farewell or depart dear ones.

319. 'Drawing a gourd from a similar sample' [依样画葫芦] *yīyànghuáhúlú*. Referring to people who imitate, or follow a precedence.

320. 'Set oneself as an example' [以身作则] *yǐshēn-zuòzé*. This is an important concept in Chinese psyche.

321. 'A tooth for a tooth' [以牙还牙] *yǐyá -huányá*. An eye for an eye.

322. 'Punish one to warn a hundred' [以一警百] *yǐyī-jǐngbǎi*. Punish one to serve as a warning and deterrent to others.

323. 'Relax and wait for events to develop' [以逸待劳] *yǐyidàiláo*. When the enemy is already under siege; relax and wait for the situation to wear them out—one of the 36 stratagems (refer to p. 235).

324. 'When you drink the water, think of the source' [饮水思源] *yǐnshuǐ-sīyuán*. A common phrase used to remind people not to forget those who have helped them in their life.

325. 'Bring a wolf into the house' [引狼入室] *yǐnlángrùshì*. Knowingly or unknowingly bring in an unwelcome or dangerous element into our midst.

326. 'Money could get the devils to work the mill' [有钱能使鬼推磨] *yǒuqián néng shǐ guǐtuīmó*. This is often cited when money 'works' wonders. It also shows the importance of using money where it is effective.

327. 'Leisurely and carefree, not a worry in the world' [悠哉游哉] *yōuzāi- yóuzāi*.

328. 'Has the eye without the eyeball' [有眼无珠] *yǒuyánwúzhū*. Unable to recognise an important personality.

329. 'What you need you would have' [应有尽有] *yīngyǒu-jìnyǒu*. To have everything necessary.

330. 'Brave but lacks tactics' [有勇无谋] *yǒuyǎng-wúmóu*. Used to describe a person, brave but acts without any plan or strategy.

331. 'When there is a will there is a way' [有志者事竟成] *yǒuzhìzhě shìjìngchéng*. Frequently used words of encouragement, to urge someone not to give up.

332. 'An un-faceted jade does not become a gem' [玉不琢不成器] *yùbùzhuò bùchéngqì*. People need education, training and discipline to become valuable.

333. 'When you are prepared you could averts peril' [有备无患] *yǒubèi-wúhuàn*. Be prepared, just in case.

334. 'When injustice and blame are revenged with more injustice and blame, when will the cycle of recrimination ends?' [冤怨相报何时了?] *yuānyuàn xiāngbào héshíliǎo*. Statement often made when trying to settle with long feuds between rival parties or nations. Often cited by Buddhists as part of their efforts not to harm any life.

335. 'No argument with the world' [与世无争] *yúshì-wúzhēng*. Referring to peace loving, contended person with a placid manner, not wanting to argue or fight with anyone.

336. 'Intend to capture someone, yet release him on purpose' [欲擒故纵] *yùqíngùzòng*. This is a war of attrition. It involves 'Exhaust the enemy's energy, dim his fighting spirit' [累其气力, 消其斗志] *lèiqíqìlì, xiāoqídòuzhì*. Should the strategy succeed, the eventual battle will be much easier, with fewer casualties—one of the 36 stratagems (refer to p. 237).

337. 'Make friends with those far away, attack those who are near' [远交近攻] *yuǎnjiāo-jìngōng*. This is often used in marketing. In terms of logistics it is much easier to attack a place nearby than a place far away. This is a strategy to attack those who are near or within capability, while appeasing those further away, to prevent those forming alliances, one of the 36 stratagems (refer to p. 237).

338. 'Water from a distance is not useful to save a nearby fire' [远水难救近火] *yuǎnshuǐ nánjiù jìnhuǒ*. Resources difficult to access are useless to solve an urgent problem. Comes from the saying 'Water from a distance is not useful to save a nearby fire, a relative living faraway is not as good as someone living in the neighbourhood' [远水难救近火, 远亲不如近邻]. In times of urgent need, a relative living far away is not able to give immediate help a neighbour could.

339. 'Blame yourself as you would blame others, forgive others as you would forgive yourself' [责人之心责己, 恕己之心恕人] *zérén zhīxīn zéjǐ, shùjǐ zhīxīn shùrén*. This even-handed approach is often contrary to normal practice.

340. 'Able to figure out the awaiting date' [指日可待] *zhǐrì-kědài*. Something hopeful and imminent

341. 'Admonish the Japonica while pointing at the mulberry' [指桑骂槐] *zhǐsāng màhuái*. Very often the enemy suffers psychologically when they are inferred, even though the words are not directed at them'. This is one of the 36 stratagems (refer to p. 238).

342. 'Theorising military strategies on paper' [纸上谈兵] *zhǐshàng-tánbīng*. Commonly used to describe people who have little idea of practical realities. Also refer to untested or unproven ideas or theories.

343. 'Deceiving oneself as well as others' [自欺欺人] *zìqī-qīrén*.

344. 'Strengthen oneself, become increasingly self reliant' [自强不息] *zìqiángbùxī*. Constantly striving to improve.

345. 'Things happen naturally' [自然而然] *zìránn'érrán*. Let event takes its own course, used when situation should not be coerced, it will happen as a matter of course, naturally.

346. 'Self interests and self gains' [自私自利] *zìsī-zìlì*. Describing someone utterly selfish.

347. 'Falling into a trap by himself' [自投罗网] *zìtóu-luówǎng*. Normally not requiring much effort by the pursuer.

348. 'Self sacrifice' [自我牺牲] *zìwǒ-xīshēng*. A much honoured virtue.

349. 'Killing or destroying each other' [自相残杀] *zìxiāng-cánshā*.

350. 'A penetrating spear versus an impenetrable armour' [自相矛盾] *zìxiāng-máodùn*. A salesman was selling a spear which he claims could penetrate anything. At the same time he sells an armour that he claims is impenetrable by anything. These claims are contradictory.

351. 'Doing something wrong himself and suffer the consequences' [自作自受] *zìzuò-zìshòu*. Referring to someone creating unnecessary problems for himself.

352. 'Three in the morning and four in the evening' [朝三暮四] *zhāosān- mùsì*. Playing fast and loose, tricks or swindles.

353. 'Get rid of the roots to rid the weeds' [斩草除根] *zhāncǎo-chúgèn*. Thoroughly—destroying the enemy completely, including getting rid of any offspring. From 'weeding without removing the roots, weeds grow again in spring' [斩草不除根, 春风吹又生].

354. 'Know the person, know his face, but does not know his heart' [知人知面不知心] *zhīrén zhīmiàn bùzhīxīn*. Comes from the saying 'Draw a dragon, a tiger, it is difficult to draw the bones; know the person, know his face, but does not know his heart' [画龙画虎难画骨, 知人知面不知心].

355. 'Taking a deer as a horse' [指鹿为马] *zhǐlùwéimǎ*. An emperor once pointed to a deer and called it a horse; his officials just agreed that it was. It points to the ridiculous state of affair that people just agree to authorities without questioning.

356. 'Totally loyal and devoted' [忠心耿耿] *zhōngxīn-gěnggěng*.

357. 'Loyal statement hurts the ear' [忠言逆耳] *zhōngyán-nì'ěr*. Truth hurts. Those who need help are the least likely to listen or accept the truth.

358. 'Escape is the best strategy' [走为上计] *zǒuwéishāngjì.*
When all else fail, escape is the best policy—one of the 36
stratagems (refer to p. 239).

359. 'Sit and not work would eat up a whole mountain of
reserves' [坐吃山空] *zuòchī-shānkōng.* Expenditure without income would deplete resources.

360. 'Being uneasy sitting or standing' [坐立不安] *zuòlì-bù'ān.*
Restless, unsettled.

361. 'Observing the sky from a well' [坐井观天] *zuòjing-
guāntiān.* Having a very limited outlook or view point
—tunnel vision.

362. 'Sit to enjoy the results of other's hard work' [坐享其成]
zuòxiǎngqíchéng. In reality reaping rewards without any
effort.

363. 'Tie itself into a self-made cocoon' [作茧自缚] *zuòjiǎn-zìfù.*
To get entangled by one's own making.

364. 'Sometimes threatening and sometimes benevolent' [作威
作福] *zuòwēi-zuòfú.* Referring to someone showing off or
abusing his power.

365. 'Thieves live in fear of exposure' [做贼心虚] *zuòzéixīnxū.*
Thieves in this context include people who cheat on others,
or do not do things ethically.

Numerous websites are available on Chinese proverbs, including:

Chinese classic story—parable in Chinese and English translation:
www.chinapage.com/story/story.html
Quotation from Chinese classics
www.chinapage.com/quote/quote.html
List of Chinese proverbs
www.en2.wikipedia.org/wiki/Chinese_proverbs#Mandarin_proverbs

CHINESE LITERATURE

Ethnic Chinese with background in the language would be able to read, to various degrees, books, magazines, or browse the Internet in Chinese. However texts written in classical Chinese 文言文 *wényánwén* require a certain level of training in the language.

The most competent would indeed read Chinese classics in 文言文 *wényanwén*, appreciating to the full the meanings and nuances. They would have no problem in using the 365 proverbs listed above.

Some would be able to use the proverbs listed, and certainly understand them when used, or be able to find out the meanings from dictionaries. They could read Chinese classics but would rather read texts transposed into modern Chinese [白话文] *báihuàwén*. This is particularly so for difficult text such as yìjīng (p. 398).

For those who have limited knowledge of written Chinese their source of Chinese literature would be in English. Though they might have heard of some of the proverbs they would be wondering what it all means. Nevertheless it is never too late to learn Chinese language or culture, be it in Chinese or English. Translations tend to differ. This is evident when one reads different versions of Lǎozǐ's Dàodéjīng, or the Confucius texts.

In reality one seldom quotes from the literature in everyday life, especially when the social circle does not appreciate them.

QUOTABLE QUOTES

When situation arises it is nevertheless relevant to quote from the classics. It is relevant to bear in mind that these quotes were made centuries ago, when conditions were substantially different. The only element that remains unchanged is human nature. The quotations below from famous classics are grouped according to their applications whenever possible.

EDUCATION

For centuries education has been central to Chinese tradition and family lives. The Imperial examination for civil service was introduced about 1,500 years ago (p. 182), enlisting the best and brightest for top government jobs.

The following saying depicts the mood of scholars.

'*Nobody bothers when you study for ten years next to the window, once you are successful the whole world would know!*' [十年窗下无人问, 一举成名天下知].

Indeed education or the lack of it was the distinct parameter that separated the ruling class from the ruled. Education henceforth provided a proven pathway to good job, fame and fortune. No other pursuit provides such hopes, aspirations and opportunities.

The Chinese have a high respect or reverence for scholars. Few people, not even billionaires or film stars, could command the same degree of respect.

The Confucian and Dàoist preaching of self-cultivation further emphasise the importance of scholarship. The often-used term 'cultivated gentleman' [君子] *jūnzǐ*, an ideal personality, is someone educated, culturally refined, able to overcome some of the human weaknesses. He would be highly respected by the people. Even today, scholars as well as teachers are held in high regards amongst the Chinese community. The Confucianists regard education as an effective means to address and solve social-political, as well as inter-personal problems.

Chinese families are familiar with the story of the mother of a great Chinese scholar Mèngzǐ [孟子] (p. 164), who relocated her house three times to provide the environment for learning. When Mèngzǐ was a young boy, they lived next to a graveyard. Mèngzǐ would play games imitating the ceremonial and burial rites they often saw. His mother then decided to move, they went to a house next to the marketplace. There Mèngzǐ imitated the behaviour of cunning business practice, bartering and trading, haggling over every bit. His mother decided that this was not what she liked and moved once again, this time close to a school. When Mèngzǐ was in the environment of students reciting texts, he too, wanted to study.

Another story relates to her teaching her son a lesson. One day when she was weaving a piece of cloth[24] she saw her son playing truant, sneaking home. She called him over, ripped off the almost finished piece, whereby the son was horrified by so much wasted energies and efforts; she explained to him that if he does not complete his studies, he would end up being the same as the strip of ripped cloth—good for nothing!

It is note worthy that an encyclopaedia was produced in the 14th century, during the reign of Yǒng Lè [永乐], born as Zhū Dì [朱棣], (1360-1424) (p. 178): The Yong Le Encyclopaedia [永乐大典] *Yǒnglè Dàdiǎn*, an encyclopaedia of some 22,877 volumes, compiled by about 3,000 people, totalling some 380 million words was produced (pp. 146, 178).

Sayings that deal with education abound. Examples include:

'A*s you eat till an old age you learn till an old age.*' [吃到老学到老] There is always something to learn no matter how old you are.

'*Pay attention to the intent and meaning when you read, a word is worth a thousand pieces of gold.*' [读书须用意，一字值千金].

'*Knowledge is when one knows the limitation of his knowledge.*' [知之为知之，不知为不知，是知也] Confucius—The Analects.

---

[24] In those days cloth was hand woven, literally strand by strand, requiring a lot of time, precision and patience.

'*Be humble enough to ask, seek knowledge.*' [不耻下问] Confucius—The Analects.

'*In the company of two others, there is always someone who could be my teacher. Select what is good and learn from it. Whatever is not good correct it.*' [三人行必有我师焉. 择其善者而学之, 其不善者而改之] Confucius—The Analects.

'*He who leans without thinking is lost; he who thinks without learning is in danger.*' [学而不思则罔, 思而不学则殆] Confucius—The Analects.

'*When students are not strictly taught, the teacher has not put in enough effort.*' [教不严, 师之惰] Three Worded Text.

'*The mother of Mèngzǐ, chose her neighbourhood.*' [昔孟母, 择邻处] Three Worded Texts.

'*Isn't it a pleasure to speak of learning and its application?*' [学而时习之, 不亦说乎?] Confucius—The Analects

'*There is no limit to learning*' [学无止境] Chinese proverb.

'*Learn under a single person, used on ten thousand people*' [学在一人之下, 用在万人之上].

'*Even though the family is poor, one still studies unceasingly.*' [家虽贫, 学不辍].

'*If a person does not learn, he would not have the sense of righteousness.*' [人不学, 不知义] Three Worded Text.

'*Everything else is inferior, only learning is superior.*' [万般皆下品, 唯有读书高].

'Bringing up a child without educating him is the fault of the father.' [养不教, 父之过] Three Worded Texts.

'A piece of jade if left uncarved, does not become a gem.' [玉不琢, 不成器] Three Worded Texts.

'If a person does not learn when he is young, what could he do when he gets older?' [幼不学, 老何为] Three Worded Texts.

'When the son doesn't learn, she cut off the piece of painstakingly woven cloth.' [子不学, 断机杼] The Worded Texts.

'It is not right that children do not receive education.' [子不学, 非所宜] Three Worded Texts.

'There are three things in learning, the heart needs to be there, the eyes need to be there, the mouth needs to be there. If the heart is not there the eyes wouldn't read carefully, if the heart and eyes are not there, reading would not lead to memory, even if it does, not for long. Amongst the three things, it is most important that the heart be there.' by Zhū Xī [读书有三到, 谓心到, 眼到, 口到. 心不在此, 则眼不看仔细, 心眼即不专一, 却只漫浪诵读, 决不能记, 记不能久也. 三到之中, 心到最急. —— 朱熹]

'Our lives are limited, but knowledge is unlimited.' by Zhuāngzǐ. [吾生也有涯, 而知也无涯. —— 庄子]

The importance of education in Chinese psyche cannot be over-emphasised. It is not uncommon for parents to sell off their business or property, borrow from friends or relatives, to finance the education of their children. This is particularly so for higher education, especially studying overseas!

Consistent with the spirit of the mother of Mèngzǐ, it is not uncommon for parents to buy a house in a good school zone; the choice of a school zone for the children overrides other personal choices, such as beach front, good scenery, easy access to work, etc. Education is still the pathway for social mobility. This is particularly so for migrants in a new country, where relevant training provides access and acceptability to the local community.

This emphasis on excellence in education is reflected in better than average performance amongst many ethnic Chinese students in high schools, colleges and universities. In many occasions their academic achievements seem to be significantly higher than their population percentage.

Government

There is a huge collection of quotations pertaining to politics and government. They include Confucius (p. 159), Lǎo Zǐ (p. 160), etc, some of which are listed under philosophy. We present here quotations from Mèngzǐ (p. 164), depicting his audience Mèngzǐ had with the Emperor (all powerful in those days), the wisdom is still relevant today.

'If your majesty administer a just and humane government, it would result in fewer criminals to be punished, minimal taxes to be collected; the fields would he ploughed deeper and easier for planting. The strong and healthy people would in their leisure be involved in self-cultivation, in matters such as filial piety, sibling affection, loyalty and trust. If they engage in these activities, they would be able to look after their parents and families; outside the family they would better serve their elders and superiors. These people will be able to defeat the kingdoms of Qin and Chu.' Mèngzǐ [王如施仁政于民, 省刑罚, 薄税, 深耕易耨; 壮者以暇日修其孝悌忠信, 入以事其父兄, 出以事其长上, 可使制梃以撻秦楚之坚甲利兵矣!]

231

'Those rulers tax so much of their people's time to the extent that they are unable to attend to the field so as to support their parents. Parents starve and freeze, families fall apart. These rulers actually trap and bury their own people. If Your Majesty would come to their aid, who will oppose you? Do not doubt the ancient proverb: 'The benevolent man has no opponent.' Mèngzǐ [彼夺其民時, 使不得耕耨以养其父母, 父母冻饿, 兄弟妻子离散. 彼陷溺其民, 王往而征之, 夫谁與王敵!' 故曰:『仁者无敵.』 王请勿疑.]

A little further, the conversation turned to:

The king asked: 'What is the difference between inaction and inability?' Mèngzǐ replied: 'If you were to leap over the North Sea taking Mt. Tai under your arm, obviously you would say: 'I am unable', this is indeed an inability. If you refuse to snap a tree branch for an elder while saying 'I am unable,' this is simply inaction, rather than inability. Not leaping over the North Sea taking Mount Tai does not deny him to be a king amongst kings. Refusing to snap a branch is not a king of kings.' [不为者與不能者之形何以異?' 曰: '挟太山以超北海, 语人曰: 『我不能.』 是诚不能也, 为长者折枝语人曰:『我不能.』 是不为也, 非不能也. 故王之不王, 非挟太山以超北海之类也; 王之不王, 是折枝之类也.]

'Take care of our elders, the common people will do the same for their elders. Nurture our young, the common folks will nurture their young—the kingdom will be held in your palm. The Book of Odes says: His example influenced his wife, reached his siblings, such that he could manage His country and community.' [老吾老, 以及人之老; 幼吾幼, 以及人之幼; 天下可运于掌. 诗云: 『刑于寡妻, 至于兄弟, 以御于家邦.』]

'*Extend your heart to others, and extend sufficient compassion to take care of all those in the four seas. Otherwise you will not even be able to take care of your own wife and children. The ancients surpassed all others by none other than this: Their good deeds extended everywhere and nothing more. Now your have enough compassion for the animals, yet it does not reach the people. Isn't that something?'* [言举斯心加诸彼而已. 故推恩足以保四海, 不推恩无以保妻子; 古之人所以大过人者无他焉, 善推其所为而已矣. 今恩足以及禽兽, 而功不至于百姓者, 独何與?]

'*Weight an object; we would know what is light and heavy. Measure an object we know its long or short. All things are like this, in particular the mind, so would you please measure it, King? Your majesty builds up armament, endanger soldiers, create problems and blame other heads of state. Does this give you pleasure?'* [权, 然后知轻重; 度, 然后知長短, 物皆然, 心为甚. 王请度之. 抑王興甲兵, 危士臣, 构怨于诸侯, 然后快于心與?]

'*Not really, how could I get pleasure out of this? I do it to fulfil my desire'. Mèngzǐ: 'Could we please listen to your desires?' the emperor smiled without giving a reply. Mèngzǐ continued: 'Aren't all your sumptuous meals insufficient for your appetite? Isn't the myriad of colours insufficient for your eyes? Isn't the voice insufficient for your ears? Have you not enough servants to serve you? Your majesty's numerous ministers can certainly get all these things for you, so how can you still want more?'* [王曰: '否. 吾何快于是! 將以求吾所大欲也.' 曰: '王之所大欲, 可得闻與?' 王笑而不言. 曰: '为肥甘不足以口與? 轻不足于礼與? 抑为采色不足视于目與? 声音不足擦于耳與? 便嬖不足使令于前與? 王之诸臣, 皆足以供之. 而王豈为是哉?]

'The king said: 'No, I don't want all these.' 'Then we know what it is you really want,' said Mèngzǐ, 'you want to expand your territory, gain control over Qin and Chu, rule the Middle Kingdom, restrain the four outlying states. To do the things to get what you crave is like climbing a tree to catch fish.' [曰: '否. 吾不为是也.' 曰: '然则王之所大欲, 可知已. 欲辟土地, 朝秦楚, 中国, 而撫四夷也. 以若所为, 求若所欲, 猶緣木而求魚也.']

MILITARY

Numerous works on military strategy were made throughout the centuries. These include

'General description of eight battles set up'	八阵总述
'Interesting strategies in a hundred battles'	百战奇略
'The Thirty-six strategies'	三十六计
'Sunzi's (p. 170) Art of War'	孙子兵法
'Wei Gong's military moves'	卫公兵法辑本
'Wu's military tactics'	吴子兵法
'Zeng Hu military management'	曾胡治兵语录
'Zhu Geliang's (p. 178) military records'	诸葛亮将苑

Most of these are unknown to the west. With the exception of Sūn Zǐ's Art of war, they probably have not been translated into English. We would like to focus on two main sources, the thirty six stratagems and 'The Art of War' [孙子兵法] *sūnzǐ bīngfǎ* by Sūn Zǐ, the military strategist who wrote the book.

Strategies for military applications are equally useful in arenas such as business, divorce, and politics.

THE THIRTY SIX STRATAGEMS

Most of these stratagems were listed in the 365 proverbs (p. 188).

1. 'Deceive the Heavens to cross the ocean' [瞒天过海] *mántiān-guòhǎi*. This involves operations under cover. The enemy is normally not aware of what is happening.

2. 'Besiege the state of Wei to rescue the state of Zhao' [围魏救赵] *wéiwèi-jiùzhào*. Dealing with military is like dealing with water. Water can be directed. It can also be diverted into more than one stream to reduce its impact. This strategy involves diverting the enemy's resources by forcing it to defend another place under siege.

3. 'Killing a person with a borrowed knife' [借刀杀人] *jièdāo-shārén*. This is used when the enemy is well defined, while a third party is still hesitating who to ally with. The strategy involves using the third party to attack the enemy.

4. 'Relax and wait for events to develop' [以逸待劳] *yǐyi-dàiláo*. When the enemy is already under siege, relax and wait for the situation to wear itself out.

5. 'To raid when there is a fire' [趁火打劫] *chènhuǒ-dǎjié*. Striking is most effective when the target or enemy is in disarray.

6. Create noise in the East but attack the West' [声东击西] shēngdōng-jīxī A tactic designed to distract attention prior to attack. The strategy works as long as the enemy's intelligence does not discover it.

7. 'Fabricating something out of nothing' [无中生有] *wúzhōng-shēngyǒu* Creating credible illusions, false images or rumours.

8. 'Secretly reaching Chén Cāng' [暗渡陈仓] *àndùchéncāng*. This comes from a proverb 'be seen to be repairing the Zhan road, secretly reaching Chen Cang'. There were two routes to Chen Cang. The attacker sent men to repair the Zhan road, giving the false impression that this was the route for the attack. While the defender mobilises his forces to defend this

route, the attacker secretly send his army to reach Chen Cang by the other route.

9. 'Watch the fire ablaze across the bank' [隔岸观火] *Gé'àn guānhuǒ*. When the enemy is in disarray, there is no better joy than quietly observing the forces tearing themselves apart from within.

10. 'Hidden knife within a smiling face' [笑里藏刀] *xiàolǐ cángdāo*. This is practised by 'smiling assassins, confidence tricksters, as well as a whole range of people who win over the confidence of customers' while hiding their real intentions.

11. 'Sacrifice a pear to get a plum' [李代桃僵] *lǐdàitáojiāng*. In any warfare there are bound to be casualties, the strategy then is to re-allocate resources, to sacrifice one person or resource for another.

12. 'Conveniently lead away the goat' [顺手牵羊] *shùnshǒu qiānyáng*. The strategy involves exploitation of the enemy's imperfection to gain advantage. The benefits might not be material gains; it could be intelligence, loyalty or an overall improvement of strategic position or strength. This is normally done by stealth, without anyone noticing.

13. 'Beating the grass would scare the snake' [打草惊蛇] *dǎcǎo jīngshé*. Beating the grass, the natural environment of the snake, would result in two outcomes. First of all it would reveal the habitat, i.e. strength and weaknesses of the snake. Secondly it would also warn the snake of the disturbance and impending danger. Unthoughtful attack on the enemy would unnecessarily warn them of imminent danger.

14. 'Borrow a corpse to bring back life [借尸还魂] *jièshīhuánhún*. In this context corpse refer to something otherwise useless, but when craftily used could boost one's position or influence. A classic example is to use the name of a descendant of a deceased popular leader as a front line leader. As

long as the descendant is not powerful in his own right this fits the criteria.

15. 'Lure the tiger to leave the mountain' [调虎离山] *tiáohǔ-líshān*. Tiger refers to a strong enemy, while mountain refers to his natural habitat or environment favourable to him. The mission is to get the tiger out of his natural habitat. This can be done by diversion, seduction or other tactics.

16. 'Intend to capture it, yet release on purpose' [欲擒故纵] *yùqíngùzòng*. This is a war of attrition. It involves pursuing the enemy 'Exhaust the enemy's energy, dim his fighting spirit' [累其气力, 消其斗志] *lèiqíqìlì, xiāoqídòuzhì*. Should the strategy succeed, the eventual battle will be much easier, with fewer casualties (refer to proverb 336, p. 222).

17. 'Throw bricks to attract gems' [抛砖引玉] *pāozhuānyǐnyù*. Gems in this context refer to the overall objective.

18. 'To catch the thieves, arrest the chief [擒贼擒王] *qínzéi qínwáng*. This highlights the importance of dealing with the leader rather than rank and file.

19. 'Pull out the firewood from under the cauldron [釜底抽薪] *fǔdǐ chōuxīn* When the enemy is strong, weaken it by wearing off its support (refer to p. 195).

20. 'Groping fish in troubled waters' [混水摸鱼] *hùnshuǐ-móyú*. This is a classic situation, attack when there is confusion within the enemy territory, where leadership is not clear.

21. 'The cicada shedding off its shell' [金蝉脱壳] *jīnchán tuōké*. This refers to withdrawal from the scene without the enemy or friends' suspicion. This is in contrast to a panic retreat.

22. 'Close the door to catch the thieves' [关门捉贼] *guānmén-zhuōzéi*. When there is only a small group being trapped, they could be surrounded and caught.

23. 'Make friends with those far away, attack those who are near' [远交近攻] *yuǎnjiāo-jìngōng* In terms of logistics it is much easier to attack a place nearby than a place far away.

This is a strategy to attack those who are near or within capability, while appeasing those further away, to prevent them forming alliances. Once that territory is occupied it can be used as a base for further expansion.

24. 'Borrowing a route to attack the country of Guo' [假途伐虢] *jiătúfáguó*. Comes from 左传 *zuǒ zhuàn*, whereby the country of Lu was used as a route to attack the country of Guo, a bigger power. However once Guo was eliminated, Lu lost an ally and was subsequently conquered.

25. 'Changing the beam and the column' [偷梁换柱] *tōuliáng-huánzhù*. The beam and the column remains the main thrust of a house. Changing them however does not change the outward appearance. This refers to structural change without creating suspicion.

26. 'Admonish the Japonica while pointing at the mulberry' [指桑骂槐] *zhǐsāng màhuái*. Very often the enemy suffers psychologically when they are inferred, even though the words of attack are not directed at them'.

27. 'Act silly but not insane' [假痴不颠] *jiǎchībùdiān*. Very often there is little point to disclose one's true strength, to keep the enemy off-guard.

28. 'Pull the ladder after climbing up the house' [上屋抽梯] *shàngwūchōuti*. The strategy involves luring the enemy to a place, then cutting off their supplies.

29. 'Flower blooming on the tree' [树上开花] *shùshàngkāihuā*. This involves creating the impression of strength through situations or circumstances.

30. 'Becoming the host rather than the guest' [反客为主] *fǎnkè-wéizhǔ*. This strategy is a gradual move over a period of time. It involves getting invited as a guest, identifying the host's weakness, seizes the opportunity to take over, as well as consolidation of power.

31. 'Pretty girls strategy' [美人计] *měirénjì*. The term originally comes from another book on military strategy 六韬 *liù tāo*. The use of sexual seduction has been common for a very long time.

32. 'Creating an illusion of an unguarded, vacated city' [空城计] *kōngchéngjì* Create the impression of weakness when you are weak, create doubts where it is already doubtful. When the defence of a city is poor and the surrounding enemy is strong, try deception. Open the door wide; give the impression that the enemy could be ambushed if they go in.

33. 'Create mutual suspicion' [反间计] *fǎnjiānjì* This involves creation of false information through the enemy's spies.

34. 'Self-torture to convince the enemy' [苦肉计] *kǔuròujì*. Normal people would not create self harm. Evidence of torture is therefore an effective weapon used in warfare.

35. 'Create chain reaction' [连环计] *liánhuánjì*. When the enemy is strong it is dangerous to directly challenge it. It is better to create attrition within the enemy to weaken them.

36. 'Escape is the best strategy' [走为上计] *zǒuwéishàngjì*. When all else fail, escape is the best strategy.

孙子兵法

Sūn Zǐ 's Art of War [孙子兵法] *Sūnzǐ bīngfǎ*

Written towards the end of 'Spring and Autumn' period (p. 130), Sūn Zǐ (p. 170) presented his thesis on military strategy, known as the 'Art of War' to the King of Wú [吴], who promptly appointed him a general. He led an army to conquer the Kingdom of Chǔ [楚].

Written 2,500 years ago, the 'Art of War' gave a comprehensive analysis of war strategy. It was certainly the first to highlight the importance of many aspects of military planning and strategy, including the use of spies. The whole thesis is quite short, containing 13 chapters as follows:

Let us look at chapter one, which gives a general overview.

'*Warfare is of vital importance to the State. It is a matter of life and death, survive or perish, something that cannot be ignored. It is governed by five factors, in determining field conditions.*' [兵者, 国之大事, 死生之地, 存亡之道, 不可不察也. 故經之以五, 校之以計, 而索其情].

'*Factors to be considered are The Morality, Heaven, Earth, Command and Techniques.*' [一曰道, 二曰天, 三曰地, 四曰將, 五曰法].

'*Morality unifies the people with the ruler, they willingly live or die together with him. Celestial factors signify yīn-yáng, cold or hot, times and seasons. Terrestrial factors include high or low, far or near, dangerous or easy paths; open area or narrow passes; the chances of life or death. Command stands for the virtues of wisdom, trust, benevolence, courage and discipline. Techniques include marshalling of the army, the ranking of*

240

officers and soldiers, the maintenance of supply lines and the control of military expenditure.' [道者, 令民于上同意者也, 可與之死, 可與之生, 民不詭也. 天者, 阴阳, 寒暑, 時制也. 地者, 高下, 遠近, 險易, 广狹, 死生也. 將者, 智, 信, 仁, 勇, 严也. 法者, 曲制, 官道, 主用也].

'The general who listens to me will be victorious, retain him; he who does not listen to me will fail, remove him.' [將听吾计, 用之必胜, 留之; 將不听吾计, 用之必敗, 去之].

'Warfare is an art of deception. Be seen to be unable, when you are ready to attack; be seen to be inactive when you mobilise your forces; be seen to be far when you are near, be seen to be near when you are far away. Tempt the enemy if he seeks some advantage. Crush him when he is in disarray. Be prepared if he is formidable and solid. Evade him if his force is superior.' [兵者, 诡道也. 故能而示之不能, 用而示之不用, 近而示之远, 远而示之近. 利而诱之, 乱而取之, 实而贝之, 强而避之].

'Provoke him if he gets angry easily. Promote his arrogance if he is humble. Wear him down when he needs to take a rest. Create division if his forces are united. Attack him when he is least prepared, appear where he least expects it. These are military tactics for victory not to be divulged.' [怒而挠之, 卑而骄之, 佚而劳之, 亲而离之, 攻其不备, 出其不意. 此兵家之胜, 不可先传也].

Chapter 3 highlights strategies for attack.

'In military tactics, the best outcome is to take the enemy country intact; to destroy it would not be so good. To capture an entire army would be better than destroying it, to capture an entire regiment, a detachment or a company would be better than destroying them. Hence to fight and conquer every time is not the

best outcome; the best outcome is victory without fighting.' [凡用兵之法, 全国为上, 破国次之; 全军为上, 破军次之; 全旅为上, 破旅次之; 全卒为上, 破卒次之; 全伍为上, 破伍次之. 是故百战百胜, 非善之善也; 不战而屈人之兵, 善之善者也].

'The best tactic is to undermine the enemy's war plans; next in order would be to undermine the enemy's alliances and allies, next would be to attack the enemy in the field; the worst tactic is to besiege cities. Only besiege a city if there is no other option. It takes at least three months to prepare the ordnance, equipment and various infrastructures for war, piling up mounds over the walls take another three months.' [故上兵伐谋, 其次伐交, 其次伐兵, 其下攻城. 攻城之法为不得已. 修橹轒辒, 具器械, 三月而後成, 距闉, 又三月而後已].

'A general unable to control his irritation might launch an assault like swarming ants, one-third of his men could be lost while the town is still not taken. Such are the dangers of a siege. The skilful leader subdues the enemy without fighting; captures their cities without laying siege; conquer their kingdoms without lengthy battles. When his forces are intact he is a force to be reckoned with. His military is still strong while he triumphs. This is the attack stratagem' [将不胜其忿，而蚁附之，杀士三分之一，而城不拔者，此攻之灾也。故善用兵者，屈人之兵而非战也。拔人之城而非攻也，破人之国而非久也，必以全争于天下，故兵不顿，而利可全，此谋攻之法也].

'As a general rule, if our forces are ten times more than the enemy, we surround them, if we are five to one, we attack them; if we are two to one, we divide them. If we are equal in numbers we have to be extra careful, if our numbers are less we should avoid the enemy; if we are inferior in other ways we should flee from the enemy.' [故用兵之法, 十则围之, 五则攻之, 倍则分

之，敌则能战之，少则能逃之，不若则能避之．故小敌之坚，大敌之擒也].

'The general is the bulwark of the State; if the bulwark is sound the State is strong; if the bulwark is defective, the State is weak.' [夫將者，国之辅也．辅周则国必强，辅隙则国必弱].

'There are three ways in which a ruler can bring down his army: ordering the army to advance when he is not aware that they cannot advance, to retreat when he is not aware that they cannot retreat, amounts to gruelling the army. Running an army in the same way as he administers a kingdom, without understanding the specific conditions in the army causes restlessness. Appointing army officers without knowing military principles undermines the confidence of the soldiers.' 故君之所以患于军者三：不知军之不可以进而谓之进，不知军之不可以退而谓之退，是为縻军；不知三军之事，而同三军之政者，则军士惑矣；不知三军之权，而同三军之任].

'But when the army is restless and distrustful, trouble is sure to come from the other feudal princes. This would bring anarchy into the army, and flinging victory away.' [则军士疑矣．三军既惑且疑，则诸侯之难至矣，是谓乱军引胜].

'There are five conditions for victory: He who knows whether it is winnable or not winnable would win. He who could understand the strength of solders would win. He who instils the same aspirations through his rank and file would win. He who prepares himself, rather than speculating wins. An able general operating without interference from his emperor wins.' [故知胜有五：知可以战與不可以战者胜，识众寡之用者胜，上下同欲者胜，以虞待不虞者胜，将能而君不御者胜．此五者，知胜之道也].

'If you know yourself and the enemy well, you are bound to win the battles. If you know yourself but not the enemy, your chances of victory or defeat are equal. If you do not know the enemy or yourself, you will be defeated.' [知己知彼，百战不殆；不知彼而知己，一胜一负；不知彼不知己，每战必殆].

The last chapter deals with the use of spies.

'Marshalling a hundred thousand soldiers through great distances requires heavy expenditure and national resources. Internal and external disturbances result in men dropping off along the way. As many as seven hundred thousand families will need to contribute in their labour. Hostile armies may face each other for years, striving for the victory which could be decided in a single day.' [凡兴师十万，出征千里，百姓之费，公家之奉，日费千金．内外骚动，怠于道路，不得操事者，七十万家．相守数年，以争一日之胜].

'To be unaware of enemy condition so as to save a hundred ounces of gold is the height of inhumanity. He who does so is not a leader, not a servant to his king, and no master of victory. The famous generals and wise leaders who strike and conquer, and achieve more than ordinary men, acquire knowledge beforehand. This prior knowledge cannot be extracted from supernatural spirits; it cannot be obtained or inferred from experience, or deduced by calculation. It can only be obtained from other men.' [而爱爵禄百金，不知敌之情者，不仁之至也．非人之将也，非主之佐也，非胜之主也．故明君贤将，所以动而胜人，成功出于众者，先知也．先知者，不可取于鬼神，不可象于事，不可验于度．必取于人，知敌之情者也].

'Hence the use of spies, of whom there are five types: local spies; internal spies; converted spies; doomed spies; and surviving spies. When all these spies are at work, we know the entire

secret, a gift from divine sources, and a treasure to the Emperor.' [故用间有五: 有因间, 有内间, 有反间, 有死间, 有生间. 五间俱起, 莫知其道, 是谓神纪, 人君之宝也].

'Local spies are recruited from people of a local area; internal spies are officials of the enemy. Converted spies people from the enemy who have joined us; doomed spies are those who could be reported by us back to their masters after they have created some problems; surviving spies are those captured from the enemy camp.' [因间者, 因其乡人而用之. 内间者, 因其官人而用之. 反间者, 因其敌间而用之. 死间者, 为誑事于外, 令吾闻知之, 而傳于敌间也. 生间者, 反报也].

'In the military there is nothing more intimate than spies, no award higher than that given to spies, no business more secretive than that of spies. Spies without integrity would not be useful. Those who are not straightforward and forthright cannot be managed. Those who are not subtle would not obtain the truth.' [故三军之事, 莫亲于间, 赏莫厚于间, 事莫密于间. 非圣智不能用间, 非仁义不能使间, 非微妙不能得间之实. 微哉! 微哉!]

Even though military technology and weaponry has advanced considerably since then, the basic strategy, based on human nature, remains the same. Numerous books have been written on Sūn Zǐ. In addition to military strategy, some authors focus on the application to business and management.[25]

POPULAR READING MATERIALS
There would be numerous other books of interests that could be discussed. The following is the summary of some popular classics,

---

[25] For example, Khoo Kheng-Hor, *Sun Tzu & Management*, Pelanduk Publications, Malaysia 2003.

most of which have already been translated into English. Most of them have a definite impact on the outlook and value judgement of the Chinese in their own ways.

'The True Story of Ah Q' [阿Q正传]

Written in 1921-1922 in Beijing by Lǔ Xùn [鲁迅] (p. 164) with rural countryside after 1911 revolution as the background. *The Story of Ah Q* depicts a homeless, landless, downtrodden labourer, who suffers all sorts of hardship and exploitation. Yet in spite of all this adversities he portrays 'spiritual victory', bragging of his past, dreaming of the future. His weakness and helplessness reflects the dilemma of Chinese people at that time, confronted with realism brought by the West.

'The White Snake Story' [白蛇傳] *Báishézhuàn*

This is a popular tale from the 'Five dynasties period' (p. 143). The White snake was curious about human life and transformed herself into a beautiful girl. She met a young scholar and they fell in love. One day she drank wine and reverted to her original shape …

Càigéntán [菜根谭]

This is a book on 'self cultivation' is written by Hóng Yìngmíng [洪应明] (p. 157), a scholar from the seventeenth century, during the Míng dynasty (p. 146). The book consists of three hundred and sixty 'words of wisdom', some of which are as follows:

'Human sentiment changes all the time, the pathways in life go up and down. When we come across an impasse, it is relevant to know how to retreat; when the going is smooth,

we should remember to make way for others.' (35) [人情反
覆, 世路崎岖. 行不去处, 须知退一步之法: 行得去处,
务加让三分之功].

*'To remain serene in a tranquil environment does not really
attain serenity. To attain serenity in a noisy environment is
real achievement of serenity according to nature. To be
happy in a joyous environment is not real happiness. To be
happy in an adverse environment reflects true happiness, an
expression of his body and soul.'* (88) [静中静非真静, 动处
静得来, 才是性天之静. 乐处乐非真乐, 苦中乐得来, 才
是心体之真机].

*'A heart that harms others is not permissible; a heart on the
alert is indispensable. This is sound advice for those who
ignore the need to be on the alert in a 'survival'
environment. I would rather that others deceive me, rather
than exposing the plot beforehand. This advice is for those
who are excessively on guard and tend to have biased
judgement. Keep these two in mind, and you would be alert
and upright.'* (129) [害人之心不可有, 防人之心不可无,
此戒疏于虑也; 宁受人之欺, 毋逆人之诈, 此警伤于察也,
二语并存精明而浑厚矣].

*'Do not be too mean when you employ people; otherwise you
would drive away those who could help you. Do not be
overjoyed and believe in praises, otherwise you would only
attract those who flatter you, rather than those who tell the
truth.'* (210) [用人不宜克, 刻则思效者去; 交友不宜滥,
滥则贡谀者来].

*'Observe people with unbiased, cool eyes; listen to others
with clear, cool ears, feel with unperturbed emotions, reason*

with a clear head and cool heart.' (206) [冷眼观人, 冷耳听语, 冷情当感, 冷心思理].

'To keep a pair of calm, cold eyes in times of hustle and bustle could avoid unnecessary worries. To retain your passion at heart when you are down and weary would be a source of fun and joy.' (284) [热闹中着一冷眼, 便省许多苦心思; 冷落处存一热心, 便得许多真趣味].

'Creation of the Gods' [封神演义] *fēng shén yǎnyì*

Written by Xú Zhōnglín [徐钟琳] from the Yuán dynasty (p. 145) is one of the most popular mythical classics. It begins with the pilgrimage of King Zhōu 周, Shāng [商] dynasty (p. 128) to worship the Goddess Nǔ Wā [女娲], the creator of mankind in Chinese mythology. Charmed by the beauty of the goddess, the emperor wrote poems to express his deep love for the goddess. The infuriated goddess decided to punish the king and bring an end to the Shāng dynasty.

'A Dream of Red Mansions' [红楼梦] *hónglóumèng*

A novel written by Cáo Xuěqín [曹雪芹] (p. 154) at the beginning of Qīng [清] dynasty (p. 148) (about 1790). This is a long series of 80 episodes, involving more than 400 characters. It depicts life in huge, extended families with grandiose, love, tragedy, fame, as well as jostling for attention and positions.

'Tales of Liaozhai' [聊斋志异] *liáozhāizhìyì*

Written by Pú Sōnglíng [蒲松龄] from the Qīng [清] dynasty (p. 148). An interesting novel with intrigues of mystical, spiritual encounters. Fox-fairies, strange spirits abound.

'The Peony Pavilion' [牡丹亭] *mùdāntíng*

Written by Tāng Xiǎnzǔ [汤显祖] from the 16th century. It portrays the romantic love story between Du Liniang and Liu Mengmei, depicting the desire for free loves in a feudal environment. With more than 160 characters and 55 scenes, the plot is complicated; it portrays social life in the Míng dynasty.

'The Scholars' [儒林外史] *rǔlínwàishǐ*

A satiric novel written by Wú Jìngzì [吴敬梓] from Qīng dynasty. It narrates two candidates who struggled throughout their lives to pass the Imperial examination for civil service. The author exposes the absurdity and decadence of scholars produced by the system, the emptiness and corrupt nature of the society and administration.

'Romance of the Three Kingdoms' [三国演义] *sānguóyǎnyì*

Written by Luó Guanzhōng [罗贯中] (p. 164) from the Míng dynasty, the novel relates the political and military intrigues between the three powers from the Eastern Hàn to the three kingdoms. The vivid and lively descriptions brought about well known household personalities such as Kōng Míng [孔明] (p. 178), Cáo Cāo [曹操] (p. 153), Liú Bèi [刘备] (p. 162), Guān Gōng [关公] (p. 156) and Zhāng Fēi [张飞] (p. 175).

'Three Worded Text' [三字经] *sānzìjīng*

A sort of poetry consisting of three words each, covering a whole range of general knowledge, designed to be recited and memorised by children.

'The Historical Records' [史记] *shǐjì*

Written in early Hàn (206-220 BC) by Sīmǎ Qian [司马迁] (p. 168). This is the earliest comprehensive account of early Chinese history from legendary times to early Hàn periods (refer to p. 126).

'The Tales of Water Margin' [水浒传] *shuǐhǔzhuàn*

Written by Shī Nài'ān [施耐奄] (p. 167) in the beginning of Míng empire, this is a very popular novel. The novel describes how 108 men and women who are oppressed by corrupt officials rise up. The heroes rob the rich and give to the poor, the plot emphasises the importance of loyalty, brotherhood, love for justice, etc at a time of feudal warlords.

'The Almanac' [通书] *tōng shū*

This is one of the oldest annuals on earth. Printed versions are annually published since the 9th century.[26] This is about the most widely used and read book amongst the Chinese, a sort of guide for the families.

Although not many truly understand this book to the full, there is always some useful information that could be easily understood. The 2003 issue from Hong Kong's 广经堂 *Guǎngjīngtáng* include:

1. Outlook of the year according to the Chinese calendar.
2. Determination of zodiac signs based on age.
3. Compatibility of zodiac signs
4. Charts for determining personal parameters for the year

---

[26] *T'ung Shu*, edited and translated by Martin Palmer, Vinpress, Malaysia 1986.

5. Astrology information.
6. Two-hundred year Chinese (Lunar)—Western (Solar) calendar equivalence to check zodiac signs.
7. Choosing an auspicious day.
8. Yellow emperor's poem of the four seasons.
9. How to cast a horoscope.
10. Positions of the planets.
11. Implications or forecast based on physical sensation.
12. Charms.
13. Five determining elements
14. Information on the 60 Celestial and Terrestrial factor combinations.
15. Dreams interpretation according to Zhou Gong.
16. The 'season segments' jié [节] with actual timing of sunrise and sunset.
17. Foetus development
18. Various divination methods
19. Lyrics on physiogamy [相法歌诀] *xiàngfǎ gējué*
20. The most common hundred Chinese surnames.
21. Divination based on words and numbers [诸葛拼字艺术妙算] *zhūgé pīnzì yìshù miaosuàn*
22. Pronunciation of common English words.
23. Dialogue between Confucius and a little precocious child.
24. Disciples of Confucius.
25. Tips on business.
26. Formal family addresses
27. Formats for invitation cards
28. Lunar eclipse
29. Rise and fall of sea tides
30. Twenty four illustrated stories of filial piety [二十四孝图说] *èrshísì xiào túshuō*
31. Collection of popular proverbs, idioms and quotations for guiding human conduct [增广贤文] *zēng guǎng xián wén.*

32. Zhu Zi's principles and guide for home management [朱子治家格言] *zhūzǐ zhìjiā gēyán*
33. Chinese calligraphy.
34. The Thousand Character Classic written in four calligraphic styles.
35. Liú Bó Wēn's [刘伯温] (p. 164) poem of cookies (from Míng dynasty, accurately predicted the future).
36. Auspicious and inauspicious days of the year for each month.
37. Charts for the identification of Terrestrial and Celestial factors for a particular day.
38. Details analysis (down to hours) on any particular day, based on yīn-yáng wǔxíng.
39. Outlook for next year.

There are several techniques of divination described in the book. However these are all designed for the laymen, not the experts.

'Diagrams of rubbing the back' [推背图] *tuī bèi tú*

People in the West have heard of Nostradamus, the sixteenth century French prophet. A book written in China by Lǐ Chūnfēng [李淳风] (p. 160) and Yuán Tiāngāng [袁天罡] (p. 175), during the reign of Táng Tàizōng [唐太宗] (599-649) gave incredibly accurate forecast.

Written about one thousand three hundred years ago, the book consisted of sixty illustrated diagrams, each with lyrics and descriptions in a cryptic style. Each scenario uses a 'Celestial Stem and Terrestrial Branch' (refer to Chapter Eight) used in Chinese calendar, as well as a scenario from I-ching (refer to Chapter Ten). Each scenario accurately predicted events in Chinese history from the Táng dynasty onwards. It accurately predicted that there would be 21 emperors in the Táng dynasty from the Li family, with one of them not from within the family.

It also forecasted the rise of Wǔ Zétiān [武则天] (p. 173), the only ruling empress in the history of China, and so on.

The book has yet to be translated into English, since it is extremely difficult to do so. This is evident when we look at scenario 39, which depicts a bird standing on top of a mountain, with the rising sun at the bottom.

The lyrics: 'Bird without leg, moon in the mountain' [鸟无足 山有月].
'The sun rises, everyone cries' [旭初升 人都哭].
The description: 'Disharmony in December' [十二月中气不和].

'Sparrows to the mountain in the South, traps to the mountain in the North' [南山有雀北山罗].
'One morning cries from metal rooster is heard' [一朝听得金鸡叫].
'The sea is lifeless, the day is over' [大海沉沉日已过].

The writings are cryptic. The Chinese character of a legless bird with a mountain is the character 'Island' 岛. Hence the event refers to an Island nation. The island nation is linked to the rising sun, hence Japan. When a million soldiers invaded China with unprecedented cruelty and inhumanity, everyone cries.

In December of 1941, the Japanese talked peace in the United States, while secretly attacking Pearl Harbour, fits the description 'Disharmony in December.'

There are sparrows (small birds) south of the mountain, referring to small nations in Southeast Asia being captured. In the picture there is certainly an eagle that could trap Japan, coming from the North, symbolising the United States. (Incidentally the word 'Luo' [罗] is also the first word of the Chinese name for President Roosevelt, the U.S. president who subdued Japan.

Japan surrendered in August 1945. This corresponds to the Chinese calendar year of rooster. The month of surrender was August, a metal month (refer to Chapter nine).

The sea is lifeless when Japanese troops surrender unconditionally. 'ri' [日] refers either to the day, or in this case to Japan [日本].

While the earlier scenarios depict events from the various dynasties, the later scenarios could probably describe events outside China.

'Journey to the West.' [西遊记] *xīyóují*

This is a novel written by Wú Chéng'ēn [吴承恩] (p. 172). It is popular amongst children, who is often fascinated by the magical powers of the monkey god Sūn Wukōng [孙悟空]. Written during the Míng Dynasty, the highly imaginative story relates the adventures of the monk Táng Sánzàng [唐三藏] (p. 173), and his three disciples, the monkey god Sūn Wùkōng [孙悟空], Zhū Bājiè [猪八戒] and Shā Zēng [沙憎] on his way to India in search of Buddhist scripts. The chapters relate the birth of the monkey god and his rebellion against Heaven, their journey to the West where they came across all sorts of demons and monsters, crossed the fiery mountain and eventually arrived at their destination.

'The Classics of Filial Piety' [孝经] *Xiàojīng*

This text contains eighteen short chapters focussing on traditional values of filial piety.

'Strategies of the Warring State' [战国策] *zhànguócé*

During the Warring States (p. 131) the warlords clashed with each other. In this era of intensive 'dog-eat-dog' warfare, a whole range of military strategists emerged, each trying to sell their expertise to the warlords. They were only given one chance, and no mistake was allowed. The 'Strategies of the Warring States' is a collection of works of these military strategists in 33 volumes. It is also a vivid description of aspects of history during this period.

'Zhen Guan Governance' [贞观政要] *zhēnguān zhèngyào*

Written by Wú Jìng 吴兢 (p. 172) in the Táng dynasty, this book describes in a narrative form the rule of Táng Tàizōng 唐太宗: the most outstanding emperor of the Táng dynasty. This has become a 'guide book' for Chinese rulers over the centuries. It looks at the intrigues of people in power, the importance of self discipline, delegation of power, trust, fair and firm dealings, as well as constant vigilance. Most of the philosophy and approach in politics is still valid till this day (refer to p. 161).

'The Book of Zhuāngzǐ' [庄子] *Zhuāngzǐ*

Written in the 4th century BC, it is considered to be the second most important text in Dàoism after Lǎo Zǐ (p. 160). Out of the 33 chapters, only the first seven are thought to be written by Zhuāngzǐ (p. 179), the rest are varied in nature, probably added by others. Unlike Lǎozǐ, who dealt with wisdom in the real world, Zhuāngzǐ presented his philosophy in metaphysics style, long before the coming of Buddhism in China. The chapters consist of a mixture of philosophic discussions, anecdotes or parables

255

One category of books not found in Western literature are stories based on martial arts, known as 武俠小说 *wǔxiáxiǎoshuō*. Based on the general principles of fighting against injustice, these stories portray fraternity, righteousness, as well as revenge. They normally involve martial arts experts acting as individuals or in groups. The plots involve considerable strategies, intrigues, joys and tribulations. These warfare stories catch the imagination of generations of readers.

There is a huge volume of websites dedicated to various aspects of Chinese literature. Some of them are general, while others are devoted to one or two of the text, such as the Analects, Tales of Water Margin, Dàodéjīng or Sūn Zi's Art of War.

Most of the original Chinese texts could be downloaded from various sites, though English translations of these texts are not always available on the net.

Chinese classics—English text: *www.merechina.com/culture/*
Chinese classical literature: *zhongwen.com/gudian.htm*
Chinese literature classics: *www.chinapage.com/classic1.html*

Five Chinese Classics Translated by Charles Muller
www.hm.tyg.jp/~acmuller/fiveclassics.htm
The Chinese classics: *www.sacred-texts.com/cfu/*

This painting of the word 'blessed' [福] *fú consists of a butterfly, a bird, some flowers, plants, beautifully laid out.*

CHINESE POETRY

Chinese poetry is sometimes called 'poetry and songs' shīgē [诗歌]*, as poetry and songs are closely associated. Though some poems have been transposed as songs, most of the poems are recited, known as lǎngsòng* [朗诵]*.*

Chinese literature is incomplete without its poetry. Many of the poets were rulers and statesmen, right from early times. Emperors such as Cáo Cāo [曹操] (p. 153), Lǐ Shìmín [李世民] (p. 161); generals such as Yuè Fēi [岳飞] (p. 175) were also poets.

Due to the 'Imperial examination' system (refer to p. 180), many top civil servants, including prime ministers, were also poets. They include Wáng Ānshí [王安石] (p. 171), Qū Yuán [屈原] (p. 166), amongst others.

The best approach to Chinese poetry is to look at the poems themselves. Out of the thousands of poetry written through the centuries, we have selected six well-known poems, listed according to pīnyīn alphabetical order.

1. 'Bird' [鳥] *niǎo* by Bái Jūyì [白居易] (p. 152).
2. 'Sympathy with farmers' [悯农] *mǐnnóng* by Lǐ Shēn [李绅]
3. 'Song of the Wanderer' [遊子吟] *yóuzǐyín* by Mèng Jiāo [孟郊]
4. 'In the still of the night' [静夜思] *jìngyèshī* by Lǐ Bái [李白] (p. 160).
5. 'A poem in seven paces' [七步诗] *qībùshī* by Cāo Zhí [曹植] (p. 154).
6. Prelude to 'Water melody' [水调歌头] *shuǐdiào gētóu* by Sū Dōngpō [苏东坡] (p. 169).

The first poem is from a Táng dynasty poet Bái Jūyì [白居易] (p. 152).

'Bird'

[鳥] *niǎo*

谁道群生性命微 *shéi dào qúnshēng xìngmìng wēi*
一般骨肉一般皮 *yībān gǔròu yībān pí*
Who says that the lives of the animals are not important?
Just like us they too have flesh and skin

劝君莫打枝头鸟 *quàn jūn mòdǎ zhītóu niǎo*
子在巢中望母归. *zǐ zài cháozhōng wàng mǔ guī*
Please do not shoot at the bird on the tree top
The chicks in the nest are waiting for their mother to return

The second poem is by Lǐ Shēn [李绅]. It highlights the sweat and toil required to produce food, something that tends to be taken for granted today.

'Sympathy with Farmers'
[悯农] *mǐnnóng*

鋤禾日当午 *chúhé rìdāngwǔ*
汗粒禾下土. *hànlì héxiàtǔ*
At noon the hoe digs into the ground ...
Drops of sweat fall and blend with the soil

谁知盘中餐 *shéi zhī pánzhōng cān*
粒粒皆辛苦. *lìlì jiē xīnkǔ*
Who would know that every grain from the plate
Comes with much sweat and toil?

The next poem is typical of Chinese mothers, reflecting their immeasurable care and love for their children. It is written by Mèng Jiāo [孟郊].

'Song of the Wanderer'
[遊子吟] *yóuzǐyín*

慈母手中线 *címǔ shǒuzhōngxiàn*
遊子身上衣. *yóuzǐ shēnshàngyī*
The threads in the hands of a tender loving mother
Sewing the coat of her departing son

临行密密缝 *línxíng mìmì féng*
意恐迟迟归. *yìkǒng chíchí guī*
Before he left she stitched his coat neatly and tight
Fearing that he might be slow to return

谁言寸草心 *Shuíyán cùncǎoxīn*
报得三春晖. *bàode sānchūnhuī*
Who would say that his young and tender[27] heart
Could ever repay the radiance and warmth[28]

Lǐ Bái 李白 (p. 160) from the Táng dynasty is one of the best known Chinese poets. The following is one of his best known, even amongst school children.

'In the Still of the Night'
[静夜思] *jìngyèshī*

床前明月光 *chuángqián míngyuèguāng*
疑是地上霜. *yíshì dìshàngshuāng*
In front of my bed is the bright moonlight..
The ground seems to be covered with frost

举头望明月 *jǔtóu wàng míngyuè*
低头思故乡. *dītóu sīgùxiāng*
Lifting my head I see the bright moon....
Casting down, I think of my homeland.

The next poem was mentioned in Chapter five, a popular poem written by Cāo Zhí [曹植] (p. 154). It is often quoted whenever there is a dispute amongst family members.

---

[27] The poet used inch long grass to depict tenderness.
[28] Warmth is compared to the radiance from three Spring seasons.

'A Poem in Seven Paces'
[七步诗] qībùshī

煮豆燃豆萁 zhǔdòu rándòuqí
豆在釜中泣. dòuzài fǔzhōngqì
The bean stalks burn to cook beans[29]...
The beans in the pot sob:

本是同根生 běnshì tónggēnshēng,
相煎何太急 xiāng jiān hétài jí
We come from the same roots!
why do we fry each other in such haste?

The last poem chosen comes from Sū Dōngpō [苏东坡] (p. 169), one of the best known literary figures in the Sòng dynasty. The poem was written on a Mid-Autumn festival night, when the moon was full and bright.

Prelude to 'Water Melody'
[水调歌头] shuǐdiào gētóu

明月几时有 míngyuè jǐshíyǒu
把酒问青天 bǎjiǔ wènqīngtián
When will the moon be clear and bright?
With a glass of wine I ask the blue sky

不知天上宫阙 búzhī tiánshàng gōngquè
今夕是何年 jīnxī shì hénián
I do not know up in the heavenly palace
What year is it tonight?

---

[29] It is important to note that the stock and the bean come from the very same plant.

我欲乘风归去 *wǒyù chéngfēng guīù*
又恐琼楼玉宇 *yòukǒng qiónglóu yùyǔ*
I would like to ride the wind to return
Yet I fear the crystal and jade mansions

高处不胜寒 *gāochù búshènghán*
起舞弄轻影 *qǐwǔ nòngqīngyǐng*
何似在人间 *hésì zài rénjiān*
These places are much too high and freezing.
Dancing with my light shadows…
It does not feel to be in the human realm

转朱阁, 低绮户 *zhuǎnzhūgé, dīqǐhù*
照无眠, 不应有恨 *zhàowúmián búyīng yǒuhèn*
Moving around in the scarlet mansion …
Beneath the carved windows
Dazzling lights shines upon the insomniacs
Why should I bear any grudge?

人有悲欢离合 *rényǒu bēihuān líhé*
月有阴晴圆缺 *yuèyǒu yīnqíng yuánquē*
Men experience sorrow, joy, separation or reunion.
The moon may be dim or bright … Full or wane

此事古难全 *cǐshì gǔnánquán*
但愿人长久 *dànyuàn rénchángjiǔ*
千里共婵娟 *qiānlǐ gòngchánjuān*
These matters are difficult to be perfect …
Since the beginning of time
May we all be blessed with long lives?
Share the loveliness[30] … Thousands of miles apart.

---

[30] Depicted as the lovely Goddess of moon.

SELECTION OF FIFTY POEMS

We have selected fifty popular or interesting poems for listing. For the enthusiasts there are literally thousands more, covering a broad spectrum of topics such as family, human relationship, love, nature, patriotism, war, wine, etc.

1. 'Grief by the Riverside' [哀江头] *āi jiāng tóu* by Dù Fǔ [杜甫] (p. 155).
2. 'Octagonal Battle Formation' [八阵图] *bā zhèn tú* by Dù Fǔ [杜甫] (p. 155).
3. 'A Song of War Chariots' [兵车行] *bīngchēxíng* by Dù Fǔ [杜甫] (p. 155).
4. 'Poem of Sorrow and Resentment' [悲愤诗] *bēi fèn shī* by Cài Wénjī [蔡文姬] (p. 153).
5. 'The Divination Expert' [卜算子] *bǔ suàn zǐ* by Lǐ Zhīyì [李之仪]
6. 'Song of Everlasting Sorrow' [长恨歌] *chánghèngé* by Bái Jūyì [白居易] (p. 152).
7. 'Dedicated to Xiao Yu' [赐萧禹] *cì xiāo yǔ* by Lǐ Shìmín [李世民] (p. 161).
8. 'Asleep in Spring' [春眠] *chūnmián* by Mèng Hàorán [孟浩然] (p. 164).
9. 'Spring Day' [春日] *chūnrì* by Zhū Xī [朱熹] (p. 179).
10. 'Scaling the Heron Lodge' [登鹳雀楼] *dēng guànquèlóu* by Wáng Zhīhuàn [王之涣] (p. 172).
11. 'Duǎngēxíng' [短歌行] by Cáo Cāo [曹操] (p. 153).
12. 'Anchoring at Night at Maple bridge' [枫桥夜泊] *fēngqiáo yèbó* by Zhāng Jì [张继]
13. 'Complaints in the Lady's Chamber' [闺怨] *guī yuàn* by Wáng Chānglíng [王昌龄]
14. 'The Yellow Crane Mansion' [黄鹤楼] *huáng hè lóu* by Cuī Hào [崔颢]

15. 'The Eighteen Beats of Hu Flute' [胡笳十八拍] *hú jiā shíbā pāi* by Cài Wénjī [蔡文姬] (p. 153).

16. 'Coming Home Anecdote' [回乡偶书] *huíxiāng oǔshū* by Hè zhīzhāng [贺知章]

17. 'The Beauty' [佳人] *jiārén* by Dù Fǔ [杜甫] (p. 155).

18. 'Bring in the Wine' [将进酒] *jiāng jìn jiǔ* by Lǐ Bái [李白] (p. 160).

19. 'The Golden Threaded Garment' [金缕衣] *jìnlóuyi* by Dù Qiūniáng [杜秋娘]

20. 'In the Still of the Night' [静夜思] *jìngyèshī* by Lǐ Bái [李白] (p. 160).

21. 'Waves Ripple on Sand' [浪淘沙] *làng táo shā* by Liú Yǔxí [刘禹锡]

22. 'Leyou Prairies' [乐游原] *lè yóu yuán* by Lǐ Shāngyǐn [李商隐]

23. 'The Lament' [离骚] *lísāo* by Qū Yuán [屈原] (p. 166).

24. 'A song of Liangzhou' [凉洲词] *liángzhōu cí* by Wáng Hàn [王翰]

25. 'The Whole River is Red' [满江红] *mǎnjiānghóng* by Yuè Fēi [岳飞] (p. 175).

26. 'Sympathy with Farmers' [悯农] *mǐnnóng* by Lǐ Shēn [李绅]

27. 'Battle of Cibi' [念奴娇] niàn nú jiāo by Sū Dōngpō [苏东坡] (p. 169).

28. 'Bird' [鸟] *niǎo* by Bái Jūyì [白居易] (p. 152).

29. 'Púsà Mán' [菩萨蛮] by Wéi Zhuāng [韦庄]

30. 'A poem in seven paces' [七步诗] *qībùshī* by Cáo Zhí [曹植] (p. 154).

31. 'Qīng Mīng' [清明] by Dù Mù [杜牧]

32. 'Song of Beach in Autumn' [秋浦歌] *qiū pǔ gē* by Lǐ Bái [李白] (p. 160).

33. 'Autumn Night' [秋夕] *qiū xī* by Dù Mù [杜牧]

34. 'Encouragement to Study' [劝学] *quàn xué* by Yán Zhēnqīng [颜真卿] (p. 174).

35. 'Stroll in the Mountain' [山行] *shānxíng* by Dù Mù [杜牧]
36. 'Retaining Guests in the Mountains' [山中留客] *shānzhōng liukè* by Zhāng Xù [张旭] (p. 176).
37. 'Forlorn' [声声慢] *shēng shēng màn* by Lǐ Qīngzhào [李清照] (p. 161).
38. Prelude to 'Water Melody' [水调歌头] *shuǐdiào gētóu* by Sū Dōngpō [苏东坡] (p. 169).
39. 'Send Off' [送别] *sòngbié* by Wang Wei [王维] (p. 171).
40. 'About the Village in South of Du City' [题都城南庄] *tí dūchéng nánzhuāng* by Cuī Hù [崔护].
41. 'About the Western Forest Wall' [题西林壁] *tí xīlíngbì* by Sū Dōngpō [苏东坡] (p. 169).
42. 'Gazing at the Moon, Thinking Far Away' [望月怀远] *wàngyuè huáiyuǎn* by Zhāng Jiǔlíng [张九龄].
43. 'Passing through Jiangling' [下江陵] *xiàjiānglīng* by Lǐ Bái [李白] (p. 160).
44. 'Newly Wed Lady' [新嫁娘] *xīnjiàniáng* by Wáng Jiàn [王建] (p. 171).
45. 'Not Meeting the Recluse' [寻隐者不遇] *xún yǐnzhě búyù* by Jiǎ Dǎo [贾岛].
46. 'Memories of South of the River' [忆江南] *yì jiāngnán* by Bái Jūyì [白居易] (p. 152).
47. 'Drinking Alone by Moonlight' [月下独酌] *yuèxià dúzhuó* by Lǐ Bái [李白] (p. 160).
48. 'Song of the Wanderer' [游子吟] *yóuzǐyín* by Mèng Jiāo [孟郊] (p. 258).
49. 'Early Departure for Baidi City' [早发白帝城] *zāofā báidì chéng* by Lǐ Bái [李白] (p. 160).
50. 'Mocking at Myself' [自嘲] *zì cháo* by Lǔ Xùn [鲁迅] (p. 164).

COUPLED POEMS [对联] *duìlián*

A unique form of literature is the 'coupled poems' or 对联 *duìlián*. These are written by specialists on special paper, framed or mounted on walls at homes and offices.

There are normally two corresponding phrases. The rules for writing 'paired phrases' are:

1. The number of words in both phrases must be the same.
2. The type of word in each phrase must correspond. For example, if the first word in the first phrase is a noun, the first word in the second phrase is also a noun. If the second word in the first phrase is a verb, the second word in the second phrase must also be a verb, etc.
3. The coupled poems as a whole should convey a message, or be meaningful.

This is a common 'coupled poem' for the newly weds. 幸福生活 *xìngfú shēnghuó* could be translated as 'Blessed and happy life', while 美满姻缘 *měimǎn yīnyuán* would mean 'Beautiful, fulfilling faithful union'

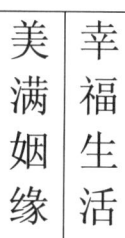

A pair of 'coupled poem' commonly used for birthdays would be 寿比南山 *shòu bǐ nán shān* 'to live as long as the 'Nan' mountain' 福如東海 *fú rú dōng hǎi* 'Blessed as the Oceans of the East' (refer to p. 305 for more details).

The Chinese theme for this book

漂洋過海，落地生根

'crossing the oceans, taking roots'
piāoyáng guòhǎi, luòdì shēnggēn

is also coupled phrases. It can be extended as a
longer 'coupled poem'.

Crossing the oceans in simple, unassuming
circumstances,
really settled down when one comes to terms
with oneself.
cǎocǎo piāoyáng guòhǎi wúduōtāwèn,
zhēnzhēn luòdìshēnggēn yǒuwéizìduì

— Zhao Zhen

真真落地生根有唯自对

草草漂洋过海无多他问

Some Cultural Practices

IN THIS CHAPTER WE WOULD like to look at Dàoist (Taoist) and Confucianist teachings, as a factor in Chinese mindset and cultural practice. We would approach Dàoism from a philosophical, rather than spiritual or religious outlook. The second part of this chapter looks into some of the cultural norms and practices, moulded by centuries of traditions and customs.

Dàodéjīng [道德经] (Tao Te Ching)
This is the source-book of Dàoism (Taoism). The word dào or Tao 道 is found in a variety of literature. There are books on 'Tao of power', 'Tao of peace', 'Tao of love', and so on. What does dào mean?

道

The character 道 *dào* is depicted as the head 首 *shǒu*, on legs 辶 *zǒu*. The head symbolises the mind, thinking or reasoning, while the leg implies moving or advancement. Together the word *dào* could be interpreted as logic going with every path of action.

The Dàodéjīng is hence a book dealing with logic, nature, human nature. It provides an insight into 'the way' or 道 *dào* to do things, as well as the cultivation of 'morality' or 德 *dé*. It is written by

Lǎozǐ [老子] (p. 160), from the kingdom of Chǔ [楚] during Spring and Autumn period (refer to p. 129).

Dàodéjīng as enunciated by Lǎozǐ (604 BC) emphasised on human conduct and character. It stressed on the cultivation of inner self. Possibly the earliest book on metaphysics, it deals with how one could harmonise with oneself and with nature. The text borders between philosophy and religion. Dàodéjīng is one of the most translated Chinese texts available.[31]

In Dàodéjīng there are 81 chapters. The chapters are short, averaging around 50 words.

The texts are hard to comprehend, some of them in apparent contradiction at the first glance. Translations are difficult; they vary considerably, as opinions differ. Our interpretations[32] from selected chapters should not be taken too literally.

Chapter 2 talks about duality in nature and dynamic balance between yīn and yáng.

'We know beauty as beauty, yet ugliness exists. We know goodness as goodness, yet there exists evil.' [天下皆知美之为美, 斯恶已. 皆知善之为善, 斯不善已].

'In this way existence and non-existence give rise to each other, difficulty and ease complement each other. Long and short contrast, High and low mutually attract. Pitch and tone harmonise together, Future and past follow one another.' [故有无相生, 难易相成, 长短相形, 高下相倾, 音声相和, 前後相随].

Chapter 7 emphasises selflessness.

---

[31] For example, R.L. Wing, *The Tao of Power*, Aquarius Press, London; Diane Dreher, *The Tao of Peace*, Mandala Press, London, etc.

[32] Translations are made contextually, not literally or word for word.

'The Heaven and Earth are everlasting. They exist forever, because they do not exit for themselves. For that alone they live eternally.' [天地长久. 天地所以能长且久者, 以其不自生, 故能长生].

'Therefore wise men put themselves last, and yet they are first. They leave themselves out, yet they stay within. Is it not because they are without self-interest, that their self-interest is fulfilled?' [是以人後其身, 而身先. 外其身, 而身存. 非以其无私邪, 故能成其私?]

Chapter 8 dwells into value judgement, ranking properties of water as having the highest amongst them.

'The highest form of goodness is that of water. It benefits all things, but does not compete with them. It stays in places loathed by men, one that is close to Dào, the divine path.' [上善若水, 善利万物, 而不争. 处众人之所恶, 故几於道].

'A dwelling is judged by its location. The heart is judged by its depth, relationship is judged by its benevolence; words are judged by their credibility, leadership is judged by its effectiveness, work is judged by its result, operation is judged by its timeliness. There is no resentment when there is no argument.' [居善地, 心善渊, 与善仁, 言善信, 正善治, 事善能, 动善时. 夫唯不争, 故无尤].

Chapter 9 talks about the inevitability of decline.

'To take all you could is never as good as to stop when you should. Though you can guard it and be alert, you cannot

hold on to it forever.' [持而盈之, 不如其己; 揣而锐之, 不可常保].

'A house filled with riches cannot be kept for ever. Pride in wealth and prestige is the way to self-destruction.' [金玉满堂, 莫之能守. 富贵而骄, 自遗其咎].

'Withdraw when the work is done, is the nature of dào. [功成身退, 天之道].

Chapter 17 talks about power, influence and subtle authority.

'Governance is best if the people are not even aware that it exists. Next come leaders who are loved and honoured. Those who are feared by the people rank next, and those who are ridiculed last.' [太上, 不知有之; 其次, 亲而譽之; 其次, 畏之; 其次, 侮之].

'If you do not trust others, others will not trust you. When the command comes from afar and the mission accomplished, the people would say 'we did it naturally.' [信不足焉, 有不信焉. 悠兮其贵言. 功成事遂, 百姓皆谓: 「我自然」].

Chapter 29 emphasises the importance of leaving nature as it is, rather than interfering with it.

'I do not see anyone who seeks to dominate the World and act on it will ever succeed. The world is a sacred instrument, not meant to be handled, not designed to be seized.' [将欲取天下而为之, 吾见其不得已. 天下神器, 不可为也, 不可执也].

'Those who act on it fail, those who seize it cannot retain. It is the enlightened who leave things as they are who have

270

nothing to loose; who do not possess it, have nothing lost.' [为者败之，执者失之. 是以圣人无为，故无败; 无执，故无失].

'Therefore things either lead or are being led, they could be active or passive; strong or weak, some carry on, while others loose heart. An enlightened avoids any extremes, extravagance and excess.' [故物或行或随; 或嘘或吹; 或强或羸; 或载或隳. 是以圣人去甚，去奢，去泰].

Chapter 33 talks about inner strength of men.

'He who knows others is astute, he who knows himself understands. He who wins over others has strength; he who wins over himself is powerful. He who is contented is blessed; he who perseveres aspires to pursue. He who maintains his position endures; he who dies but does not perish lives on eternally.' [知人者智，自知者明. 胜人者有力，自胜者强. 知足者富，强行者有志. 不失其所者久，死而不亡者寿].

A stone carving of Lǎozǐ, made in Sòng dynasty, found in 'Qīng Yuán' mountain [清源山], *in* Quánzhōu [泉州], *Fújiàn Province* [福建省] (refer to p. 103).

Chapter 48 talks about the limits of action, leading to the utopia of inaction.

'Pursue learning and knowledge, pursue further everyday. Pursue the Dào, remove (fixed ideas) from it everyday.

Remove it again and again, till there is nothing left. Do nothing, yet nothing is left undone. To understand the events and non-events in the world, does not amount to understanding the world.' [为学日益, 为道日损. 损之又损, 以至于无为. 无为而无不为. 取天下常以无事, 及其有事, 不足以取天下].

Chapter 54 discusses self-cultivation.

'Those good at establishing are not uprooted. Those good at grasping do not let things slip away. This is honoured for generations to come.' [善建者不拔, 善抱者不脱, 子孙以祭祀不輟].

'Cultivate your inner self, its values are real. Cultivate your family, its values are abundant, Cultivate your community, its values last long. Cultivate your nation, its values are rich. Cultivate the world, its values are universal.' [修之于身, 其德乃真; 修之于家, 其德乃馀; 修之于乡, 其德乃長; 修之于邦, 其德乃丰; 修之于天下, 其德乃普].

'Therefore observe yourself through self, observe your family through the family, observe the community through the community, observe your nation through the nation, observe the world through the world. How would I know the world? through these.' [故以身观身, 以家观家, 以乡观乡, 以邦观邦, 以天下观天下. 吾何以知天下然哉? 以此].

Chapter 63 deals with management of issues.

'Do without doing, achieve without achieving, taste without savouring. Whether it is big or small, many or few, reply

ill-will with kindness.' [为无为, 事无事, 味无味. 大小多少, 报怨以德].

'Deal with difficult issues when it is still easy, Solve big problems when they are small. The cultivated gentleman does not take great actions, in this way he becomes great.' [图难于其易, 为大于其细; 天下难事, 必作于易, 天下大事, 必作于细. 是以圣人終不为大, 故能成其大].

'Those who promise easily are hard to be believed, the easier to promise the harder it is. Therefore the sage finds it difficult to promise, and they have no difficulty to be believed.' [夫轻诺必寡信, 多易必多难. 是以圣人犹难之, 故終无难矣].

The first part of chapter 64 discusses the issue of nature, where time is required to build up events or products. It also emphasise the timeliness of operations.

'What is at peace is easy to hold, Events that are yet to happen are easy to plan for.' [其安易持, 其未兆易谋].

'What is rigid is easily broken, Things that are small are easily scattered, Problems are best dealt with before they emerge, Order is best put in place before there is chaos.' [其脆易泮, 其微易散, 为之於未有治之於未乱].

'A tree of wide girdle grows from a tiny seed, A tower of nine stories is built from the ground, A journey of a thousand miles begins with the first step.' [合抱之木生於毫末, 九层之台起於累土, 千里之行始於足下].

Chapter 67 looks at the power of compassion.

> '*I hold three treasures to protect and uphold: The first is compassion, the second moderation, and the third is to overcome the urge to be the first in the world.*' [夫我有三宝而持之, 一曰慈, 二曰俭, 三曰不敢为天下先].

> '*With compassion one becomes courageous; with moderation one looks far, overcoming the urge to be first, one cultivates leadership.*' [慈故能勇, 俭故能广, 不敢为天下先, 故能成器长].

Chapter 73 looks at some of the situations inherent in nature.

> '*Those who are bold and daring end up dead, those who are bold but do not dare survive. Both of them may bring benefit or harm.*' [勇于敢则杀, 勇于不敢则活. 此兩者, 或利或害].

> '*How does one know the evil of nature? Even cultivated gentleman finds it difficult. The Dào of nature does not argue but wins, does not speak but responds, comes without being invited, takes its time in its strategies. The network of nature is vast, it is loose, but nothing slips through.*' [天之所惡, 孰知其故? 是以人犹南之. 天之道, 不争而善胜, 不言而善应, 不召而自來, 然而善谋. 天網恢恢, 疏而不失].

Chapter 79 deals with resolution of conflict.

> '*Even when a conflict is settled, there would be residual resentment. This must be resolved.*' [和大怨, 必有馀怨;安可以为善?]

'Therefore the sage works on the agreement, and does not blame others. Those with morals work to uphold the contract, those without morals work to dismantle it. The Dào of nature does not favour anyone; it only works with good people.' [是以圣人执左契, 而不责于人. 有德司契, 无德司徹. 天道无亲, 常與善人].

Chapter 80 gives an insight into the ideal social and political set up.

'A small country with a small population. Where people are neighbours, people are armed, but arms not used. People value their lives, and do not wander far. Though there are boats and carriages, there is no need for them. Though there are weapons and soldiers, there is no need to display them. The people tie knots[33] and use them.' [小国寡民. 使有什伯之. 器而不用; 使民重死而不遠徙. 虽有舟輿, 无所乘之, 虽有甲兵, 无所陈之. 使民复結繩而用之].

'Enjoy the food, clothing is fine and homes are secure. Find pleasure in the customs. The neighbouring countries living so close, that people hear their sounds of life.[34] The people living, growing and dying in harmony, without getting into each other's way.' [甘其食, 美其服, 安其居, 乐其俗. 鄰国相望, 鸡犬之声相闻, 民至老死, 不相往來].

Confucius Studies [儒家学术] *rujiāxuéshù*

Chinese culture is invariably associated with Confucius teachings. Confucius (p. 159) dedicated his lifetime to teaching and learning. He contributed significantly to the study of yìjīng, his teachings were

---

[33] The system of knotted ropes comes from an ancient system of mathematics and memory cache. The abacus was developed from rows of knotted ropes.

[34] Represented by crowing of rooster and barking of dogs.

recorded by his students, which were then passed down throughout the generations.

Zhū Xī [朱熹] (p. 179), the great scholar of Southern Sòng dynasty (p. 143) compiled four classics texts 四书 sìshū, later became the standard text for the study of Confucianism. The texts, together with notes written by Zhū Xī, subsequently became the text for the all important Civil service examination in China. The four texts total about 53,000 words became extremely influential in the political, social and academic life of Chinese for centuries.

A statue of Confucius, in a Confucius temple in Yunan province.

The four texts are the 'Analects' [论语] lúnyǔ, Great Studies [大学] dàxué, Doctrine of the Mean [中庸] Zhōngyōng, as well as Mèngzǐ [孟子].

Most of these are words of wisdom, dealing with the inter-personal relationships. These range from relationship between the ruler and his people, interaction between teacher and student, harmony in the family, etc. The importance of knowing oneself, moderation in all matters, and learning itself are often emphasised. Some of his teachings might seem common sense today. Some of moral values would be controversial or irrelevant in today's circum-stances. The fact that these principles were enunciated and discussed two thousand and five hundred years ago indicated a highly develop-ed social order and sophistication of the society at that time. Their inclusion as syllabus for 'Imperial examinations' assured that all civil servants have a good understanding of social studies.

The Analects [论语] *lùnyǔ*

Literally translated as the 'theoretical discussions', the 'Analects' is a series of conversations recorded by disciples of Confucius. It provides an insight into Confucius teachings, his vision of an 'ideal' society governed by an enlightened ruler who governs by 'humanity, benevolence' [仁] *rén* and 'righteousness' [义] *yi*. The following are quotations translated from the 'Analects'. Other than chapter one, the rest are not quoted in entire paragraphs.

Chapter 1 (The entire chapter)

'Isn't it a pleasure to speak of learning and its application?'
'Is it not delightful to have friends visiting from far?'
Doesn't a cultivated man feel perfectly all right even though others do not take note of him?' [学而时习之, 不亦说乎?
有朋自远方来, 不亦乐乎? 人不知而不愠, 不亦君子乎?]

'Those who are filial do not offend their superiors. If they do not offend their superiors, they would not cause havoc. The cultivated man sticks to his basic principles, from which all things develop. Those who are filial have deep-rooted benevolence.' [其为人也孝弟, 而好犯上者, 鲜矣; 不好犯上, 而好作乱者, 未之有也. 君子务本, 本立而道生. 孝弟也者, 其为仁之本与!]

'I examine myself daily on three matters. Have I been dishonest in business? Have I been untrustworthy to friends? Have I practised what I preach?' [吾日三省吾身—为人谋而不忠乎? 于朋友交而不信乎? 传不习乎?]

'To rule a country attention must be paid to issues and credibility, be thrifty, love *the people, employ them at the appro-*

priate time.' [道千乘之国, 敬事而信, 节用而爱人, 使民以时].

'A person should be filial at home, respect his elders outside. Be earnest and trustworthy. Love the people, cultivate benevolence. At his spare time, learn to cultivate himself.' [弟子, 入则孝, 出则弟, 谨而信, 凡爱众, 而亲仁. 行有余力, 则以学文].

'Liberate from the love of beauty. Serve his parents to the best of his ability. Devote to serve his superiors. Be true and sincere in his words to his friends. Even if he were not considered 'learned', I would say that he is.' [贤贤易色; 事父母, 能竭其力; 事君, 能致其身; 于朋友交, 言而有信. 虽曰未学, 吾必谓之学矣].

'If a cultivated man does not take thing seriously he is not held in high esteem, his learning would not be solid. Be loyal and trustworthy. There is no friend who is as good as oneself. When you have faults, do not hesitate to correct them.' [君子不重, 则不威; 学则不固. 主忠信. 无友不如己者. 过则勿惮改].

'Be respectful to a person's funeral rites, remember them long after they are gone, and the spiritual virtue of the people will be returned many folds.' [慎终, 追远, 民德归厚矣].

'When our master visits a country, he learns all about its government. Does he seek out or is his information given to him?' Zi Gong (one of the disciples): 'Our master is warm, good, and courteous, examines himself, does not compete with others and gets his information. The master's way of seeking information, is different from that of others.' [夫子

至於是邦也, 必闻其政, 求之与? 抑与之与? 子贡曰: '夫子温, 良, 恭, 俭, 让以得之. 夫子之求之也, 其诸异乎人之求之与?']

'While the father is alive, observe his ambition; when the father has passed away, observe his conduct. If he does not deviate from his father's teaching for three years he would be considered filial.' [父在, 观其志; 父没, 观其行; 三年无改於父之道, 可谓孝矣].

'In practising etiquette, harmony is of utmost importance. According to good ancient kings this is good virtue, practised to a big or small extent. Yet there would be situations when it is not applicable; emphasises on harmony alone while ignoring social etiquette is also not practical.' [礼之用, 和为贵. 先王之道, 斯为美; 小大由之. 有所不行, 知和而和, 不以礼节之, 亦不可行也].

'When trusts established are based on virtues, what is spoken can be repeated. When respect is shown according to customs, shame and disgrace are kept at bay. If you do not lose the relationship, you can be his guides.' [信近於义, 言可复也. 恭近於礼, 远耻辱也. 因不失其亲, 亦可宗也].

'The cultivated gentleman does not eat to satisfy his appetite, he does not live to seek peace, he is earnest in his pursuit, careful in his speech; he acknowledges that it is correct to observe proper ways. He could be said to love learning.' [君子食无求饱, 居无求安, 敏於事而慎於言, 就有道而正焉, 可谓好学也已].

'What do you think of the poor who is not greedy, and is not frown upon; the rich who is not arrogant?' The Master replied: 'This is all right; it is not as good as the poor who is *happy, or the rich who observes etiquette.' Zi Gong: 'It is said in the Book of Poetry, 'You cut and shape, facet and polish.'—the meaning is the same.' Master: 'Granted! I can begin to talk about the odes. I only need to relate one point, and the rest is understood.'* ['贫而无谄, 富而无骄, 何如?' 子曰: '可也; 未若贫而乐, 富而好礼者也.' 子贡曰: '诗云: '如切如磋, 如琢如磨', 其斯之谓与?' 子曰: '赐也, 始可与言诗已矣, 告诸往而知来者.']

'I am not concerned by anyone not knowing me; I am concerned that I do not know him.' [不患人之不己之, 患不知人也].

The other chapters

'At fifteen, my ambition was to learn and acquire knowledge. At thirty, I have established myself. At forty, I had no doubts. At fifty, I understand destiny. At sixty, my ears are receptive to the truth. At seventy, I could do what my heart desired, without infringing on etiquette.' [吾十有五而志于学, 三十而立, 四十而不惑, 五十而知天命, 六十而耳顺, 七十而从心所欲, 不逾矩].

'A cultivated gentleman acts before he speaks, and speaks according to his actions thereafter.' [先行其言而后从之].

'He who learns without thinking is lost; he who thinks without learning is in danger.' [学而不思则罔, 思而不学则殆].

'Wealth and honour are what men seek. If they are not acquired in the proper way, they should not be acquired at all. Poverty and low-down situation are what men dislike. If these cannot be avoided in the proper way, they should not be avoided. 'If a cultivated gentleman abandons his virtues,

wouldn't the evil man be famous?' [富与贵, 是人之所欲也; 不以其道得之, 不处也. 贫与贱, 是人之恶也; 不以其道得之, 不去也. 君子去仁, 恶者成名?]

'The cultivated gentleman in the world does not suit himself to anything; he pursues what is right.' [君子之於天下也, 无适也, 无莫也, 义之於比].

'In the company of two others, there is always someone who could be my teacher. Select what is good and learn from it. Whatever is not good correct it.' [三人行必有我師焉. 择其善者而学之, 其不善者而改之].

'Do not do to others what you do not want for yourself.' [己所不欲, 勿施於人].

Great Learning [大学] *Dàxué*
Once again we will only go through the first chapter of Great Learning in detail.

'The objective of the Great learning is to highlight the virtues, to be associated to the people, and only ends with excellence.' [大学之道在明明德, 在亲民, 在止於至善].

'When you know when to stop then you would stabilise; when you are stable you would be calm and tranquil; when you are calm then you feel secure; when you are secure you could then deliberate; after due deliberation you would achieve.' [知止而後有定; 定而後能静; 静而後能安; 安而後能虑; 虑而後能得].

'Matters have beginning and end, events start and finish. To know the sequence and order of importance would bring us close to Dào.' [物有本末; 事有终始. 知所先後则近道矣].

281

'From ancient times those who want to be a leader or ruler, need to put his own house in order; to put his house in order; he needs to cultivate his own morals; to cultivate his own morals, he needs to put his heart right. To put his heart right, he needs to be sincere. When he is sincere, he would reach out to his knowledge. Extension of knowledge leads to the investigation of things.' [古之欲明明德於天下者欲治其国者, 先齐其家; 欲齐其家者, 先修其身; 欲修其身者, 先正其心; 欲正其心者, 先诚其意, 欲诚其意者先致其知. 致知在格物].

In the reverse order, you only reach out to your knowledge when you are sincere; you would be sincere when your heart is right; when your heart is right you would get your morals correct; it is only when your morals are all right, your house is in order; when your house is in good order, you can then rule the state.

'One gets to know after things are investigated. With true knowledge one gets more sincere. With sincerity the heart and mind is more forthright. One then cultivates when the heart is righteous. Cultivated people then manage their families. When the family is looked after one then run the country. Their country properly run would lead to peace.' [物格而後知至. 知至而後意诚。意诚而後心正. 心正而後身修. 身修而後家齐. 家齐而後国治. 国治而後天下平].

'From the Emperor down to the commoner, self-cultivation is the basis of all things.' [自天子以至於庶人台是皆以修身为本].

Other Chapters

'Listen to complaints, I am just like any others. It is neces-
sary to resolve matters so that there is no complaint.' Do not
let unscrupulous people defend themselves to no end;
Respect people's wishes, deal with the root cause.' [听讼,
吾犹人也. 必也, 使无讼乎? 无情者, 不得尽其辞, 大畏
民志. 此谓知本].

'Wealth adorns a house, virtues adorn an individual. A
broadminded person leads to a healthy body. Therefore the
cultivated gentleman needs to make his intentions sincere.'
[富润屋, 德润身. 心广体胖. 故君子必诚其意].

'The cultivation of a person amounts to cultivating the
mind.' An angry man will not conduct his affairs fairly in an
environment of fear, extreme pleasure, sorrow or distress.'
[所谓修身在正其心者: 身有所忿, 则不得其正. 有所恐
惧, 则不得其正. 有所好乐, 则不得其正. 有所忧患, 则
不得其正].

'When the heart is not there, he looks without seeing; hears
without listening; eats without savouring.' [心不在焉, 视而
不见, 听而不闻, 食而不知其味].

Doctrine of the Mean [中庸] *Zhōngyōng*

Note that the word 'mean' refers to statistical mean, i.e. equally far
from two extremes, rather than being spiteful. 'Doctrine of the Mean'
emphasises the need to avoid from extreme viewpoints and
measures. This is evident from the introduction. We only look at the
first chapter in detail.

'Without leaning on either side (central in position) is called
'Central'. Without making changes is called 'Ordinary'.

Pursuing 'Central' [中] zhōng *is the correct pathway for things in this world, pursuing 'ordinary'* [庸] yōng *would be the guiding principles regulating all things under the sun.'* [子程子曰,「不偏之谓中; 不易之谓庸.」中者, 天下之正道. 庸者, 天下之定理].

'What Heaven confers is 'nature'. What leads nature is Dào. Dào is cultivated by 'education'. [天命之谓性; 率性之谓道; 修道之谓教].

'That which is called Dào cannot be separated at any instant. What can be separated from nature is not the Dào. Therefore the Cultivated gentleman cautions himself in any thing that he does not see with his own eyes, or hears with his own ears.' [道也者, 不可须臾离也; 可离, 非道也. 是故君子戒慎乎其所不睹, 恐惧乎其所不闻].

'Do not underestimate the visibility of the hidden; do not underestimate the apparent nature of anything subtle. Therefore the Cultivated gentleman is cautious when he is alone.' [莫见乎隐, 莫显乎微. 故君子慎其独也].

'When the emotions of joy, anger, sorrow and pleasure are dormant, it is called 'Mean'. When they arise to their appropriate levels, it is called 'harmony.' The 'Mean' is the root of all things under the sky. Harmony is the manifestation of Dào through all things under the sky.' [喜, 怒, 哀, 乐之未发, 谓之中. 发而皆中节, 谓之和. 中也者, 天下之大本也. 和也者, 天下之达道也].

'When the 'mean' and harmony are balanced, Heaven and Earth are in their proper positions and a myriad of things flourish.' [致中和, 天地位焉, 万物育焉].

Other chapters

'Cultivated gentleman practises moderation, while the uncultivated man goes against it. Cultivated gentleman practises moderation because he is always with it; uncultivated man does not observe it to his own detriment.' [君子, 中庸; 小人, 反中庸. 君子之中庸也, 君子而时中. 小人之中庸也, 小人而无忌惮也].

'How far-reaching the 'mean' can be! Very few people are able to maintain it for long.' [中庸其至矣乎! 民鲜能久矣].

'There are five universal obligations in this world, carried out in 3 ways. These are the relationship obligation between the ruler and the ruled, between father and child, between husband and wife, between siblings, and between friends. The three entities of wisdom, benevolence and courage are universal virtues. These virtues are therefore displayed by the same person.' [天下之达道五, 所以行之者三, 曰: 君臣也, 父子也, 夫妇也, 昆弟也, 朋友之交也. 五者, 天下之达道也. 知, 仁, 勇三者, 天下之达德也. 所以行之者一也].

'Some know it at birth; some acquire it through learning and some get to know it through life experience. Nonetheless, the knowledge once acquired is the same. Some are comfortable in practicing it, some benefit from its practice, and some struggle strenuously to practise it. But when he succeeds, the result is the same.' [或生而知之; 或学而知之; 或困而知之: 及其知之, 一也. 或安而行之; 或利而行之; 或勉强而行之: 及其成功, 一也].　　,

'To be fond of study is to be close to knowledge. To put it into practice is to approach benevolence. To understand shame is to be close to courage. When you understand all these three,

you know how to cultivate your character; when you know how to cultivate your character, you know how to deal with others; when you know how to deal with others, you know how to govern a country.' [好学近乎知. 力行近乎仁. 知耻近乎勇. 知斯三者, 则知所以修身. 知所以修身, 则知所以治人. 知所以治人, 则知所以治天下国家矣].

'To govern a country *there are 9 general rules to follow. These are: self-cultivation; respect people of good character; caring for relatives; respect high officials; be kind and considerate towards junior officials; treat the commoner as your children; make craftsman feel welcome; welcome foreign guests and embracing the nobles.'* [凡为天下国家有九经, 曰: 修身也, 尊贤也, 亲亲也, 敬大臣也, 体群臣也, 子庶民也, 来百工也, 柔远人也, 怀诸侯也].

'Cultivate your character; you build up your Dào. Respect people of good character you do not feel lost. Care for your relatives, there would be no friction with your family and siblings. Respect high officials and you will not make serious errors. Being kind and considerate to junior officials you get grateful returns for your courtesy. Treat commoners as your children, the masses would *encourage each other. Make the craftsman feel welcome; there will be ample skilled resources. Welcome foreign guests, people would flock to you from all directions. Embrace the nobles, the people will have a healthy fear and respect for them.'* [修身, 则道立. 尊贤, 则不惑. 亲亲, 则诸父昆弟不怨. 敬大臣, 则不眩. 体群臣, 则士之报体重. 子庶民, 则百姓劝. 来百工, 则财用足. 柔远人, 则四方归之. 怀诸侯, 则天下畏之].

The Book of Mèngzǐ [孟子]

The last of the 'four classics' [四书] *sìshū* is the book of Mèngzǐ.

The influence of Confucius and Mèngzǐ on Chinese governance over the centuries cannot be under-estimated. However moral dictums, though powerful, are insufficient to maintain social order. Contemporary Chinese societies favour a combination of legalistic system, enforceable by law, as well as retaining elements of Confucianism ideals. Some aspects of Confucianism, in particular the position of women in society, have been discarded.

The Five Classics Scripts [五经] *wǔjīng*

The five classics scripts are 'the book of change' [易经] *yìjīng*, 'the Book of History' [书经] *shūjīng*, 'the book of Odes' [诗经] *shījīng*, 'the Book of Rites' [礼记] *lǐjì* and 'Annals of Spring and Autumn' [春秋] *chūnqīu*. A short description of the texts is given below.

The Book of Change [易经] *yìjīng*

This book is better known as I-Ching in the west. It is one of the earliest book and most influential book on the Chinese psyche. This is the most important text dealing with metaphysics as well as changes in nature. This book is discussed in detail in Chapter Ten.

The Book of Documents [书经] *shūjīng*

The book of documents is a book of 26,000 words, compiled by Confucius. This is a set of documents such as speeches, laws relating to ancient history of China from Xià [夏] (About 2205-1752 BC) to Zhōu [周] dynasties (1027-249 BC). The book is regarded as a valuable source book for governance and early civilisation.

The Book of Odes [诗经] *shījīng*

Also translated as the Book of Poetry, this is a collection of ancient poetry, ranging from early Zhōu [周] (11th century BC) to 'Spring and Autumn' period (p. 129). The 305 poetry collection could be categorised into 3 categories, 风 *fēng*, relating to music and poetry from the general population, 雅 *yǎ*, pertaining to Imperial court and its surroundings, as well as 颂 *sòng*, words of praise in religious ceremonies. Themes range from conquest, hunting, and romance to daily life. Confucius is regarded as the editor of the book.

The Book of Rites [礼记] *lǐjì*
This was written during the Warring States (p. 131) to early Hàn period (p. 133). This is a good reference text on early social situation, ceremonies, rites, education and music in China. These books on philosophy and rituals documented early social etiquettes and rituals in ancient China.

The Annals of Spring and Autumn [春秋] *chūnqiū*
This was the first annual record of China, reportedly written or compiled by Confucius. The story comprised 242 years, started at 722 BC and ended at 481 BC.

COMMON CULTURAL NORMS AND PRACTICES
This second part of the chapter looks into some of the cultural norms and practices.

Ethnic Chinese living in environments where Chinese is not the majority seek to be treated as equals. While acquiring the mainstream culture through formal education at school, there is also the awareness that there could be differences in outlook.

It is therefore interesting to look at the social etiquettes, comparing them wherever possible with Western norms.

Culture
The word 'culture' originates from the Latin word *colere*: to till, cultivate, culture imparts unique identities to an ethnic group, be it behaviour, clothing, customs, expressions, food, language, literature, music, religion, or other traditions.

Culture [文化] *wénhuà* is an abstract entity that challenges a precise definition. Cultural heritage is conceptually complex, difficult to be defined, and permeates all aspects of human civilisation.

It serves as a benchmark for behaviour within a community, ranging from attitudes, dispute settlement, hierarchy, as well as a host of what is and what is not socially acceptable. It sets parameters by which members of the group communicate and react with each other.

At a higher level, culture reflects refinement in human thoughts, aesthetic values and judgement systems.

CHINESE SOCIAL ETIQUETTES

The Chinese society and family is rather structured, with distinct hierarchical relationships.

Confucius etiquettes are quite elaborate, covering aspects of relationship between the ruler and his subjects, between man and wife as well as between a man and his compatriots. Codes of practice were written in books such as 'The book of rites' 礼记 lǐjì, 'rites and rituals' 仪礼 yìlǐ. They outline in detail the standards to help court officials and ordinary people to behave in a civilised manner. Though most of the imperial rituals are no longer relevant, a great proportion of the human relationship etiquettes are still very much in place, a notable exception is the position of women.

HIERARCHY OF RELATIONSHIPS

The fundamental difference is that emphasis is placed in the greater social entity rather than self. This is evident when we examine how an address is written.

If we write, for example,

Mr. Peter Chang,
22, High Street,
Willetton,
Western Australia
Australia

The address written in Chinese on an envelope is exactly the opposite, namely

> Australia
> Western Australia
> Willetton,
> 22, High Street,
> Mr. Peter Chang (To receive)

We have seen earlier on that in a Chinese naming system the Surname is always placed first and the given name last. Inversion of this system in Western countries is often a source of great confusion and embarrassment.

FAMILY TERMINOLOGY

Traditionally, when there were three or four generations used to live in the same compound, when there are tens or possibly more than a hundred people that one needs to recognise and address correctly, only a hierarchical system could avoid the confusion.

First of all it is extremely rude to address one's elder by his or her name.

Right at the early age, the child is taught to call his father [爸爸] *bàba* and mother [妈妈] *māma*. In addition a distinction is made between a person younger or elder than him or her, for example:

Elder Brother	[哥哥] *gēge*
Younger Brother	[弟弟] *dìdi*
Elder Sister	[姐姐] *jiějie*
Younger sister	[妹妹] *mèimei*

If there were four brothers, each of them would be addressed according to their 'hierarchy', for example, eldest brother, second brother, etc. In this way all brothers are identified without any error. The same applies to sisters.

When it comes to cousins, a distinction is made between cousins from father's siblings, (addressed with the prefix 堂 *táng*, and mother's siblings, addressed with the prefix 表 *biǎo*. For example a cousin brother, son of your father's sibling elder than you would be your 堂哥 *tánggē* or 堂弟 *tángdì* if he is younger than you. However the son of a brother of your mother's sibling would be your 表哥 *biǎogē* or 表弟 *biǎodì*. An easy way to remember is your 堂 *táng* brother or sister shares the same surname as you.

When a couple get married, the two families would be 亲家 *qīnjiā*. The husband is called 丈夫 *zhàngfū* or 先生 *xiānshēng* (same words as Mr.), while the wife is called 妻子 *qīzǐ* or 太太 *tàitai*. In China they are called 爱人 *àirén* 'loved person'.

When your sister gets married, there would be a 姐夫 *jiěfū*, the husband of your elder sister, or a 妹夫 *mèifū*, the husband of your younger sister. When your elder brother gets married, his wife would be your 嫂 *sǎo*. Her exact title depends on the position of your brother. For example If your third elder brother sāngē gets married, his wife would be your third sister in-law (brother's wife) 三嫂 *sānsáo*. The wife of your younger brother is your 弟妇 *dìfù*.

A whole range of vocabulary exists to precisely identify an uncle, as shown in the following table.

Elder brother of your father	伯伯	*bóbo*
Younger brother of your father	叔叔	*shūshu*
Brother of your mother	舅父	*jiùfù*
Husband of a sister of your father	姑丈	*gūzhàng*
Husband of a sister of your mother	姨丈	*yízhàng*

Hence your third 叔 *shū* should be the third amongst your father's brothers, younger than your father; your second 姑丈 *gūzhàng* would be the husband of the second sister of your father.

The list for aunts are as follows:

Sister of your father	姑 *gū*
Sister of your mother	姨 *yí*
Wife of your father's elder brother bóbo	伯母 *bómǔ*
Wife of the your father's younger brother shūshu	叔母 *shūmǔ*
Wife of the your mother's brother jiùfù	舅母 *jiùmǔ*

It is not uncommon that a traditional ethnic Chinese does not know his uncle or aunt's real name.

Terms used for the younger generation are as follows:

Son	儿子 *érzǐ*
Daughter	女儿 *nǚ'ér*
Son-in-law	女婿 *nǚxù*
Daughter-in-law	媳妇 *xífù*
Nephew (Brother's son)	侄儿 *zhí'ér*
Niece (Brother's daughter)	侄女 *zhínǚ*
Nephew (Sister's son)	外甥 *wàishēng*
Niece (sister's daughter)	外甥女 *wàishēngnǚ*

The entire terminology became somewhat obsolete in China when the one child policy is adopted. There would be no siblings, no spouses of siblings. By the next generation there would be no uncles and aunts, and therefore no cousins. However the system is very much intact outside China.

Even to someone totally unrelated, it is quite normal to address a more senior person using the terms 'uncle' or 'auntie', for example 'Uncle Lim' or 'Auntie Tracy'. Such practice imparts a feeling of familiarity, comradeship and being courteous or polite.

FORMAL SALUTATIONS

A person is officially addressed by his or her surname, with an appropriate title. Common titles include:

Mr.   先生 *xiānshēng*
Mrs. 太太 *tàitai*
Ms   女士 *nǚshì*
Miss 小姐 *xiǎojiě*

It is good to know the surname of the person you are about to address. Mr. Chen is addressed as 陈先生 *Chén Xiānshēng*. Confusing the surname with the given name would be a disaster.

Other titles are associated with professions or job designations. Mr. Wang, a teacher, is addressed as 王老师 *Wáng Lǎoshī*, while Mr. Wang, the Manager is addressed as 王经理 *Wáng Jīnglǐ*. As these are official titles it is important to remember the person's status (often shown on the name card). Hierarchy is important in countries such as China and you risk ruffling feathers if a person's due respect is not paid to him.

FORMAL TITLES

A list of titles in alphabetical order is given below.

Ambassador 大使 *dàshǐ*
Accountant 会计师 *kuàijishī*
Adviser 顾问 *gùwèn*
Association/Society President 会长 *huìzhǎng*
Chairman 主席 *zhǔxi*
Chairman of Board of Directors 董事长 *dǒngshìzhǎng*
City Mayor 市长 *shìzhǎng*
College Principal 院长 *yuànzhǎng*
Company boss 老闆 *lǎobǎn*
Company Director 董事 *dǒngshì*

Consul 领事 *lǐngshì*
Consultant 顾问 *gùwèn*
Doctorate (Ph.D.) 博士 *bóshì*
Engineer 工程师 *gōngchéngshī*
Factory Chief 厂长 *chǎngzhǎng*
Lawyer 律师 *lǜshī*
Lecturer 讲师 *jiǎngshī*
Manager 经理 *jīnglǐ*
Master (for example martial arts) 师父 *shīfù*
Medical Doctor 医生 *yīshēng*
Minister 部长 *bùzhǎng*
Miss 小姐 *xiǎojiě*
Mrs. 太太 *tàitai*
President of Corporation 董事长 *dǒngshìzhǎng*
Priest 牧师 *mùshī*, 神父 *shénfù*
Prime Minister 总理 *zǒnglǐ*
Professor 教授 *jiàoshòu*
School principal 校长 *xiàozhǎng*
Student 学生 *xuéshēng* or 同学 *tóngxué*
Teacher 老师 *lǎoshī* or 先生 *xiānshēng*
The Chief (semi-formal address) 老总 *lǎozǒng*

There are certain government appointment or job titles that are unique to China. These confer certain status as well as authority to the holders. They include:

Director of Department 处长 *chùzhǎng*
Head of Bureau 局长 *júzhǎng*
Head of District 区长 *qúzhǎng*
Head of Ministry 厅长 *tīngzhǎng*
Head of Section 科长 *kēzhǎng*
Governor of a Province 省长 *shěngzhǎng*
Secretary 书记 *shūjì*

In general the person in charge is addressed as 主任 *zhǔren.* The word 总 *zǒng* means overall. The chief engineer, for example, is called 总工程师 *zǒngōngchéngshī.* The word fù 副 means deputy. The deputy governor of a province should be addressed as 副省长 *fùshěngzhǎng.* Normally the word 老 *lǎo* is used for someone you are familiar with, while the word 小 *xiǎo* used for someone generally younger or from the younger generation.

Just as in the case of any other naming system, when you are unsure, please ask!

Arranged in pīnyīn alphabetical order, the formal addresses are as follows. The terms marked with * are commonly used only in China.

bóshì 博士 Someone with a doctorate degree.
bùzhǎng 部长 Minister
chǎngzhǎng 厂长 Chief Executive of the factory
chùzhǎng 处长* Director, Head of Department
dàshǐ 大使 Ambassador
dōngshì 董事 Company Director
dǒngshìzhǎng 董事长 Chairman of Board of Directors/President
gōngchéngshī 工程师 Engineer
gùwèn 顾问 Consultant, Adviser
huìzhǎng 会长 Association President
jiǎngshī 讲师 Lecturer
jiàoshòu 教授 Professor
jīnglǐ 经理 Manager
júzhǎng 局长* Head of Bureau
kēzhǎng 科长* Section head
kuàijìshī 会计师 Accountant
lǎobǎn 老闆 Boss of a company
lǎoshī 老师 Teacher
lǎozǒng 老总 The Chief (semi-formal address)
lǐngshì 领事 Consul

lùshī 律师 Lawyer
mùshī 牧师 Priest
qūzhǎng 区长* District Head
shénfù 神父 Catholic priest
shěngzhǎng 省长* Provincial Governor
shīfu 师父 Master (for example martial arts)
shìzhǎng 市长 City Mayor
shūjì 书记* Secretary
tàitai 太太 Mrs.
tīngzhǎng 厅长 Head of Ministry
xiānshēng 先生 Teacher
xiǎojiě 小姐 Miss
xiàozhǎng 校长 School principal
xuéshēng 学生 Student
yīshēng 医生 Medical Doctor
yuànzhǎng 院长 College Principal
zhǔrèn 主任 Director, Head
zhǔxí 主席 Chairman
zǒnglí 总理 Prime Minister

BASIC SOCIAL PHRASEOLOGY

The difference between a cultivated gentleman and others is in the heart. The cultivated gentleman has deep rooted benevolence and courtesy. — Mèngzǐ
[君子所以异于人者，以其存心也. 君子以仁存心，以礼存心].

Some of the concepts in Chinese society are poorly understood, though used quite often. As there is no precise word in English, it is better to understand the concept rather than insisting on a precise translation. Some of these terms originated from Confucius teachings, and are still widely used today.

bàoqiàn [抱歉] Is used when you need to apologise. This are commonly used words.

bùhǎoyìsī [不好意思] Used when you are embarrassed, or used as a polite reply when you are provided with some service.

bùyòngkèqì [不用客气] Used when you do not wish your guest to feel too formal or restricted; also used as a reply, when someone says 'thank you'.

gānbēi [干杯] Literally means 'drying up the cup'. The English equivalent would be 'bottoms up'. This phrase is used often in dinners celebrating a happy event.

guānxì [关系] Literally translated as relationship, Guan Xi refers to connection, connectivity or networking. It is imperative in societies where confidence or trust between individuals is crucial and important when favours are returned as part of the deals. Very often the guānxi is valued and honoured at all costs. It is also important to verify claims of guānxi, as the degree varies.

guānxīn [关心] or guānhuái [关怀] Used to express concern or care about someone's welfare.

kèqì [客气] Literally means courteous or polite. In practice, it is used to express appreciation of the hospitality of one's host.

lǐ [礼] Lǐ is more than courtesy. It implies practice of the whole spectrum of social etiquette and social norms expected as proper behaviour and good manners.

liǎn [脸] Literally means 'face'. It refers to how others judge you, not just how pretty or handsome you actually look. Socially it indicates how much respect a person commands. See 'Face giving' shǎngliǎn [赏脸]

méiguānxì [没关系] This means 'doesn't matter', not lack of relationship.

qiānxū [谦虚] is one of the cherished values amongst the Chinese. Interpreted as humbleness, it actually combines values of humility, sense of proportion, as well as the need to avoid being seen as 'Show off'. Indeed when someone says that he knows very little, it could be a case of humbleness rather than a lack of knowledge, particularly when the person speaks to elders. This could cause unfortunate results in Western Society when a person with such behaviour could sometimes be perceived as ignorant, disinterested, or even-non cooperative.

qǐng [请] Please. Also means 'invite'.

rén [仁] or réncí [仁慈] This has been variously translated as benevolence, humane, kindness, merciful and so on.

rěn [忍] Endure, tolerate. A word frequently used when faced with an adverse or unpleasant, unjust situation.
'Endurance' is conceptualised as having the 'sharp edge of the knife' rèn [刃] on the heart xīn [心]. The 'need' to endure hardships is part of the Chinese 'psyche'.

忍

rénqíng [人情] Literally meaning 'human sentiment', it implies that human dimension should always be part of any transaction. 'Rénqíng' is reciprocal, and mutual obligation is the norm. It is linked to the practice of giving face. Rénqíng shìgù [人情世故] refers to the art of human relationship. (Also refer to proverb No. 191, p. 207).

shàn [善] Shàn is variously translated as kind, good, fine, etc. The exact term depends on the context.

shǎngliǎn [赏脸] Face giving
The need to 'Save Face' in Asian cultures is well known, but poorly understood. Chinese tend to appraise the overall situation, in particular human relationships and sensitivities, rather than making decisions based strictly on legalistic considerations. Often steps are taken well beyond the required legal or even moral considerations, so as not to bring about an embarrassing situation. The Western concept of 'damn what others think' does not apply to Chinese psyche.

In an environment where the legal, social or political framework is not as transparent, face saving measures could also camouflage more than what meets the eyes. Things could be swept under the carpet in the name of 'Face giving'

At times the need to 'save face' is misunderstood as not being 'straightforward', 'beating around the bush' or 'getting to the point' (Indeed avoiding direct confrontation in the interest of face saving could lead to other complications, such as reluctance to complain or take positive action.

Failure to understand this is sometimes the source of problem or constraint when dealing with business in certain Asian countries. There are different ways to ask the same question, each having a different impact on the listener, who correspondingly respond in an appropriate manner. Practical application needs to be balanced with cultural sensitivities.

On the higher level involving the family, loss of face is associated with family honour. Traditionally strict social censure is applied to family members. This is somewhat less emphasised nowadays.

sònglǐ [送礼] Literally meaning 'Presenting gifts'. It is quite normal to present an appropriate gift. Amongst the Chinese, presentation of gifts has become a cultural phenomenon, in particular during festivals such as Chinese New Year.

wènhòu [问候] Used when you wish to convey your concern, or send your regards to someone through another person.

xièxie [谢谢] Thank you very much. This is one of the first words a foreigner learns.

xìnrèn [信任] This literally means 'Trust.' People dealing with Asian businessmen find that establishing mutual trust is as important as signing written contracts. Indeed the unwritten belief in reciprocal duties and responsibilities towards each other are at times more relevant or valuable than legal rights and obligations. This is particularly so in countries where the legal framework is not watertight, subject to interpretation by officials and not too easily enforced in practice.

In some countries and situations, the weight attached to written contracts is not the same as that in Australia, Europe or North America. Companies over-depending on legal rights without mutual trusts soon get bogged down in long-winded conflicts and disputes.

More importantly, the maintenance of excellent personal relationship is central to the continuance of good commercial relationship. The degree of trust on the local operator is often the single biggest factor on whether the business venture succeeds or otherwise.

yì [义] Yì Evokes the idea of someone morally correct, honest, courteous, someone fighting for a just cause. This has been variously translated as righteousness, justice, and so on.

yuánliàng [原谅] Used when you make a mistake and ask to be forgiven. Non Chinese speaking with incorrect intonation are often forgiven 'yuánliàng'.

zūnzhòng [尊重] Respect. Used quite often in formal address, for example the Honourable is often translated as zūnzhòngde [尊重的].

TABOOS

Like any other race the Chinese has their fair share of taboos, some of them are related to the language and culture.

❖ Death is a taboo which is not to be discussed in 'joyous' occasions such as Chinese New Year, weddings or birthdays.

❖ The number 'four' [四] sì phonetically sounds so much like 'death' [死] sǐ, that the number four, fourteen, forty-four, etc, are avoided as far as possible. Given a choice a Chinese would not buy house No. 4 of a given street.

- ❖ In the company of fishermen or sailors, do not turn the fish over at meal times. It symbolises boats capsized.
- ❖ Never buy a clock as a present for any Chinese friend. The word 'clock' [钟] *zhōng*, has similar sound with the 'end' [终] *zhōng*. Giving a clock as a gift 送钟 *sòngzhōng* sounds the same as 送终 *sòngzhōng*, being present at the bedside when a person takes his last breath.
- ❖ Never buy a green hat for any male married friend, as wearing a green hat [绿帽] *lǜmào* has the same meaning that his wife commits adultery.

FAMILY

We saw earlier on from the Great Learning of Confucius that those who want to be a leader or ruler need to put his own house or family in order. In typical Confucian tradition the family was always regarded as the foundation of the state, the source of social values.

As we have seen earlier traditional Chinese families are hierarchical, as is evident from ways relatives are addressed. This structured environment provided individuals with a first hand experience with the demands of respect, love, upholding of family honour and values. These values are then naturally extended to the society and the nation. Indeed the word 'country' [国家] *guójiā* consists of two words, the 'Nation' [国] *guó*, and the 'family' [家] *jiā*. It implies a natural progression from family to country.

Families tend to deal with problems internally. As the saying goes: 家丑不可外扬 *jiāchǒu bùkě wàiyáng* (proverb No. 106, p. 199) — Ugly aspects of the family are not broadcast outside, equivalent to dirty linen is not laundered in public.

Very often breach of codes of behaviour is best dealt with by talking to family elders. As a rule families avoid bringing the matter to court or in public, some of the disputes can be settled at the level.

In Chinese terminology there is the 'small me' [小我] *xiǎo wǒ* and the 'big me' [大我] *dàwǒ*, when one is compared to a bigger

301

entity, be it the family, the society or the Nation. Very often the society expect, and the individual consents to, a certain degree of self-sacrifice in favour of bigger me (my larger community).

Confucianism promotes filial piety and respect for authority; it also stipulates the responsibilities of rulers and parents to their subjects or children.

Family values came under attack from Mao Zedong during the Cultural Revolution, whereby family loyalties were condemned as vestiges of feudal past against absolute loyalty to Socialism, the Party and Country.

Family values in China is somewhat distorted under the one child system. The child tends to become the center of the family, and in some cases, spoilt and pampered. This is particularly so in the second generation when the two grand parents and parents put all their hopes and energies on one grandchild/child. Nevertheless traditional values are still upheld in most families.

POSITION OF WOMEN

About a century ago, the feet of young girls were tightly bound, to keep them physically small. As their feet were actually deformed, the women could not walk properly. They had to take tiny steps and wobbled when they walked. The wobbling and slightly swaying gait made the women look dainty. The binding of feet to fit in a three inch shoe has been made illegal.

Many of the traditional believe and practices are today obsolete or simply out of place. Binding of the feet to fit in a three inch shoe is now unheard of. Gone are the days when women have their feet bound so that they look dainty.

GENDER DIFFERENTIATION [重男轻女]

The desire to have males in the family to carry on the family line (through surnames) is well known. In China, this has serious impact, where the policy of one child is enforced. When the only child allowed to be born into the family is a female, some families could worry that the family surname will not survive continuity. Female infanticide had been reported to occur to enable the family to have another chance of getting a male baby.

Decades ago a woman has three men to follow in her lifetime:

1. 'Follow the father before marriage'　　未婚从父
2. 'Follow the husband after marriage'　　即嫁从夫
3. 'Follow the son when the husband dies'　夫死从子

Tradition dictates that the father looks after his daughter before her marriage, the husband looks after his wife, and the son is expected to look after his mother during her widowhood. Even today there are widows who would rather, or insist, that they stay with their sons rather than their daughters in their old age. This could lead to strained family dynamics amongst the siblings.

Gender differentiation is disregarded by the more educated and enlightened, in particular the overseas Chinese. Gone are the days when sons are given more opportunities in education in preference to the daughter. Nevertheless the inherent inequality (including psychological) in traditional family and social structure contrasts sharply with equal opportunities in modern societies.

Education leads to career and financial independence, resulting in social equality as well as joint leadership and management of the family, society and country.

Gone are the days when parents decide who their young daughter should marry, based on the advice of match makers. Young girls seek their own partners, based largely on their own values and judgment.

As most women seek their own careers, co-responsibility for running the home and family is the trend. This contrasts sharply with the earlier system whereby the man worked outside the home, whilst the woman is entirely responsible for domestic affairs.

Nowadays it is socially more 'aceeptable' for young widows to remarry (unless their personal circumstances are such). Equality amongst the sexes is the norm; government welfare system has established a new set of equality standards.

The practice of Chinese culture varies tremendously from country to country, and certainly changes over time and circumstances. In this era of equality gender differentiation it is certainly a thing of the past.

WORDS OF CONGRATULATION

We end this chapter with how the Chinese express words of congratulations. Certain phrases and sayings are used more commonly than others, depending on occasions. These sayings are often seen on plaques in businesses, homes, etc. They are also found in congratulatory messages in newspapers as well as greeting cards.

Traditional characters, rather than simplified ones, are normally used. A variety of type fonts are used for the following writings. Note that it is extremely difficult to provide precise and 'true to the spirit' translations.

The following are examples of how congratulations are expressed for

- ❖ Appointment/Election to office
- ❖ Birthday
- ❖ Business
- ❖ Weddings

APPOINTMENT/ELECTION TO OFFICE

為國為民 *wéi guó wéi mín*
For the country, for the people

任勞任怨 *rèn láo rèn yuàn*
Taking the responsibility and the blames without complaints

造福人群 *zào fú rén qún*
Bringing prosperity to the people

民主之光 *mín zhǔ zhī guāng*
Pride of democracy

民族之光 *mín zú zhī guāng*
Pride of the race

萬眾共欽 *wàn zhòng gòng qīn*
Admired and respected by thousands of people

BIRTHDAY

壽比南山 *shòu bǐ nán shān*
To live as long as the Mountain in the South[35]

福如東海 *fú rú dōng hǎi*
Blessed as the Oceans of the East[36]

福壽康寧 *fú shòu kāng níng*
Blessed, long life, health and peace

萬壽無疆 *wàn shòu wú jīang*
Long, long life without boundary

BUSINESS

大展鴻圖 *dà zhǎn hóng tú*
Ever expanding business

輔導工商 *fǔ dǎo gōng shāng*
Guiding commerce and Industry

---

[35] [shòubǐnánshān] is often used together with [fúrúdōnghǎi].
[36] [fúrúdōnghǎi] is often used together with [shòubǐnánshān].

駿業崇隆 *jùn yè chóng lóng*
Prestige and grand business

如日東昇 *rú rì dóng shēng*
Like the sun rising from the east

欣欣向榮 *xīn xīn xiàng róng*
Thriving and flourishing business

萬商雲集 *wàn shāng yún ji*
Congregation of thousands of business

展翅高飛 *zhǎn chí gāo fēi*
Soaring to great heights

蒸蒸日上 *zhēng zhēng rì shàng*
Business flourishing by the day

WEDDINGS

百年好合 *bái nián hǎo hé*
Loving and living together for a hundred years

美滿家庭 *měi mǎn jiā ting*
Beautiful and fulfilling family

天缘巧合 *tiān yuán qiǎo hé*
Brought together by heavenly destiny

心心相印 *xīn xīn xiāng yìn*
Two loving hearts resonating on each other

永结同心 *yǒng jié tóng xīn*
United together for ever, heart to heart

In Search of Chinese Psyche: Revisiting Ancient Paradigms

知

Know, Knowledge [知] *zhī* is represented by two components, 矢 *shǐ,* an arrow 'word radical' signifying targetting, transmitting, sending, and 口 *kǒu,* the mouth. Before tape recorders, photocopiers, phones, faxes, emails were invented; knowledge was passed on by words of mouth.

THIS CHAPTER SEEKS TO IDENTIFY some of the underlying 'logic', 'believes', or 'traditions' that consciously or subconsciously affects the Chinese psyche. To do this we need to visit three very ancient paradigms, the yīn-yáng theory, the five determinant elements, as well as the 'Celestial Stems' and 'Terrestrial Branches'. All these are fundamental to virtually every single Chinese practices such as Feng Shui, the art of 'Destiny Analysis', Chinese medicine, Martial arts, Chinese art, food, and so on.

The term 'psyche' refers to the human mind in their underlying thoughts and behaviour. Applied to a social or ethnic group, it refers to mental characteristics typical of the group, society, race, people or nation.

Is there any underlying philosophy that influence Chinese thought, on a conscious or sub-conscious level? Is there any perception that could be cultivated formally at school, at home, or acquired informally amongst peers and friends? Would there be any social pressures that require an ethnic Chinese to conform to certain norms?

To a large extent this depends on the home environment, in particular their exposure to the Chinese language and culture.

Though an Overseas ethnic Chinese may not be able to quote words of wisdom, there would certainly be elements that are somehow assimilated through family practice, tradition and ethics. These may not be fully explained at home or formally taught.

> 智
> Knowledge [知] *zhī*, worthy of being applied everyday [日] *rī* becomes Wisdom [智] *zhì*.

CHINESE CULTURAL PRACTICES

In a multicultural society there are distinctive habits or events that other communities associate the Chinese with, in particular the Chinese educated. Cultural activities, in addition to Chinese names, language, history as well as literature, stand out as social features that make the Chinese 'Chinese'. These could include:

- Chinese cooking
- Chinese festivals, in particular Chinese New Year.
- Chinese horoscope and Chinese calendar
- Chinese medicine, including acupuncture
- Divination (forecasting)
- Feng Shui
- Martial arts, including lion dance, dragon dance and Taiji
- Physiogamy (face reading)
- Chinese calligraphy, painting, pottery and other handicrafts.
- Traditional customs such as Chinese marriage, wedding ceremony, celebration of newborn at the age of one month.
- Chinese songs and dances.

As Chinese horoscope, divination and Feng Shui requires background understanding of basic concepts such as yīn-yáng [阴阳] and five elements, it is crucial to have a grasp of these concepts before these topics are discussed in the next chapters. This chapter comprises three sections. Section one discusses the yīn-yáng [阴阳] concept. Section two looks at the five determinant elements, unique to Chinese culture. Section three is dedicated to another ancient Chinese concept, the 'Celestial Stem' and the 'Terrestrial Branches'.

SECTION ONE

The Yīn-Yáng Theory

In Chinese philosophy, there exists a duality in everything, represented by the yīn-yáng concept. The yīn-yáng [阴阳] represents a balance between 'Female' [阴] *yīn* and 'Male' [阳] *yáng*. This balance is applicable to a whole spectrum of situations ranging from astronomy to Chinese medicine, from digital technology to events in nature.

(Note that other than the common radical, the word yīn [阴] has the moon as its component while the word yáng [阳] has the sun. The sun and the moon represent two forms of light, one dazzling bright, the other comfortable, warm glow)

This duality of yīn and yāng is better understood if we look at the simplicity of extremely complex scenarios, be it man-made or created by God.

Yīn-Yáng and its Endless Creativity

Take the Information Technology, perhaps the most important development in the 20th Century and beyond. A whole range of our present day activities would not be possible without it. Home and office computers analyse complex data, trends, projections, reports, complete with texts, graphics, sounds, videos, animations, as well as interaction at extremely fast speeds. With appropriate software, we could also simulate scenarios, carry out product development, market research, and more importantly make decisions!

Through the Internet we connect with millions of individuals or enterprises anywhere in the World. Communication through websites, email, and videoconference dramatically changes personal lives and business practices.

Few people realise that at the fundamental 'machine language' level texts, pictures, sounds, videos and animation are known to the computer as a series of ons and offs, plus or minus, represented as 0 or 1. A digitised picture, for example, is represented by a matrix of dots across the screen; each dot assigned a code representing the colour and tone. It is obvious that in the final analysis, a fascinating picture is no more than a matrix of dots, represented by 0 or 1 in an organised and sequential manner.

Once this is appreciated, it is easy to understand how image processing software uses the speed and power of the computer to edit pictures, whereby images could be merged, superimposed, or modified to obtain the effects of colour, stroke, light, shade, contrasts, smudging, and so on.

Similarly digitised voice or sounds can also be represented by a series of 0 and 1. Modern mobile phones are digitised, so that they can link with computers and other digital equipment. Digital television provides interaction with the viewer. Indeed a whole range of hitherto unrelated activities such as computerised graphics design, animation, simulation, picture and sound production, MP3, printing, artificial intelligence, on-line trading and education, is evolving at an incredibly fast rate—based on simple 0 and 1.

Indeed anything digital, from television to palm-top, from photography to animation, arises from the simple binary, yīn-yáng system.

Yīn-Yáng Concepts

Having looked at a an interesting contemporary application of the centuries old concept of duality, let us see if we could find words that adequately contain the following notions inherent in yīn-yáng concepts.

The argument might seem to be paradoxical or contradictory at first glance.

Yīn and Yáng are Equal and Opposite

This is expressed as 阴阳对立 *yīn-yáng duìlì*. Recognition of the equality and opposing nature of the two entities is crucial to the appreciation of balance of power, as well as interdependence of things in nature. This applies across the whole spectrum of parameters. For example when yīn is associated with females and yáng associated with males the two are equal and opposite.

Yīn and Yáng are Well Defined

This is expressed as 阴阳属性 *yīn-yáng shǔxìng*. Every entity, parts of human body, food material, physical concepts such as heat and cold, high and low, directions, taste, etc, is either yīn or yáng The yīn or yáng aspect in nature is distinct, definite and consistent. For example outer surface is always designated as yáng and inner surface designated yīn.

Yīn and Yáng are 'Rooted' from Each Other

This is expressed as 'taking mutual roots' [阴阳互根] *yīnyáng hūgēng*. Without yīn there is no yáng and without yáng there is no yīn. Once again this is obvious in partnership, be it marital or business. It follows that for it to work yīn-yáng controls each other, restrains each other and work together as a coherent entity. Within yáng there is a touch of yīn and within yīn there is always a tinge of yáng. If we take yáng as male, the outer part, for example the skin is yáng while the inner part yīn within the same entity.

311

Yīn and Yáng are in Dynamic Equilibrium

This is expressed as Dynamic equilibrium [阴阳消长] *yīnyáng xiāozhǎng*. Mutual dependence and restraint requires compromises, give and take. This dynamic equilibrium is only attained when the energies are balanced, just as the force of electrons and protons must be balanced for matter to be stable. This unity, mutual restraint and interdependence cannot be over-emphasised.

The Evolving Nature of Yīn-Yáng

This is expressed as 阴阳转化 *yīnyáng zhuǎnhuà*. Take the example of human moods or economic cycle; there are periods of ups and downs. Periods of growth would inevitably give rise to recession. Recession cannot last and is always followed by growth.

Consider the following:

Success only exists where there is failure to be compared with. Brightness is only meaningful if one has experienced darkness. If one surface of the earth were to face the sun all the time there would be brightness always, but probably no one would think that it is bright, since there is no darkness to contrast with.

Rather than dealing with familiar but simplistic, absolute values such as good and evil, right and wrong, the real world requires interpretation of relative values of yīn and yáng.

This is why we only appreciate happiness when we can compare it to sadness. If there were only good people in this world, how would one know what it is to be bad?

In practice yīn or yáng would be relative values. In other words there is simply no absolute truth or value. Duality or polarity refers to different facets of the same feature. They refer to both sides of the same coins, not different coins.

PRACTICAL IMPLICATIONS

This view of life permeates all aspects of Chinese thinking. In practical terms

❖ It implies that whatever happens, there is always the opposite side of the coin.

❖ It highlights the importance of harmony and balance. This is translated into compromise and negotiation.

❖ It emphasises on relative rather than absolute values. The propensity to think in relative, rather than absolute terms results in a more contextual, cyclical, rather than linear thought process.

❖ It highlights combination of possibilities, rather than simple, straight forward yes/no answer.

❖ It infers that nothing is permanent, everything being subject to continuous change. Someone who is relatively weak today could well be your competitor one day. Someone powerful today could loose all his influence and authority one day. Long term stability, rather than short term advantage, should be the ultimate objective.

❖ It favours moderation in preference to extremes. This is one of the central themes of Confucius thoughts.

❖ It demonstrates the equality and counter-dependence of factors.

A combination of these considerations permeates all aspects of our lives.

A good example of the acceptance of mutual coexistence of yīn and yáng is the present Chinese political and economic realities. To the uninitiated it is difficult to rationalise how Capitalism thrives (officially or unofficially) under the Communism in China, how a diametrically opposing system as different as Hong Kong can coexist within the overall Chinese framework. The yīn-yáng theory makes such situations conceptually as well as psychologically comfortable. Yīn and yáng depend on each other, give rise to each other, restrain on each other, contain a bit of each other in a cyclical, ever changing manner.

The yīn-yáng concept is perhaps best depicted in the typical 太极 *tàijí* symbol.

There are numerous websites dedicated to yīn-yáng [阴阳] interaction, including:

Chinese philosophy – yin and yang:
   www.wsu.edu:8080/~dee/CHPHIL/YINYANG.HTM
Chinese cultural studies – Yin and Yang in Medical Theory:
   acc6.its.brooklyn.cuny.edu/~phalsall/texts/yinyang.html
Feng Shui – Yin and Yang theory:
   www.168fengshui.com/Articles/Article_yinyang.htm

SECTION TWO

The Five Determinant Elements, wǔxíng [五行]

One the left are the Chinese characters for the five determinant elements: metal, wood, water, fire and earth.

The five elements interact with each other. There is a cycle of growth and a cycle of generation, which ensures that the elements are properly balanced and in harmony.

Almost every item in nature can be classified into one of the five elements. These include acupuncture points, colours, directions, food, internal organs, medicine, music, personalities, shapes, sounds, tastes, etc.

314

The yīn-yáng duality concept is in itself insufficient to represent forces in nature, or portray interaction of forces at play in a home or business environment.

Parallel to the concept of yīn-yáng duality is the notion of 'five determinant elements' [五行] *wǔxíng*, designed to balance various forces in nature. This notion would be known, but not necessarily understood in depth by the average ethnic Chinese

Experience throughout the millenniums indicate that parameters in nature could be categorised into five types of determinant elements, represented by wood [木] *mù*, fire [火] *huǒ*, metal [金] *jīn*, water [水] *shuǐ* and earth [土] *tǔ*.

Originating from nature, the five basic determinants could be conceptualised in relation to the season of the year as follows:

WOOD 木

WOOD represents germination and growth, the emergence or renewal phase in a cycle.

The *WOOD* 'energy' [气] *qì* is particularly significant in spring, when vegetative growth takes off. *WOOD* signifies growth after a phase of dormancy. It also implies competition, as thousands of others seek to grow within the same space and time.

Taking into account the yīn-yáng theory', there would be a yīn Wood and a yáng *WOOD*. Yáng *WOOD* is represented by tall, tough Oak or Jarrah trees, and yīn Wood, represented by grass and flowers or shrubs. Note that yin and yáng are equal in importance.

It is possible to link determining elements to time and space. As emergence and growth are associated *with* the Sun, which rises from the East; Wood is therefore associated with east in terms of space. The associated colour is green, typical of vegetation. In general *WOOD* signifies growth and order. Its energy is inherently not very mobile, it tends to develop on-site. The associated organ is liver, the taste sour.

315

FIRE 火

The *FIRE* 'energy' [气] *qì* represents vigour, heat, particularly significant in summer, when vegetative growth has reached its peak. A situation is said to reach the *FIRE* status when it reaches its plateau, with very little room for further growth or expansion. *FIRE* feeds on *WOOD*.

Once again there is yáng *FIRE*, represented by bright, dazzling sunlight or forest fire, as well as yīn *FIRE*, represented by moonlight or candlelight, imparting warmth rather than heat. Both are equal in importance.

In terms of space *FIRE* is represented by South, where warmth comes from. The associated colour is red. In general *FIRE* signifies blaze. The energy is inherently mobile; it tends to move upwards. The associated organ is heart, the taste bitter.

METAL 金

The *METAL* 'energy' [气] *qì* represents autumn, when vegetation growth has ceased; resources are now diverted into fruits or seeds, ready for harvesting for the next generation. This is a time when wood is cut or pruned and leaves shed.

Not surprisingly there is yáng *METAL*, represented by iron and steel, as well as yīn *METAL*, depicted by softer jewellery or malleable metals.

In terms of space *METAL* is linked to West, where the sun sets. The associated colour is white or greys, typically of polished iron and steel. In general *METAL* signifies change, the energy is calm. The associated organ is lung, the taste astringent.

WATER 水

WATER (liquid or ice) 'energy' [气] *qì* represents winter, when vegetation goes to into a period of minimal growth. Animals hibernate. This is a time of low activity when plant and animals survive on reserves, expanding minimal energy. This energy flows downwards, in sharp contrast with the *FIRE* energy, which moves upwards.

As we would imagine, there is yáng *WATER*, represented by torrents, water falls and oceans, and yīn *WATER*, portrayed as mist or dew.

In terms of space, water looks towards North. Its colour is black. In general *WATER* signifies descend and flow, the energy is fluid; the associated organ is kidney, the taste salty.

EARTH 土

To complete the equilibrium of energies, there is *EARTH*, whose 'energy' [气] *qì* is interspersed amongst all the four seasons. While the first two months of spring are considered *WOOD*, the third month is deemed to be *EARTH*, a month of transition after the vigour of WOOD, before the onset of summer.

Similarly the first two months of summer would be FIRE, while the third month is *EARTH*, before heading for autumn. The first two months of autumn would be *METAL*, while the last month *EARTH*. Finally the first two months of winter would be *WATER*, while the last month *EARTH*.

True to the doctrine of yīn-yáng [阴阳], there is yáng earth, represented by rocks, bricks and walls, as well as yīn earth, such as swamps and farmland. Yáng *EARTH* is used for buildings and bridges; yīn *EARTH* supports agriculture.

EARTH sits in the Central location. The colour is yellowish brown. In general *EARTH* signifies nurture; the energy has low mobility, though it is not considered static. It has the ability to nurture and digest. The associated organ is spleen, the taste sweet.

It is important to note that none of the determinants are particularly desirable or undesirable. It is the balance of forces that counts, not individual values.

APPLICATIONS

Central to the applications is the concept of balance of forces in nature and avoidance of excesses. This is critical to the practice of good health, harmony with the environment, and so on.

The five elements are used in a wide range of applications include Feng Shui, Chinese medicine, physiogamy and personality analysis. If you know a person's dominant element (refer to chapter 9), you have a fair idea of his or her personality. We present here an application in personality profiling.

PERSONALITY PROFILING

Wood Personality

Wood symbolises growth and expansion, just like trees or shrubs. To survive in this competitive environment one has to be steadfast, organised, practical, and innovative, to face the challenge. The personality traits include:

'Humane, benevolent, kind' [仁慈] *réncí*; 'Serious, no nonsense, stick to the points' [严肃] *yánsù*; 'Moody' [情绪] *qíngxù*; 'Organised, routinised' [规律] *guīlǜ*; 'Sticking to one's princeples' [原则] *yuánzé*; 'Inflexible, rigid' [死板] *sǐbǎn*; 'Sincere and honest' [朴实] *pūshí*; 'High moral integrity' [骨气] *gúqì*; 'Sympathetic to others' [同情] *tóngqíng*.

People lacking in wood elements could be the opposite of the above. They tend to be weak in their opinions, lack of determination, do not have strong points of view and disorganised. Those with excessive wood element are often strong minded, inflexible, intolerant of other's opinion, somewhat biased or prejudiced.

Fire Personality

Fire symbolises upward movement, expansion, as well as self expression. Fire is dazzling and brilliant, though transient in nature. The personality traits include:

'Good etiquette; well mannered' [礼] *lǐ*; 'Impatient' [性急] *xìngjí*; 'Imaginative and artistic' [幻想] *huànxiǎng*; 'Curious' [好奇] *hàoqí*; 'Enthusiastic and passionate' [热情] *rèqíng*; 'Quick, agile, nimble' [敏捷] *mǐnjié*; 'Self-respect' [自尊] *zìzūn*; 'Hospitable' [好客] *hàokè*; 'Loves cultural pursuits' [文化] *wénhuà*.

People lacking in fire element are generally not easily excited, have little self confidence and is in no mood to show off. Those with excessive fire are impulsive, attention seeking, easily excitable, restless or even aggressive, with a tendency for unpredictable and rapid change. Their impatience may progress to quick temper.

Earth Personality

The earth symbolises consolidation. It has an enormous carrying capacity. It is extremely stable, static and reacts slowly but steadily. It is also very reliable, selfless and sincere. The personality traits include:

'Trustworthy, reliable' [信] *xìn*; 'Honesty' [诚实] *chéngshí*; 'Stability rather than change' [稳固] *wěngù*; 'Loyal and considerate' [忠厚] *zhōnghòu*; 'Forgiving, including others' [包涵] *bāohán*; 'Practical, pragmatic' [实际] *shíjì*; 'Accumulate within (keeping things to oneself)' [内聚] *nèijù*; 'Lenient (not petty)' [宽大] *kuāndà*; 'Prepared to undertake responsibility' [承担] *chéngdān*.

People lacking in earth element tend to be selfish, lack sincerity, and rather self-centred, as well as lack of trust and sincerity. Those with excessive earth elements are likely to be stubborn, not flexible, and slow to react, keen to maintain status quo rather than change. They do not change their mind often once it is made.

Metal Personality

Metal symbolises restructure and reorganisation. Metal is extracted from earth, whereby the whole environment needs to be reorganised, throwing away most of the materials, leaving only a small quantity of metal. As such one needs to be decisive, firm, strong, prepared to cull or get rid of unnecessary products. The personality traits are:

'Righteousness; justice' [义] *yì*; 'Sharp and penetrating (in action as well as words)' [锐利] *ruìlì*; 'Radical, ready for rapid advance' [急进] *jíjìn*; 'Firm, determined' [坚强] *jiānqiáng*; 'Reform or restructure' [改革] *gǎigé*; 'Purge or eliminate' [肃杀] *sùshā*; 'Seek justice' [正义] *zhèngyì*; 'Happy-go-lucky' [乐天] *lètiān*; 'Humour' [幽默] *yōumò*.

People lacking in metal tend to negotiate rather than confront. They tend to refrain from vigorous reforms or changes, are non-exertive and do not exert authority. People having excess metal elements are resolute, fighting injustice at tremendous costs; they have tremendous courage, organisation and discipline. They tend to be ruthless, brave but somewhat unthoughtful.

Water Personality

Water symbolises free flowing, uninhibited spirit. As an entity it could adapt itself to any shape or form. This brings about flexibility and creativity. The personality traits include:

'Intelligent' [智] *zhì*; 'Uninhibited, free spirit' [自由] *zìyóu*; 'Constantly changing his mind, unstable' [不稳定] *bùwěndìng*; 'Flexible, adaptable' [灵活] *línghuó*; 'Creative' [创作] *chuàngzuò*; 'Adaptable, go along as one pleases' [随意] *suíyì*; 'Lively, active' [活跃] *huóyào*; 'Spread around, disseminate' [传播] *chuánbō*; 'Casual' [随便] *suíbiàn*.

People lacking in water tend to be rigid rather than flexible, they lack good sense and intuition. People with excessive water tend to be over smart, tricky and scheming. They tend to be dreamers rather than realists, changing their mind far too often.

A PLACE FOR EVERYONE

It is obvious that there is a place for all types of personalities, or combinations for them. Wood people provides growth, fire people further expands and develops it, earth people consolidates, metal people reorganises and extracts it, while water people set it free and the cycle begins again.

Distribution of Five Elements in Space and Time

The five determinants are distributed in a cyclic fashion. Note that the positions of North, South East and West are different from Western concepts. The months are taken from Chinese calendar (refer to Chapter 9).

South East	South			South West
East	↗	**FIRE** [火] Summer Apr-May	↘	West
	WOOD [木] Spring Jan-Feb	**EARTH** [土] Mar, Jun, Sep, Dec	**METAL** [金] Autumn July-Aug	
	↖	**WATER** [水] Winter Oct-Nov	↙	
North East	North			North West

This presentation forms the basis of Feng Shui studies, when elements from the eight trigrams are added (refer to Chapter ten).

Balance of Forces—Control and Generation

It is evident that things in nature are intricately balanced; the accumulation or depletion of any of these elements would only bring about disaster. These are brought about by two mechanisms, control and generation.

Balance of Forces—Control

The five determining elements control each other in a master – slave cyclic relationship as follows:

Cycle of Control

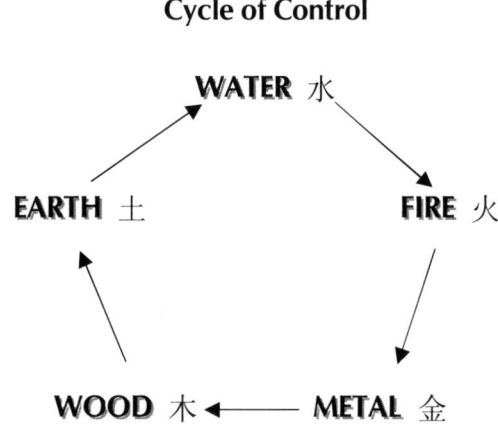

In simple terms, water puts out fire, fire melts metal, metal chops wood, wood breaks up earth (through its roots), earth blocks water (through embankment as well as absorption).

The cycle maintains a balance of forces in nature, ensures that every determining element is not in excess.

RESISTANCE TO CONTROL

It is important that it is the relative strength that counts. It is true that *WATER* puts out fire, but strong fire could evaporate water. *FIRE* melts metal, but the *FIRE* needs to be strong, the temperature high to be effective. *METAL* chops wood, provided the metal is strong and

WOOD relatively weak. *WOOD* breaks up earth, but strong earth such as stones is hardly penetrable by *WOOD*. *EARTH* blocks water, but *EARTH* would collapse when *WATER* is ferocious.

Balance of Forces—Generation

Concurrently another cycle, the cycle of generation (also depicted as Cycle of Birth) ensures that each determining element is promoted. This is the parent-child relationship, whereby the parent gives birth to the child.

Cycle of Generation

WATER 水

METAL 金   WOOD 木

EARTH 土 ⟵——————— FIRE 火

In this cycle, a determining element derives from its parents, and promotes the activity of the child.

For example if WATER is the parent, it promotes the growth of WOOD (the child). WOOD supports fire, ashes from FIRE builds up earth. EARTH gives rise to METAL in the ground, while METAL produces water.[37]

---

[37] Metal producing water is rather difficult to explain. People familiar with chemistry would know that in the Periodic Table Hydrogen dioxide is water, in the same way that any other metal, say Calcium or Iron, forms oxides. Therefore water is derived from a metal like element. Some people explain this relationship in terms of *Qi*.

Both the control and generation cycles are showed in this figure. The cycle on outer circle indicates generation, while the inner arrows indicate controls.

The cycle of generation (promotion) runs parallel to the cycle of control (destruction). In this way forces are balanced and harmonised. Note that nothing is static and the world is in dynamic equilibrium of forces.

APPLICATIONS
It is commonly known that while we get along well with some people, we tend to clash with others due to personality differences.

The cycle of control gives an explanation of personality clashes. If we take the year of birth for example, the following would result:

- 'Wood' clashes with 'Metal'
- 'Fire' clashes with 'water':

More details are found in p. 371.

REMEDIES
Whether in Chinese medicine, Feng Shui or horoscopes, it is possible to achieve rebalance.

For an element that is too strong, introduce the 'master' that curbs its strength. A second method is to introduce the 'child', which would exhaust the parent's energy. A third alternative is to introduce a 'slave', restraining which would also drain off a lot of its energy. For example:

If **Wood** were too strong, introduce **Metal** to curb; generate **Fire** to exhaust wood energy or let wood restrain **Earth** to drain off wood energy.

If **Fire** were too strong, introduce **Water** to curb; generate **Earth** or exhaust fire energy or let fire restrain **Metal** to drain off fire energy.

If **Earth** were too strong, introduce **Wood** to curb; generate **Metal** to exhaust earth energy or let earth restrain **Water** to drain off earth energy.

If **Metal** were too strong, introduce **Fire** to curb; generate **Water** to exhaust metal energy or let metal restrain **Wood** to drain off metal energy.

If **Water** were too strong, introduce **Earth** to curb; generate **Wood** to exhaust water energy or let water restrain **Fire** to drain off water energy.

On the other hand, if an element is too weak, we could introduce the equivalent partner to support, or the generating element to produce more. For example

If **Wood** were too weak, introduce its parent **Water** to generate more, or another **Wood** to support it.

If **Fire** is too weak, introduce its parent **Wood** to generate more, or another **Fire** to support it.

If **Earth** were too weak, introduce its parent **Fire** to generate more, or another **Earth** to support it.

If **Metal** were too weak, introduce its parent **Earth** to generate more, or another **Metal** to support it.

If **Water** were too weak, introduce its parent **Metal** to generate more, or another **Water** to support it.

In personality profiling, the relative strength of a particular element determines the extent of which he is affected by the profile. For a 'wood' person, 'water' element would support him or her, while 'metal' would weaken his or her 'wood' features.

Terms often used in these contexts include:

Self: Self, partners and associates
Child: The product of generation or birth
Parent: The entity that generate self
Master: The entity that controls self
Slave: The entity that is controlled by self

The relationship between the five determinants can be summarised in the table below.

	WOOD	**FIRE**	**EARTH**	**METAL**	**WATER**
WOOD	Self	Child	Slave	Master	Parent
FIRE	Parent	Self	Child	Slave	Master
EARTH	Master	Parent	Self	Child	Slave
METAL	Slave	Master	Parent	Self	Child
WATER	Child	Slave	Master	Parent	Self

APPLICATIONS

The balance between the five determinants forms the basis of many Chinese practices such as Chinese medicine, Feng Shui, the 'life destiny analysis', 'divination', and so on. Life destiny analysis is considered in the next chapter.

An Exercise in Restoring Balance

It is relevant to note that most people have a combination of most of the five elements. When a child is born, it is a practice to take into consideration the balance of the five elements in the birth data.

Should a certain element be lacking, a word containing the missing element would be chosen as part of the child's name.

Wen Yan Zhang [张文炎] *was told that the word* 炎 Yan *was chosen for his name as he lacked fire in his inherent profile. Such is the influence of yīn-yáng wu-xing on some parents!*

The concept of yīn-yáng and 'five determinant elements' wǔxíng is important in Chinese culture. This provides interconnectivity to a huge matrix of parameters including space, time, direction, anatomy, taste, nature, mood, etc, forming a powerful tool for the informed. It provides the possibility of harmonising these factors into a coherent system for consideration. The information is vital in the fields of Chinese medicine, fēngshuǐ, divination, forecasting human life cycles, physiogamy (face reading), etc. The impact on Chinese culture and civilisation, though not well documented, cannot be underestimated. (A word of caution, interpretation of linkages and its inferences is not always easy or accurate, even for the trained and experienced).

People familiar with yīnyáng-wǔxíng tend to develop lateral thinking, the ability to associate events with cause and effects, as well as the ability to work through apparently complicated scenarios.

One of the 'source books' of Chinese philosophy is the I-Ching [易经] yìjīng. Probably the earliest book that is still widely read on earth today, the yìjīng provides the philosophical foundation for the Chinese. Better known as the Book of Change, it analyses the inevitability and nature of changes, transformation from one scenario to another, the cyclic and sometimes predictable nature of these changes. Though not all Chinese actually understand the yìjīng, its underlying principal could be inherent in their thinking. This will be discussed in Chapter 10.

SECTION THREE

CELESTIAL STEMS AND TERRESTRIAL BRANCHES
Another concept frequently encountered is 'Celestial Stems and Terrestrial Branches' [天干地支] *tiāngán-dìzhī*. There are two components, the 'Celestial Stem' [天干] *tiángān* and the 'Terrestrial Branches' [地支] *dìzhī*.

I. **CELESTIAL STEMS** [天干] *tiāngān*
   The 'Celestial Stem' is derived from yīn-yáng and the five determinant elements as follows:

Wood	yáng	甲	*jiǎ*
Wood	yīn	乙	*yǐ*
Fire	yáng	丙	*bǐng*
Fire	yīn	丁	*dīng*
Earth	yáng	戊	*wù*
Earth	yīn	己	*jǐ*
Metal	yáng	庚	*gēng*
Metal	yīn	辛	*xīn*
Water	yáng	壬	*rén*
Water	yīn	癸	*guǐ*

Note that once again yáng alternates with yīn in the sequence.

Refinement of the Five Determinants Elements
The five elements which we have seen in the last section can be refined.

Wood Personality
There are two types of 'WOOD', the 'yáng' woods [甲] *jiǎ* include tall hard-wood trees, while yīn wood [乙] *yǐ* includes grass and shrubs. The yáng wood reaches for the sky, resolute

and bold. The yīn wood are more humble, but resilient. Both types of wood thrive under competition. It is not correct to think that the tall and mighty yáng wood is better than yīn wood, the grass. Should there be a strong wind the strong and mighty tree could snap or be uprooted, while the humble grass still survives, it quickly recovers when the wind passes.

In terms of personality, 'wood' represents growth, development. People with yáng wood [甲] *jiǎ*, just like tall trees are deep rooted in his own believes, his own right with righteousness and strong moral values. They include 'Humane, benevolent, kind characters' [仁慈] *réncí*; 'serious, no nonsense, stick to the points' [严肃] *yánsù*. They tend to be 'moody' [情绪] *qíngxù*; 'organised, routinised' [规律] *guīlù*; 'stick to their principles' [原则] *yuánzé*, 'Inflexible, rigid' [死板] *sǐbǎn*, 'Sincere and honest' [朴实] *pūshí*. They have 'high moral integrity' [骨气] *gúqì* and are 'sympathetic to others' [同情] *tóngqíng*. They do not like to beat around the bush, like to be upfront and forthright, firm in their beliefs.

Examples of yáng Wood [甲] *jiǎ* personalities include the Sòng dynasty general Yuè Fēi (p. 175) and Elvis Presley.

People with yīn wood have similar growth and development personalities, but are less rigid, more flexible and negotiable in their outlook. They are able to survive even in strong winds that would uproot the yáng wood. Just as the grass, the yīn wood people would survive even if stepped upon, as long as their roots are not affected. They tend to encroach on others during their growth and development.

Examples of yīn Wood [乙] *yǐ* personalities include Kublai Khan (p. 160) and Diana, Princess of Wales.

Fire Personality

There are two types of 'FIRE', the yáng fire [丙] *bǐng* include sunlight, volcanoes and forest fire. The yīn fire [丁] *dīng* include

329

moonlight and candles. The yáng fire is powerful, energetic, generates lots of heat, and could be destructive. The yīn fire on the other hand, produces warmth, not heat. It is generally non destructive, though not as forceful as the yáng fire.

In terms of personality, people with 'fire' are generally 'well mannered' [礼] lǐ; 'Impatient' [性急] xìngjí; 'Imaginative and artistic' [幻想] huànxiǎng; 'Curious' [好奇] hàoqí; 'Enthusiastic and passionate' [热情] rèqíng; 'quick, agile, nimble' [敏捷] mǐnjié. They have a sense of 'self-respect' [自尊] zìzūn, are 'sociable, hospitable' [好客] hàokè and like cultural pursuits [文化] wénhuà.

Yáng fire personality is symbolised by the dazzling sun. They could be powerful, hot tempered, impulsive, and do not give sufficient time for strategy and planning. They tend to be energetic, interested or involved in a broad range of activities. They have good understanding of situations, though their temperamental tendencies create unnecessary problems.

Examples of yáng Fire [丙] bǐng personalities include Albert Einstein and Bruce Lee.

People with yīn fire personality, on the other hand, are more refined, sympathetic, and more intricate in planning and thinking, though not as impressive in presenting their ideas. They are warm rather than dazzling. They are better at planning, strategy, and wait for the opportune moment. Just like the candle, they are prepared to sacrifice themselves to provide warmth.

Examples of yīn fire [丁] dīng personalities include Mao Zedong and Margaret Thatcher.

Earth Personality

There are two types of 'EARTH', the yáng earth [戊] wù, includes boulders and stone, while the yīn earth [己] jǐ includes marshland or rice fields. Yáng earth obviously has the strength and bearing capacity, excellent for buildings or to undertake heavy load. Yīn earth, on the other hand, is soft and provides the environment for crops.

In general the earth people are 'trustworthy, reliable' [信] *xìn*; 'honest' [诚实] *chéngshí*; 'stable' [稳固] *wěngù*; 'loyal and considerate' [忠厚] *zhōnghòu*. They also tend to be 'lenient (not petty)' [宽大] *kuāndà*, 'include others' [包涵] *bāohán* and 'practical, pragmatic' [实际] *shíjì*. They have an ability to 'accumulate within (keeping things to oneself)' [内聚] *nèijù* and are 'prepared to undertake responsibility' [承担] *chéngdān*.

People with Yáng earth personality tend to be steady in their approach. They represent dry, strong, unyielding rocks, solid and stable. They would only undertake things on a strong, solid basis, taking their time. Once a decision is made, they do not waver; have the confidence and responsibility to see it through. They are trusted and trustworthy.

Examples of yáng Earth [戊] *wù* personalities include Genghis Khan (p. 156) and Emperor Kāng Xī (p. 151).

Those with Yīn earth personality tend to be gentle and quiet. They represent wetland or farm land, capable of supporting a variety of life and crops. In other words, there are resourceful, talented, quick to assimilate and dispense 'nutrients'. They are flexible, adaptable, and quick to appraise conditions and adapt themselves to changing situations. They tend to be suspicious or skeptical.

Examples of yīn Earth [己] *jǐ* personalities include Emperor Hàn Wǔdì (p. 163) and Chou En Lai (p. 178).

Metal Personality

There are two kinds of 'METAL', the yáng metal [庚] *gēng* are tough, of which swords are made of, while yīn metal [辛] *xīn* are more malleable, used for jewelry and ornamentals. Yáng metal withstands high heat. They are tough and can be used to cut or chop materials. Yīn metal, on the other hand, is soft and malleable, highly decorative, excellent for making jewelry.

In terms of personalities metal people tend to seek or impose justice [正义] *zhèngyì*; they are 'sharp and penetrating (in action as well as words)' [锐利] *ruìlì*; 'Radical, willing, ready and able for rapid advance' [急进] *jíjìn*. They are normally 'firm, determined' [坚强] *jiānqiáng*; seek 'reform or restructure' [改革] *gǎigé*; 'prepared to cull, purge or eliminate' [肃杀] *sùshā*. They are in general 'happy-go-lucky' [乐天] *lètiān* with a sense of humour [幽默] *yōumò*.

People with yáng metal [庚] *gēng* personality are decisive, tough, non malleable, not compromising. They are sharp, strong willed, bold and daring, hate to be losers. They would act with a sense of righteousness, justice and fairness, willing to help the down-trodden and the helpless.

Examples of yáng metal [庚] *gēng* personalities include Emperor Tóng Zhì (p. 152) and Richard Nixon.

Those with yīn metal [辛] *xīn* is symbolised by metals that are tough yet malleable. They are less 'offensive', more amicable, negotiable, subtle, though equally decisive. Their judgment tends to be swayed by emotion or sentiment. They also tend to be vane.

Examples of yīn metal [辛] *xīn* include J. F. Kennedy and Marilyn Monroe.

Water Personality

There are two kinds of 'WATER', the yáng water [壬] *rén* flows like torrents and rivers, while the yīn water [癸] *guǐ* is best depicted as dew or drizzle. Yáng water is powerful and energetic, and can be very destructive; its power needs to be restrained. Yīn water, on the other hand is still rather than active. Nevertheless it moistens surfaces, producing a serene, limited outcome without destruction.

In terms of personality 'water' people are known to be 'Intelligent' [智] *zhì*; extremely 'Flexible, adaptable' [灵活] *línghuó*; with an 'uninhibited, free spirit' [自由] *zìyóu*; 'constantly changing his mind, unstable' [不稳定] *bùwěndìng*. They also have high 'adaptability, go along as one pleases' [随意] *suíyì*, 'casual' [随便] *suíbiàn*. They are 'creative' [创作] *chuàngzuò*, 'lively, active' [活跃] *huóyào*, and 'like to disseminate their ideas' [传播] *chuánbō*.

People with yáng water personality tend to be extrovert; headstrong, good at grasping opportunities. Just like a big river that flows over large areas, the yáng water people tend to be confident, looking forward to the future rather than the past, and are keen in a broad range of activities. They are diplomatic and flexible in their approaches.

Examples of yáng Water [壬] *rén* personalities include Sun Yat San (p. 170) and George Bush Sr.

Those with yīn water personality tend to be more easy-going, helpful, pragmatic, full of imagination, though at times impractical. They are more cool-headed and considerate, more sensitive to the needs of the environment.

Examples of yīn Water [癸] *guǐ* personalities include the Sòng dynasty poet Sū Dōngpō (p. 169) and Wáng Ānshí (p. 171).

CELESTIAL STEM CLASHES

As expected, the FIRE elements 丙 *bǐng*, 丁 *dīng*, would clash with the WATER elements 壬 *rén*, 癸 *guǐ*. At the same time the WOOD elements 甲 *jiǎ*, 乙 *yǐ*, would clash with the METAL elements 庚 *gēng*, 辛 *xīn* (refer to Chapter 9 for more details).

II. TERRESTRIAL BRANCHES [地支] *dìzhī*

Most ethnic Chinese would know what zodiac year they are born in, for example year of the dragon, ox, etc. Not many realise that this refers to the 'Terrestrial Branch' [地支] *dìzhī* component. It is made up of twelve entities, each represented by a zodiac sign. Each of the symbols has a distinct yīn-yáng as well as 'Five Elements' [五行] *wǔxíng* combination. These entities, together with their yīn-yáng and five elements are as follows:

Animal	Name		Yīn-yáng	Elements
Rat	zǐ	子	yáng	Water
Ox	chǒu	丑	yīn	Water/Earth
Tiger	yín	寅	yáng	Wood
Rabbit	mǎo	卯	yīn	Wood
Dragon	chén	辰	yáng	Wood/Earth
Snake	sì	巳	yīn	Fire
Horse	wǔ	午	yáng	Fire
Goat	wèi	未	yīn	Fire/Earth
Monkey	shēn	申	yáng	Metal
Rooster	yǒu	酉	yīn	Metal
Dog	xū	戌	yáng	Metal/Earth
Pig	hài	亥	yīn	Water

Note that once again a yáng entity alternates with a yīn entity in the sequence. Each of these signs is invariably associated with some personality traits, characters, etc, consistent with zodiac features. Each have their own strengths and weaknesses, there being no overall winner!

Combination of Celestial Stem and Terrestrial Branches

Combination of Celestial Stem and Terrestrial Branches produce a whole range of parameters necessary for Chinese zodiac signs, Chinese calendar, mapping life destiny, divination, etc.

Since there are five determinant elements and twelve earthly branches, there would be sixty stem-branch combinations go in a definite, continuous sequence as follows:

1.	'Wood-rat'	甲子	*jiǎzǐ*
2.	'Wood-ox'	乙丑	*yǐchǒu*
3.	'Fire-tiger'	丙寅	*bǐngyín*
4.	'Fire-rabbit'	丁卯	*dīngmǎo*
5.	'Earth-dragon'	戊辰	*wùchén*
6.	'Earth-snake'	己巳	*jǐsì*
7.	'Metal-horse'	庚午	*gēngwǔ*
8.	'Metal-goat'	辛未	*xīnwèi*
9.	'Water-monkey'	壬申	*rénshēn*
10.	'Water-rooster'	癸酉	*guǐyǒu*
11.	'Wood-dog'	甲戌	*jiǎxū*
12.	'Wood-pig'	乙亥	*yǐhài*
13.	'Fire-rat'	丙子	*bǐngzǐ*
14.	'Fire-ox'	丁丑	*dīngchǒu*
15.	'Earth-tiger'	戊寅	*wùyín*
16.	'Earth-rabbit'	己卯	*jǐmǎo*
17.	'Metal-dragon'	庚辰	*gēngchén*
18.	'Metal-snake'	辛巳	*xīnsì*
19.	'Water-horse'	壬午	*rénwǔ*
20.	'Water-goat'	癸未	*guǐwèi*
21.	'Wood-monkey'	甲申	*jiǎshēn*
22.	'Wood-rooster'	乙酉	*yǐyǒu*
23.	'Fire-dog'	丙戌	*bǐngxū*
24.	'Fire-pig'	丁亥	*dīnghài*
25.	'Earth-rat'	戊子	*wùzǐ*
26.	'Earth-ox'	己丑	*jǐchǒu*
27.	'Metal-tiger'	庚寅	*gēngyín*
28.	'Metal-rabbit'	辛卯	*xīnmǎo*
29.	'Water-dragon'	壬辰	*rénchén*

30. 'Water-snake'   癸巳   *guǐsì*
31. 'Wood-horse'   甲午   *jiǎwǔ*
32. 'Wood-goat'   乙未   *yǐwèi*
33. 'Metal-monkey'   丙申   *bǐngshēn*
34. 'Metal-rooster'   丁酉   *dīngyǒu*
35. 'Earth-dog'   戊戌   *wùxū*
36. 'Earth-pig'   己亥   *jǐhài*
37. 'Metal-rat'   庚子   *gēngzǐ*
38. 'Metal-ox'   辛丑   *xīnchǒu*
39. 'Water-tiger'   壬寅   *rényín*
40. 'Water-rabbit'   癸卯   *guǐmǎo*
41. 'Wood-dragon'   甲辰   *jiǎchén*
42. 'Wood-snake'   乙巳   *yǐsì*
43. 'Fire-horse'   丙午   *bǐngwǔ*
44. 'Fire-goat'   丁未   *dīngwèi*
45. 'Earth-monkey'   戊申   *wùshēn*
46. 'Earth-rooster'   己酉   *jǐyǒu*
47. 'Metal-dog'   庚戌   *gēngxū*
48. 'Metal-pig'   辛亥   *xīnhài*
49. 'Water-rat'   壬子   *rénzǐ*
50. 'Water-ox'   癸丑   *guǐchǒu*
51. 'Wood-tiger'   甲寅   *jiǎyín*
52. 'Wood-rabbit'   乙卯   *yǐmǎo*
53. 'Fire-dragon'   丙辰   *bǐngchén*
54. 'Fire-snake'   丁巳   *dīngsì*
55. 'Earth-horse'   戊午   *wùwǔ*
56. 'Earth-goat'   己未   *jǐwèi*
57. 'Metal-monkey'   庚申   *gēngshēn*
58. 'Metal-rooster'   辛酉   *xīnyǒu*
59. 'Water-dog'   壬戌   *rénxū*
60. 'Water-pig'   癸亥   *guǐhài*

Relationship between a Celestial Stem and Terrestrial Branch

This relationship between the 'Celestial Stem' [天干] *tiāngán* and the 'Terrestrial Branch' [地支] *dìzhī*, expressed in terms of yīn-yáng and the five determinant elements is important. Whether the stem and branch controls, harmonises, or support each other gives an indication of the general state of affairs. Taking the first twelve combinations as examples, we have:

'Wood-rat':	Wood-water (support)	甲子 *jiǎzǐ*
'Wood-ox':	Wood-earth (control)	乙丑 *yǐchǒu*
'Fire-tiger':	Fire-wood (support)	丙寅 *bǐngyín*
'Fire-rabbit':	Fire-wood (support)	丁卯 *dīngmǎo*
'Earth-dragon'	Earth-earth (harmony)	戊辰 *wùchén*
'Earth-snake':	Earth-fire (support)	己巳 *jǐsì*
'Metal-horse':	Metal-fire (control)	庚午 *gēngwǔ*
'Metal-goat':	Metal-earth (support)	辛未 *xīnwèi*
'Water-monkey':	Water-metal (support)	壬申 *rénshēn*
'Water-rooster':	Water-metal (support)	癸酉 *guǐyǒu*
'Wood-dog':	Wood-earth (control)	甲戌 *jiǎxū*
'Wood-pig':	Wood-water (support)	乙亥 *yǐhài*

It is obvious that relationship is not happy when one controls the other, but will be great when one supports the other.

The sixty combinations start with 'Wood-rat' [甲子] *jiǎzǐ* and ends with 'Water-pig' [癸亥] *guǐhài*. The year in which 'Wood-rat' [甲子] *jiǎzǐ* commences, for example in 1924, 1984, 2044, are regarded as beginning of new cycle.

Websites dedicated to 'tiāngān-dìzhī' include:

Heavenly stem and earthly branches:
http://www.hko.gov.hk/gts/time/stemsandbranches.htm
Establishment and uses of heavenly stems and earthly branches:
http://www.hiakz.com/establishment.asp

The 'Pillars of Destiny':
An Application of the Ancient Paradigms

天

the word 'big' [大] *dà* is easily visualised by a person stretching his arms, showing how big he is. The word 'sky' or 'heaven' [天] *tiān* consists of a horizontal stroke 一 capping the word 'big' [大] *dà*. As the saying goes, the sky is the limit.

THIS CHAPTER BUILDS ON KNOWLEDGE gained from the three paradigms, the yīn-yáng [阴阳], the 'five determinant elements' [五行] *wǔxíng*, as well as 'Celestial Stems and Terrestrial Branches' [天干地支] *tiāngán-dìzhī*.

In this chapter we look at how these paradigms form the basis of one of the Chinese 'psyche'. We compare the workings of Chinese and Western calendars, as well as approaches to zodiacs.

One of the unique practices that distinguish many Chinese homes and businesses is these metaphysical practices.

The 'analysis of life destiny' [算命] *suànmìng* is a topic that is fascinating and interesting. In this chapter we would look at the workings of the 'four pillars' [四柱] *sìzhù*, used to map the personality profiles as well as 'Analysis of destinies', including the ups and downs in our lives.

338

THE CHINESE CALENDAR

We are used to calendar systems based on numbers, such as the 11th hour on the third day of the 6th month of the year 2006. Could you imagine a date without numbers? Can you imagine a calendar system that tells you precisely the prevailing determining elements, the balance of forces in nature, rather than just numbers? Well the traditional Chinese calendar system does just that.

We know that the Gregorian calendar denotes the historical importance of Jesus Christ, while the Moslem dates started with Prophet Mohammad's journey to Medina in 622. The Chinese calendar, on the other hand does not denote any historical or personality importance. Each year, month, day or hour is represented by a combination of 'Celestial Stem' [天干] *tiāngán* and 'Terrestrial Branch' [地支] *dìzhī*. The system provides an important set of parameters, pertaining to the interaction between environmental factors. In other words the calendar system takes into account the forces in nature at work.

The traditional starting year for the Chinese calendar is 2637 BC, making the year 2006 the 4643rd year. It goes on a sixty-year cycle, starts with 'Wood-rat' [甲子] *jiǎzǐ*, the first of the Celestial Stem and Terrestrial Branch, and ends with 'Water-pig' [癸亥] *guǐhài*, the last Celestial Stem and Terrestrial Branch (refer to the previous chapter for the complete listing of all sixty years). The present sixty-year cycle started on 2 February 1984, ends in the year 2023.

What is Your Chinese Zodiac Sign?

Chinese zodiac signs are based on the year, rather than the month. The signs for the years from 1924 to 2021 are as follows.

'Wood-rat'	甲子 *jiǎzǐ*	05/02/1924 – 23/01/1925
'Wood-ox'	乙丑 *yǐchǒu*	24/01/1925 – 12/02/1926
'Fire-tiger'	丙寅 *bǐngyín*	13/02/1926 – 01/02/1927
'Fire-rabbit'	丁卯 *dīngmǎo*	02/02/1927 – 22/01/1928

'Earth-dragon'	戊辰	*wùchén*	23/01/1928 – 09/02/1929
'Earth-snake'	己巳	*jǐsì*	10/02/1929 – 29/01/1930
'Metal-horse'	庚午	*gēngwǔ*	30/01/1930 – 16/02/1931
'Metal-goat'	辛未	*xīnwèi*	17/02/1931 – 05/02/1932
'Water-monkey'	壬申	*rénshēn*	06/02/1932 – 25/01/1933
'Water-rooster'	癸酉	*guǐyǒu*	26/01/1933 – 13/02/1934
'Wood-dog'	甲戌	*jiǎxū*	14/02/1934 – 03/02/1935
'Wood-pig'	乙亥	*yǐhài*	04/02/1935 – 23/01/1936
'Fire-rat'	丙子	*bǐngzǐ*	24/01/1936 – 10/02/1937
'Fire-ox'	丁丑	*dīngchǒu*	11/02/1937 – 30/01/1938
'Earth-tiger'	戊寅	*wùyín*	31/01/1938 – 18/02/1939
'Earth-rabbit'	己卯	*jǐmǎo*	19/02/1939 – 07/02/1940
'Metal-dragon'	庚辰	*gēngchén*	08/02/1940 – 26/01/1941
'Metal-snake'	辛巳	*xīnsì*	27/01/1941 – 14/02/1942
'Water-horse'	壬午	*rénwǔ*	15/02/1942 – 04/02/1943
'Water-goat'	癸未	*guǐwèi*	05/02/1943 – 24/01/1944
'Wood-monkey'	甲申	*jiǎshēn*	25/01/1944 – 12/02/1945
'Wood-rooster'	乙酉	*yǐyǒu*	13/02/1945 – 01/02/1946
'Fire-dog'	丙戌	*bǐngxū*	02/02/1946 – 21/01/1947
'Fire-pig'	丁亥	*dīnghài*	22/01/1947 – 09/02/1948
'Earth-rat '	戊子	*wùzǐ*	10/02/1948 – 28/01/1949
'Earth-ox'	己丑	*jǐchǒu*	29/01/1949 – 16/02/1950
'Metal-tiger'	庚寅	*gēngyín*	17/02/1950 – 05/02/1951
'Metal-rabbit'	辛卯	*xīnmǎo*	06/02/1951 – 26/01/1952
'Water-dragon'	壬辰	*rénchén*	27/01/1952 – 13/02/1953
'Water-snake'	癸巳	*guǐsì*	14/02/1953 – 02/02/1954
'Wood-horse'	甲午	*jiǎwǔ*	03/02/1954 – 23/01/1955
'Wood-goat'	乙未	*yǐwèi*	24/01/1955 – 11/02/1956
'Fire-monkey'	丙申	*bǐngshēn*	12/02/1956 – 30/01/1957
'Fire-rooster'	丁酉	*dīngyǒu*	31/01/1957 – 17/02/1958
'Earth-dog'	戊戌	*wùxū*	18/02/1958 – 07/02/1959
'Earth-pig'	己亥	*jǐhài*	08/02/1959 – 27/01/1960
'Metal-rat'	庚子	*gēngzǐ*	28/01/1960 – 14/02/1961

'Metal-ox'	辛丑	*xīnchǒu*	15/02/1961 – 04/02/1962
'Water-tiger'	壬寅	*rényín*	05/02/1962 – 24/01/1963
'Water-rabbit'	癸卯	*guǐmaǒ*	25/01/1963 – 12/02/1964
'Wood-dragon'	甲辰	*jiǎchén*	13/02/1964 – 01/02/1965
'Wood-snake'	乙巳	*yǐsì*	02/02/1965 – 20/01/1966
'Fire-horse'	丙午	*bǐngwǔ*	21/01/1966 – 08/02/1967
'Fire-goat'	丁未	*dīngwèi*	09/02/1967 – 29/01/1968
'Earth-monkey'	戊申	*wùshēn*	30/01/1968 – 16/02/1969
'Earth-rooster'	己酉	*jǐyǒu*	17/02/1969 – 05/02/1970
'Metal-dog'	庚戌	*gēngxū*	06/02/1970 – 26/01/1971
'Metal-pig'	辛亥	*xīnhài*	27/01/1971 – 14/02/1972
'Water-rat'	壬子	*rénzǐ*	15/02/1972 – 02/02/1973
'Water-ox'	癸丑	*guǐchǒu*	03/02/1973 – 22/01/1974
'Wood-tiger'	甲寅	*jiǎyín*	23/01/1974 – 10/02/1975
'Wood-rabbit'	乙卯	*yǐmǎo*	11/02/1975 – 30/01/1976
'Fire-dragon'	丙辰	*bǐngchén*	31/01/1976 – 17/02/1977
'Fire-snake'	丁巳	*dīngsì*	18/02/1977 – 06/02/1978
'Earth-horse'	戊午	*wùwǔ*	07/02/1978 – 27/01/1979
'Earth-goat'	己未	*jǐwèi*	28/01/1979 – 15/02/1980
'Metal-monkey'	庚申	*gēngshēn*	16/02/1980 – 04/02/1981
'Metal-rooster'	辛酉	*xīnyǒu*	05/02/1981 – 24/01/1982
'Water-dog'	壬戌	*rénxū*	25/01/1982– 12/02/1983
'Water-pig'	癸亥	*guǐhài*	13/02/1983 – 01/02/1984
'Wood-rat'	甲子	*jiǎzǐ*	02/02/1984 – 19/02/1985
'Wood-ox'	乙丑	*yǐchǒu*	20/02/1985 – 08/02/1986
'Fire-tiger'	丙寅	*bǐngyín*	09/02/1986 – 28/01/1987
'Fire-rabbit'	丁卯	*dīngmǎo*	29/01/1987 – 16/02/1988
'Earth-dragon'	戊辰	*wùchén*	17/02/1988 – 05/02/1989
'Earth-snake'	己巳	*jǐsì*	06/02/1989 – 26/01/1990
'Metal-horse'	庚午	*gēngwǔ*	27/01/1990 – 14/02/1991
'Metal-goat'	辛未	*xīnwèi*	15/02/1991 – 03/02/1992
'Water-monkey'	壬申	*rénshēn*	04/02/1992 – 22/01/1993
'Water-rooster'	癸酉	*guǐyǒu*	23/01/1993 – 09/02/1994

'Wood-dog'	甲戌	*jiǎxū*	10/02/1994 – 30/01/1995
'Wood-pig'	乙亥	*yǐhài*	31/01/1995 – 18/02/1996
'Fire-rat'	丙子	*bǐngzǐ*	19/02/1996 – 06/02/1997
'Fire-ox'	丁丑	*dīngchǒu*	07/02/1997 – 27/01/1998
'Earth-tiger'	戊寅	*wùyín*	28/01/1998 – 15/02/1999
'Earth-rabbit'	己卯	*jǐmǎo*	16/02/1999 – 04/02/2000
'Metal-dragon'	庚辰	*gēngchén*	05/02/2000 – 23/01/2001
'Metal-snake'	辛巳	*xīnsì*	24/01/2001 – 11/02/2002
'Water-horse'	壬午	*réwǔ*	12/02/2002 – 31/01/2003
'Water-goat'	癸未	*guǐwèi*	01/02/2003 – 21/01/2004
'Wood-monkey'	甲申	*jiǎshēn*	22/01/2004 – 08/02/2005
'Wood-rooster'	乙酉	*yǐyǒu*	09/02/2005 – 28/01/2006
'Fire-dog'	丙戌	*bǐngxū*	29/01/2006 – 17/02/2007
'Fire-pig'	丁亥	*dīnghài*	18/02/2007 – 06/02/2008
'Earth-rat'	戊子	*wùzǐ*	07/02/2008 – 25/01/2009
'Earth-ox'	己丑	*jǐchǒu*	26/01/2009 – 13/02/2010
'Metal-tiger'	庚寅	*gēngyín*	14/02/2010 – 02/02/2011
'Metal-rabbit'	辛卯	*xīnmǎo*	03/02/2011 – 22/01/2012
'Water-dragon'	壬辰	*rénchén*	23/01/2012 – 09/02/2013
'Water-snake'	癸巳	*guǐsì*	10/02/2013 – 30/01/2014
'Wood-horse'	甲午	*jiǎwǔ*	31/01/2014 – 18/02/2015
'Wood-goat '	乙未	*yǐwèi*	19/02/2015 – 07/02/2016
'Fire-monkey'	丙申	*bǐngshēn*	08/02/2016 – 27/01/2017
'Fire-rooster'	丁酉	*dīngyǒu*	28/01/2017 – 15/02/2018
'Earth-dog'	戊戌	*wùxū*	16/02/2018 – 04/02/2019
'Earth-pig'	己亥	*jǐhài*	05/02/2019 – 24/01/2020
'Metal-rat'	庚子	*gēngzǐ*	25/01/2020 – 11/02/2021

It is relevant to note that Masters working out pillars of destiny uses the day marking the 'Beginning of Spring' [立春] *lìchūn* as the start of the Chinese New Year, rather than the first day of Chinese calendar (refer to p. 374).

CHINESE ZODIAC INTERPRETATIONS

Hundreds of books and websites have been written on Chinese zodiac signs. Theodora Lau,[38] for example, gives detailed analysis of character profile, personality types, affinity or conflict with other zodiac personalities. She also describes various relationships: within the family, as a teacher, a lover and spouse, a business partner, a boss, a friend and colleague, an opponent, or the mediator.

The 'Celestial Stem' [天干] *tiāngān* produces five determinant elements of 'wood', 'fire', 'earth', 'metal' and 'water. When this is taken into account a given zodiac sign could be differentiated into five types. For example rather than having 'tiger', five types of tigers, 'wood-tiger', 'fire-tiger', 'earth-tiger', 'metal-tiger' and 'water-tiger' can be distinguished. These should be read as additional part of the overall zodiac sign. A good source of information on the impact of the five determinant elements on Chinese zodiacs comes from the traditional interpretations of sixty life destiny combinations.

It is interesting to link zodiac interpretations directly to the animals chosen to represent them. A very brief description of each of the zodiac signs is given in the following pages. On their own they are too general and limited, as only the year is taken into account, when all four parameters, the year, month, day and hour, provide useful information (refer to p. 381). It is only when all parameters are considered that interesting data could be interpreted.

The cycle of zodiac signs are illustrated as follows (moving clockwise, starting with the rat):

---

[38] Lau, Theodora. *The Chinese Horoscopes Guide to Relationships: Love and Marriage, Friendship and Business*, Souvenir Press, Canada, 1995.

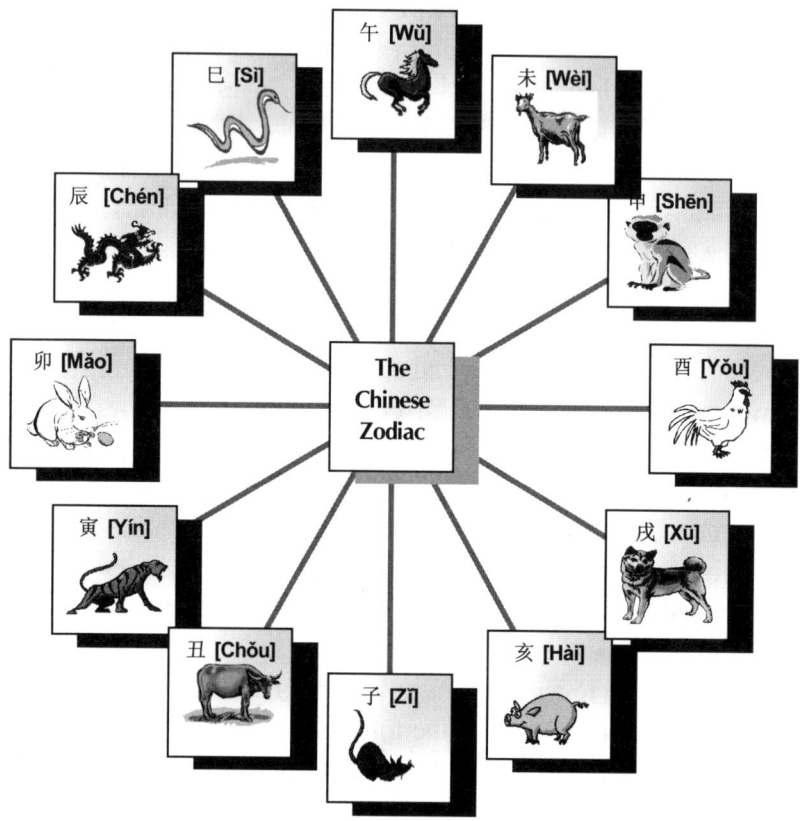

Note that the zodiac interpretations, including combination with five determinant elements, are of little value to a professional 'life destiny' analyst.

Further information could be obtained from *www.woosee.com/zpsz/zipingrumen/shengnian.htm* (In Chinese) (Note that the translation is extremely difficult and only serves as a guide).

The zodiac cycle is more meaningfully presented in the following table. As we shall see later, this table illustrates the relationships between the various Terrestrial components. (Compare with the diagram in p. 321. Refer to p. 334 for the relationship between the zodiac signs and the five elements).

sì [巳] Snake (Fire)	wǔ [午] Horse (Fire)	wèi [未] Goat (Earth)	shēn [申] Monkey (Metal)
chén [辰] Dragon (Earth)			yǒu [酉] Rooster (Metal)
mǎo [卯] Rabbit (Wood)			xū [戌] Dog (Earth)
yín [寅] Tiger (Wood)	chǒu [丑] Ox (Earth)	zǐ [子] Rat (Water)	hài [亥] Pig (Water)

INTERPRETATIONS ACCORDING TO ANIMAL TRAITS

'Wood-rat'   甲子 *jiǎzǐ*   5 Feb 1924 - 23 Jan 1925
'Fire-rat'   丙子 *bǐngzǐ*   24 Jan 1936 - 10 Feb 1937
'Earth-rat' 戊子 *wùzǐ*   10 Feb 1948 - 28 Jan 1949
'Metal-rat' 庚子 *gēngzǐ*   28 Jan 1960 - 14 Feb 1961
'Water-rat' 壬子 *rénzǐ*   15 Feb 1972 - 2 Feb 1973

'Wood-rat'   甲子 *jiǎzǐ*   2 Feb 1984 - 19 Feb 1985
'Fire-rat'   丙子 *bǐngzǐ*   19 Feb 1996 - 6 Feb 1997
'Earth-rat' 戊子 *wùzǐ*   7 Feb 2008 - 25 Jan 2009
'Metal-rat' 庚子 *gēngzǐ*   25 Jan 2020 - 11 Feb 2021
'Water-rat' 壬子 *rénzǐ*   11 Feb 2032 - 20 Jan 2033

The Rats [子] *zǐ*

The rat [鼠] *shǔ* is known as 子 *zǐ* in the 'Terrestrial Branch' [地支] *dìzhī* naming system. In nature, the rat

345

- Survives in a wide range of habitat, i.e. highly adaptable to the environment, not too demanding on food source or the living habitat.
- Is found wherever human beings are found, live in the same habitat as human or human created habitat such as grain silos
- Converges where there is food, including non-edible materials such as wood or electrical wires.
- Is apparently optimistic, cheerful
- Is smart, nimble, creative and imaginative in their effort to get food or getting out of trapped situations, highly intuitive.
- Is curious, energetic, always exploring.
- Has good memory
- Not constrained by 'fixed environment, think outside the square.

As rat is a yáng water element, it has a certain degree of adaptability. It is able to deal with a wide range of people and situations. It can 'go with the tide', and in general get along well with people.

People born under the rat sign are generally regarded as clever, quick witted, curious, creative, optimistic, cheerful and sensitive. They are energetic, curious but careful.

They are by nature alert and suspicious, until trust and confidence is established. They have good observation and analytical abilities. They are often gifted with good memory.

When combined with the 'Celestial Stem' [天干] tiāngān, five aspects of rat could be established.

'Wood-rat' [甲子] jiǎzǐ 1924, 1984. Described as 'Rat in the attics' [屋上之鼠] wūshàngzhīshǔ. Some of the characteristics include 'quick wit, intelligent and capable' [伶俐聪明贤能] língli cōngmíng xiánnéng.

'Fire-rat' [丙子] bǐngzǐ 1936, 1996. Described as 'Rat in the field' [田内之鼠] tiánnèizhīshǔ. Some of the characteristics include 'living according to one's status and ability, happiness ensues' [守己安分, 幸福遁来] *shǒujǐ'ānfen, xìngfúdùnlái.*

'Earth-rat' [戊子] *wùzǐ* 1948, 2008. Described as 'Rat in the grain silo' [仓内之鼠] *cāngnèizhīshǔ.* Some of the characteristics include 'excellence in planning and computation, good in physical as well as intellectual pursuits' [计算聪明, 精通文武] *jìsuàn cōngmíng, jīngtōngwénwǔ.*

'Metal-rat' [庚子] *gēngzǐ* 1960, 2020. Described as 'Rat along the roof beam' [梁上之鼠] *liángshàngzhīshǔ.* Some of the characteristics include 'Respected and stable, does not lack material needs' [尊重安稳, 衣禄无亏] *zūnzhòng'ānwěn, yīlùwúkuī.*

'Water-rat' [壬子] *rénzǐ* 1912, 1972. Described as' Rat in the hills' [山上之鼠] *shānshàngzhīshǔ.* Some of the characteristics include 'Difficulties in earlier age, by midlife there is ample supplies' [幼年有灾, 中年衣食足用] *yòuniányǒuzāi, zhōngnián yīshí zúyòng.*

'Wood-ox'	乙丑	*yǐchǒu*	24 Jan 1925 - 12 Feb 1926
'Fire-ox'	丁丑	*dīngchǒu*	11 Feb 1937 - 30 Jan 1938
'Earth-ox'	已丑	*jǐchǒu*	29 Jan 1949 - 16 Feb 1950
'Metal-ox'	辛丑	*xīnchǒu*	15 Feb 1961 - 4 Feb 1962
'Water-ox'	癸丑	*guǐchǒu*	3 Feb 1973 - 22 Jan 1974
'Wood-ox'	乙丑	*yǐchǒu*	20 Feb 1985 - 8 Feb 1986
'Fire-ox'	丁丑	*dīngchǒu*	7 Feb 1997 - 27 Jan 1998
'Earth-ox'	已丑	*jǐchǒu*	26 Jan 2009 - 13 Feb 2010
'Metal-ox'	辛丑	*xīnchǒu*	12 Feb 2021 - 31 Jan 2022
'Water-ox'	癸丑	*guǐchǒu*	31 Jan 2033 - 18 Feb 2034

The Oxen [丑] *chǒu*

The ox [牛] *niú* is known as 丑 *chǒu* in the 'Terrestrial Branch' [地支] *dìzhī* naming system. In nature, the ox:

- Toils throughout its life (especially in earlier times), pulling heavy burdens.
- Is honest, steadfast, serious, single-minded in its job
- Is serious, takes no nonsense, charges on when provoked.
- Regurgitates its food, take its time to digest
- Has close association with man (especially in earlier days), reliable, loyal to man. Is useful to man even after its death for its meat, hide, bones, etc.
- Does not change once its mind is made up. Stick to routines.
- When challenged, might charge like a 'bull' without changing directions.

As the ox is a yīn earth/water element, there is a certain degree of conservative nature inherent with earth element, readiness to accept responsibility and hard work, but not as flexible and negotiable as the rat.

People born under the ox sign are generally regarded as honest, inflexible amounting to stubbornness, responsible, living up to his or her believes and principal. They would complete their tasks even in the face of tremendous odds and work load.

They are loyal and reliable, ready and willing to work hard or undertake responsibilities. They are conscientious in their work. Though they might appear conservative, they have their own ideas and principles. They might take time to rethink or regurgitate, giving the misleading impression that they are slow to reach conclusions or indecisive. However once an opinion is made, they seldom change their mind.

When combined with the 'Celestial Stem' [天干] tiāngān, five aspects of ox could be established.

'Wood-ox' [乙丑] yǐchǒu 1925, 1985. Described as 'Ox of the ocean' [海内之牛] hǎinèizhīniú. Some of the characteristics include 'As a person very generous, likes spring breeze (occasion

348

to be happy or joyous)' [为人慷慨, 喜爱春风] *wéirén kǎngkai, xi'ài chūnfēng.*

'Fire-ox' [丁丑] *dīngchǒu* 1937, 1997. Described as 'Ox of the lakes' [湖内之牛] *húnèizhīniú.* Some of the characteristics include 'Harmonious as a person, plentiful in material supply' [为人和睦, 衣禄不少] *wéirén hémù, yīlùbùshǎo.*

jǐchǒu [己丑] 'Earth-ox' 1949, 2009. Described as 'Ox within the paddock' [栏内之牛] *lánnèizhīniú.* Some of the characteristics include 'Quick with the mouth but uncomplicated at heart. Gifted in the arts, capable' [口快心直, 通文艺有才能] *kǒukuài xīnzhí, tōng wényì yǒu cáinéng.*

'Metal-ox' [辛丑] *xīnchǒu* 1901, 1961. Described as 'Ox along the way' [路途之牛] *lùtuzhīniú.* Some of the characteristics include 'Mild tempered and mannered' [心性温和] *xīnxìng wēnhé.*

'Water-ox' [癸丑] *guǐchǒu* 1913, 1973. Described as 'Ox in the paddock' [栏内之牛] *lánnèizhīniú.* Some of the characteristics include 'Respected through his life, does not cause any trouble' [一生尊重, 不惹是非] *yīshēng zūnzhòng, bùrě shìfēi.*

'Fire-tiger'	丙寅	*bǐngyín*	13 Feb 1926 - 1 Feb 1927
'Earth-tiger'	戊寅	*wùyín*	31 Jan 1938 - 18 Feb 1939
'Metal-tiger'	庚寅	*gēngyín*	17 Feb 1950 - 5 Feb 1951
'Water-tiger'	壬寅	*rényín*	5 Feb 1962 - 24 Jan 1963
'Wood-tiger'	甲寅	*jiǎyín*	23 Jan 1974 - 10 Feb 1975
'Fire-tiger'	丙寅	*bǐngyín*	9 Feb 1986 - 28 Jan 1987
'Earth-tiger'	戊寅	*wùyín*	28 Jan 1998 - 15 Feb 1999
'Metal-tiger'	庚寅	*gēngyín*	14 Feb 2010 - 2 Feb 2011
'Water-tiger'	壬寅	*rényín*	1 Feb 2022 - 21 Jan 2023
'Wood-tiger'	甲寅	*jiǎyín*	19 Feb 2034 - 7 Feb 2035

The Tigers [寅] *yín*

The tiger [虎] *hǔ* is known as 寅 *yín* in the 'Terrestrial Branch' [地支] *dìzhī* naming system. In nature, the tiger:

- Is King of the jungle, Is ferocious, ruthless
- Acts alone, does not hunt in groups. Needs a space to roam, does not get along well with another in the same territory.
- Create environment for others to take into account.
- Has very high self esteem, very confident of one's ability
- Active, tend to be impulsive.
- Does not give up until the pursuit is completed.
- Takes calculated risk in every undertaking, be prepared for any eventuality.
- Bold, brave, prepared to take challenges.

As the tiger is a yáng wood element, there is a certain degree of aggressive aspect to the personality, they are not afraid to challenge others or to be challenged. They have strong ambitions and like to be recognised or acknowledged.

People born under the tiger sign are generally regarded as independent, strong willed, active and optimistic. They are in general self-made people; self confident, hard working, and pursue something right till the end.

They tend to be unpredictable, not refined, aggressive and impatient. They are cautious, though they tend to regret after certain actions (verbal and physical) are made. They stick to their principles and believe, even if they clash with others on occasions. They like to work independently without supervision.

When combined with the 'Celestial Stem' [天干] *tiāngān*, five aspects of tigers could be established.

'Wood-tiger' [甲寅] *jiǎyín* 1914, 1974. Described as 'Standing tiger' [立定之虎] *lìdìngzhīhǔ*. Some of the characteristics include 'An honest person, would be important or esteemed' [为人诚实,利官近贵] *wéirénchéngshí, lìguānjīnguì*.

'Fire-tiger' [丙寅] *bǐngyín* 1926, 1986. Described as 'Tiger in the jungle' [山林之虎] *shānlínzhīhǔ*. Some of the characteristics include 'Not too certain about his intentions, the mouth is quick but the lips stiff'[39] [心性不定，口快舌硬] *xīnxìng bùdìng, kǒukuài shéyìng.*

'Earth-tiger' [戊寅] *wùyín* 1938, 1998. Described as 'Tiger roaming through the mountain' [过山之虎] *guòshānzhīhǔ.* Some of the characteristics include 'As a person he is aggressive, easy to move quick and easy to cool down' [为人猛烈，易快易冷] *wéirén měngliè, yìkuàiyìlěng.*

'Metal-tiger' [庚寅] *gēngyín* 1950, 2010. Described as 'Tiger emerging from the mountain' [出山之虎] *chūshānzhī hǔ.* Some of the characteristics include 'Impatient by nature, saying without meaning to act on it' [人心性急，有口无心] *rénxīn xìngjí, yǒukǒuwúxīn.*

'Water-tiger' [壬寅] *rényín* 1912, 1962. Described as 'Tiger roaming through the forest' [过林之虎] *guòlínzhīhǔ.* Some of the characteristics include 'Quick with the mouth, but uncomplicated at heart. Does not hide things from others' [口快心直，有事不藏] *kǒukuài xīnzhí, yǒushì bùcāng.*

'Fire-rabbit'	丁卯	*dīngmǎo*	2 Feb 1927 - 22 Jan 1928
'Earth-rabbit'	己卯	*jǐmǎo*	19 Feb 1939 - 7 Feb 1940
'Metal-rabbit'	辛卯	*xīnmǎo*	6 Feb 1951 - 26 Jan 1952
'Water-rabbit'	癸卯	*guǐmǎo*	25 Jan 1963 - 12 Feb 1964
'Wood-rabbit'	乙卯	*yǐmǎo*	11 Feb 1975 - 30 Jan 1976
'Fire-rabbit'	丁卯	*dīngmǎo*	29 Jan 1987 - 16 Feb 1988
'Earth-rabbit'	己卯	*jǐmǎo*	16 Feb 1999 - 4 Feb 2000
'Metal-rabbit'	辛卯	*xīnmǎo*	3 Feb 2011 - 22 Jan 2012
'Water-rabbit'	癸卯	*guǐmǎo*	22 Jan 2023 - 9 Feb 2024
'Wood-rabbit'	乙卯	*yǐmǎo*	8 Feb 2035 - 27 Jan 3206

The Rabbits [卯] *mǎo*

The rabbit [兔] *tù* is known as 卯 *mǎo* in the 'Terrestrial Branch' [地支] *dìzhī* naming system. In nature, the rabbit:

---

[39] Quick with blunt words.

- Is alert of any potential enemy, with a strong hearing capability and good sense of smell.
- Is quick to respond, reacts fast to any environmental change.
- Looks relaxed, but even at rest is highly instinctive, escapes quickly.
- Is mild mannered, not aggressive, not equipped with claws or other weapons.
- Is cute, lovable, friendly, approachable, and easy to get along with.
- Is a pacifist. It does not create enemies, makes friends easily.

As the rabbit is a yīn wood element, there is gentle and warm caring environment to growth. They grow and develop without being assertive, as they generally value human relationships, do not impose on others or create enemies. True as a 'wood' person, the rabbit is at times moody, and keep their inner thoughts and feelings to themselves.

People born under the rabbit sign are generally regarded as peace loving, gentle and quite. They are instinctive, quick thinking and respond quickly. They are highly sensitive.

They are good natured and do not take unnecessarily risks. By nature they are kind hearted and do not undermine the interests of others. They do not seek argument or confrontation with others. As such they lead a peaceful life.

In spite of their appearances they are normally well prepared, thinking things through, working out exit strategy prior to action.

When combined with the 'Celestial Stem' [天干] tiāngān, five aspects of rabbits could be established.

'Wood-rabbit' [乙卯] yǐmǎo 1915, 1975. Described as 'the rabbit who has the dào' [得道之兔] dédàozhītù. Some of the characteristic include 'Great aspirations, clever schemes and plans' [志气轩昂，计谋巧妙] zhìqì xuān'áng, jìmóu qiǎomiào.

'Fire-rabbit' [丁卯] *dīngmǎo* 1827, 1987. Described as 'Rabbit gazing at the moon' [望月之兔] *wàngyuèzhītù*. Some of the characteristics include 'always working, clever and intelligent'[手足不停, 性巧聪明] *shǒuzú bù tíng, xìngqiǎo cōngmíng.*

'Earth-rabbit' [己卯] *jǐmǎo* 1939, 1999. Described as 'Rabbit in the forest' [山林之兔] *shānlínzhītù*. Some of the characteristics include 'Fun loving, not bullied by others' [嬉戏不受人所欺] *xǐxì bùshòu rén suǒqī.*

'Metal-rabbit' [辛卯] *xīnmǎo* 1951, 2011. Described as 'Rabbit in the toad hole' [蟾窟之兔] *chánkūzhītù*. Some of the characteristics include 'Prone to be important or esteemed, even the body is at rest, the mind does not rest' [利官近贵, 身闲心不闲] *lìguān jìnguì, shēnxián xīnbùxián.*

'Water-rabbit' [癸卯] *guǐmǎo* 1903, 1963. Described as 'Rabbit emerging from a forest' [出林之兔] *chūlínzhītù*. Some of the characteristics include 'High income, high expenditure, good life in late years' [多收入多支出, 晚景兴隆] *duōshōurù duōzhīchū, wǎnjǐng xìnglóng.*

'Earth-dragon'	戊辰	*wùchén*	23 Jan 1928 - 9 Feb 1929
'Metal-dragon'	庚辰	*gēngchén*	8 Feb 1940 - 26 Jan 1941
'Water-dragon'	壬辰	*rénchén*	27 Jan 1952 - 13 Feb 1953
'Wood-dragon'	甲辰	*jiǎchén*	13 Feb 1964 - 1 Feb 1965
'Fire-dragon'	丙辰	*bǐngchén*	31 Jan 1976 - 17 Feb 1977
'Earth-dragon'	戊辰	*wùchén*	17 Feb 1988 - 5 Feb 1989
'Metal-dragon'	庚辰	*gēngchén*	5 Feb 2000 - 23 Jan 2001
'Water-dragon'	壬辰	*rénchén*	23 Jan 2012 - 9 Feb 2013
'Wood-dragon'	甲辰	*jiǎchén*	10 Feb 2024 - 28 Jan 2025
'Fire-dragon'	丙辰	*bǐngchén*	28 Jan 2036 - 14 Feb 2037

The Dragons [辰] *chén*

The dragon [龙] *lóng*, a legendary animal in Chinese mythology, is known as [辰] *chén* in the 'Terrestrial Branch' [地支] *dìzhī* naming system. The dragon:

353

- Is highly noble, associated with kings
- Is benevolent and kind
- Is one of the four animals of good omen
- Is not inhibited by normal constraints, limited only by hard work and imagination
- Tend to attract attention
- Is independent, doing what it likes, doesn't like supervision.
- Reacts aggressively when betrayed by others or down-trodden.

As the dragon is a yáng wood-earth element, it combines the growth aspects of wood with a down to earth attitude. Dragon people grow in stature, which gives them a certain degree of respect, charisma and leadership. They combine imagination, idealism and vision with practical realities.

People born under the dragon sign are generally regarded as peace loving, honourable, respectable, outstanding in their own ways. They are energetic and enthusiastic, with a strong sense of principles and conviction.

They are self confident, take calculated risks. They are active; tend to be self-centered, somewhat impatient and intolerant of inefficiencies and stupidity. They are decisive, not deceiving. They thrive in an environment that requires innovation, creativity, particularly when they are given the freedom to act.

When combined with the 'Celestial Stem' [天干] *tiāngān*, five aspects of dragons could be established.

'Wood-dragon' [甲辰] *jiǎchén* 1904, 1964. Described as 'Dragon resting in a deep pool' [伏潭之龙] *fútánzhīlóng*. Some of the characteristics include 'Ample food and clothing, a life of peace and ease' [衣食丰足, 一生清闲] *yīshí fēngzú, yīshēng qīngxián.*

'Fire-dragon' [丙辰] *bǐngchén* 1916, 1976. Described as 'Dragon in the sky.' [天上之龙] *tiānshàngzhīlóng.* Some of the characteristics include 'The body is at rest but the mind still works, like to make friends' [身闲心劳, 好交朋友] *shēnxián xīnláo, hàojiāo péngyǒu.*

'Earth-dragon' [戊辰] *wùchén* 1928, 1988. Described as 'Noble and warm dragon' [清温之龙] *qīngwēnzhīlóng.* Some of the characteristics include 'Like Spring breeze, prone to be an important or esteemed person' [喜气春风, 利官近贵] *xiqì-chūnfēng, lìguān jìnguì.*

'Metal-dragon' [庚辰] *gēngchén* 1940, 2000. Described as 'A dragon with a nature of forgiveness' [恕性之龙] *shùxìng-zhīlóng.* Some of the characteristics include 'Would be important or esteemed, reaping both reputation and benefits' [利官近贵, 名利双全] *lìguān jìnguì, mínglìshuāngquán.*

'Water-dragon' [壬辰] *rénchén* 1952, 2012. Described as 'A dragon that manipulates the rain' [行雨之龙] *xíngyǔzhīlóng.* Some of the characteristics include 'As a person he works and toils, the hands and legs do not get to rest' [为人劳碌, 手足无停] *wéirén láolù, shǒuzúwútíng.*

'Earth-snake'	己巳 *jǐsì*	10 Feb 1929 - 29 Jan 1930	
'Metal-snake'	辛巳 *xīnsì*	27 Jan 1941 - 14 Feb 1942	
'Water-snake'	癸巳 *guǐsì*	14 Feb 1953 - 2 Feb 1954	
'Wood-snake'	乙巳 *yǐsì*	2 Feb 1965 - 20 Jan 1966	
'Fire-snake'	丁巳 *dīngsì*	18 Feb 1977 - 6 Feb 1978	

'Earth-snake'	己巳 *jǐsì*	6 Feb 1989 - 26 Jan 1990	
'Metal-snake'	辛巳 *xīnsì*	24 Jan 2001 - 11 Feb 2002	
'Water-rabbit'	癸巳 *guǐsì*	10 Feb 2013 - 30 Jan 2014	
'Wood-snake'	乙巳 *yǐsì*	29 Jan 2025 - 16 Feb 2026	
'Fire-snake'	丁巳 *dīngsì*	15 Feb 2037 - 3 Feb 2038	

The Snakes [巳] *sì*

The snake [蛇] *shé* is known as 巳 *sì* in the 'Terrestrial Branch' [地支] *dìzhī* naming system. In nature, the snake:

- Is able to display and charm the prey or enemy, sometimes gives an impressive performance.
- Displays charm and elegance.
- Might look inactive on the surface. It actually stays alert, reacts fast when the time comes.
- Is exciting as well as dangerous at the same time.
- Is cool on the outside, alert on the inside. Contemplative and private.
- Acts on instincts, intuitive and introspective. Keen and intelligent. Acts independently, based on personal judgment.
- Thrives in a wide range of environments from the ocean, the forest, to the desert.
- Able to seize opportunity, waits for the opportune moment before striking.

As the snake is a yīn fire element, it generates inner warmth while outwardly appearing indifferent or cool. It calmly observes its surrounding environment while completing the assigned task. People born under the snake sign are regarded as charming, intuitive and rather introvert. They are intelligent though contemplative and private. As they do not express their emotions or inner feelings they could be misinterpreted or misunderstood.

In general they are independent in thoughts and action. On the whole they are stable and diplomatic. In particular they are on the alert, defensive against any potential attacks.

When combined with the 'Celestial Stem' [天干] *tiāngān*, five aspects of snakes could be established.

'Wood-snake' [乙巳] *yǐsì* 1905, 1965. Described as 'Snake coming out of the den' [出穴之蛇] *chūxuézhīshé*. Some of the characteristics include 'Helping others without getting any credits, doing good deeds without mentioning it' [救人无功, 做好不说] *jiùrén wúgōng, zuóhǎo bùshuō*.

'Fire-snake' [丁巳] *dīngsì* 1917, 1977. Described as 'Snake within the embankment' [塘内之蛇] *tángnèizhīshé*. Some of the characteristics include 'Strong character and natural disposition, does not go along well socially' [禀性刚强, 不顺人情] *bǐngxìng gāngqiáng, bùshùnrénqíng*.

'Earth-snake' [己巳] *jǐsì* 1929, 1989. Described as 'A snake with good luck and fortune' [福气之蛇] *fúqìzhīshé*. Some of the characteristics include 'Clever and quick-witted with opportunity to fame' [聪明伶俐, 有功名之分] *cōngmíng línglì, yǒu gōng-míng zhīfēn*.

'Metal-snake' [辛巳] *xīnsì* 1941, 2001. Described as 'A snake hibernating in winter' [冬藏之蛇] *dōngcángzhīshé*. Some of the characteristics include 'Have plans and strategies, instantly adapt to changing environment' [有机谋, 随机应变] *yǒujìmóu, suíjīyīngbiàn*.

'Water-snake' [癸巳] *guǐsì* 1953, 2013. Described as 'Snake amongst the grass' [草中之蛇] *cǎozhōngzhīshé*. Some of the characteristics include 'Intelligent and quick witted, assemble together the riches and disperse them' [伶俐聪明, 财谷聚散] *línglì cōngmíng, cáigǔ jùsàn*.

'Metal-horse'	庚午	*gēngwǔ*	30 Jan 1930 - 16 Feb 1931
'Water-horse'	壬午	*rénwǔ*	15 Feb 1942 - 4 Jan 1943
'Wood-horse'	甲午	*jiǎwǔ*	3 Feb 1954 - 23 Jan 1955
'Fire-horse'	丙午	*bǐngwǔ*	21 Jan 1966 - 8 Feb 1967
'Earth-horse'	戊午	*wùwǔ*	7 Feb 1978 - 27 Jan 1979
'Metal-horse'	庚午	*gēngwǔ*	27 Jan 1990 - 14 Feb 1991
'Water-horse'	壬午	*rénwǔ*	12 Feb 2002 - 31 Jan 2003
'Wood-horse'	甲午	*jiǎwǔ*	31 Jan 2014 - 18 Feb 2015
'Fire-horse'	丙午	*bǐngwǔ*	27 Feb 2026 - 5 Feb 2027
'Earth-horse'	戊午	*wùwǔ*	4 Feb 2038 - 23 Jan 2039

The Horses [午] *wǔ*

The horse [马] *mǎ* is known as 午 *wǔ* in the 'Terrestrial Branch' [地支] *dìzhī* naming system. In nature, the horse:

- Is active, quick, speedy, being the fastest domesticated animal
- Is lively, animated, full of energy, cannot keep still, hard to settle down.
- By nature does not want to be restrained in any way. Tend to be restless if confined.
- Tends to stop over obstacles, rather than going around.
- Is the symbol of mobility (till vehicles were invented).
- Cannot sustain high speeds over long distances, prefers quick success rather than long, drawn-out slog.
- Likes free expression.
- More demanding on feed and maintenance

As the horse is a yáng fire element, it is a symbol of high energy and intense activity. As fire does not last when there is nothing to burn, it also reflects a hasty or impulsive nature, as well as eagerness to achieve results quickly.

People born under the horse sign is generally regarded as generally optimistic, enjoy their freedom, and are quick to react to events and opportunities. They are expressive, do not hide or hold their feelings readily, and like to be in the limelight.

They accept challenge, though at times their minds and ideas changes rather abruptly. They are elegant, sharp minded, independent with a strong sense of self confidence. However they tend to loose interest in the face of difficulties.

When combined with the 'Celestial Stem' [天干] *tiāngān*, five aspects of horses could be established.

'Wood-horse' [甲午] *jiǎwǔ* 1954, 2014. Described as 'Horse in the clouds' [云中之马] *yúnzhōngzhīmǎ*. Some of the characteristics include 'polite and good natured, make lots of friends' [为人和气, 交朋群友] *wéirénhéqì, jiǎopéng qúnyǒu*.

'Fire-horse' [丙午] *bǐngwǔ* 1906, 1966. Described as 'A horse on the road' [行路之马] *xínglùzhīmǎ*. Some of the characteristics include 'Easy and relaxed life, no worry in the mind' [为人清闲, 心不忧不住] *wēirénqīngxián, xīnbùyōubùzhù*.

'Earth-horse' [戊午] *wùwǔ* 1918, 1978. Described as 'Horse in the stable' [厩内之马] *jiùnèizhīmǎ*. Some of the characteristics include 'strong aspirations, gentle character' [志气宽宏, 温良性格] *zhìqìkuānhóng, wēnliáng xìnggé*.

'Metal-horse' [庚午] *gēngwǔ* 1930, 1990. Described as 'Horse in the hall' [堂里之马] *tánglǐzhīmǎ*. Some of the characteristics include 'Quick at the mouth but uncomplicated at heart. Prone to be important or esteemed' [口快心直, 利官近贵] *kǒukuàixīnzhí, lìguān jìnguì*.

'Water-horse' [壬午] *rénwǔ* 1942, 2002. Described as 'Horse in the army' [军中之马] *jūnzhōngzhīmǎ*. Some of the characteristics include 'Thrifty and hardworking, breaking up dangers and disasters' [为人勤俭, 灾厄可折] *wéirén qínjiǎn, zāiwéikězhé*.

'Metal-goat'	辛未	*xīnwèi*	17 Feb 1931 - 5 Feb 1932
'Water-goat'	癸未	*guǐwèi*	5 Feb 1943 - 24 Jan 1944
'Wood-goat'	乙未	*yǐwèi*	24 Jan 1955 - 11 Feb 1956
'Fire-goat'	丁未	*dīngwèi*	9 Feb 1967 - 29 Jan 1968
'Earth-goat'	己未	*jǐwèi*	28 Jan 1979 - 15 Feb 1980
'Metal-goat'	辛未	*xīnwèi*	15 Feb 1991 - 3 Feb 1992
'Water-goat'	癸未	*guǐwèi*	1 Feb 2003 - 21 Jan 2004
'Wood-goat'	乙未	*yǐwèi*	19 Feb 2015 - 7 Feb 2016
'Fire-goat'	丁未	*dīngwèi*	6 Feb 2027 - 25 Jan 2028
'Earth-goat'	己未	*jǐwèi*	24 Jan 2039 - 11 Feb 2040

The Goats [未] *wèi*

The goat [羊] *yáng* is known as 未 *wèi* in the 'Terrestrial Branch' [地支] *dìzhī* naming system. In nature, the goat:

● Is a tame, domesticated animal
● Is peace living, has no argument with anyone. All it seeks is to be left alone.
● Lives in a flock, is gregarious has strong interpersonal skills.
● Looks tame and mild in temperament externally. Peace loving; does not pick up fights. When provoked would fight to the end.
● Has good fighting spirit individually, each to be treated with due respect.
● Is a hardy animal, not demanding on food or other living conditions, resilient, flexible and adaptable.
● Disciplined, respects the leader of the flock.
● Is quiet and tolerant, not obvious at first.

As the goat is a yīn fire-earth element, it combines the warm, sympathetic temperament with down to earth reality. It is considerate, not easily agitated, practical, observant and analytical.

People born under the goat sign are generally regarded as peace loving, harmonious, honest, hardworking and tolerant. They also have strong opinions of their own.

They are diplomatic, sympathetic, well mannered, establish good inter-personal relationships, have strong internal ambitions and pursuits, they persevere till the end. The need to reconcile inter-personal relationships and strong internal opinion could lead to misinterpretations and misunderstanding.

When combined with the 'Celestial Stem' [天干] *tiāngān*, five aspects of horses could be established.

'Wood-goat' [乙未] *yǐwèi* 1955, 2015. Described as 'Respected goat' [敬重之羊] *jìngzhòngzhīyáng*. Characteristics include 'Good looks, diligent, thrifty when young' [容貌端正, 少年勤俭] *róngmàoduānzhèng, shàoniánqínjiǎn.*

'Fire-goat' [丁未] *dīngwèi* 1907, 1967. Described as 'The lost goat from the flock' [失群之羊] *shiqúnzhīyáng.* Some of the characteristics include 'Mood swing with a sharp tongue' [喜怒不常, 口舌能便] *xǐnù bùcháng, kǒushé néngbiàn.*

'Earth-goat' [己未] *jǐwèi* 1919, 1979. Described as 'Goat in the meadow' [草野之羊] *cǎoyězhīyáng.* Some of the characteristics include 'Quick with words; material needs come naturally [口快舌便, 衣禄自来]' *kǒukuàishébiàn, yīlùzìlái.*

'Metal-goat' [辛未] *xīnwèi* 1931, 1991. Described as 'Goat that gets the benefits' [得禄之羊] *délùzhīyáng.* Some of the characteristics include 'a person of morals and principles, generous by nature' [为人有志气, 一生性宽] *wéirén yǒuzhìqì, yīshēng xìngkuān.*

'Water-goat' [癸未] *guǐwèi* 1943, 2003. Described as 'Goat in the flock' [群内之羊] *qúnnèizhīyáng.* Some of the characteristics include 'Emphasis on material needs, build up good foundation' [重物质, 造基础] *zhòng wùzhì, zhàojīchǔ.*

'Water-monkey' 壬申 *rénshēn* 6 Feb 1932 - 25 Jan 1933
'Wood-monkey' 甲申 *jiǎshēn* 25 Jan 1944 - 12 Feb 1945
'Fire-monkey' 丙申 *bǐngshēn* 12 Feb 1956 - 30 Jan 1957
'Earth-monkey' 戊申 *wùshēn* 30 Jan 1968 - 16 Feb 1969
'Metal-monkey' 庚申 *gēngshēn* 16 Feb 1980 - 4 Feb 1981

'Water-monkey' 壬申 *rénshēn* 4 Feb 1992 - 22 Jan 1993
'Wood-monkey' 甲申 *jiǎshēn* 22 Jan 2004 - 8 Feb 2005
'Fire-monkey' 丙申 *bǐngshēn* 8 Feb 2016 - 27 Jan 2017
'Earth-monkey' 戊申 *wùshēn* 26 Jan 2028 - 12 Feb 2029
'Metal-monkey' 庚申 *gēngshēn* 12 Feb 2040 - 31 Jan 2041

The Monkeys [申] *shēn*

The monkey [猴] *hóu* is known as 申 *shēn* in the 'Terrestrial Branch' [地支] *dìzhī* naming system. In nature, the monkey

- Is active, lively, playful, changes its mind quite often.
- Has a keen sense of observation and analysis, reacts fast.
- According to Charles Darwin, men evolved from monkeys. Monkey would have the closest mental capacity to men.
- Is capable of doing all sorts of tricks, good at covering up
- Is intelligent, resourceful, temperamental, can be impulsive
- Has leadership ability, able to seize opportunities
- Is thoughtful, able to see through traps, capable of planning.

As the monkey is a yáng metal element, they could bring about reforms or changes. They could also bring unnecessary turbulence and disturbances. In general they have leadership qualities, and are able to seize good opportunities.

A person born under the monkey sign is generally regarded as active, always thinking, intelligent, resourceful and temperamental. They generally have lots of ideas, imaginative. They also tend to change course or plans, giving an impression of being unsettled or lacking in patience.

They like limelight. In general they are able to seize opportunities, analysing and responding to changing situations quickly. They are also good at arguing and defending themselves.

When combined with the 'Celestial Stem' [天干] *tiāngān*, five aspects of monkeys could be established.

'Wood-monkey' [甲申] *jiǎshēn* 1944, 2004. Described as 'Monkey crossing the trees' [过树之猴] *guòshùzhīhóu*. Some of the characteristics include 'Life is upside down in earlier years, but smooth and good in late years' [初年颠倒, 晚岁利达] *chūnián diāndǎo, wǎnsuì lìdá*.

'Fire-monkey' [丙申] *bǐngshēn* 1956, 2016. Described as 'Monkey in the mountain' [山上之猴] *shānshàngzhīhóu*. Some of the characteristics include 'Toil in the early years, prosperous in late years' [早年劳碌, 晚景兴旺] *zǎonián láolù, wǎnjǐng xìngwàng*.

'Earth-monkey' [戊申] *wùshēn* 1908, 1968. Described as 'The independent monkey' [独立之猴] *dúlìzhīhóu*. Some of the characteristics include 'Impatient, changes often when undertaking a task' [为人性急, 作事反覆] *wéirén xìngjí, zuòshì fǎnfù*.

'Metal-monkey' *gēngshēn* [庚申] 1920, 1980. Described as 'The fruit eating Monkey' [食果之猴] *shíguǒzhīhóu*. Some of the characteristics include 'Always at work, prone to be an important or esteemed person' [手足不停, 利官近贵] *shǒuzúbùtíng, lìguān jìnguì*.

'Water-monkey' [壬申] *rénshēn* 1932, 1992: Described as 'A dainty monkey' [清秀之猴] *qīngxiùzhīhóu*. Some of the characteristics include 'Clever and intelligent, able to work out strategies and make multiple changes' [性巧聪明, 机谋多变] *xìngqiǎo cōngmíng, jìmóu duō biàn*.

'Water-rooster'	癸酉 *guǐyǒu*	26 Jan 1933 - 13 Feb 1934	
'Wood-rooster'	乙酉 *yǐyǒu*	13 Feb 1945 - 1 Feb 1946	
'Fire-rooster'	丁酉 *dīngyǒu*	31 Jan 1957 - 17 Feb 1958	
'Earth-rooster'	己酉 *jǐyǒu*	17 Feb 1969 - 5 Feb 1970	
'Metal-rooster'	辛酉 *xīnyǒu*	5 Feb 1981 - 24 Jan 1982	
'Water-rooster'	癸酉 *guǐyǒu*	23 Jan 1993 - 9 Feb 1994	
'Wood-rooster'	乙酉 *yǐyǒu*	9 Feb 2005 - 28 Jan 2006	
'Fire-rooster'	丁酉 *dīngyǒu*	28 Jan 2017 - 15 Feb 2018	
'Earth-rooster'	己酉 *jǐyǒu*	13 Feb 2029 - 1 Feb 2030	
'Metal-rooster'	辛酉 *xīnyǒu*	1 Feb 2041 - 21 Jan 2042	

The Roosters [酉] *yǒu*

The rooster [鸡] *jī* is known as 酉 *yǒu* in the 'Terrestrial Branch' [地支] *dìzhī* naming system. In nature, the rooster:

● Crows every morning during dawn, irrespective of the weather, a symbol of reliability, dependability, loyalty and dedication to work.

- Would not run away from its enemy, but stand up to fight, a symbol of bravery and fighting spirits.
- Calls others when there is feed, a symbol of benevolence, gregarious nature and team spirit.
- Is busy looking for food all the time, a symbol of hard working attitude. Is not unduly worry about work load.
- Is elegant looking, does not like its feathers to be ruffled. Is concerned about physical appearance.
- Works on the land all the time, very sensitive to the environment.

As the rooster is a yīn metal element, it provides a gentler, less offensive means of reform and restructuring. It also contains elements of ambition and seeking limelight.

People born under the rooster sign are generally regarded as hardworking, reliable, dependable, considerate.

They are also sensitive, reacts fast, think ahead of others. They tend to be concerned and worried, giving an impression of poor communication and impatience. Being active and self confident, they have a good understanding of the environment.

When combined with the 'Celestial Stem' [天干] *tiāngān*, five aspects of rooster could be established.

'Wood-rooster' [乙酉] *yǐyǒu* 1945, 2005. Described as 'The rooster that crows at noon' [唱午之鸡] *chàngwǔzhījī*. Some of the characteristics include 'Quick at the mouth but uncomplicated at heart, dignified aspirations' [口快心直, 志气轩昂] *kǒukuàixīnzhí, zhìqìxuān'áng*.

'Fire-rooster' [丁酉] *dīngyǒu* 1957, 2017. Described as 'the Independent rooster' [独立之鸡] *dúlìzhījī*. Some of the characteristics include 'Emphasis on feelings and kindness or benevolence, prone to be an esteemed or important person' [多情重恩, 利官近贵] *duōqíng zhòng'ēn, lìguān jìnguì*.

'Earth-rooster' [己酉] *jǐyǒu* 1919, 1979. Described as 'The rooster that announces the arrival of dawn' bàoxiǎozhījī 报晓之鸡. Some of the characteristics include 'Intelligent and clever, good provision of material needs' [心性聪明, 衣禄有足] *xīnxìng cōngmíng, yīlù yǒuzú*.

'Metal-rooster' [辛酉] *xīnyǒu* 1921, 1981. Described as 'The rooster in the cage' [笼藏之鸡] *lóngcángzhījī*. Some of the characteristics include 'the mouth is capable, the tongue changes, highly respected' [口能舌便, 高人敬重] *kǒunéng shébiàn, gāorén jìngzhòng*.

'Water-rooster' [癸酉] *guǐyǒu* 1933, 1993. Described as 'The rooster that is resting' [栖宿之鸡] *qīsùzhījī*. Some of the characteristics include 'Fair and just, the mouth is ready and the tongue capable' [心直公平, 口便舌能] *xīnzhí gōngpíng, kǒubiàn shénéng*.

'Wood-dog'	甲戌	*jiǎxū*	14 Feb 1934 - 3 Feb 1935
'Fire-dog'	丙戌	*bǐngxū*	2 Feb 1946 - 21 Jan 1947
'Earth-dog'	戊戌	*wùxū*	18 Feb 1958 - 7 Feb 1959
'Metal-dog'	庚戌	*gēngxū*	6 Feb 1970 - 26 Jan 1971
'Water-dog'	壬戌	*rénxū*	25 Jan 1982 - 12 Feb 1983
'Wood-dog'	甲戌	*jiǎxū*	10 Feb 1994 - 30 Jan 1995
'Fire-dog'	丙戌	*bǐngxū*	29 Jan 2006 - 17 Feb 2007
'Earth-dog'	戊戌	*wùxū*	16 Feb 2018 - 4 Feb 2019
'Metal-dog'	庚戌	*gēngxū*	2 Feb 2030 - 22 Jan 2031
'Water-dog'	壬戌	*rénxū*	22 Jan 2042 - 9 Feb 2043

The Dogs [戌] *xū*

The dog [狗] *gǒu* is known as 戌 *xū* in the 'Terrestrial Branch' [地支] *dìzhī* naming system. In nature, the dog:

● Forms part of human household or establishment such as farms. Is assured of protection and food from men in return for its services or companionship.

365

- Is loyal, dependable, does not leave the owner for another. Has a strong sense of duty and responsibility.
- Takes instructions, work as required, understands his role.
- Has good fighting spirit
- Has a good sense of hearing and smell, sensitive to the environment, sharp in their judgment.
- Is alert, cautious. Able to access situations such as danger, opportunities, etc. Able to make on the spot judgement.
- Has inherent intelligence to be trained for a variety of tasks.

As the dog is a yáng metal-earth element, it combines the decisiveness for organisation, with down to earth pragmatism and realities.

People born under the dog sign are generally regarded as loyal, trustworthy, considerate, candid, energetic. They would play their part efficiently in the overall plan of schemes. They are also prepared to sacrifice for others.

They tend to be sentimental, understand their role and play their part. They are loyal in their relationships, do not like to change the environment unnecessarily. Appreciated by superiors for their dedication and loyalty. They are generally sociable and likable. They could be decisive, though at times impulsive.

When combined with the 'Celestial Stem' [天干] tiāngān, five aspects of dog could be established.

'Wood-dog' [甲戌] jiǎxū 1934, 1994. Described as 'The dog that guards' [守身之狗] shǒushēnzhīgǒu. Some of the characteristics include 'the mouth is quick the tongue easy, the body is at rest but the mind is not' [口快舌便, 身闲心不闲] kǒukuàishébiàn, shēnxiánxīnbùxián.

'Fire-dog' [丙戌] bǐngxū 1946, 2006. Described as 'The dog that goes to sleep by itself' [自眠之狗] zìmiánzhīgǒu. Some of the characteristics include 'hardworking in the earlier years, prosperous in later years' [前运勤劳, 晚年荣华] *qiányùn qínláo, wānnián rónghuá.*

'Earth-dog' [戊戌] *wùxū* 1958, 2018. Described as 'The dog that enters the mountain' [进山之狗] *jìnshānzhīgǒu.* Some of the characteristics include 'Operating as an independent, getting prosperous in late years' [自营自立, 晚景得财] *zìyíng zìlì, wǎnjǐng décái.*

'Metal-dog' [庚戌] *gēngxū* 1910, 1970. Described as 'Dog in the temple' [寺观之狗] *sìguānzhīgǒu.* Characteristics include 'Happy go lucky, would be esteemed or important' [为人快活, 利官近贵] *wéirún kuàihuó, lìguān jìnguì.*

'Water-dog' [壬戌] *rénxū* 1922, 1982. Described as 'The dog that looks after the house' *gùjiāzhīgǒu* [顾家之狗]. Some of the characteristics include 'Ordinary early years, prosperous late years' [早年平常, 晚年兴旺] *zǎoniánpíngcháng, wǎnnián xìngwàng.*

'Wood-pig'	乙亥	*yǐhài*	4 Feb 1935 - 23 Jan 1936
'Fire-pig'	丁亥	*dīnghài*	22 Jan 1947 - 9 Feb 1948
'Earth-pig'	己亥	*jǐhài*	8 Feb 1959 - 27 Jan 1960
'Metal-pig'	辛亥	*xīnhài*	27 Jan 1971 - 14 Feb 1972
'Water-pig'	癸亥	*guǐhài*	13 Feb 1983 - 1 Feb 1984
'Wood-pig'	乙亥	*yǐhài*	31 Jan 1995 - 18 Feb 1996
'Fire-pig'	丁亥	*dīnghài*	18 Feb 2007 - 6 Feb 2008
'Earth-pig'	己亥	*jǐhài*	5 Feb 2019 - 24 Jan 2020
'Metal-pig'	辛亥	*xīnhài*	23 Jan 2031 - 10 Feb 2032
'Water-pig'	癸亥	*guǐhài*	10 Feb 2043 - 29 Jan 2044

The Pigs [亥] *hài*

The pig [猪] *zhū* is known as [亥] *hài* in the 'Terrestrial Branch' [地支] *dìzhī* naming system. In nature, the pig:

● Is not demanding on feeds or living environment. Tolerant of others.

- Is one of the fastest growing farm animals, thanks to strong digestive system and long intestines
- Does what it enjoys, independent of others.
- Peace loving, relaxed, does not seek a fight. Like to be left alone.
- Steady and resolute, honest, strong willed.
- Has a good and strong body, muscles and bone structure

As the pig is a yīn water element, it portrays the easy going, easy to get along, non-confrontational attributes. As a whole 'pig' people are negotiable.

People born under the 'pig' sign is generally regarded as resolute, relaxed, optimistic, easy to get along with, though occasionally blunt. However they do not seek limelight or attention.

They are also people of principles, often speaking the truth without beating round the bush, often without too much concern about people who could be offended. They tend to be discouraged in times of difficulties, and self conscious of the consequences.

When combined with the 'Celestial Stem' tiāngān 天干, five aspects of pig could be established.

'Wood-pig' [乙亥] yǐhài 1935, 1995. Described as 'The pig that passes by' [过往之猪] guòwǎngzhīzhū. Some of the characteristics include 'Easy to get along with, a person with good intentions' [为人和顺, 存心中正] wéirén héshùn, cúnxīn zhōngzhèng.

'Fire-pig' [丁亥] dīnghài 1947, 2007. Described as 'The pig that passes by the land' [过土之猪] guòtǔzhīzhū. Some of the characteristics include 'Clever and intelligent, independent in its ways' [性巧聪明, 自立自营] xìngqiǎo cōngmíng, zìlìzìyíng.

'Earth-pig' [己亥] jǐhài 1959, 2019. Described as 'The pig in a Dàoist temple' [道院之猪] dàoyuànzhīzhū. Some of the characteristics include 'Clever and quick witted, ample supply of food and clothing' [巧计伶俐, 衣食安稳] *qiǎojìlínglì, yīshí'ānwěn.*

'Metal-pig' [辛亥] *xīnhài* 1911, 1971. Described as 'The pig in the ring' [圈里之猪] *quānlǐzhīzhū.* Some of the characteristics include 'Not involve in other's business, like to seek a variety of things' [不惹闲事, 百事谋求] *bùrěxiánshì, bǎishìmóuqiú.*

'Water-pig' [癸亥] *guǐhài* 1923, 1983. Described as 'The pig under the forest' [林下之猪] *línxiàzhīzhū.* Some of the characteristics include 'A straight and firm person, does not go along to please others' [为人刚直, 不顺人情] *wéirén gāngzhí, bùshùn rénqíng.*

Websites: Websites that look into tiāngān aspects of Chinese zodiac signs include:

The five types of pigs:
www.chinavoc.com/zodiac/pig/five.asp
Lovegevity:
www.usbridalguide.com/special/chinesehoroscopes/Snake.htm

WHEN ZODIAC SIGNS MEET

When two zodiac signs meet, they could be compatible with each other, clashes with one another, or just getting along.

Note that this is a simplistic analysis, since it take into consideration only one of the eight elements that could be analysed.

COMPATABILITY CHARTS

The compatibility chart for the zodiac signs are divided in three groups as follows:

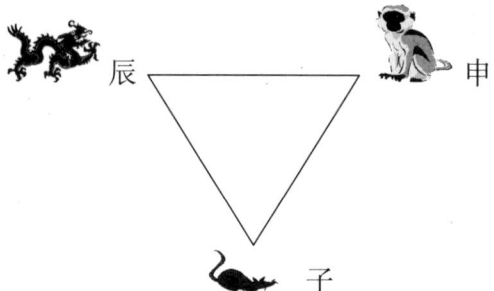

Rat is compatible with dragon and monkey.

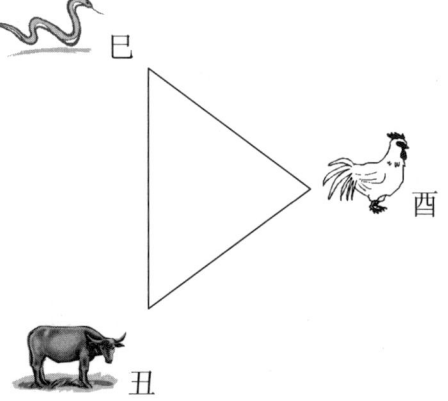

Ox is compatible with Snake and Rooster.

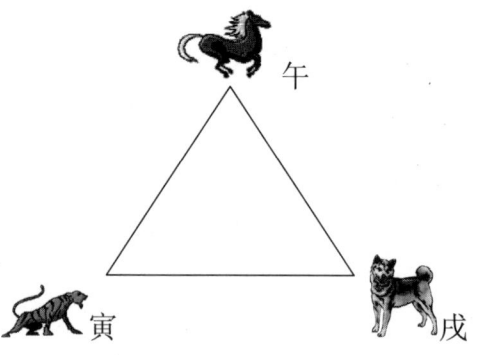

Tiger is compatible with Horse and Dog.

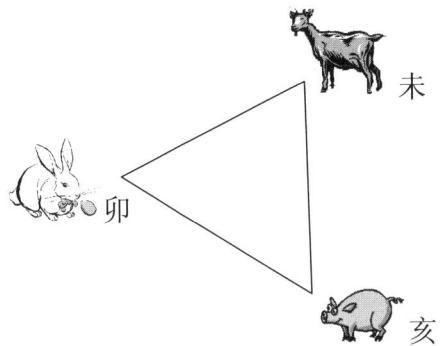

Rabbit is compatible with Goat and Pig

WHEN ZODIAC SIGNS CLASH

However powerful it is, every sign has its opponent; this is simply the balance of nature. Parallel to the compatibility chart is the incompatibility chart, where the zodiac signs clash.

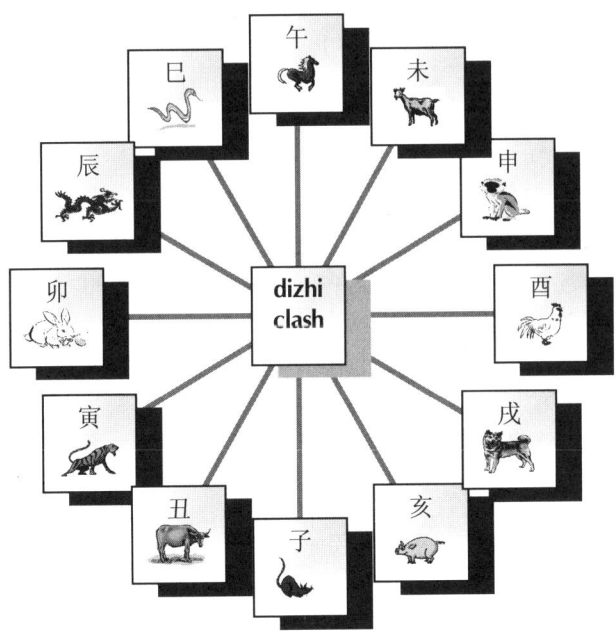

371

The table of zodiac incompatibility is easily worked out by taking the sign diametrically opposite. As we have seen on p. 324, 'Wood' clashes with 'metal' and 'fire' clashes with 'water. It is often acknowledged that:

❖ Rat (yáng water) clashes with horse (yáng fire)
❖ Ox (yīn water-earth) clashes with goat (yīn fire-earth)
❖ Tiger (yáng wood) clashes with monkey (yáng metal)
❖ Rabbit (yīn wood) clashes with Rooster (yīn metal)
❖ Dragon (yáng wood-earth) clashes with Dog (yáng metal-earth)
❖ Snake (yīn fire) clashes with Pig (yīn water)

Zodiac clashes or compatibility is one of the criteria used to select an auspicious date. For example if a person has a rat (water) zodiac, it is inadvisable to choose a day with a horse zodiac to host any important event, as they would clash. Auspicious events include weddings, moving into a new premise, commencing a new business, etc. The day zodiac could be found from the 'calendar of ten thousand years' [万年历] *wànniánlì*.

THE MONTH PILLAR [月柱] *yuèzhù*

Obviously the zodiac based on 'year' factor is insufficient to adequately analyse ones' personality profile or map his ups or downs.

In reality the 'analysis of life destiny' [算命] *suànmìng* involves 'four pillars' [四柱] *sìzhù*, based on parameters derived from the year, month, day and hour.

The second level of the 'four pillars' is the month pillar. The month pillar is also made of two components, the 'month celestial component', [月干] *yuègān* and the 'month terrestrial component' [月支] *yuèzhī*. The same twelve animals are used for the terrestrial component.

The 'month component' reflects the seasons of the year as follows, the number indicate Chinese calendar month. It is roughly one month before the Western calendar month.

sì [巳] 4 May Summer Fire	wǔ [午] 5 June Summer Fire	wèi [未] 6 July Sum-Aut Fire/E	Shēn [申] 7 Aug Autumn Metal
chén [辰] 3 April Spring/Sum Wood/E			yǒu [酉] 8 Sept Autumn Metal
mǎo [卯] 2 March Spring Wood			xū [戌] 9 Oct Aut/Win Metal/E
yín [寅] 1 Feb Spring Wood	chǒu [丑] 12 Jan Winter/Spr Water/E	zǐ [子] 11 Dec Winter Water	hài [亥] 10 Nov Winter Water

The 'Terrestrial components for the month' [月支] *yuèzhī* roughly correspond to Western Zodiac as follows:

sì [巳] **Taurus** 20/4 to 20/5	wǔ [午] **Gemini** 21/5 to 21/6	wèi [未] **Cancer** 22/6 to 21/7	shēn [申] **Leo** 22/7 to 21/8
chén [辰] **Aries** 21/3 to 19/4			yǒu [酉] **Virgo** 22/8 to 22/9
mǎo [卯] **Pisces** 20/2 to 20/3			xū [戌] **Libra** 23/9 to 22/10
yín [寅] **Aquarius** 21/1 to 19/2	chǒu [丑] **Capricorn** 22/12 to 20/1	zǐ [子] **Sagittarius** 22/11 to 21/12	hài [亥] **Scorpio** 23/10 to 21/11

The relationship between Chinese and Western calendar month is approximate. The personality profile in terms of [天干地支] *tiángān-dìzhī* for the Chinese 'month' zodiac is the same as that for the 'year'.

It is certainly possible to take advantage of both Chinese and Western zodiac signs, by combining the Chinese zodiac year with Western zodiac month, giving 144 combinations, rather than just 12. The zodiac analysis would be at least twelve times more refined and precise. For example we could have rat-virgo, rat-libra, ox-leo, ox-virgo, etc. If we further add the five determinant elements, there would be 60×12 or 720 combinations.

THE TWENTY-FOUR PERIOD SEGMENTS

A more detail description is made up of 'twenty-four period segments' [节] *jié*. Typically a segment occurs every fifteen days throughout the four seasons of the year. The segments were originally designed as a guide to farmers, the segment names or characteristics themselves indicate the weather and its relationship to agriculture. These 'period segments' are considered in weather forecast. The segments are:

1. 'Beginning of spring' [立春] *lìchūn*. Around 5 February. The start of all activities.
2. 'Rain Water' [雨水] *yǔshuǐ*. About 20 February. The beginning of rain. At the same time snow begins to melt. If this is supplemented by rain, there would be ample water for agriculture.
3. 'Awakening of insects' [惊蜇] *jīngzhē*. About 5 March. Time when hibernating reptiles, insects become active again.
4. 'Mid spring' [春分] *chūnfēn*. About 21 March. The sun is over the Equator, with equal day and night times. Hereafter the weather gets progressively warmer.

374

5. 'Clear and bright' [清明] *qīngmíng*. About 5 April. Weather is warm and clear. Plants begin to sprout. This is also a festival day, the day when the Chinese visit their ancestors' graves to pay their respects.
6. 'Rain for the grains' [穀雨] *gǔyǔ*. About 20 April. After having sown their grains rainfall at this time is much welcome.
7. 'Beginning of summer' [立夏] *lìxià*. About 5 May. The weather gets progressively warmer.
8. 'Partially filled grains' [小满] *xiǎomán*. About 21 May. Summer grains are partially filled, and could be harvested in the near future.
9. 'Seed sowing' [芒种] *mángzhòng*. About 6 June. Time to sow winter grains, especially those requiring a longer time to ripen.
10. 'Summer Solstice' [夏至] *xiàzhì*. About 21 June. Summer Solstice, the longest day and shortest night in the Northern Hemisphere, is also the warmest day
11. 'Slight Heat' [小暑] *xiǎoshǔ*. About 7 July. Weather gets warmer, though still not too warm. Grains quality will be affected if the weather is too warm at this time of the year.
12. 'Great Heat' [大暑] *dàshǔ*. About 23 July. The weather is at his hottest, the air sultry.
13. 'Beginning of autumn' [立秋] *lìqiū*. About 7 August. Ripening of crops at this time.
14. 'End of heat' [处暑] *chùshǔ*. About 23 August. Accumulated heat in the house over the past two months would dissipate.
15. 'White dew' [白露] *báilù*. About 8 September. Surface moisture forms dew, forming a white, glittering surface, while the weather gets cool.
16. 'Autumn Equinox' [秋分] *qiūfēn*. About 23 September. Equal periods of day and night, the sun having returned to the equator. From now on night gets progressively longer.

17. 'Cold dew' [寒露] *hánlù*. About 8 October. Frost appears, the weather gets distinctly colder. Trees shed their leaves, migrating birds fly south to a warmer climate. Chrysanthemum blossoms.

18. 'Frost descends' [霜降] *shuāngjiàng*. About 23 October. Frost forms, winter is approaching.

19. 'Beginning of winter' [立冬] *lìdōng*. About 7 November. Crops have been harvested and stored for the winter.

20. 'Slight snow' [小雪] *xiǎoxuě*. About 22 November. The sky becoming grey, beginning of snow fall.

21. 'Big snow' [大雪] *dàxuě*. About 7 December. Weather getting colder, more snow.

22. 'Winter solstice' [冬至] *dōngzhì*. About 22 December. Longest night and shortest day, though coldest weather is yet to come. This is also a festival day when families make little glutinous rice balls in sugary soup called Tāng Yuán [汤圆], a symbol of unity in the family.

23. 'Slight cold' [小寒] *xiǎohán*. About 6 January. Weather getting progressively colder.

24. 'Extreme cold' [大寒] *dàhán*. About 22 January. This is around Chinese New Year and about the coldest day of the year. Ponds and lakes are frozen. After this day weather gets warmer and another season begins.

The start of the month cycles could be seen from the following table. Note that the start of the four seasons is at the corner of the table.

sì [巳] 4 **May** lìxià [立夏]	wǔ [午] 5 **June** mángzhòng [芒种]	wèi [未] 6 **July** xiǎoshǔ [小暑]	Shēn [申] 7 **Aug** lìqiū [立秋]
chén [辰] 3 **Feb** qīngmíng [清明]			yǒu [酉] 8 **Sept** báilù [白露]
mǎo [卯] 2 **Jan** jīngzhē [惊蜇]			xū [戌] 9 **Oct** hánlù [寒露]
yín [寅] 1 **Dec** lìchūn [立春]	chǒu [丑] 12 **Jan** xiǎohán [小寒]	zǐ [子] 11 **Dec** dàxuě [大雪]	hài [亥] 10 **Nov** lìdōng [立冬]

Obviously these twenty-four period segments are meaningless for people living in the tropics. They are relatively unimportant for those living in the cities. These seasons are reversed for those living in the Southern hemisphere. The period segments are carefully compiled and maintained, as they are crucial in determining the exact 'Celestial Stems and Terrestrial Branches' [天干地支] *tiángān-dìzhī* components.

THE DAY PILLAR [日柱] *rìzhù*

The third component, and the most important in 'pillars of destiny' analysis, is actually the day pillar.

The day pillar is made of the same two components, the 'day celestial component' [日干] *rìgān* and the 'day terrestrial component' [日支] *rìzhī*. They are organised in a sequential manner in the same way as the 'year pillar' or 'month pillar'.

The configuration for any particular day could only be obtained from published Chinese calendar, the 'calendar of ten thousand

377

years' [万年历] *wànniánlì*, or from certain computer software. For example the 31 July 2000 would be

Year:	'Metal-dragon'	庚辰	*gēngchén*
Month:	'Water-goat'	癸未	*guǐwèi*
Day:	'Metal-tiger'	庚寅	*gēngyín*

The 'day celestial component' of day pillar [日干] *rìgān* (more commonly known as 'determinant component' [日主] *rìzhǔ*) is central to the analysis of 'pillars of destiny'. The personality profiles based on elements of wood, fire, earth, metal and fire described in p. 318 refers to the 'day celestial component' [日干] *rìgān*.

A child born on the date in the example above would be considered a yáng metal gēng 庚 person, based on the "day celestial component".

This is a critical parameter to be considered, known as the "determinant component" in this book. The strength of this component as well as the interaction with the changing environment throughout life forms the basis of "life destiny analysis".

THE HOUR PILLAR [时柱] *shízhù*

The hour pillar is similarly made of two components, the 'hour celestial component' [时干] *shígān* and the 'hour terrestrial component' [时支] *shízhī*. They are organised as follows:

sì [巳] **Snake** 9 am - 11 am	wǔ [午] **Horse** 11 am - 1 pm	wèi [未] **Goat** 1 pm - 3 pm	shēn [申] **Monkey** 3 pm - 5 pm
chén [辰] **Dragon** 7 am - 9 am			yǒu [酉] **Rooster** 5 pm - 7 pm
mǎo [卯] **Rabbit** 5 am - 7 am			xū [戌] **Dog** 7 pm - 9 pm
yín [寅] **Tiger** 3 am - 5 am	chǒu [丑] **Ox** 1 am - 3 am	zǐ [子] **Rat** 11 pm - 1 am	hài [亥] **Pig** 9 pm - 11 pm

Note that the Chinese day begins at 11 pm. at night rather than midnight, its mid-point.

People familiar with Chinese medicine or acupuncture would know that the vital energy qi, of each organ is active during certain times[40], corresponding to the hourly pillars.

COMBINING THE FOUR PILLARS
What makes the Chinese zodiac distinct from any others is the combination of the four pillars.

Everyone is unique in that he or she is born at a particular time in history when you are under the particular combination of determining elements. There are four parameters to determine anyone's birth, the year, the month, the day and the hour.

ANALYSIS OF LIFE DESTINY [算命] *suànmìng*
A common saying in Chinese linking life destiny, ups and downs in life, as well as fēngshuǐ is 'First is the destiny [命] *mìng*, next comes the destiny cycle [运] *yùn*, fēngshuǐ ranks third [一命二运三风水]

---

[40] C. Rogers: *An Introduction to the Study of Acupuncture: The Five Keys*, Morgan Printing, 1986.

379

yīmìng èryùn sānfēngshuǐ. In simple English, it means that the most important determinant in life is your 'life destiny', which is fixed at the time of birth. That 'life destiny' would interact with the changing time parameters (ten year cycles, year, month, day and hour) to generate the second determinant affecting your life. The third determinant that could affect the quality of life is the fēngshuǐ.

The 'eight characters' [八字] *bāzì* comprises the year, the month, the day and the hour pillars, each composed of two characters, the 天干 *tiāngán* and the 地支 *dìzhī*. The gender of the person and place of birth are also taken into account. Once these details are known, the results are basically the same whoever one consults. One does not need to be a clairvoyant or acquire other supernatural gift to be an analysis. All it requires is a study of 'life destiny analysis' [命理学] *mìnglǐxué*. The analysis would be the same for a given time, be it in the past, present or future.

Several schools of life readings analysis have been established, the most famous of which would be Xú Zǐpíng [徐子平] (p. 173), whose art is aptly known the art of Zǐpíng. The system has developed to a respectable art, often consulted by true believers. Another school is the 紫微斗数 *zǐhuídǒushù*, attributed to Chén Xīyí [陈希夷].

Few people realise that a detailed analysis of the 'eight characters' [八字] *bāzì* birth data could reveal:

- ❖ One's ups and downs over the years, the details of which could be fine tuned to months or even days if necessary.
- ❖ Profile of one's personality
- ❖ Information on parents, brothers or sisters, husband or wife, children
- ❖ Types of sickness that the person is prone to
- ❖ Wealth
- ❖ Power, status
- ❖ Intelligence
- ❖ Periods of travel

* Compatibility with any other person
* Preference on occupation, feng shui direction, location, etc.

DESTINY ANALYSIS

The analysis involves:

1. Conversion of birth data into 'Celestial Stems and Terrestrial Branches' the 天干 *tiāngán* and the 地支 *dìzhī*.
2. Identify the determinant component, in particular the 'day celestial component' [日主] *rìzhǔ*.
3. Analyse data from 'five determinant elements' [五行] *wǔxíng*
4. Establish the relationship of other components with the determinant component
5. Determining strength of determinant component [断强弱] *duàn qiángruò*.
6. Determine the favourable or unfavourable circumstances [定喜吉] *dìng xǐjí*
7. Working out cycles of destiny [论吉凶] *lún jíxiōng*.
8. Focusing on specific issues.

I. CONVERSION INTO TIANGAN-DIZHI

Before any analysis could be carried out, it is necessary to convert any birth data into the Chinese calendar, which represents the birth data in 'Celestial Stems and Terrestrial Branches' [天干地支] *tiāngán-dìzhī*. This could be found from the 'calendar of ten thousand years' [万年历] *wànniánlì*, or from certain computer software.

For example a child born on 31 July 2000 at noon would have his data presented as

Year:	'Metal-dragon'	庚辰	*gēngchén*
Month:	'Water-goat'	癸未	*guǐwèi*
Day:	'Metal-tiger'	庚寅	*gēngyín*
Hour:	'Water-horse'	壬午	*rénwǔ*

These 'eight characters' [八字] *bāzì* effectively represents the forces prevailing at his exact time of birth.

II. IDENTIFY THE DETERMINANT COMPONENT

The determinant component is a yáng metal [庚] *gēng*, based on 'day celestial component' [日主] *rìzhǔ*.

III. ANALYSE DATA FROM FIVE ELEMENTS

First of all it is possible to gain an insight into a person's personality based on the five elements of wood, fire, earth, metal and water.

The person's birth data could be viewed as:

Year:	'Metal-dragon'	庚辰 *gēngchén*	metal-earth
Month:	'Water-goat'	癸未 *guǐwèi*	water-earth
Day:	'Metal-tiger'	庚寅 *gēngyín*	metal-wood
Hour:	'Water-horse'	壬午 *rénwǔ*	water-fire

Looking at the last column there are:

1 wood; 1 fire; 2 earths; 2 metals, 2 water.

(It is relevant to bear in mind that some of the elements could be 'hidden' under 'Terrestrial Branches' [地支] *dìzhī*.)

The configuration is that of a metal person, with strong earth elements. As we will discuss later, the 'metal' element is rather strong, especially when 'earth' generates 'metal'.

Personality 'profiles' presented in the last chapter could be used as a preliminary analysis. In this case the person has a yáng metal—[庚] *gēng* personality.

Each of the five elements plays a definite role, and they all interact or influence one another.

IV. ESTABLISH THE RELATIONSHIP OF COMPONENTS

A person is often analysed in terms of the relationship between the 'determinant component'—celestial day element [日主] *rìzhǔ* and the other seven components.

A set of vocabulary describes this relationship. In the last chapter we learn that there are two mechanisms, control and generation. In p. 326 the following terminology were used to relate the five determinant elements to one another.

Self: Self, partners and associates
Child: The product of generation or birth
Parent: The entity that generate self
Master: The entity that controls self
Slave: The entity that is controlled by self

In 'destiny analysis' the professional terms are:

Self: 'Partners or competitors' 比劫 *bǐjié*
Child: 'Creation' 食伤 *shíshāng*
Parent: 'Protector' 印星 *yìnxíng*
Master: 'Power' 官杀 *guānshā*
Slave: 'Wealth' 财星 *cáixíng*

A short description of these terms are as follows:

Partners or Competitors [比劫] *bǐjié*

Just like siblings, the partner element functions either as 'associates' or 'rivals/competitors' depending on circumstances. They could prop up the 'determinant element' [日主] *rìzhǔ* when it is weak, as siblings do. However when there is plenty of wealth around they become competitors. Depending on circumstances they might also compete for the same 'love' ones.

The relationship between the 'determinant component' [日主] *rìzhǔ* and bǐjié [比劫] is considered to be 'associates' [比肩]

bǐjiān when both belong to the same yīn-yáng signs. They are considered to be 'competitor' [劫财] *jiécái* when they belong to different yīn-yáng signs.

Creation [食伤] *shíshāng*
In our context the 'Creation' refers to the imaginative faculty, the ability to create something out of nothing, endowed at the time of birth. A person born with strong 食伤 *shíshāng* would be imaginative, creative, to a certain extent non-conforming. Normally people strong in 'Creation' are good designers, artists, authors, able to capture the imagination of audience or readers. To be effective the 'determinant component' [日主] *rìzhǔ* needs to be strong. However excessive 'Creation' is not good for anyone, as it drains or exhaust the 日主 *rìzhǔ*, making the latter weak.

The 食伤 *shíshāng* is the element that the 'determinant element' [日主] *rìzhǔ* generates. If the 日主 *rìzhǔ* were

'wood'	the 'Creation' element is	'fire'
'fire'	the 'Creation' element is	'earth'
'earth'	the 'Creation' element is	'metal'
'metal'	the 'Creation' element is	'water'
'water'	the 'Creation' element is	'wood'

The relationship between the 'determinant component' [日主] *rìzhǔ* and 食伤 *shíshāng* is considered to be 食神 *shíshén* when both belong to the same yīn-yáng signs. They are considered to be 伤官 *shāngguān* when they belong to different yīn-yáng signs.

Protector [印星] *yìnxíng*
In our context the 'Protector', 'Power booster' or 'Inheritance' are resources inherited from the parents at the time of birth. A person born with strong 印星 *yìnxíng* is intelligent, suitable for

academic work, research or jobs requiring analysis. Normally people strong in 'Protector' are more matured in his approach, able to plan, and exercise self restraint. As the name implies, the 'Protector' provides additional resources to the 'determinant component' [日主] *rìzhǔ*. However, excessive 'protector' is not good for anyone, as the 'Protector' restrains 'Creation'.

The 'Protector' [印星] *yìnxíng* is the element that gives rise to the 'determinant component' [日主] *rìzhǔ*. If the 日主 *rìzhǔ* is

'wood'	the 'Protector' element is	'water'
'fire'	the 'Protector' element is	'wood'
'earth'	the 'Protector' element is	'fire'
'metal'	the 'Protector' element is	'earth'
'water'	the 'Protector' element is	'metal'

The relationship between the 'determinant component' [日主] *rìzhǔ* and the 印星 *yìnxíng* is considered to be 偏印 *piānyìn* when both belong to the same yīn-yáng signs. They are considered to be 正印 *zhèngyìn* when they belong to different yīn-yáng signs.

Power [官星] *guānxíng*

In our context the 'Power' has the propensity to curb the potential of the 'determinant component' [日主] *rìzhǔ* at the time of birth. Though strong 'Power' [官星] *guānxíng* is beneficial when the 'determinant component' is too strong, the 'Power' could be disastrous when the 'determinant component' is itself weak. Normally people strong in 'Power' are able to impose discipline, firm in his leadership, commands respect from his staff. Excessive 'Power' is not good for anyone. The poor 日主*rìzhǔ* is over regulated, not given a chance to grow.

The 'Power' [官星] *guānxíng* is the element that controls the 'determinant component' [日主] *rìzhǔ*. If the 日主 *rìzhǔ* were

385

'wood'	the 'Power' element is	'metal'
'fire'	the 'Power' element is	'water'
'earth'	the 'Power' element is	'wood'
'metal'	the 'Power' element is	'fire'
'water'	the 'Power' element is	'earth'

The relationship between the 'determinant component' and 官星 *guānxíng* is considered to be 七杀 *qīshā* when both belong to the same yīn-yáng signs. It is 正官 *zhèngguān* when they belong to different yīn-yáng signs.

Wealth [财星] *cáixíng*
In our context 'Wealth' is the ability or propensity to accumulate wealth, endowed at the time of birth. A person born with strong 'Wealth' [财星] *cáixíng* could be in a position of accumulating wealth or managing wealth. He or she is suitable to manage wealth, such as accountants and bank managers. Normally people strong in 'Wealth' are good businessmen, able to seize opportunities at the correct time. To be effective the 'determinant component' needs to be strong. However excessive 'Wealth' is not good for anyone. It weakens the 'determinant element' [日主] *rìzhǔ*.

The 'Wealth' is the element that the 日主 *rìzhǔ* controls. If the 日主 *rìzhǔ* were

'wood'	the 'wealth' element is	'earth'
'fire'	the 'wealth' element is	'metal'
'earth'	the 'wealth' element is	'water'
'metal'	the 'wealth' element is	'wood'
'water'	the 'wealth' element is	'fire'

They relationship between the 'determinant component' and the 财星 *cáixíng* is considered to be 偏财 *piāncái* when both belong to the same yīn-yáng signs. They are considered to be 正 財 *zhèngcái* when they belong to different yīn-yáng signs.

These relationships are critical to the analysis of life destiny. Taking the same example above, the four pillars are

Year:	'Metal-dragon'	庚辰	*gēngchén*
Month:	'Water-goat'	癸未	*guǐwèi*
Day:	'Metal-tiger'	庚寅	*gēngyín*
Hour:	'Water-horse'	壬午	*rénwǔ*

The relationship between the components from p. 385 are as follows:

Year:	bǐjiān	比肩	(gēng 庚	chén	辰)	piānyìn	偏印
Month:	shāngguān	伤官	(guǐ 癸	wèi	未)	zhèngyìn	正印
Day:			(gēng 庚	yín	寅)	piāncái	偏财
Hour:	shíshén	食神	(rén 壬	wǔ	午)	zhèngguān	正官

To an analyst the component relationship provides a wealth of information. The personality profile of an individual is not only determined by the 'five elements' of metal, fire, water, wood and water, but also by the component relationships.

The relationship between a man and his wife, as well as other women, could be analysed from his 'Wealth' [财星] *cáixíng* properties. The relationship between a woman and her husband, as well as other man, could be analysed from her 'Power' [官星] *guānxíng* properties. These include the marriages, phase of one's life favourable to relationships, etc.

Whether a person is destined to be in a position of power, fame, whether he has great literary or other talents, etc, could be deciphered from these data.

CHOOSING A CAREER

Personality profiling based on 'five elements' 'relationships of components' as well as 'strength of determinant component' would roughly identify the strength and weakness, interest, as well as types of careers.

Some Chinese families tend to equate success in life with wealth accumulation through business. However the reality is that not everyone is suited to handle money, or be a businessman. Depending on his inherent ability, his potential could be under-utilised if his only option is business or money making.

Ideally a good career should allow 'the development to the full, the human personality'. Being excellent professional or successful artists could be just as gratifying. The Chinese saying 'in every profession there emerges a top Imperial scholar' [行行出状元] *hánghāng chū zhuàngyuán* is worth taking note.

V. STRENTH OF 'DETERMINANT COMPONENT' [断强弱]
duàn qiángruò

The relative strength of 'determinant component' [日主] *rìzhǔ* is central to the success or otherwise of one's pursuit. A reasonably strong 'determinant component' is essential to take advantage of elements such as 'Wealth' [财星] *cáixíng*. Chinese philosophy generally seeks moderation, rather than extremes. In the inter-action between various components of the pillars, the best out-come is not a powerful or a weak 'determinant component', but one that is moderate.

Various factors influence the strength of components. One of the key considerations lies in the relation of 'determinant com-ponent' with the season of the year. The effect of season on the five elements is as follows: The numbers indicate strength levels from 1 to 5, 1 being the strongest.

During Spring, the months of 寅 *yín,* 卯 *mǎo*

1. 'Wood' is 'prosperous' [旺] *wàng*
2. 'Fire' is 'strong' [相] *xiàng*
3. 'Water' is 'inactive' [休] *xiū*
4. 'Metal' is 'imprisoned' [囚] *qiú*
5. 'Earth' is 'dead' [死] *sǐ*

During Summer, the months of 巳 *sì,* 午 *wǔ*

1. 'Fire' is 'prosperous' [旺] *wàng*
2. 'Earth' is 'strong' [相] *xiàng*
3. 'Wood' is 'inactive' [休] *xiū*
4. 'Water' is 'imprisoned' [囚] *qiú*
5. 'Metal' is 'dead' [死] *sǐ*

During Autumn, the months of 申 *shēn,* 酉 *yǒu*

1. 'Metal' is 'prosperous' [旺] *wàng*
2. 'Water' is 'strong' [相] *xiàng*
3. 'Earth' is 'inactive' [休] *xiū*
4. 'Fire' is 'imprisoned' [囚] *qiú*
5. 'Wood' is 'dead' [死] *sǐ*

During Winter, the months of 亥 *hài,* 子 *zǐ*

1. 'Water' is 'prosperous' [旺] *wàng*
2. 'Wood' is 'strong' [相] *xiàng*
3. 'Metal' is 'inactive' [休] *xiū*
4. 'Earth' is 'imprisoned' [囚] *qiú*
5. 'Fire' is 'dead' [死] *sǐ*

During the change-over months of 辰 *chén,* 未 *wèi,* 戌 *xū,* 丑 *chǒu*

1. 'Earth' is 'prosperous' [旺] *wàng*
2. 'Metal' is 'strong' [相] *xìang*
3. 'Fire' is 'inactive' [休] *xiū*
4. 'Wood' is 'imprisoned' [囚] *qiú*
5. 'Water' is 'dead' [死] *sǐ*

The association between the five determinant elements and [天干地支] *tiángān-dìzhī* are:

Wood: 甲 *jiǎ*, 乙 *yǐ*, 寅 *yín*, 卯 *mǎo*
Fire: 丙 *bǐng*, 丁 *dīng*, 巳 *sì*, 午 *wǔ*
Earth: 戊 *wù*, 已 *jǐ*, 辰 *chén*, 未 *wèi*, 戌 *xū*, 丑 *chǒu*
Metal: 庚 *gēng*, 辛 *xīn*, 申 *shēn*, 酉 *yǒu*
Water: 壬 *rén*, 癸 *guǐ*, 亥 *hài*, 子 *zǐ*

In addition to the season factor, the 'determinant component' could be strengthened by having more 'Partners' (associates, friends) or 'Protectors' (boosters, resources) (p. 383).

VI. Determine the Favourable or Unfavourable Circumstances

[定喜吉] *dìng xǐjí*
Depending on the strength of the 'determinant component' [日主] *rìzhǔ*, the numbers of each element, as well as interaction between them, it is possible to work out circumstances favourable or unfavourable to self.

The cycles of control and generation cycles are central to strengthening or weakening a component. The cycle on outer circle indicates generation, while the inner arrows indicate controls.

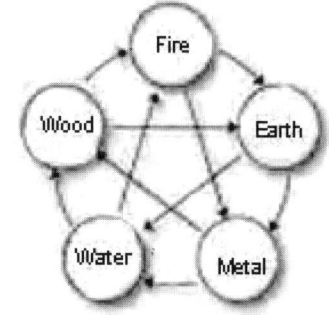

True to the Chinese philosophy of moderation, a weak 'determinant component' needs to be strengthened, over powerful 'determinant component' needs to be weakened.

If the 'determinant component' [日主] *rìzhǔ* is strong, the favourable elements would be the 'Creation' [食伤] *shíshāng*, which would exhaust the [日主] *rìzhǔ* energy. A second option is the 'Power' [官星] *guānxíng* to curb its strength. A third alternative is the 'Wealth' [财星] *cáixíng*, which would also drain off a lot of its energy. The unfavourable elements would be 'Protector' [印星] *yìnxíng* and 'Partner' [比劫] *bǐjié*.

If the 'determinant component' [日主] *rìzhǔ* is too weak, the favourable elements would be 'Protector' [印星] *yìnxíng* and 'Partner' [比劫] *bǐjié*. The unfavourable elements would be the 'Creation' [食伤] *shíshāng*, the 'Power' [官星] *guānxíng* and the 'Wealth' [财星] *cáixíng*.

Please note that there are exceptions to the rule, in particular when the 'determinant component' is exceptionally strong or weak.

In practice allowances need to be given to interaction of components, giving rise to 'mergers', 'acquisitions', 'alliances', 'restraints'. For example 寅 *yín*, 卯 *mǎo*, 辰 *chén* merge to form powerful wood energies.

VII. WORK OUT THE CYCLE OF DESTINY [论吉凶] *lún jíxiōng*

The 'eight characters' [八字] *bāzì* as it stands reflect the conditions at the time of birth.

It is obvious that no one would be lucky throughout his life. A person with good 'wealth' element normally makes his wealth during a certain period, not throughout his life.

There would be good and bad years. The 'life destiny analysis' stipulates that a given set of 'eight characters' [八字] *bāzì* interacts with the changing environment throughout his life. In nature nothing is static, environmental parameters are dynamic, continuously changing on a cyclical, predicable basis.

Normally the cycle changes every ten years, according to the 'Celestial Stem' tiāngān cycles. It could be envisaged as another pillar, the 'cycle' [运] yùn pillar.

Let us refer to the person born as described in p. 381. The birth data could be viewed as:

Year:	'Metal-dragon'	庚辰	gēngchén
Month:	'Water-goat'	癸未	guǐwèi
Day:	'Metal-tiger'	庚寅	gēngyín
Hour:	'Water-horse'	壬午	rénwǔ

First of all let us determine the strength of determinant component [断强弱] duàn qiángruò. A metal element [庚] gēng born in the month of 未 wèi would be strong (p. 390), particularly when there is another metal to support it, and two earth components to produce more.

Having determined his strength, we can then work out the elements favourable or unfavourable to metal the 'determinant' element [庚] gēng. 'Water' or 'Fire' would be favourable; we could also consider 'Wood'. 'Earth' and 'Metal' unfavourable.

We can then work out the cycles of destiny [论吉凶] lùn jíxiōng. Without going into theoretical details, the life cycles would depend on whether the person is a male or a female. As a theoretical analysis, let us take the first four cycles (ten years per cycle) of his or her life.

If the person were a male, his cycle pillar would be under the influence of:

'Wood-monkey'	甲申	jiǎshēn
'Wood-rooster'	乙酉	yǐyǒu
'Fire-dog'	丙戌	bǐngxū
'Fire-pig'	丁亥	dīnghài

His wellbeing during his first cycle would depend on the interaction of his inherent 'eight characters' with 'Wood-monkey' [甲申] *jiǎshēn*, the second cycle would depend on the interaction with 'Wood-rooster' [乙酉] *yǐyǒu*, and so on.

As a general rule, the 'Celestial Stem' [天干] *tiāngān*, in this case yáng 'wood' [甲] *jiǎ* from 甲申 *jiǎshēn* determines the first five years, while the 'Terrestrial Branch' [地支] *dìzhī*, in this case yáng 'metal' [申] *shēn* would rule the second five years.

As his is a 'metal' personality with strong 'earth' elements, the 'metal' is strong and needs to be 'weakened'. He would do well in the fourth cycle; the 'fire' element would control 'metal', while the 'water' element from 'pig' would also drain off energy from 'metal'.

In reality elements from the 'Terrestrial Branches' could merge. The merger could occur during the cycles when the appropriate components meet. In the example above during the third cycle 寅 *yín*, 午 *wǔ* and 戌 *xū* merge to form 'fire', making it favourable.

If the person were a female, her cycle pillar (ten years per cycle) would be:

'Water-horse'	壬午	*rénwǔ*
'Metal-snake'	辛巳	*xīnsì*
'Metal-dragon'	庚辰	*gēngchén*
'Earth rabbit'	己卯	*jǐmǎo*

Her wellbeing during her first cycle would depend on the interaction of her inherent or 'eight characters' with 'Water-horse' [壬午] *rénwǔ*, the second cycle would depend on the interaction with 'Metal-snake' [辛巳] *xīnsì* and so on.

She needs to be careful in her second and third cycles, as there would be excessive 'metal' and 'earth' elements, leading to massive imbalance, or inadequacies in other elements.

Mergers of the 'Terrestrial Branches' occur during the second cycle, with 巳 *sì*, 午 *wǔ*, 未 *wèi* forming strong 'fire'; as well as in the fourth cycle, with 寅 *yín*, 卯 *mǎo*, 辰 *chén* forming powerful 'wood'.

It is also possible to have an idea of periods in life during which one is more likely to acquire wealth, power, prestige, prone to accidents, and so on.

THE TIME DIMENSION

In addition to the original elemental configuration at birth as well as the ten year cycle, the influence of the particular year in question is important. The 天干 *tiāngān* and 地支 *dìzhī* elements of the ruling year interacts with the original configuration. The term 'paramount ruler' [太岁] *tàisuì* is given, as the emperor cannot be offended. The year would be unfavourable (unless there are other elements to balance it), if the configuration clashes with the 'paramount ruler).

Quite often it is also necessary to work out details down to individual years or months. Theoretically it is possible to work out the interactions to a 'day' or even 'hour' level, though this is considered too time consuming and frivolous.

VIII. SPECIFIC ISSUES

A whole range of interesting parameters could be worked out from the 'eight characters' [八字] *bāzì*. Whether a person has the potential to be wealthy, powerful, creative, intelligent, famous, etc could be worked out. Other topics of interest include his or her love or marriage life, compatibility with husband or wife, relationship with parent, sibling, children, and so on.

To the believers there are identifiable phases in life when they are more likely to acquire wealth, fame, disaster, etc, could also be worked out.

How much of life is destined would be highly debatable. It is also dangerous to be psychologically or physically over-dependent on these forecast. In the final analysis, success only comes with lots of sweat and toil, in addition to 'luck' or 'destiny'.

SUPPLEMENTARY INFORMATION

Some practitioners transform the birth data to a set of hexagrams (refer to chapter ten). The interaction between various components within the hexagram, as well as the implication of the line change (refer to p. 430) provide additional information. The person born as described in p. 381 with the birth data of

Year:	'Metal-dragon'	庚辰 *gēngchén*	metal-earth
Month:	'Water-goat'	癸未 *guǐwèi*	water-earth
Day:	'Metal-tiger'	庚寅 *gēngyín*	metal-wood
Hour:	'Water-horse'	壬午 *rénwǔ*	water-fire

would be transformed from the hexagram 'Perseverance' [雷风恒] *léifēng-hēng* (p. 435) to the hexagram 'Great Power' [雷天大壯] *léitiān-dàzhuàng* (p. 435).

MATCHING INDIVIDUALS

The system has wide applications in personal relationships, in particular matching the compatibility or 'complementarities' of couples. It was widely used in older days when couples were matched or arranged, often at quite a young age. Modern couples select their future spouse based on love as well as other factors. However marriages could end up in divorce when the inherent profiles do not match.

Compatibility is based on the needs of a person's 'four pillars'. If a man lacks or need a certain element, say 'wood', if 'wood' is the strength of his partner, then he would benefit from her strength. At the same time if she lacks 'fire' and 'fire' is found in her partner, then she would also benefit. In this case the couple is mutually supporting

395

and compatible. (There are also other compatibility factors, depending on criteria of judgment).

In modern times the same system could be used in human resource management. It is useful to supplement information from *curricula vitae*, to profile the personalities or to match the compatibility of working partners or senior staff. In this way harmonious working relationship is ensured at the top management level.

At a corporate level it could be used in company mergers, acquisition, just as in the case of personal relationships.

ANALYSIS OF NATIONS

The analysis works for individuals as well as nations, if we could accurately pin down the critical time in history in terms of four pillars when an event occurs.

An excellent book on analysis of the destiny of China[41] was written by an anonymous author under the pen name of Liǔ Chí [柳 迟], analysing in detail the birth characteristics of China. It is significant to note that the defining moment in history was taken to be 2 pm, 1 October, 1949, when Mao Zedong was elected to be the Chairman and the government formed, rather than 3 pm, when the announcement and celebration was made. The difference is subtle but highly critical, as the analysis patterns would be different. According to the author, the birth data of China is:

Year:	'Earth-ox'	己丑	*jǐchǒu*
Month:	'Water-rooster'	癸酉	*guǐyǒu*
Day:	'Wood-rat'	甲子	*jiǎzǐ*
Hour:	'Metal-goat'	辛未	*xīnwèi*

To those who are familiar, this is indeed a powerful set of eight characters. Nevertheless there are periods of ups and downs; the initial years would be difficult and tumultuous.

---

[41] 国运（关于中华人民共和国八子的推算）—通行 Publisher, H.K., 1996.

LEADERSHIP PROFILE

As the fortunes of countries or corporate entity depend on their leadership, the pillars of destiny of the relevant political and corporate leaders are also taken into account. In analysing a nation's or company's profile, we need to analyse the leadership as well as relevant nation/company during the period.

Though personality profiles are yet to be scientifically tested rigorously, empirical or circumstantial evidence over the centuries provide sufficient confidence on the system.

OTHER INTERESTING WORKS

Raymond Lo used the 'four pillars' [四柱] *sìzhù* analysis to predict the emergence and outcome of important events such as the Gulf War, the resignation of Margaret Thatcher and the fall of President Mikhail Gorbachev.[42] He also authored a series of books on this fascinating subject.[43]

Many traditional Chinese acknowledge the omnipotence of 'God' compared to men. The proverb 'Man puts in his efforts, the Heaven makes it a success' [谋事在人, 成事在天] (p. 204) *móushìzàirén, chéng shìzàitiān*, recognises the fact that at times events are beyond the control of men. This however does not mean that a man should not put in all his effort to make things happen.

---

[42] Raymond Lo: *Feng Shui & Destiny for Managers*, Times Book International, 1966.

[43] Raymond Lo: *Feng Shui—The Pillars of Destiny*. Times Editions Pte. Ltd. 1994

Living in a Continuously Changing World

As WE HAVE SEEN IN the last chapter, even if we were doing nothing, the 'time' parameter, with the associated 阴阳五行 *yīn-yáng wǔxíng* cycle revolves, their presence felt, impacting on outcome of events happening at a particular time. In other words the world is continuously changing.

This chapter looks into how the traditional Chinese understand and cope with changes, through the eyes of yìjīng [易经], one of the oldest books in the world. Yìjīng has tremendous impact in the Chinese psyche, as it is the source of many of the paradigms. The chapter also looks at an application of yìjīng, the art of 'Divination', when men are confronted with unknown outcome.

Yìjīng [易经]

If there is anything inherently true in this world, it is the fact that all things are subject to change.

Technological advances lead to changes in our environment, lifestyle, our basic understanding of ourselves at a molecular or genetic level, as well as our perception of universe.

Yìjīng is undoubtedly a book of substance. The book is difficult to comprehend, subject to interpretation, and requires considerable lateral thinking. Its theory, logic or philosophy is used in a wide range of applications directly or indirectly, with or without the users being aware of it.

Yìjīng is also known as zhōuyì [周易] to the practitioners. More commonly known as the book of change or I-Ching, this is a book that is not well understood by most people, including people who are well educated in Chinese. Translations of the book in English vary tremendously depending on the author's background and command of the Chinese language.

While yìjīng is hardly known in the West, in China numerous scholars contributed to the topic. They range from Emperors Fú Xī [伏羲] (p. 155) and Zhōu Wénwáng [周文王] (p. 178), to Confucius (p. 159) and Zhū Xī [朱熹] (p. 179). Other less known personalities include Huì Dòng [惠栋] (p. 158), Lǐ Dǐngzhà [李鼎诈] (p. 160) and Shào Kāngjié [邵康节] (p. 167) and Wèi Bóyáng [魏伯阳] (p.172).

Most people today benefit from developments in the binary system, which leads to development of computer as well as information technology. When the inventor, Gottfried Wilhelm Leibniz, the seventeenth-century German mathematician saw the sixty-four hexagram from Yijing, he recognised his own binary arithmetic was already in use 5,000 years before in the East.

Some Interesting Scenarios

Before we discuss yìjīng proper, it is interesting to look at a book which assigns yìjīng scenarios for each year. This is an interesting book, not well known to many, entitled 皇极经世书*huáng jíjīng shìshū* written by Shào Kángjié [邵康节] (1011-1077) (p. 167). As a matter of interest the following general scenarios have been listed.

2000:	'Small errors'	雷山小过	*léishānxiǎoguò*
2001:	'Gradual buildup'	风山渐	*fēngshān-jiàn*
2002:	'Extreme Difficulties'	水山蹇	*shuǐshān-jiǎn*
2003:	'Restrain'	艮为山	*gènwéishān*
2004:	'Humility'	地山谦	*dìshān-qīan*

2005:	'Conflict, Opposition'	天地否	*tiandì-pǐ*
2006:	'Assembling'	泽地萃	*zédicuì*
2007:	'Advance, Progress'	火地晋	*huǒdì-jìn*
2008:	'Excitement'	雷地豫	*léidì-yù*
2009:	'Contemplation'	风地观	*fēngdì-guān*

Needless to say, the interpretation or relevance of these scenarios is subject to disputes. These scenarios should not be taken too seriously, as conditions differ for each country and individuals. Nevertheless the above scenarios serve as a good start for the understanding of yìjīng.

The yìjīng scenarios are made up of six lines, each being either yīn or yáng. The six lines constitute a hexagram, which depicts certain scenarios, such as 'Extreme difficulties', 'Contemplation', 'Advance' etc. At a higher level, it is not the general concept of these scenario, but interaction of forces that constitute that scenario that is analysed. This is discussed at the end of this chapter.

The ability to forecast events, to link various parameters in a coherent whole is why one of the oldest books written in the world still attracting so much attention and research. It also explains why the book is able to mesmerise and retain scholars throughout the centuries.

To gain an insight into the workings of yìjīng, it is relevant to discuss the concepts inherent in the book, the notion of cyclic nature of events, the propensity for change in nature, as well as the cause-effect relationship.

Cyclic Nature of Events

Events are relative and contrasting in nature; an example would be day and night, represented by yīn and yáng. There would be 'positive' to contrast with the 'negative'. (One could not judge anything being bad without comparing to good things).

Events are also cyclic, for example the four seasons, represented by four determining elements, 'Wood' (spring), 'Fire' (summer), 'Metal' (autumn), 'Water' (winter), with the remaining element 'Earth' interspersed. The more we realise and accept this truism in nature the easier it is to harmonise with the glorious rhythmic process, rather than having to endure its inevitability.

Women as a whole live their lives in physiological cycles, and probably understand the rhythmic process better than men. In particular mothers have profound experiences in child bearing, when they witness life cycle in an intimate, physiological, emotional and spiritual manner. For that matter they are more intuitive and have a better feel for cyclic changes. They would go with the tide, experience for themselves and bring it to fruition.

Indeed both natural and man-made events go through cycles. Business cycles follow a certain pattern. Technology goes through shorter and shorter life cycles. The associated products development, training, services and infrastructure go through a similar pattern.

Inherent Propensity for Change

If there is anything that is certain as sun rises in the morning, it is that yīn-yáng [阴阳] interaction change continuously. Indeed nothing should be considered static and everything is subject to continuous change. These changes occur both in the micro and macro scenarios. The rate of change increases with technology and accelerated transmission of information. Not only are changes occurring at increasingly higher frequencies, but also the nature or impact of change is becoming more and more intense. The ability to adapt to change is the key to survival.

If events were prone to the inevitability of cyclic change, timing would be crucial in decision making. It is critical because the relative weights of criteria for judgment or consideration change with time.

The inherent dynamism is part of the effects of cyclic nature in the universe, and forms the basis of evolution.

The Cause-Effect Relationship

As a scenario changes, the associated parameters will necessarily change. Whether a change is natural or as a result of artificial intervention, there is always a cause-effect relationship, as stated by the Third law of Newton.

HEXAGRAM PRESENTATION

We would like to present five hexagrams listed at the beginning of this chapter in 皇极经世书 *huáng jíjīng shìshū*. The hexagram (6 lines symbol) is given, as well as the binary symbol. Emphasis is placed on readings for relationship and business.

Numbers such as 001-010 is explained at a later section.

Note that this is only an abridged introductory version, intended to create an initial interest in the study of this fascinating subject.

A more advanced interpretation of the hexagrams involves analysis of components that made up the hexagram. A brief description is seen at the end of this chapter.

Hexagram Example 1

 **'Extreme Difficulties' 001-010**
[水山蹇] *shuǐshān-jiǎn*

This hexagram is described as 'Water-mountain-Extreme difficulties' [水山蹇] *shuǐshān-jiǎn*. It could be portrayed as having to navigate through a mountain with perilous abyss all over the place. One has to be extremely careful, as one false step would mean either dropping off the mountain or drown in deep pits!

'The sequence of hexagrams' Xùguàzhuàn [序卦传] writes: 'Disobedience of rules invariably lead to all sorts of difficulties' [乖 必有难, 故受之以蹇]. It implies that one is in such a difficult situation due to not following certain rules.

Just like the 'five determinant elements', each hexagram is associated in space and time.

In this hexagram, there is advantage to the south west; as there are obstacles to the north east [利西南, 不利东北]. It is also the time to seek guidance and help from someone experienced and knowledgeable [利见大人, 贞吉].

It is also important to be able to stop in the face of danger, rather than blindly carrying on [见险而能止, 知矣哉].

Finally, the image depicts the cultivated gentleman turning around and engage in self cultivation [君子以反身修德]. Righteous persistence brings good fortune.

The hexagram paints a scenario of 'extreme danger', and gives some ideas of how to get out of it. Now that there is danger everywhere; you have to tread very carefully. Obstacles must be overcome before you can advance any further.

Could this be the result of your own doing? Are you the source of some of these obstacles? Identification of the cause is crucial; otherwise no remedial actions could work. There are good reasons to ask yourself a lot of hard questions.

Keywords in the hexagram 'Extreme difficulties' [水山蹇] *shuǐshān-jiǎn* include Danger, Difficulties, Hazardous, Obstacles, Obstruction, Pitfall, Seek help.

When Applied to Business Environment: you seem to be surrounded by a series of obstacles and difficulties. Keep cool; identify the source of problems, including any internal factors. Be willing to listen, collect feedback. Do not get into any new ventures or projects just to get out of present constraints. The situation is critical, hazardous and should not be negotiated alone. Scale down the operation. Seek help, rather than attempting to salvage the situation single handedly. Swallow your pride.

When Applied to Relationship: This is a trying time as relationship moves to a very rocky patch. Is your attitude, hope, or expectation that is blocking other possibilities in your life? Review the situation;

look into any factors, such as attitude or behaviour that could have caused it. Do not run away from the problem, however painful it could be. Avoid blaming others, be positive. Seek help from friends or professional counselors. Despite the fact that you seem to be facing tremendous problems, this is a good time for self-cultivation and development.

On a more positive note you could also see this as an opportunity rather than a problem. Do not give up the relationship easily in face of a problem. This may be the time to build up your self-esteem, build up your confidence to face future challenges.

Hexagram Example 2

☷☶ **'Humility' 001-000**
[地山谦] *dìshān-qīan*

This hexagram is described as 'Earth-mountain Humility' [地山谦] *dìshān-qīan*. It could be portrayed as the mighty mountain hidden under the earth, not visible, not boasting of its might, but certainly there and powerful.

'The sequence of hexagrams' xùguàzhuàn [序卦传] writes: 'People who are destined for great things have a sense of humility, in spite of the immense prestige' [大有者不可以盈，故受之以谦].

When a person of high position is humble, he commands tremendous respect, and bargains from a position of moral strength. 'Humility brings about success: [谦，亨].

When humility rules, the hexagram speaks of the Celestial (the powerful and strong) way of radiating brightness and success downwards, and the Terrestrial (the small and weak) way of emitting its influence upwards [天道下济而光明，地道卑而上行]. There is excellent communication when arrogance is not around. This is evident as 'the Celestial path trims the excesses, and augment the modest; the Terrestrial path becomes more filled and bring up the humble' [天道亏盈而益谦，地道变盈而流谦].

404

Finally, the image depicts the cultivated gentleman donates his surplus to those in need, thereby striking a new balance [君子以裒多益寡, 称物平施].

Keywords in the understanding of the hexagram 'Humility' [地山谦] *dìshān-qiān* include Considerate, Humility, Humble, Moderation, Modesty and Moral authority.

When Applied to Business Environment: Humility and moral strength, whether as a corporation or as individuals have the power to change status quo. There is hence an opportunity to co-operate with companies or individuals who share or respect these values. In terms of consumer acceptance and marketing this is a definite plus. At a management level, modesty in high position would bring about better outcome.

When Applied to Relationship: This is the time when relationship develops beyond physical (including sexual) dimensions. Nurture the relationship to a new level, be yourself, physically and spiritually. You would arrive at a new equilibrium.

Hexagram Example 3
☰☷ 'Conflict, Opposition' 000-111
[天地否] *tiandì-pǐ*

The hexagram is described 'Heaven-earth-Opposition' [天地否] *tiāndì-pǐ*. At first glance the 'Heaven' and 'Earth' are in their rightful position, and everything should be all right. However in this static position 'Heaven' could only moves further upward and 'Earth' sinks further downwards. The situation would be good if the 'Heaven' energy moves downwards and the 'Earth' energy moves up, so that there is some exchange or mutual influence. It is important to realise that yìjīng deals with dynamic, not static positions.

'The sequence of hexagrams' xùguàzhuàn [序卦传] writes: 'Nothing could function perpetually, opposition sets in' [物不可以终

通, 故受之以否]. After a period of peace, invariably disagreement develops. Over a period of time two parties would reach a new equilibrium, whereby they are diametrically opposite. This is a stand-still phase, where nothing works.

The hexagram speaks of 'Opposition, evil forces operating, unfavourable to the nature of cultivated gentlemen, the good and great withdraws, and the inferior advances' [否: 否之匪人, 不利君子贞, 大往小来].

This is also the time when the 'Heaven' does not communicate with or understands the 'Earth', everything stagnates [天地不交, 而万物不通也].

Finally, the image depicts the cultivated gentleman withdraws into himself and conceals his true self. In this manner he avoids the disasters, and does not want to be honoured or associated with it [君子以俭德辟难, 不可荣以禄].

Keywords in the hexagram 'Heaven-earth-Opposition' [天地否] *tiāndì-pǐ* include Disagreement, Disobedience, Obstruction, Opposition, Stagnation and Standstill.

When Applied to Business Environment: A period of stagnation, depression or decline. There is disharmony, dishonesty as well as lack of co-ordination. There is obviously a problem in your business. This is a time to do a thorough review of your objectives and plans, to identify the root cause of the problem. Do not take any risk, make major decisions, or get embroiled in unnecessary arguments. Do not compromise on your business ethics or moral values, though following the 'trend' could be very tempting. In the long run there is no short cut to succeed. Do not get embroiled with unethical practices.

When Applied to Relationship: What you see or sense could be just a façade. Behind the scene there could be a breakdown of mutual understanding and trust. There could be undercurrent or some other factors that you are not aware of. Somehow you have lost your sense of judgment. Withdraw from the group if possible; remain faithful to your true principles. Do not be tempted by peers or 'idols'. Be extremely cautious and careful. Do not commit yourself.

Hexagram Example 4
☳☷ 'Excitement, Joy' 000-100
[雷地豫] *léidì-yù*

This hexagram is described as 'Thunder-earth Excitement' [雷地豫] *léidì-yù*. It can be depicted as thunder (excitement) emerging from the ground, resulting in much excitement and joy.

'The sequence of hexagrams' xùguàzhuàn [序卦传] writes: 'With great achievement and humility, there is much joy, followed by enthusiasm within the circle' [有大而能谦, 必豫, 故受之以豫].

The spirit of enthusiasm and joy sustains the collective psyche, the leadership structure. It provides an underlying unity and sense of purpose.

'The heaven and earth moves in unison. The sun and the moon keep their courses, and the four seasons do not change their appointed times. The sage go along with the movements, the people follow. Punishment would be light, as the people obey his leadership. Great indeed are the times of 'excitement' [天地以顺动, 故日月不过, 而四时不忒; 圣人以顺动, 则刑罚清而民服. 豫之时义大矣哉!]

'Thunder energy bursts from the earth into heaven. The ancient kings honour the heaven by joyous activities, offer appropriate sacrifices, in remembrance of their ancestors' [雷出地奋, 豫. 先王以作乐崇德, 殷荐之上帝, 以配祖考].

When Applied to Business Environment: It is time to galvanise the troop; excite them to get things moving. Enthusiasm and common sense of purpose and direction enables staff and management to move as a single entity. In the process it is important to look after individual needs and personal appreciation. Your leadership is much appreciated and unquestioned. It is an opportunity to follow the natural course of action.

When Applied to Relationship: Passion sets in; it is time to follow your heart and inner feelings. Feeling of joy and enthusiasm is contagious. Do something that you both enjoy, try a new activity, there is plenty of good feelings. Express yourself freely, get moving. Your relationship would succeed, the relationship are in total accord. Your values and objectives are compatible.

Keywords in the hexagram 'Thunder-earth Excitement' [雷地豫] *léidì-yù* include Anticipation, Arousal, Energise, Enthusiasm, Excitement and Joy.

Hexagram Example 5

'Contemplation' 000-011

[风地观] *fēngdì-guān*

The hexagram is described as 'Wind-earth-Contemplation' [风地观] *fēngdì-guān*. Conceptually it could be portrayed as gentle wind blowing over the earth, observing and contemplating as it blows along.

'The sequence of hexagrams' xùguàzhuàn [序卦传] writes: 'With things develop and prosper, they could be observed' [物大然后可观, 故受之以观].

The hexagram speaks of 'Contemplation, the worshiper has washed his hands but has not made the offerings. Good credibility, the people look up to him' [观: 盥而不荐, 有孚颙若].

Finally the wind blows over the earth: contemplation. The ancient kings inspect all parts of the kingdom, to observe his people and teach them [风行地上, 观; 先王以省方, 观民设教].

Keywords in the hexagram 'Wind-earth-Contemplation' [风地观] *fēngdì-guān* include Being seen, Contemplation, Inspect, Looking from above, Observation, Reflection, Review, Scanning and Viewpoint.

When Applied to Business Environment: This is the time when a company or an individual takes an environmental scan. Once that is done we have a good, clear picture and understanding of forces at work. This is a good time to review strategies, products and services, as well as making long term plans. It is also a good time to look into streaming operations, making it more efficient and simpler.

When the wind blows it blows far and freely, reflecting wide reaching panoramic view and conclusions. Wait until you have done your survey, it is not time to act yet.

This is a time to scan the business environment, observe how others perform in the market place, compare and contrast options and priorities.

When Applied to Relationship: Things are developing well. You can afford to sit back, contemplate and review the situation. You might find new facets of relationship that you have taken for granted. Your prospective might even change. Take a good hard look at your relationship, review the events of late, and explore new directions.

We emphasise once again that this is only a short description of the hexagrams. No mention is made on the individual lines constituting each of the hexagrams, though they are important in interpretations of scenarios.

THE HEXAGRAMS

We note from the scenario descriptions earlier on that scenarios are described as combinations of certain entities. For example

'Extreme difficulties' is depicted by 'Water-mountain-Extreme difficulties' [水山蹇] *shuǐshān-jiǎn*, water pits on mountain tops.

'Humility' is depicted by 'Earth-mountain-Humility' [地山谦] *dìshān-qīan*, mountain under the earth

'Conflict', 'Opposition' is depicted by 'heaven-earth-Opposition' [天地否] *tiāndì-pǐ*, the sky moving upwards and the earth sinking further below.

'Excitement' is depicted by 'thunder-earth-Excitement' [雷地豫] *léidì-yù*, energy coming from the earth.

'Contemplation' is depicted by 'Wind-earth-Contemplation' [风地观] *fēngdì-gūan*, gentle wind observing landscape as it blows.

Each of the scenarios, depicted by a hexagram, is made of two trigrams. It is therefore relevant to gain an insight into the basic concepts of Yìjīng trigrams.

THE TRIGRAMS

The South Korean flag, featuring four trigrams of heaven, earth, fire and water, together with the yīn-yáng symbol.

At the fundamental level a trigram is composed of three lines, known as 爻 *yáo*, each line being yīn or yáng. Traditionally yīn is depicted as a broken line — — and yáng is depicted as a continuous line ———. In binary code we could represent yīn as 0 and yáng as 1. These three 'lines' [爻] *yáo* forms the basis of Yìjīng study and analysis.

The three yīn or yáng lines make 8 possible combinations. In the system below '1' refers to a continuous yáng line, while '0' refer to a broken or yīn line. The numbering system starts from bottom. 100 means that the bottom line is yáng, followed by two yīn lines.

      111 'Heaven, Creative'   乾 *qián*
      110 'Joy'   兑 *duì*
      101 'Clarity, Fire'   离 *lí*

100 'Thunder, Energy'　震　*zhèn*
000 'Earth, Receptive'　坤　*kūn*
001 'Stillness, Mountain'　艮　*gèn*
010 'Danger, Water'　坎　*kǎn*
011 'Wind, Penetration'　巽　*xùn*

Note that there could be more than one concept for a trigram. For example 011 could be interpreted as 'wind', 'penetration', 'wood', 'influence', etc.

Descriptions of the trigrams are as follows:

THE EIGHT BASIC TRIGRAMS

111 'Heaven, Creative' [乾] *qián*

Qián is the creative trigram, with three yáng lines. It is associated with the Father and Heaven. Though blessed with qualities of strength, creativity and command, it is important to remember that this trigram is co-generated with　坤　*kūn* 000, the Mother Earth.

Keywords associated with qián [乾] include Assertive, Authority, Creative, Father, Heaven, and Power.

000 'Receptive, Earth' [坤] *kūn*

As we have seen earlier, kūn represents the receptive trigram of Mother Earth. In human relationship, kūn is associated with the caring, nurturing mother.

The three yīn lines of Mother Earth imply a situation that is safe and gentle. It is receptive to ideas, sensitive to changes, intuitive, willing and prepared to accept burdens.

The pure yīn trigram has the inherent strength to buffer, absorb, and endure tremendous trials and tribulations. It also signifies peace and devotion.

Kūn is the direct complement to qián, the creative. If qián represents time, then kūn is best interpreted as space. The creativity of qián needs kūn to mature or be brought to fruition.

Keywords that are associated with 坤 *kūn* include Care, Earth, Mother, Nurture, Going Along, and Receptive.

Once the Heaven and Earth, the 'Father' and 'Mother' are established as two base lines, we can then look into combinations of these two. Yìjīng believes that yīn-yáng [阴阳] attracts, the sons take after the mother and the daughters take after the father.

Derivatives from 000 Trigram [坤] *kūn*
These are obtained when broken yīn lines are replaced by yáng lines.

☳ 100 'Thunder, Energy' [震] *zhèn*
When the mother takes one unbroken line from the father (always starting from the bottom), we have the first trigram zhèn. This is the first trigram to have a yáng entity. A degree of excitement or agitation occurs, which adds spice to the otherwise calm and peaceful earth. Zhèn imparts a jolt to the peace and tranquility from below. This represents volatile energy, associated with rousing thunder, vibration, and dramatic change. Zhèn represents the eldest son.

Note that the strength coming from yáng is only incipient and is therefore transient. Its two outer lines are weak.

Keywords associated with 震 *zhèn* would be Arousing, Eldest Son, Jolting, Shaking, Shocking, and Thunder.

☵ 010 'Water, Danger, Fluidity' [坎] *kǎn*
If the energy were transferred from the bottom to the middle line, we have kān, representing the middle son. It is associated with fluidity and a certain degree of unfathomable danger, in any shape or form.

A yáng line in between two yīn lines, water or fluidity is one of the most fascinating of the trigrams. It represents strength within, flexibility without. Strength comes from the fact that water cannot be easily destroyed, it can certainly change its form or shape into steam or ice, but as an entity it is indestructible. Its inner strength is easily seen when water is compressed, as used in hydraulics.

Very often inner strength is easily mistaken by the apparent, outer weakness. As the saying goes: Still water runs deep! As we have seen in p. 269, Lǎozǐ associates water with the entity closest to Dào.

Keywords associated with 坎 *kān* include Abyss, Danger, Fluidity, Middle Son, Unfathomable, and Water.

☶ 001 'Stillness, Mountain, Restrain' [艮] *gèn*

When the yáng energy reaches the top, we have gèn, represents the youngest son. Symbolised by Mountain, gèn represents restrain, calm or stillness.

Gèn has a solid yáng line on top, with yielding yīn lines below, signifying restrain. Very often the trigram and its combinations teach us that when we have reached a certain plateau, it would be time to pause and rethink, to evaluate the whole situation. This has tremendous implications in daily life, social or business cycles and activities.

Keywords associated with 艮 *gèn* would include Arrest, Keeping still, Mountain, Restrain, Stillness, and Youngest son.

Derivatives from 111 Trigram [乾] *qián*

These are obtained when firm yáng lines are replaced by yīn lines.

When the bottom line from 乾 *qián* 111 is replaced with a yīn line we get:

☴ 011 'Gentle Influence, Wind, Penetration' [巽] *xùn*

This trigram has a yīn line that sweeps from below, penetrating even the hard and strong yáng lines. The other entity that has similar properties would be plant roots, equally penetrating and mobile beneath the hard surface. Xùn also represents vegetation.

Xùn represents the eldest daughter, with her gentle yet persisting influence.

In personal life xùn pertains to persuasion. In business the obvious association would be advertising. Other activities would include Music. Xùn is inherently penetrating, be it in sound, pictures, videos, or the Internet.

Keywords associated with 巽 *xùn* would include Eldest Daughter, Gentle, Influence, Penetration, Wind etc.

101 'Clarity, Fire' [离] *lí*
This occurs when the broken line moves to the middle.

This is a very interesting trigram. Lí has a weak yīn line at the centre, though it appears strong externally with yáng lines. In other words, fire is itself hollow; it survives only when there is something to feed on. Though dazzling and brilliant, it is a passing event; the effects are temporary and transient. One needs to remember that it cannot survive on its own.

Lí represents the middle daughter, represented as fire, brilliance, clarity.

Lí is associated with brilliant performance, burst of success.

Key words associated with 离 *lí* include Beauty, Brilliance, Clarity, Clinging, Dazzling, Fire, and Middle Daughter.

Last but not least we have

110 'Joy, Wetland' [兑] *duì*
Duì represents the youngest daughter, full of joy, pleasure and humour.

This is visualised as wet land, water over earth. The pool of water sits on solid ground. It is definable in shape, and is serves as a joyful, pleasurable site. In other words it combines the attributes of Earth and water, without the dangers of the latter. It points to the lighter side of life in an otherwise serious world.

Duì would infer celebrations, success, etc.

Keywords associated with 兌 *duì* include Celebration, Happiness, Humour, Joy, and Youngest Daughter.

The eight possible combinations are shown in the 八卦 bāguà diagram. This symbol is frequently found in objects pertaining to Feng Shui.

TIME DIMENSION

Trigrams and hexagrams can be linked to a number of dimensions such as time, space, colour, numbers, and so on. As an exercise let us look at the 'time' dimension.

Since there are 8 trigrams and 24 hours in a day, each trigram reigns for 3 hours as follows:

'Thunder' [震] *zhèn*: 6 am
Dawn sweeps away the stillness of the night. Sunrise, represented by newly awaken energy, 震 zhèn. Life begins to stir anew, propagated by the energy coming from below.

'Gentle Influence' [巽] *xùn*: 9 am
Gentle, penetrating wind energy 巽 xùn that consolidates the surroundings into realities. The day awakens further and realities of life become increasingly apparent.

'Clarity' [离] *lí*: Noon
This is the time of 离 lí. 'Clarity' enables all entities to perceive, relate and interact with one another. (Please note that perception and interactions are not confined to the physical dimensions. Importantly it involves contemplation from within).

'Receptive' [坤] *kūn*: 3 pm

When things are getting settled, 'Earth' 坤 kūn, sets in, signalling a phase of consolidation, bringing things to fruition. Kūn also signifies fellowship.

'Joy' [兌] *duì*: 6 pm

The daily work is concluded, and the time of reckoning has come. This is the time of harvesting the day's work, the time of 兌 duì. We have reached the evening, a stark contrast to morning. Duì represents joy, in expectation of the harvest of the day's work. Hidden within this joy is a tinge of sadness; after all, successful outcome does not happen everyday. Duì marks the end of day time activities.

'Creative' [乾] *qián*: 9 pm

Night has arrived; the active part of life is over. We have reached the realm of 乾 qián the creative. The day has ended, with pleasures and joys. Before we retire for the day, it is time to contemplate over the day's events, a serious moment of thought before we sleep.

'Danger' [坎] *kǎn*: Midnight

In the still of the night we have 坎 kǎn, the active water, and the abysmal. This is the time when interaction with the moon is significant. Just as the line is firm at the centre, life at this point withdraws to a subconscious state. Sleep replaces consciousness.

'Stillness' [艮] *gèn*: 3 am

Early morning, this is the time of 艮 gèn, or stillness. Subconsciously it is the completion of yesterday and preparation for a brand new day.

We are back to 'Thunder' [震] *zhèn* by 6 am.

As we can see each trigram has its place in the time of the day. A day that unfolds, gets into reality, becoming clear, interacts, consolidates, comes into fruition, and enters into a phase of contemplation, sub consciousness and finally stillness.

Without going into the theoretical details, at another level, the trigrams could be associated with the seasons of the month in the same order, whereby we have:

100	Spring	'Arousing thunder'	震	*zhèn*
011	Spring-Summer	'Gentle wind'	巽	*xùn*
101	Summer	'Fire, heat, clarity'	离	*lí*
000	Summer-autumn	'Earth'	坤	*kŭn*
110	Autumn	'Joy, harvest'	兌	*duì*
111	Autumn-winter	'Creative'	乾	*qián*
010	Winter	'Water, ice, Danger'	坎	*kăn*
001	Winter-spring	'Stillness'	艮	*gèn*

It is obvious that the seasons could also be translated into months of the year.

This supplements information provided by 'Five Determining Element', forming an interlocking matrix.

The trigrams could be linked to various other parameters if we take the rotation of Sun into consideration. It would be difficult to compile a comprehensive list of all parameters. What we have described could be summarised as:

001 'Stillness' [艮] *gèn*

Person: Youngest Son	Symbol: Mountain
Property: Stillness, restrain	Time: 3 am
Season; Winter-Spring	Direction: North-East
Body: Hand	

100 '**Thunder**' [震] *zhèn*

Person: Eldest Son	Symbol: Thunder
Property: Arousing, vibration	Time: 6 am
Season; Spring	Direction: East
Body: Foot	

011 '**Influence**' [巽] *xùn*

Person: Eldest daughter	Symbol: Wind, vegetation
Property: Gentle, permeation	Time: 9 am
Season: Spring-Summer	Direction: South East
Body: Thigh	

101 '**Clarity**' [离] *lí*

Person: Middle daughter	Symbol: Fire
Property: Brilliance, clarity	Time: Midday
Season: Summer	Direction: South
Body: Eye	

000 '**Receptive**' [坤] *kūn*

Person: Mother	Symbol: Earth
Property: Receptive, fruition	Time: 3 pm
Season: Summer /autumn	Direction: South West
Body: Stomach	

110 '**Joy**' [兑] *duì*

Person: Youngest daughter	Symbol: Still water
Property: Joy, Harvest	Time: 6 pm
Season: Autumn	Direction: West
Body: Mouth	

111 '**Creative**' [乾] *qián*

Person: Father	Symbol: Sky, Heaven
Property: Creative	Time: 9 pm
Season: Autumn-Winter	Direction: North-West
Body: Head	

010 '**Danger**' [坎] *kǎn*

Person: Middle Son	Symbol: Water
Property: Danger, unfathomable	Time: Midnight
Season: Winter	Direction: North
Body: Ear	

As could be expected, all these would interlock into the overall network of directions, time, space, colour, parts of body, etc. It is only when different entities are inter-related that a whole spectrum of activities such as 'Feng Shui', 'Divination', 'Destiny Mapping', could be worked out, transposing natural, man-made, psychological, celestial, terrestrial, human-relationship or any other dimensions, in space and in time!

The vigour of yìjīng lies in its ability to link a whole matrix of seemingly unrelated entities such as time, space, our internal organs, direction, relationship, etc, into a coherent whole.

The trigrams are often represented as follows:

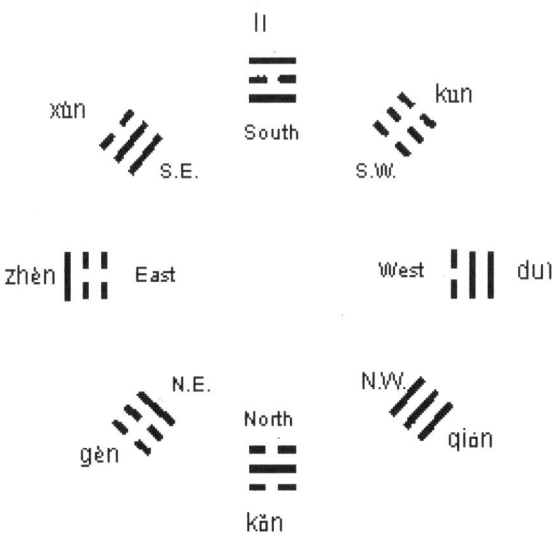

FENG SHUI REPRESENTATION

People familiar with Feng Shui would be able to interpret numbers expressed in 'nine squares'; the basic one could be expressed as:

South East		South		South West
East	**4**	**9**	**2**	West
	3	**5**	**7**	
	8	**1**	**6**	
North East		North		North West

(It is interesting to note that the sum of numbers added horizontally, vertically or diagonally all add up to 15.)

The diagram could be more meaningfully presented as:

South East	South			South West
East	**4** ☰ 'Wind' xùn [巽]	**9** ☲ 'Fire' lí [离]	**2** ☷ 'Earth' kūn [坤]	West
	3 ☳ 'Thunder' zhèn [震]	**5**	**7** ☱ 'Joy' duì [兑]	
	8 ☶ 'Mountain' gèn [艮]	**1** ☵ 'Water' kǎn [坎]	**6** ☰ 'Heaven' qián [乾]	
North East	North			North West

THE TIME DIMENSION

True to the Yìjīng principles, Feng Shui is subject to time constraints. A popular school of Feng Shui divides time into three cycles 三元 *sānyúan* of sixty years each. Within the one hundred and eighty years there would be nine 'Cycles', 'Age' or 'Period' [运] *yùn*, each 'Cycle' lasting twenty years.

The years 1984-2003 belongs to the 7th 'cycle' [运] *yùn*, while the years 2004-2023 belong to the 8th cycle, Age 8, or Period 8.

Within each period the numbers are rearranged in a certain way, according to luò shū 洛书, The numbers for the 7th cycle and 8th cycle are as follows:

7th Cycle, Age or Period

South East	South			South West
East	**6**	**2**	**4**	West
	5	**7**	**9**	
	1	**3**	**8**	
North East	North			North West

8th Cycle, Age or Period

South East	South			South West
East	**7**	**3**	**5**	West
	6	**8**	**1**	
	2	**4**	**9**	
North East	North			North West

421

A lot of information could be obtained when the trigram, rather than the number it is represented, is analysed.

For example in 'cycle seven' (1984-2003), the hexagram 兌 *duì* moves to the centre and dominates the scenario. 兌 *duì* signifies 'mouth'; mouth implies communication. During this period, industries associated with communication, such as the Internet, mobile phone, etc, had a significant boost. 兌 *duì* also signifies 'young lady'; during this period, young women climb to positions of influence.

In the present 'cycle eight' (2004-2023), the hexagram 艮 *gèn* moves to the centre stage. As 艮 *gèn* signifies young men, this period already witness young men in positions of power in China, Russia, Singapore, United Kingdom, United States, and so on. 艮 *gèn* also signifies 'hand'; hand should imply something mechanical, something that manipulates. What this could mean is yet to be seen. Could this be the years when 'robotics' enter our lives?

WHEN TRIGRAMS COMBINE

When two trigrams combine, a hexagram is formed; the 'upper trigram' is called 上卦 *shàngguà*, while the lower trigram 下卦 *xiàguà*. Once again the relationship between the upper and lower entities, in terms of yīn-yáng the five elements wǔxíng, is highly significant.

Each of the hexagrams represents a unique scenario. The translated names of each hexagram vary, depending on the authors. The use of a particular name does not imply that other names are inappropriate; it all depends on the circumstances.

The hexagrams have been studied in detail throughout the centuries, and used in countless occasions to explain, predict, or otherwise analyse situations.

APPLICATIONS

Zhōuyì [周易], yìjīng refined by Zhōu Wénwáng [周文王] (p. 178), is used quite extensively in divination or forecasting, known as bǔguà [卜卦].

Very often we find ourselves in a position where we are faced with the unknown while having to make a decision. In business, where we ponder what the prospects are, where we stand *vis-à-vis* a competitor, whether the decision would lead to a good outcome. 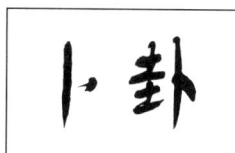 In personal relationships (family, friends or colleagues) we often wonder when we should remain cool, take initiative, or whether there are problems developing. In health matters we might wonder whether the impending medical treatment would be successful. In politics, sports or legal battles we would like to have an idea who should emerge as the victor. When we travel we would like to know whether the trip would be meaningful or successful, etc.

Some depend on their inspiration, or get the 'feel of it'. Others ask friends or consultants for professional assessment. It is however relevant to note that the person who knows the situation best could very well be yourself, since the consultant would not know your thoughts or entire life history. How wonderful would it be if you could get an indication of things to come somehow?

One of the applications of yìjīng is divination or forecasting, in which the circumstances surrounding the situation as well as possible outcome could be analysed. With good judgment, lot of common sense and ability to network various parameters, someone skilled in yìjīng could come out with interpretation of the present scenario. Very often a second hexagram is obtained at the same time, indicating possible changes, as well as things to come. The causes behind these changes would also be evident.

Yìjīng provides a powerful tool in decision making. This adds a new dimension to qualitative risk analysis, invaluable in many circumstances. The actual practice requires considerable learning and practice; the results are subject to interpretation.

It must be emphasised that the system is sound, though not fool proof, 100% accurate. Interpretation of results depends on the depth of knowledge and experience of the person.

DIVINATION

The art of divination involves three components:

1. Formulating a precise question
2. Arriving at the appropriate Yìjīng hexagrams
3. Interpretation of the hexagrams

FORMULATING A QUESTION

Questions should be precise rather than open ended. Some examples include: .

1. I applied for a job, would I be successful?
2. I have lost some valuables. Would I be able to find it this month?
3. Is my relationship with the particular person all right this year?

OBTAINING HEXAGRAMS

There are numerous methods of arriving at the hexagram or hexagrams. They include

1. Drawing from yarrow stalks
2. Tossing of Coins
3. Inspiration, known as 'plum blossom numerology' [梅花易数] méihuā yìshù
4. Random generation through computer software
5. Time data (birthday, time when an incident occurred, etc)

The date (month and day) of divination is important, as they affect the interpretations.

By far the most common method would be 'tossing of coins'. Three identical coins are used. What is critical is the concentration of mind by the person seeking answer. Focus on the question, discard any other thoughts! Hold the three coins in the palms, toss them six times.

There are four possible outcomes from each tossing of three coins:

1 Head, 2 Tails, provide a yīn line — — 0
2 Heads, 1 Tail, provide a yáng line —— 1
3 Heads provide a yīn line — — 0, changing to yáng line —— 1.
3 Tails provide a yáng line —— 1, changing to yīn — — line 0

Changing lines give a good indication of the causes of change. Very often the particular line concerned is critical in the overall interpretation.

It is important to note that the lines are built from bottom to top, not top to bottom.

INTERPRETING HEXAGRAMS

Normally two hexagrams would be obtained, the first one deals with the initial scenario, and the second one deals with the final scenario. If the first hexagram is the same as the second one, it implies that the situation is stable, 'final', not subject to changes. Should there be changes, the particular line or lines that cause the change are then analysed carefully.

As we have seen, there are sixty four hexagrams or scenarios. If we take into account the initial and final scenarios, there should be 64×64 or 4096 combinations.

Once a pair of hexagrams is obtained, it is relevant to understand the general nature of the hexagram. Consult a good book or a useful website to have a general idea of the hexagram concerned. It is not unusual to have somewhat different interpretations of the same hexagram; even the names would be different.

One would gather an excellent idea of the circumstances surrounding the scenario. One could also look at the associated hexagrams.

As an example if you have entered into a relationship with someone or a partnership with a company, you would like to know the situation and the forces surrounding it. You could do a forecast through divination.

Supposing you obtain the hexagram 'Water-mountain-Extreme difficulties' [水山蹇] *shuǐshān-jiǎn* 001-010. You could consultant books or website on its implications, (a short description is given on p. 402). This is a combination of 'Water' (you) and 'Mountain' (your partner).

A diametrically opposing scenario would emerge if we reverse the order of the lines; we would get another hexagram, 'Release from constraints' [雷水解] *léishuǐ-jiě* 010-100.

What would happen if one of the parties dishonours the partnership or agreement? It all depends on who dishonour the arrangement. If your partner changes his/her mind, the scenario then becomes 'Traveller' [火山旅] *huǒshān-lǚ* 001-101 (You are now free to roam, seek new opportunities). If you manage to disengage from the agreement the scenario becomes 'Limitation' [水泽节] *shuǐzé-jié* 110-010. (You are out of danger though there would still be various limitations).

The internal structure could further be looked into. If we discard the two outermost line from 001-010 we would get 0101. This could be further expanded to another hexagram 'Incompletion' [火水未济] *huǒshuǐ-wèijì* 010-101, indicating that at the end of the scenario the project or mission has yet to be completed.

The combinations and permutations in yìjīng are fascinating. Refer to various books for interpretations of these hexagrams.

ANALYSIS OF HEXAGRAMS

At a more advanced level, yìjīng analyses scenarios not only in terms of hexagrams themselves, but also the individual lines constituting the hexagrams.

The hexagrams are classified into eight 'palaces' gōng 宫, each belonging to a distinct 'determinant element' (refer to p. 438).

Within each hexagram, each line is either yīn or yáng. There exists a 'Subject' line [世爻] shì yáo, and a 'Response' line [应爻] yìng yáo. The 'Subject' line refers to the person seeking enquiry, and the 'Response' line refers the subject matter. The position of these lines on a hexagram is critical.

Each of the lines 爻 yáo belongs to one of the five determinant element of 'wood', 'fire', 'earth', 'metal' and 'water'. When two lines are matched they would have master-slave, parentchild or sibling relationships. These relationships for lines within a given hexagram are pre-determined.

Let us revisit the hexagrams described under 'Hexagram presentation' earlier on in this chapter.

'Water-mountain-Extreme difficulties'   [水山蹇] shuǐshān-jiǎn
'Earth-mountain-Humility'   [地山谦] dìshān-qiān
'Heaven-earth-Opposition'   [天地否] tiāndì-pǐ
'Thunder-earth-Excitement'   [雷地豫] léidì-yù
'Wind-earth-Contemplation'   [风地观] fēngdì-guān

A set of vocabulary describes this relationship. In Chapter eight we learn that there are two mechanisms, control and generation. The terms used in these contexts (p. 326) are

Self: Self, partners and associates
Child: The product of generation or birth
Parent: The entity that generate self
Master: The entity that controls self
Slave: The entity that is controlled by self

In 'divination analysis' a different set of terms, described as 'six relatives' liù qīn 六亲are used for the hexagon lines components.

Self: 'brother' line [兄弟爻] *xiōngdìyáo*, the line with the same element as self, used for 'siblings', 'colleagues', 'friends' or rivals.

Child: 'descendant' line [子孙爻] *zǐsūnyáo*, used for 'children', 'disciples', 'creations', 'aspirations'.

Parent: 'parents' line [父母爻] *fùmǔyáo*, used for 'elders', 'documentation', anything that protects oneself; 'resources', 'authority'.

Master: 'controller' line [官鬼爻] *guānguǐyáo*. It is derived from the all powerful 'imperial official' as well as 'devil', things that people fear; used for 'careers', 'status', 'power', 'sickness'.

Slave: 'wealth' line [妻财爻] *qīcáiyáo*. Used for 'wealth' or 'transactions', relationship with wife

Since each of the lines belongs to a 'five determinant element', they would interact with each other in the same manner as the five elements would (p. 322-323).

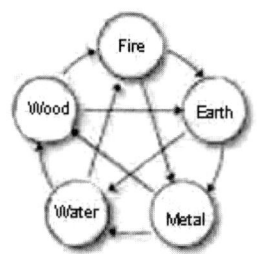

ANATOMY OF HEXAGRAMS

The hexagrams described above could now be analysed in further details, using the same hexagrams listed above. Refer to p. 438 regarding 'palace' and the corresponding element).

1. 'Water-mountain-Extreme difficulties' [水山蹇] *shuǐshān-jiǎn* (Palace of 兑 *duì* – 'Metal' element)

'descendant'	子孙 *zǐsūn*	— —	water	子水	
'parents'	父母 *fùmǔ*	———	earth	戊土	
'brother'	兄弟 *xiōngdì*	— —	metal	申金	'Subject'
'brother'	兄弟 *xiōngdì*	———	metal	申金	
'controller'	官鬼 *guānguǐ*	— —	fire	午火	
'parents'	父母 *fùmǔ*	— —	earth	辰土	'Response'

2. 'Earth-mountain-Humility' [地山谦] *dìshān-qiān*
   (Palace of 兑 *duì* – 'Metal' element)

'brother'	兄弟 *xiōngdì*	— —	metal	酉金	
'descendant'	子孙 *zǐsūn*	— —	water	亥水	'Subject'
'parents'	父母 *fùmǔ*	— —	earth	丑土	
'brother'	兄弟 *xiōngdì*	———	metal	申金	
'controller'	官鬼 *guānguǐ*	— —	fire	午火	'Response'
'parents'	父母 *fùmǔ*	— —	earth	辰土	

3. 'Heaven-earth-Opposition' [天地否] *tiāndì-pǐ*
   (Palace of 乾 *qián* – 'Metal' element)

'parents'	父母 *fùmǔ*	———	earth	戊土	'Response'
'brother'	兄弟 *xiōngdì*	———	metal	申金	
'controller'	官鬼 *guānguǐ*	———	fire	午火	
'wealth'	妻财 *qīcái*	— —	wood	卯木	'Subject'
'controller'	官鬼 *guānguǐ*	— —	fire	巳火	
'parents'	父母 *fùmǔ*	— —	earth	未土	

4. 'Thunder-earth-Excitement' [雷地豫] *léidì-yù*
   (Palace of 雷 *léi* – 'Wood' element)

'wealth'	妻财 *qīcái*	— —	earth	戊土	
'controller'	官鬼 *guānguǐ*	— —	metal	申金	
'descendant'	子孙 *zǐsūn*	———	fire	午火	'Response'
'brother'	兄弟 *xiōngdì*	— —	wood	卯木	
'descendant'	子孙 *zǐsūn*	— —	fire	巳火	
'wealth'	妻财 *qīcái*	— —	earth	未土	'Subject'

429

5. fēngdì-guān 风地观 'Wind-earth-Contemplation'
   (Palace of 乾 qián – 'Metal' element)

'wealth'	妻财 qīcái	——————	wood 卯木	
'controller'	官鬼 guānguǐ	——————	fire 巳火	
'parents'	父母 fùmǔ	— —	earth 未土	'Subject'
'wealth'	妻财 qīcái	— —	wood 卯木	
'controller'	官鬼 guānguǐ	— —	fire 巳火	
'parents'	父母 fùmǔ	— —	earth 未土	'Response'

INTERPRETATION OF HEXAGRAMS
A. 'SUBJECT' VERSUS 'RESPONSE' LINE

First of all, consider the 'Subject' line [世爻] shìyáo and the 'Response' line [应爻] yìngyáo. The 'Subject' line is directly linked to the person seeking the answer. The 'Response' line [应爻] yìngyáo would provide appropriate response to the question. Let us consider their relationships from the previous examples. (Note that the 'Subject line' is not always the line to be used in all cases).

1. In the hexagram 'Water-mountain-Extreme difficulties' [水山蹇] shuǐshān-jiǎn, the 'Response' earth line gives rise to the 'Subject' metal line. This is considered good for 'Subject', as the 'opponent' needs to support him. Good omen!

2. In the hexagram 'Earth-mountain-Humility' [地山谦] dìshān-qīan, the 'Subject' water line controls the 'Response' fire line. This is highly favourable to the 'Subject'. If the question were about the relationship between two men or companies, then the 'Subject' (person seeking answer) obviously has control or have tremendous influence over his opponent. If there was a match between Team A and Team B, and Team A is the 'Subject', it is very likely that Team A would win!

3. In the hexagram 'Heaven-earth-Opposition' [天地否] *tiāndì-pǐ*, the 'Subject' line controls the 'Response' earth line. The conclusions are the same as that in item 2.

4. In the hexagram 'Thunder-earth-Excitement' [雷地豫] *léidì-yù*, the 'Response' fire line gives rise to the 'Subject' earth line. The conclusions are the same as that in item 1.

5. In the hexagram 'Wind-earth-Contemplation' [风 地 观 *fēngdì-gūan*], the 'Subject' and 'Response' are both earth, signifying that the two are equal partners, both exist in harmony.

In reality the strength of each of these lines is influenced by interaction with other lines, the day and month of divination, as well as a lot of common sense and intuition.

B. DEFINING LINES

Though the beginner might use the 'Subject' and 'Response' lines, experienced practitioners choose a line that defines a particular situation. For example if someone enquires about status, seeking jobs, the 'controller' line [官鬼] *guāngǔi* is used. For any enquiry about wealth or business, normally the 'wealth' line [妻财] *qīcái* is the defining line. Any enquiry about education or scholarship is dealt with by the 'parents line' [父母爻] *fùmǔyáo*.

As an example if enquiry is about whether a certain project would make money, and the hexagram 'Humility' [地山谦] *dìshān-qīan* was obtained, it is unlikely that the project would be successful, as the 'wealth line' [妻财爻] *qīcáiyáo* line is absent. If the hexagram 'Wind-earth-Contemplation' was obtained, the 'wealth line' is present as a 'wood' element, and the fortunes depend on factors that would support or suppress 'wood'.

Whichever line is defining, the rules are the same. The strength of the particular line element dictates whether the outcome is good or poor. For example if that particular line is a 'wood' element, if the configuration supports or nurture 'wood' (with strong 'wood' or 'water' elements), the outcome is favourable. On the other hand if there are elements that destroys 'wood' ('metal'), or drains off wood energy ('fire' or 'earth'), the outcome is unfavourable. The interplay of the five elements decides if the outcome is favourable or otherwise.

An important factor to be considered is which of the 'six relatives' described in p. 428 is 'in charge of the World' [持世] *chí shì*. A line that coincides with the 'Subject line' [世爻] *shì yáo* is deemed to be 'in charge', and is very powerful.

C. TIME OF DIVINATION

The time of divination is also critical, as time itself has five elements, and also exerts its own influence. The month and the day of divination are critical.

If the 'element' from day or month of divination supports the 'defining line', then its situation is favourable. If the 'element' clashes with the 'defining' line, the scenario would be unfavourable. For example in the hexagram 'Humility' [地山谦] *dìshān-qīan*, and the defining line were hài 亥 'pig', the divination made in a day or month of 'snake' [巳] *sì*, the situation is unfavourable, as snake clashes with 'pig' [亥] *hài* (refer to p. 371).

In other words, the same hexagram obtained on different day or month could bring very different results or interpretations.

There is also the issue of 'void' [旬空] *xúnkōng*, whereby the particular line is effectively void.

D. CHANGING SCENARIOS

When the hexagram changes from one to another, the situation is dynamic rather than static. The situation could change for the better or for the worse, depending on the situation. The initial and final 'determinant element' of the changing line is critical to the overall picture. For example if the initial element supports the 'defining' line and the final element suppresses it, it indicates initial friendly support, ending with hostile dominance. It becomes more of an obstacle rather than a help.

The reason for the change is often given by the changing line. For example if the hexagram changes from 'Extreme difficulties' [水山蹇] *shuǐshān-jiǎn* 001-010 to 'Humility' [地山谦] *dìshān-qīan*, only one line changes.

Looking at the two hexagrams represented in their binary code, 'Water-mountain-Extreme difficulties' 001-010 to 'Earth-mountain-Humility' 001-000, only the fifth line changes from 1 to 0, or from —— to — —. It is then necessary to read the fifth line of 'Extreme difficulties', which reads:

'Even in this most desperate time, friends come to provide assistance. This cooperation would bring eventual success in your undertakings' [大蹇朋來, 以中節也]. It is then obvious that you need to organise assistance from friends, rather than solving the problem all by yourself.

Numerous other details, such as time, directions and quantities could be deciphered from hexagrams. To decipher them several other factors need to be taken into account.

EXPERIENCE COUNTS

Each of the hexagrams is a multi-dimensional, multi-faceted entity. It is a complex matrix of inter-linked parameters including time, space, person, organ, human relation, colour, sense, etc. Each of them gives a snap-shot of the environmental or human relationship scenario at a particular time. Divination techniques are quite involved. It might look simple, but could also be quite complicated. Interpretation of the same hexagram could vary tremendously.

As in the case of 'life destiny analysis', the determining elements could clash, merge, control, or restrain other elements. At the end of the day experience counts.

HEXAGRAM NAMES

There are numerous books published in English. Generally they do not provide detailed analysis of each hexagram in terms of interaction between the lines.

Translated names of the hexagrams vary tremendously, depending on their perception of the hexagram, their initial source and interpretation, as well as choice of words. The difficulty lies in the fact that some of these Chinese characters have more than one meanings, and are subject to totally different interpretations. It is better to stick to the original name in Chinese. The names that we have chosen are:

1.	'Creative'	乾为天	*qiánwéitiān*	111-111
2.	'Receptive'	坤为地	*kūnwéidì*	000-000
3.	'Difficult beginning'	水雷屯	*shuǐléi-tún*	100-010
4.	'Naivety'	山水蒙	*shānshuǐ-méng*	010-001
5.	'Needs'	水天需	*shuǐtiān-xū*	111-010
6.	'Conflict'	天水讼	*tiānshuǐ-sòng*	010-111
7.	'Commander'	地水师	*dìshuǐ-shī*	010-000
8.	'Unity'	水地比	*shuǐdì-bǐ*	000-010
9.	'Small surplus'	风天小畜	*fēngtiān-xiǎochù*	111-011
10.	'Conduct'	天泽履	*tiānzé-lǚ*	110-111
11.	'Peace'	地天泰	*dìtiān-tài*	111-000
12.	'Opposition'	天地否	*tiāndì-pǐ*	000-111
13.	'Fellowship'	天火同人	*tiānhuǒ-tóngrén*	101-111
14.	'Abundance'	火天大有	*huǒtiān-dàyōu*	101-111
15.	'Humility'	地山谦	*dìshān-qiān*	001-000
16.	'Joy'	雷地豫	*léidì-yù*	000-100
17.	'Follow'	泽雷随	*zéléi-suí*	100-110
18.	'Attrition'	山风蛊	*shānfēng-gǔ*	011-001
19.	'Supervision'	地泽临	*dìzé-lín*	110-000
20.	'Contemplate'	风地观	*fēngdì-guān*	000-011
21.	'Grinding'	火雷噬嗑	*huǒléi-shìkè*	100-101

22. 'Decoration'	山火贲	*shānhuǒ-bì*	101-001
23. 'Peeling off'	山地剥	*shāndì-bō*	000-001
24. 'Re-emergence'	地雷复	*dìléi-fù*	100-000
25. 'Reasonable'	天雷无妄	*tiānléi-wúwàng*	100-111
26. 'Big surplus'	山天大畜	*shāntiān-dàchù*	111-001
27. 'Nourishment'	山雷颐	*shānléi-yí*	100-001
28. 'Excessive'	泽风大过	*zéfēng-dàguò*	110-110
29. 'Danger'	坎为水	*kǎnwéishuǐ*	010-010
30. 'Clarity'	离为火	*líwéihuǒ*	010-010
31. 'Attraction'	泽山咸	*zéshān-xián*	001-110
32. 'Perseverance'	雷风恒	*léifēng-héng*	011-100
33. 'Retreat'	天山遁	*tiānshān-dùn*	001-111
34. 'Great Power'	雷天大壮	*léitiān-dàzhuàng*	111-100
35. 'Elevation'	火地晋	*huǒdì-jìn*	000-101
36. 'Darkening'	地火明夷	*dìhuǒ-míngyí*	101-000
37. 'Family'	风火家人	*fēnghuǒ-jiārén*	101-011
38. 'Disharmony'	火泽睽	*huǒzé-kuí*	110-101
39. 'Difficulties'	水山蹇	*shuǐshān-jiǎn*	001-010
40. 'Release'	雷水解	*léishuǐ-jiě*	010-100
41. 'Losses'	山泽损	*shānzé-sǔn*	110-001
42. 'Benefits'	风雷益	*fēngléi-yì*	100-011
43. 'Breakthrough'	泽天夬	*zétiān-guài*	111-110
44. 'Encounter'	天风姤	*tiānfēng-gòu*	011-111
45. 'Assembling'	泽地萃	*zédì-cuì*	000-110
46. 'Ascending'	地风升	*dìfēng-shēng*	000-011
47. 'Constrained'	泽水困	*zéshuǐ-kùn*	010-110
48. 'The well'	水风井	*shuǐfēng-jǐng*	011-010
49. 'Revolution'	泽火革	*zéhuǒ-gé*	101-110
50. 'Cauldron'	火风鼎	*huǒfēng-dǐng*	011-101
51. 'Thunder'	震为雷	*zhènwéiléi*	100-100
52. 'Mountain'	艮为山	*gènwéishān*	001-001
53. 'Gradual build-up'	风山渐	*fēngshān-jiàn*	001-011
54. 'Marrying maiden'	雷泽归妹	*léizé-guīmèi*	110-100

55. 'Abundance'	雷火丰	*léihuǒ-fēng*	101-100
56. 'Traveller'	火山旅	*huǒshān-lǚ*	001-101
57. 'Wind'	巽为风	*xùnwéifēng*	011-011
58. 'Joy'	兑为泽	*duìwéizé*	110-110
59. 'Dispersion'	风水涣	*fēngshuǐ-huàn*	010-011
60. 'Limitation'	水泽节	*shuǐzé-jié*	110-010
61. 'Inner truth'	风泽中孚	*fēngzé-zhōngfú*	110-011
62. 'The small persists'	雷山小过	*léishān-xiǎoguò*	001-100
63. 'After Completion'	水火即济	*shuǐhuǒ-jìjì*	101-010
64. 'Before completion'	火水未济	*huǒshuǐ-wèijì*	010-101

There are three common listings of hexagrams, namely

a. Listing by sequence
b. Listing by trigram combinations
c. Listing by 'Palaces' gōng 宫

LISTING BY SEQUENCE

.Most yìjīng books translated into English list hexagrams according to a definite sequence, depicting the succession of events or scenarios. Many yìjīng enthusiasts go by these numbers, rather than memorising the Chinese names or their various translated equivalents. The names given above are listed by sequence.

LISTING BY TRIGRAM COMBINATIONS

A listing of hexagrams by trigram combinations is found in the next page. The table is a matrix of the eight upper trigrams and eight lower trigrams. It is also customary to name the upper and lower trigrams together with the hexagram itself, for example 'fire-heaven-Abundance' [火天大有] *huǒtiān- dàyōu*.

Hexagrams Listing by Trigrams Combinations

Bottom \ Top	Qián 乾	Zhèn 震	Kǎn 坎	Gèn 艮	Kūn 坤	Xùn 巽	Lí 离	Duì 兑
111 Qián 乾	Qián 乾 (1) Creative	Dàzhuàng 大壮 (34) Great Power	xū 需 (5) Needs	Dàchù 大畜 (26) Big surplus	Tài 泰 (11) Peace	Xiǎochù 小畜 (9) Little Extra	Dàyǒu 大有 (14) Abundance	Guài 夬 (43) Decisive
100 Zhèn 震	Wúwàng 无妄 (25) Reasonable	Zhèn 震 (51) Thunder	Tún 屯 (3) Difficult beginning	Yí 颐 (27) Energise	Fù 复 (24) Re-emergence	Yì 益 (42) Benefits	Shìkè 噬嗑 (21) Grinding	Suí 随 (17) Follow
010 kǎn 坎	Sòng 讼 (6) Conflict	Jiě 解 (40) Release	kǎn 坎 (29) Danger	Méng 蒙 (4) Naivety	Shī 师 (7) Commander	Huàn 涣 (59) Dispersion	Wèijì 未济 (64) Before completion	Kùn 困 (47) Constraint
001 Gèn 艮	Tún 遁 (33) Retreat	xiǎoguò 小过 (62)	jiǎn 蹇 (39) Extreme Difficulties	Gèn 艮 (52) Mountain	qiān 谦 (15) Humility	Jiàn 渐 (53) Gradual	Lǚ 旅 (56) Traveler	Xián 咸 (31) Attraction
000 Kūn 坤	Pǐ 否 (12) Opposition	Yù 豫 (16) Joy	Bǐ 比 (8) Unity	Bō 剥 (23) Peeling off	kūn 坤 (2) Receptive	Guān 观 (20) Contemplate	Jìn 晋 (35) Elevation	Cuì 萃 (45) Sprouting
110 Xùn 巽	Gòu 姤 (44) Encounter	Héng 恒 (32) Persevere	Jǐng 井 (48) The well	Gǔ 蛊 (18) Attrition	Shēn 升 (46) Ascending	Xùn 巽 (57) Wind	Dǐng 鼎 (50) Cauldron	Dàguò 大过 (28) Excessive
101 Lí 离	Tóngrén 同人 (13) Fellowship	fēng 丰 (55) Abundance	Jìjì 既济 (63) After Completion	bi 贲 (22) Decoration	Míngyí 明夷 (36) Darkening of fire	jiārén 家人 (37) Family	Lí 离 (30) Clarity	Gé 革 (49) Revolution
011 Duì 兑	Lǚ 履 (10) Conduct	Guīmèi 归妹 (54) Marrying maiden	jié 节 (60) Limitation	Sǔn 损 (41) Losses	Lín 临 (19) Supervision	zhōngfú 中孚 (61) Inner truth	Kuí 睽 (38) Disharmony	Duì 兑 (58) Joy

Number in bracket refers to listing by sequence.

LISTING BY PALACES

This is more professional approach, where the hexagrams are listed according to their properties in terms of five determinant elements, as well as the evolution of these hexagrams. This listing is commonly found in Chinese texts.

(Number in front refers to the listing order in a particular palace. Number in bracket at the end refers to listing by sequence).

Palace of 'Creative, Heaven' [乾] *qián* (Metal element)

11.	'Creative'	乾为天	*qiánwéitiān*	111-111 (1)
12.	'Encounter'	天风姤	*tiānfēng-gòu*	011-111 (44)
13.	'Retreat'	天山遁	*tiānshān-dùn*	001-111 (33)
14.	'Opposition'	天地否	*tiāndì-pǐ*	000-111 (12)
15.	'Contemplation'	风地观	*fēngdì-guān*	000-011 (20)
16.	'Peeling off'	山地剥	*shāndì-bō*	000-001 (23)
17.	'Elevation'	火地晋	*huǒdì-jìn*	000-101 (35)
18.	'Abundance'	火天大有	*huǒtiān-dàyōu*	111-101 (14)

Palace of 'Water, Danger' [坎] *kǎn* (Water element)

21.	'Danger'	坎为水	*kǎnwéishuǐ*	010-010 (29)
22.	'Limitation'	水泽节	*shuǐzé-jié*	110-010 (60)
23.	'Difficult beginning'	水雷屯	*shuǐléi-tún*	100-001 (3)
24.	'After completion'	水火即济	*shuǐhuǒ-jìjì*	101-010 (63)
25.	'Revolution'	泽火革	*zéhuǒ-gé*	101-110 (49)
26.	'Abundance'	雷火丰	*léihuǒ-fēng*	101-100 (55)
27.	'Darkening'	地火明夷	*dìhuǒ-míngyi*	101-000 (36)
28.	'Commander'	地水师	*dìshuǐ-shī*	010-000 (7)

Palace of 'Mountain, Stillness' [艮] *gèn* (Earth element)

31.	'Mountain'	艮为山	*gènwéishān*	001-001 (52)
32.	'Decoration'	山火贲	*shānhuǒ-bì*	101-001 (22)

438

33. 'Big surplus'   山天大畜   *shāntiān-dàchù*   111-001   (26)
34. 'Losses'   山泽损   *shānzé-sǔn*   110-001   (42)
35. 'Disharmony'   火泽睽   *huǒzé-kuí*   110-101   (38)
36. 'Conduct'   天泽履   *tiānzé-lǚ*   110-111   (10)
37. 'Inner truth'   风泽中孚   *fēngzé-zhōngfú*   110-011   (61)
38. 'Gradual build-up' 风山渐   *fēngshān-jiàn*   001-011   (53)

Palace of 'Thunder' [雷] *léi* (Wood element)

41. 'Thunder'   震为雷   *zhènwéiléi*   100-100   (51)
42. 'Joy'   雷地豫   *léidì-yù*   000-100   (16)
43. 'Release'   雷水解   *léishuǐ-jiě*   010-100   (40)
44. 'Perseverance' 雷风恒   *léifēng-héng*   011-100   (32)
45. 'Ascending'   地风升   *dìfēng-shēng*   000-011   (46)
46. 'The well'   水风井   *shuǐfēng-jǐng* 011-010   (48)
47. 'Excessive'   泽风大过   *zéfēng-dàguò*   110-110   (28)
48. 'Follow'   泽雷随   *zéléi-suí*   100-110   (17)

Palace of 'Wind, Wood' [巽] *xùn* (Wood element)

51. 'Wind'   巽为风   *xùnwéifēng*   011-011 (57)
52. 'Small surplus' 风天小畜   *fēngtiān-xiǎochù*   111-011 (9)
53. 'Family'   风火家人   *fēnghuǒ-jiārén*   101-011 (37)
54. 'Benefits'   风雷益   *fēngléi-yì*   100-011 (42)
55. 'Reasonable'   天雷无妄   *tiānléi-wúwàng*   100-111 (25)
56. 'Grinding'   火雷噬嗑   *huǒléi-shìkè*   100-101 (21)
57. 'Nourishment'   山雷颐   *shānléi-yí*   100-001 (27)
58. 'Attrition'   山风蛊   *shānfēng-gǔ*   011-001 (18)

Palace of 'Fire, Clarity' [离] *lí* (Fire element)

61. 'Clarity'   离为火   *líwéihuǒ*   010-010 (30)
62. 'Traveller' 火山旅   *huǒshān-lǚ*   001-101 (56)
63. 'Cauldron'   火风鼎   *huǒfēng-dǐng*   011-101 (50)

64. 'Before completion' 火水未济 *huǒshuǐ-wèijì*   010-101 (64)
65. 'Naivety'   山水蒙   *shānshuǐ-méng* 010-001 (4)
66. 'Dispersion'   风水涣   *fēngshuǐ-huàn* 010-011 (59)
67. 'Conflict'   天水讼   *tiānshuǐ-sòng* 010-111 (6)
68. 'Fellowship'   天火同人 *tiānhuǒ-tóngrén* 101-111 (13)

Palace of 'Earth, Receptive' [坤] *kūn* (Earth element)

71. 'Receptive'   坤为地   *kūnwéidì*   000-000 (2)
72. 'Re-emergence' 地雷复   *dìléi-fù*   100-000 (24)
73. 'Supervision'   地泽临   *dìzè-lín*   110-000 (19)
74. 'Peace'   地天泰   *dìtiān-tài*   111-000 (11)
75. 'Great Power'   雷天大壮 *léitiān-dàzhuàng*   111-100 (34)
76. 'Breakthrough' 泽天夬   *zétiān-guài*   111-110 (43)
77. 'Needs'   水天需   *shuǐtiān-xū*   111-010 (5)
78. 'Unity'   水地比   *shuǐdì-bǐ*   000-010 (8)

Palace of 'Joy' [兑] *duì* (Metal element)

81. 'Joy'   兑为泽   *duìwéizé*   110-110 (58)
82. 'Constrained'   泽水困   *zéshuǐ-kùn*   010-110 (47)
83. 'Assembling'   泽地萃   *zédì-cuì*   000-110 (45)
84. 'Attraction'   泽山咸   *zéshān-xián*   001-110 (31)
85. 'Difficulties'   水山蹇   *shuǐshān-jiǎn*   001-010 (39)
86. 'Humility'   地山谦   *dìshān-qiān*   001-000 (15)
87. 'Thesmallpersists' 雷山小过 *léishān-xiǎoguò* 001-100 (62)
88. 'Marryingmaiden' 雷泽归妹 *léizé-guīmèi*   110-100 (54)

Study of Yìjīng

The study of yìjīng is fascinating, as it is applicable to a wide range of circumstances. Various books and websites are dedicated to the study of yìjīng. Some of the excellent references include I-Ching, or book of changes by Richard Wilhelm, the I-Ching Workbook, by R. L. Wing, etc.

Numerous websites are dedicated to the study of Yìjīng. Some, such as Free I-Ching Readings: *http://www.facade.com/iching/*, or Chri's free I-ching page: *www.homebrew.net/ching/* provide free I Ching readings.

Discussion groups on yìjīng are also available. The study of yìjīng has evolved as 易学 *yìxué*, pertaining to the application of yìjīng to a broad spectrum of disciplines.

Conclusion: What about the Future

WE HAVE PUT TOGETHER INFORMATION on various aspects of Chinese culture. Hopefully they provide some useful insight into facets of the roots, the mindset and psyche of ethnic Chinese throughout the world.

An understanding of the Chinese culture is interesting in several ways:

❖ Economically China grows at an impressive rate, opening up tremendous opportunities and generates great trade potential to the rest of the world. Part of the success is due to their cultural heritage, including the spirit of hardwork, sacrifice and dedication.

❖ Opportunities abound for those who could understand the Chinese better. There are those who would like to set up factories or trading operations in China. There are others who would consider contract manufacturing, manufacturing under licence, or simply trade in one of the thousands of products.

❖ Business aside, there would be those who seek to learn or acquire skills unique to China. This ranges from traditional Chinese medicine to ancient Chinese history or archaeology to Chinese martial arts.

❖ Traditional Chinese medicine, as a holistic approach to health, would certainly gain ground in the medical/health care industry worldwide. It emphasises on balance between body and mind, balance between the 'five elements' within the body system. The combination of a whole range of therapies including herbs, acupuncture, qigong, supplemented by Western medical diagnostic equipment and medical practices, would make significant contributions to health.

❖ In years to come the numerous forms of Chinese martial arts would certainly take their roots in the World, together with other martial arts from the East such as Judo, Karate and Taekwando. The blend of medicine, martial arts and philosophy, as practised in China is distinct and unique. In particular the practice of health exercises through 'controlled circulation of bio-energy' [气功] *qìgōng* would find its place in the medical, health and sports arena.

❖ In the area of arts, blending of eastern and western thoughts have brought about a new sense of vigour in paintings, sculpture, plays, architecture, music, industrial arts as well as other areas on dimensions never seen before.

❖ Chinese philosophy is a fascinating subject. Ideas and theories put forward hundreds of years ago are still valid today. Over the centuries technology has improved but the basic human thoughts and behaviour remain basically the same. In time to come, more and more of these would be translated into English, and introduced to the rest of the World.

❖ Finally the metaphysical aspects of Chinese culture, evolving around the Yijīng, 'feng shui', 'pillar of destiny', 'divination' 'physiogamy' and other myriad of practices is gaining acceptance to various degrees in different parts of the World. Now these arts are mainly practised by the 'new age' group. When more texts are translated, more people would get to know and learn about them. At the end of the day the truth prevails.

Confucius said that 'In the company of two others, there is always someone who could be my teacher. Select what is good and learn from it. Whatever is not good correct it' [三人行必有我师焉. 择其

善者学而之，其不善者而改之]. In the long run, each of us would pick and choose what is relevant and good for us, and rejects anything irrelevant or useless.

As the world gets miniaturised within a global village all groups contribute in their own ways to our collective wisdom. Indeed the long term well-being and survival of humanity as a whole depends on her ability to galvanise the collective intelligence of all citizens.

To the ethnic Chinese who does not have the opportunity to understanding their own culture, I think this book would have explained in some detail the pronunciation (in various dialects), writing (both in simplified and traditional Chinese), as well as meaning of their surnames and names. I hope they would also have gained some insight of their regions of origin and dialects.

I am confident that this book would serve as a source book on their heritage, including commonly used proverbs, quotations, history, social norms, together with some aspects of culture.

To those who work with ethnic Chinese, as friends, neighbours, colleagues, partners, I sincerely hope that this book would provide some useful information.

In the final analysis there is more in common rather than differences between Oriental and Occidental values. Whether it is Confucius or Christian teachings, the basic philosophy of humanist ideals are essentially concurrent. As mutual understanding increases, whilst the process of multi-culturalism takes root, the sense of 'oneness' prevails.

The German novelist and philosopher, Goethe once remarked,

'Orient und Occident sind nicht mehr zu trennen.'
(East and West can no longer be kept apart.)

Nowhere and at no time is this truism more obvious than the contemporary World today.

Glossary of Chinese Terms

A

蔼 [ǎi] Friendly, amicable.

爱 [ài] Love, to be fond of, to like.

碍 [ài] Hindrance, obstruction, blockage.

艾 [ài] Name of a herb (*Artemisia vulgaris*, Chinese mugwort), Surname.

安 [ān] Peace, tranquil, secure, content, calm, still, quiet, pacify.

暗 [àn] Dark, gloomy, secret, hidden

按 [àn] Restrain, control, press down, according to, in the light of

昂 [áng] Holding high, raise (head), soar, lift

澳 [ào] Used as name of places. Often refer to Australia.

B

八 [bā] Eight

八 (八字部) [bāzìbù] 'Eight' radical

爸 [bà] Father

白 [bái] White, unblemished, empty, blank, bright, clear, pure, gratuitous.

百 [bǎi] Hundred, numerous, myriad

败 [bài] Lose, lost, defeated

半 [bàn] Half, semi, incomplete

备 [bèi] Equip, prepare, get ready, provide, equip

本 [běn] Basis, foundation, origin, source, root, a measure word for books, fundamental, the current item, this

勹 (包字头) [bāozìtóu] 'Wrap' radical

苞 [bāo] Bud, calyx

帮 [bāng] Help

邦 [bāng] (M) Nation, state, country

绑 [bǎng] Tied up

包 [bāo] Wrap

宝 [bǎo] Treasure, precious

宀 (宝盖部) [bǎogàibù] 'Cover of character 宝' radical

保 [bǎo] Protect, defend, insure, guarantee, maintain, hold, keep, guard

抱 [bào] Hold, grab

北 [běi] North

备 [bèi] Equipped

本 [běn] Basis, origin

崩 [bēng] Collapse

碧 [bì] Green, blue, bluish-green jade

必 [bì] Must

币 [bì] Currency

闭 [bi] Close

边 [biān] Side

扁 [biǎn] Flat

便 [biàn] Convenient
标 [biāo] Sign, mark, label, indication, prize, award
表 [biǎo] Surface
别 [bié] Another
彬 [bīn] Courteous, refined, urbane
冰 [bīng] Ice
兵 [bīng] Soldier, army, military
丙 [bǐng] The third tián gàn
炳 [bǐng] Brilliant, bright, luminous
病 [bìng] Sick
疒 (病字旁) [bìngzìpáng] 'Sick' radical
博 [bó] Rich, immense
伯 [bó] Father's elder brother
卜 [bǔ] Divine
卜 (卜字部) [bǔzìbù] 'Divination' radical
卜卦 [bǔguà] Divination
不 [bù] No, not
部 [bù] Part of
部首 [bùshǒu] Chinese character radicals

C

才 [cái] Talent, ability, endowment, gifted, expert
财 [cái] Wealth, riches, valuables, money
彩 [cǎi] Colour, colourful, variety, lottery prize, variegated
蔡 [cài] A Chinese surname
参 [cān] Take part
苍 [cāng] Grey
仓 [cāng] Storehouse

操 [cāo] Manage, operate, exercise, act, take in hand, exercise
曹 [cáo] A Chinese surname
草 [cǎo] Grass
艹 (草字头) [cǎozìtóu] 'Grass' radical
禅 [chán] A school of Buddhism
婵 [chán] Lovely, beautiful, graceful
昌 [chāng] Flourish, prosperous
长 [cháng] Long
嫦 [cháng] The legendary goddess of the moon
常 [cháng] Frequent, always, often, common, general, constant
场 [chǎng] Venue
厂 [chǎng] Factory
厂 (厂字部) [chāngzìbù] 'Factory' radical
唱 [chàng] Sing
畅 [Chàng] Uninhibited, fluent, smooth
超 [chāo] Exceed, overtake, surpass, transcend, super, ultra.
潮 [cháo] Tide
巢 [cháo] Nest
陈 [chén]: A Chinese surname
辰 [chén] 5th terrestrial branch. Dragon
程 [chéng]: Rule, regulation, formula, journey, procedure, sequence, Chinese surname
骋 [chěng] Gallop
城 [chéng] City
成 [chéng] Become, achieved, developed, finish, complete, accomplish, become, turn into, succeed, one tenth

吃 [chī] Eat
尺 [chǐ] Foot (length)
赤 [chì] Red
翅 [chì] Wing
充 [chōng] Fill up
崇 [chóng] Lofty, Esteemed, dignified, honoured, highly regarded
虫 [chóng] Worm
虫 (虫字旁) [chóngzìpáng] 'Worm' radical
抽 [chōu] Draw out
丑 [chǒu] The second 'Terrestrial branch' element.
屮 (屮字头) [chūzìtóu] Sprout radical
出 [chū] Emerge, exit
初 [chū] Initial, beginning
刍 [chú] Fodder
除 [chú] Get rid of
楚 [chǔ] An ancient Chinese kingdom
处 [chù] Place
川 [chuān] Stream
传 [chuán] Convey, transmit
船 [chuán] Boat, ship
垂 [chuí] Drop down
春 [chūn] Spring time, joy, youth
传 [chuán] Convey, transmit, pass on, transfer, spread, disseminate, infect.
床 [chuáng] Bed
创 [chuàng] Initiate, inaugurate, begin, start, create
慈 [cí] Compassionate, kind, humane, merciful
次 [cì] Times, sequence
聪 [cōng] Intelligent, intellect, bright, clever, wise.
从 [cóng] Follow
崔 [cuī] A Chinese surname

翠 [cuì] A type of jade, jadeite
村 [cūn] Village
寸 [cùn] Inch
寸 (寸字部) [cùnzìbù] 'Inch' radical
错 [cuò] Mistake, errors

D

达 [dá] Reach, attain, achieve, realise, convey
打 [dǎ] Hit
大 [dà] Big, grand, huge, large, massive, major, great, eldest
大 (大字部) [dàzìbù] 'Big' radical
戴 [dài] Wear, put on, A Chinese surname
代 [dài] Substitute, generation
待 [dài] Wait
单 [dān] Single
卩 (单耳旁) [dan'ěrpáng] 'Single ear' radical
亻 (单人字旁) [dānrénzìpáng] 'Single person' radical
刀 [dāo] Knife
刀 (刀字部) [dāozìbù] 'Knife' radical
倒 [dǎo] Upside down
导 [dǎo] Guide
道 [dào] The way, path
到 [dào] Reached, arrived
德 [dé] Virtue, moral, ethics, character, Germany
底 [dǐ] Bottom
地 [dì] Earth, floor
第 [dì] No:
帝 [dì] Emperor
弟 [dì] Younger brother
涤 [dì] Clean, cleanse
颠 [diān] Insane

点 [diǎn] Dot
丶 (点部) [diǎnbù] 'Dot' radical
典 [diǎn] Texts
电 [diàn] Electricity
掉 [diào] Dropped, lost
跌 [diē] Fall down
段 [duàn] Segment, section
邓 [dèng] An ancient kingdom,
　　A Chinese surname
澄 [dèng] Clarify (a liquid)
底 [dǐ] Bottom
地 [dì] Earth
丁 [dīng] An able bodied man,
　　4th Celestial stem, Chinese
　　surname.
顶 [dǐng] Supports something
定 [dìng] Stable, calm
丢 [diū] Throw
冬 [dōng] Winter
夂 (冬字头) [dōngzìtóu] 'Top of
　　the character 冬' radical
东 [dōng] East
董 [dǒng] A Chinese surname,
　　董事 [dǒngshì]: director, 古
　　董 [gǔdǒng]: antique
冻 [dòng] Freeze
栋 [dòng] Pillar
动 [dòng] Move, Act
斗 [dǒu] Volume measure,
　　funnel
斗 (斗字部) [dǒuzìbù] 'Funnel'
　　radical
斗 [dòu] Compete
都 [dū] Big city
独 [dú] Independent, lone
杜 [dù] A Chinese surname
度 [dù] Degree
端 [duān] Proper, appropriate,
　　regular, terminal, extremity,
　　end.
段 [duàn] Segment, section

兑 [duì] Joy, A trigram /
　　hexagram
对 [duì] Correct
队 [duì] Troop
敦 [dūn] Honest, sincere
多 [duō] Numerous
朵 [duǒ] Bouquet
夺 [duò] Rob

E

娥 [è] Pretty lady
恩 [ēn] Kindness or benefits
　　bestowed, grace, favour
儿 [ér] Child, son
儿 (儿字部) [érzìbù] 'Child'
　　radical
耳 [ěr] Ear
贰 [èr] Two

F

发 [fā] (M) Send out, emit, issue,
　　develop
法 [fǎ] Law, method, way
发 [fà] Hair
繁 [fán] Numerous, manifold,
　　complicated
繁体字 [fántǐzì] Traditional
　　Chinese characters
凡 [fan] Ordinary, any
反 [fǎn] Revert
犭 (反犬旁) [fǎnquǎnpáng]
　　'Dog' radical
范 [fàn] Pattern, role model,
　　example; Chinese surname
饭 [fàn] Rice
方 [fāng] Square, method,
　　prescription
囗 (方筐) [fāngkuāng] 'Square
　　frame' radical

方 (方字部) [fāngzìbù] 'Square' radical
芳 [fāng] fragrant
防 [fáng] Prevent, defend
房 [fáng] Room
放 [fàng] Lay down
飞 [fēi] Fly
芬 [fēn] Fragrance
分 [fēn] Distribute
锋 [fēng] Sharp edge of a knife or tool
丰 [fēng] Abundant, plentiful
峰 [fēng] Pinnacle, mountain top, peak summit
风 [fēng] Wind
冯 [féng] A Chinese surname
凤 [fèng] Phoenix
枫 [fèng] Maple
佛 [fó] Buddhism
傅 [fù] A Chinese surname, 师傅 [shīfù]: master, expert
夫 [fū] Man
福 [fú] Blessed, good fortune
浮 [fú] Float
甫 [fǔ] A naming word
富 [fù] Wealthy, rich
妇 [fù] Women, lady
父 [fù] Father
父母爻 [fùmǔyáo] Parents, a hexagram line relationship

G

尬 [gà] Embarrassing
改 [gǎi] Change, alter
甘 [gān] Sweat, pleasant
干 [gān] Branch
尴 [gān] Awkward
敢 [gǎn] Bold, daring, courageous

刚 [gāng] Just, exact; tough, firm, hard, strong, exactly
钢 [gāng] Steel
岗 [gāng] Small hill ridge
港 [gǎng] Port
高 [gāo] Tall, high
戈 [gē] Dagger-axe
歌 [gē] Song
哥 [gē] Elder brother
革 [gé] Change, alter
各 [gè] Each and every
个 [gè] Individual
艮 [gèn] Mountain, stillness, a trigram / hexagram
庚 [gēng] Seventh 'Celestial stem'
耿 [gěng] Dedicated, loyal, devoted, just
更 [gèng] Even more
乾 [qián] Heaven, Creative – a trigram, hexagram
谦 [qiān] Humility – a hexagram
功 [gōng] Effort, work
工 [gōng] Work
宫 [gōng] Palace
工 (工字部) [gōngzìbù] 'Work' radical
龚 [gōng] A Chinese surname
公 [gōng] Public
弓 [gōng] Bow
弓 (弓字旁) [gōngzìpáng] Bow radical
共 [gòng] Shared, together
勾 [gōu] Tick off
狗 [gǒu] Dog
古 [gǔ] Ancient
姑 [gū] Aunt (Father's sister)
菇 [gū] Mushroom
骨 [gú] Bone
顾 [gù] Care, look after, attend to
挂 [guà] Hang up

449

冠 [guān] Crown, crest, hat, cap
关 [guān] Shut, close
冠 [guān] Crown
官 [guān] Officials
官鬼爻 [guānguǐyáo] Official-devil, a hexagram relationship
馆 [guǎn] Association
观 [guān] observation – a hexagram
莞 [guān] Part of the name of a place, 东莞 [Dōngguān]
管 [guǎn] In charge
惯 [guàn] Familiar
管 [guǎn] Regulate, rule
光 [guāng] Bright, light
广 [guǎng] Vast, extensive
广 (广字旁) [guǎngzìpáng] 'Broad' radical
过 [guò] Passing by
顾 [gù] Look after, attend to
归 [guī] Return
癸 [guǐ] Tenth tiangan
贵 [guì] Expensive, noble, noble, respectful word for 'your'
滚 [gǔn] Roll
郭 [guō] A Chinese surname
国 [guó] Country, nation, state
过 [guò] Cross

H

海 [hǎi] Ocean, sea
亥 [hài] The twelfth 'Terrestrial branch'
韩 [hán] A Chinese surname, Korea
函 [hán] Document
汉 [Hàn] Chinese; man, fellow, name of a dynasty.

豪 [háo] Someone outstanding, grand, heroic.
濠 [háo] Trench
好 [hǎo] Good
皓 [hào] Luminous, bright, white
好 [hào] Like
浩 [hào] Vast, grand, great
郝 [hao] A Chinese surname
何 [hé] Interrogative word
河 [hé] River
和 [hé] Harmony, peace, and, together, with, union
合 [hé] Combine, close
荷 [hé] Lotus
贺 [hè] Congratulate
鹤 [hè] Crane (bird)
黑 [hēi]
很 [hěn] Very
恨 [hèn] Hate, sorrow
亨 [hēng] Smooth going, prosperous.
横 [héng] Across, horizontal
一 (横部) [héngbù] 'Horizontal stroke' radical
衡 [héng] Measure, weight, judge
恒 [héng] Perseverance, endurance, permanent, eternal
弘 [hóng] Great grand, magnificent, expand, enlarge
红 [hóng] Red, popular, revolutionary, bonus
虹 [hóng] Rainbow
洪 [hóng] A Chinese surname, 洪水: Flood
宏 [hóng] Magnificent, grand, great, immense
鸿 [hóng] (M) Swan, Grand, great
猴 [hóu] Monkey

候 [hóu] Nobleman, high official
胡 [hú] A Chinese surname, A minority people in China, beard; reckless
狐 [hú] Fox
湖 [hú] Lake
虎 [hǔ] Tiger
户 [hù] Household
户 (户字部) [hùzìbù] 'Household' radical
花 [huā] Flower, spend, blossom, pattern
华 [huá] China, Chinese, splendid, magnificent, surname
画 [huà] Pictures, drawing
话 [huà] Language, speech
化 [huà] Change
怀 [huái] Bosom, concern
欢 [huān] Happy, exhaling, joy, pleased
还 [huán] Return
焕 [huàn] Shine, glow, brilliant, illustrious
换 [huàn] Change
患 [huàn] Scourge, trouble
幻 [huàn] Unreal
黄 [huáng] Yellow, A Chinese surname
辉 [huī] Brilliant, glorious
回 [huí] Return
慧 [huì] Intelligence, kindness, kind deeds.
卉 [huì] Varieties of grass
惠 [huì] Benefit, kindness
蕙 [huì] Orchid species
会 [huì] Meet
混 [hùn] Mixed up, unclear
火 [huǒ] Fire
火 (火字部) [huǒzìzìbù] 'Fire' radical

获 [huò] Obtain

J

几 [jī] Small table
几 (几字部) [jīzìbù] 'Small table' radical
鸡 [jī] Chicken
饥 [jī] Hungry
基 [jī] Foundation, basic
即 [ji] Immediate, reach
己 [jǐ] Self, sixth 'Celestial stem'
己 (己字部) [jǐzìbù] 'Self' radical
几 [jī] Few
记 [jì] Note, remember
吉 [jì] Auspicious, good omen
济 [jì] Relieve, help, benefit, aid
计 [jì] Compute
家 [jiā] Family, household, home, specialist
加 [jiā] Add, plus
佳 [jiā] Excellent, fine
嘉 [jiā] Excellent, fine
贾 [jiǎ] A Chinese surname
甲 [jiǎ] The first 'Celestial stem'
假 [jiǎ] Not real, false
稼 [jià] Sowing
驾 [jià] Drive
肩 [jiān] Shoulder
简 [jiǎn] Simple, brief
简体字 [jiǎntǐzì] Simplified Chinese characters
见 [jiàn] See
建 [jiàn] Build up, establish, construct, set up
廴 (建之旁) [jiànzhīpáng] 'Build' radical
拣 [jiǎn] Pick
健 [jiàn] Healthy
剑 [jiàn] Sword

451

箭 [jiàn] Arrow
塞 [jiàn] Extreme difficulties – a hexagram
将 [jiàng] Imminent
爿 (将字旁) [jiàngzìpáng] 'The side of the character 将' radical
江 [jiāng] River, A Chinese surname
姜 [jiāng] A Chinese surname
蒋 [jiǎng] A Chinese surname
教 [jiāo] Educate, religion
交 [jiāo] Exchange
姣 [jiāo] Lovable, charming, pampered, tender loving, delicate
骄 [jiāo] Proud
娇 [jiāo] Charming, tender loving
蕉 [jiāo] Banana type plant
脚 [jiǎo] Leg
角 [jiǎo] Angle
绞 [jiǎo] Twist
纟 (绞丝旁) [jiǎosīpáng] 'Silk radical'
叫 [jiào] Call
揭 [jiē] Lift off
节 [jiē] Festival
杰 [jié] Outstanding, prominent, illustrious
解 [jiē] Solve
姐 [jiě] Elder sister
借 [jiè] Borrow
金 [jīn] Gold, Metal, money, A Chinese surname
钅 (金字旁) [jīnzìpáng] 'Metal' radical
斤 [jīn] Weight measure
巾 [jīn] Napkin
巾 (巾字底) [jīnzìdǐ] 'Napkin' radical

近 [jìn] Near
尽 [jìn] Maximum
锦 [jǐn] Brocade, glorious, , embroidered work, bright
经 [jīng] Classics, book
敬 [jìng] Respect, venerate, salute, offer
精 [jīng] Refined, essence, excellent
景 [jǐng] Scenery, view
晶 [jīng] crystal
靖 [jìng] Peace, tranquillity
静 [jìng] Tranquil, quiet, still calm
酒 [jiǔ] Alcohol
九 [jiǔ] Nine
舅 [jiù] Mother's brother
旧 [jiù] Old
居 [jū] Reside
局 [jú] Situation, administrative entity
菊 [jú] Chrysanthemum
举 [jǔ] Lift up
聚 [jù] Gather, assemble, accumulate
句 [jù] Sentence
巨 [jù] Huge, giant, enormous, tremendous
娟 [juān] Grace, beauty
鹃 [juān] – 杜鹃 [dùjuān] Azalea plant
绝 [jué] Absolute, sever
军 [jūn] Military, army
君 [jūn] Gentleman, Lord, monarch, soverign
骏 [jùn] Excellent horse
俊 [jùn] Handsome

K

开 [kāi] Open, initiate

452

楷 [kǎi] Calligraphy style
刊 [kān] Magazine
坎 [kǎn] Water, danger, pit, a trigram / hexagram
康 [kāng] Health
考 [kǎo] Test
柯 [kē] A Chinese surname
可 [kě] Possible, permit
克 [kè] Overcome, subdue, restrain; gram (weight)
客 [kè] Guest
刻 [kè] Engrave
壳 [kè] Shell
空 [kōng] Void, empty
孔 [kǒng] Orifice, hole
口 [kǒu] Mouth
口 (口字部) [kǒuzìbù] 'Mouth' radical
苦 [kǔ] Bitter
快 [kuài] Quick
宽 [kuān] Broad, wide, lenient
况 [kuàng] Condition, situation
坤 [kūn] Feminine, earth, a trigram, hexagram
阔 [kuò] Vast, broad

L

来 [lái] Come, arrive
赖 [lài] Depend on, rely, A Chinese surname
兰 [lán] Orchid
懒 [lǎn] Lazy
劳 [láo] Toil, work, labour
老 [lǎo] Old
乐 [lè] Happy, cheerful; Chinese surname
雷 [léi] Thunder; Chinese surname
蕾 [lěi] Flower bud

离 [lí] Separate, clarity, a trigram, hexagram
黎 [lí] Multitude, A Chinese surname
礼 [lǐ] Etiquette, manners, social custom, rite, propriety; gift
李 [lǐ] Plum, Chinese surname
理 [lǐ] Logic, reason, principles; science
莉 [lì] – 茉莉 [mòli] Jasmine
丽 [lì] Pretty, beautiful
俐 [lì] – 伶俐 [língli] Witty, clever, intelligent, bright
利 [lì] Advantage, favourable, benefit, profit, sharp
立 [lì] Setup; upright, stand
刂 (立刀字旁) [lìdāozìpáng] 'Upright knife' radical
力 [lì] Power, force, strength
力 (力字旁) [lìzìpáng] 'Strength' radical
历 [lì] History
励 [lì] Encourage, exhort
荔 [lì] Lychee
莲 [lián] Lotus
连 [lián] Continuous, link
廉 [lián] Cheap
脸 [liǎn] Face
炼 [liàn] Heat treatment
良 [liáng] Good, fine, very
两 [liǎng] Two, both
冫 (两点水) [liǎngdiǎnshuǐ] 'Two doted water' radical
梁 [liáng] Beam, A Chinese surname
寥 [liáo] Scanty, scarce
廖 [liào] A Chinese surname
料 [liào] Material
列 [liè] Display
林 [lín] Forest, woods, A Chinese surname

邻 [lín] Neighbour
琳 [lin] Beautiful jade, gem
凌 [líng] Soaring, rising high
铃 [líng] Bell
玲 [líng] – 玲珑 [línglong] Dainty, exquisite
伶 [líng] Actor or actress
岭 [lǐng] Mountain range
刘 [liú] A Chinese surname
流 [liú] Flow
柳 [Liǔ] Willow
六 [liù] Six
亠 (六字头) [liùzìtóu] 'Top of the character 六' radical
龙 [lóng] Dragon, Imperial; Chinese surname
隆 [lóng] Thriving, prosperous, grand
楼 [lóu] Dwelling
卢 [lú] A Chinese surname
陆 [lù] Land mass, A Chinese surname
路 [lù] Road
璐 [lù] Pretty jade
露 [lù] Dew
吕 [lǔ] A Chinese surname
律 [lǜ] Regulation, law
乱 [luàn] Messy
论 [lùn] Discuss
罗 [luó] Trap, net, A Chinese surname
落 [luò] Drop down

M

妈 [mā] Mother
马 [mǎ] Horse, a common Chinese Muslim surname
马 (马字部) [mǎzìbù] 'Horse' radical
麻 [má] Hemp

骂 [mà] Scold
满 [mǎn] Full, filled, packed. Manchuria
曼 [màn] Graceful
忙 [máng] Busy
毛 [máo] Hair, fur; a ten cents, A Chinese surname
卯 [mǎo] The fourth 'Terrestrial branch'
茂 [mào] Luxuriant
梅 [méi] Plum blossom
玫 [méi] (F) Rose
美 [měi] Beautiful, pretty
妹 [mèi] Younger sister
眉 [méi] (F) Eyebrow, features
媚 [mèi] Cute, lovely
门 [mén] Door
门 (门字筐) [ménzìkuāng] Door radical
蒙 [méng] Cover up
孟 [mèng] A Chinese surname
蜜 [mì] (F) Honey
勉 [miǎn] Urge, encourage, exhort
面 [miàn] Face
苗 [miáo] Sprout
敏 [mǐn] Quick, nimble
闽 [mǐn] Fujian province
民 [mín] People, civilian, race, nationality, citizen
明 [míng] Bright, clear; understand; next
名 [míng] Name
铭 [míng] Inscription, engrave
鸣 [míng] Bird or animal cry
命 [mìng] Life
茉 [mò]: 茉莉 [mòli] Jasmine
莫 [mò] Not
母 [mǔ] Mother
木 [mù] Wood

木 (木字旁) [mùzìpáng] 'Wood'
  radical
慕 [mù] Admire, yearn for
目 [mù] Eye
目 (目字旁) [mùzìpáng] 'Eye'
  radical

N

耐 [nài] Endure
南 [nán] South
男 [nán] Male
难 [nán] Difficult
脑 [nǎo] Brain
内 [nèi] Within, inside
能 [néng] Able
妮 [nī] Girl, lass
你 [nǐ] You
年 [nián] Year
娘 [niáng] Lady, mother
鸟 [niǎo] Bird
宁 [níng] Peace, tranquil
牛 [niú] Cattle
妞 [Niu] Girl
弄 [nòng] Play with
廾 (弄字底) [nòngzìdǐ] 'Bottom
  of the character 弄' radical
努 [nǔ] Effort
女 [nǚ] Female, woman
女 (女字旁) [nǚzìpáng] 'Female'
  radical
暖 [nuǎn] Warm

O

欧 [ōu]: 欧洲 [ōuzhōu] Europe
欧阳 [ōuyáng] A Chinese
  surname

P

派 [pāi] Dispatch
潘 [pān] A Chinese surname
番 [pān] Part of the name for the
  city 番禺 [pānyú]
旁 [páng] Side
庞 [páng] Huge, enormous;
  Chinese surname
跑 [pǎo] Run
培 [péi] Cultivate
佩 [pèi] Wear (at the waist)
沛 [pèi] (M) Abundant
澎 [péng] Splash, surge, sound
  of waves
彭 [péng] A Chinese surname
蓬 [péng] Fluffy
鹏 [péng] Legendary, huge bird
朋 [péng] Friend
否 [pǐ] Opposition - a hexagram
皮 [pí] Skin
琵 [pí] Musical instrument
漂 [piāo] Float, drift
撇 [piě] Left downward stroke
丿 (撇部) [piěbù] 'Left
  downward stroke' radical
拼 [pīn] Piece together
品 [pǐn] Product, article
平 [píng] Even, level, flat; calm,
  peaceful
萍 [píng] Duckweed
苹 [píng] Apple
坡 [pō] Slope, plain
婆 [pó] Grandmother
破 [pó] Break
璞 [pǔ] Uncut jade
埔 [pǔ] Name for a place

Q

七 [qī] Seven
妻 [qī] Wife

妻财爻 [qīcáiyáo] Wife-wealth, a hexagram line relationship
齐 [qí] Orderly; even, name of a Chinese empire, A Chinese surname
琪 [qí] Pretty jade
其 [qí] That, such
奇 [qí] Strange, queer, wonderful!
琦 [qí] Fine jade; outstanding
起 [qǐ] Arise
乞 [qǐ] Beg
气 [qì] Dynamic energy
谦 [qiān] Humble, modest
千 [qiān] Thousand
乾 [qián] One of the trigrams, hexagrams
钱 [qián] Money
前 [qián] In front, former
强 [qiáng] Strength, powerful
乔 [qiáo] A Chinese surname
巧 [qiǎo] Skillful
俏 [qiào] Pretty, attractive
切 [qiè] Cut
亲 [qīn] Relative, close
钦 [qīn] Admire, esteem, respected; imperial
秦 [qín] An ancient Chinese empire, A Chinese surname
勤 [qín] Diligent, hard-working
琴 [qín] Musical instrument
情 [qíng] Sentiment, feeling, emotion, passion
清 [qīng] Clear, pure
青 [qīng] Green, blue-green
庆 [qìng] Celebrate
琼 [qióng] Fine jade, refined; Hainan
秋 [qiū] Autumn
丘 [qiū] Small hill
囚 [qiú] Prison

区 [qū] District
曲 [qǔ] Tune
去 [qù] Go
全 [quán] All
泉 [quán] Spring, source, fountain
犬 [quǎn] Canine
劝 [quàn] Advice
群 [qún] Flock (of sheep)

R

饶 [ráo] Forgive, A Chinese surname
热 [rè] Hot
人 [rén] People
人 (人字头) [rénzìtóu] 'People' radical
壬 [rén] Ninth tiangan
仁 [rén] Humane, benevolent, kind
任 [rén] Chinese surname
忍 [rěn] Tolerate
韧 [rèn] Resilient
任 [rèn] Taking up a post, appoint
日 [rì] Day, sun
日 (日字部) [rìzìbù] 'Sun' radical
融 [róng] Harmonious, compatible
容 [róng] Contain, allow, hold; appearance, look
荣 [róng] Pride, Honour, glory
蓉 [róng] – 芙蓉 Cotton rose hibiscus
榕 [róng] Name of a tree
柔 [róu] Tender, soft, gentle
肉 [ròu] Meat
如 [rú] Resemble
乳 [rǔ] Milk

阮 [ruǎn] A Chinese surname
瑞 [ruì] Auspicious, propitious
锐 [ruì] Sharp, acute
蕊 [ruǐ] Stamen or pistil
潤 [rùn] Moist, lubricate
弱 [ruò] Weak

S

三 [san] Three
凵 (三道筐) [sāndàokuāng] 'Holding cup' radical
氵 (三点水) [sāndiǎnshuǐ] 'Three doted water' radical
巛 (三枴部) [sānguǎibù] 'Three bends' radical
匚 (三筐栏) [sānkuānglán] 'Three sided frame' radical
彡 (三撇) [sānpie] 'Three downward left strokes' radical
丧 [sàng] Things associated with deceased people
嫂 [sǎo] Elder brother's wife
杀 [shā] Kill, murder
山 [shān] Mountain
山 (山字部) [shānzìbù] 'Mountain' radical
珊 [shān] Coral
汕 [shàn] Part of the name of a placc, 汕头[Shàntóu]
赏 [shǎng] Give, award
上 [shàng] Above, upper
韶 [sháo] Pretty
邵 [Shào] A Chinese surname
少 [shào] Youth
蛇 [shé] Snake
社 [shè] Society
绅 [shēn] Gentleman
申 [shēn] The ninth 'Terrestrial branch'

深 [shēn] Deep
身 [shēn] Body
神 [shén] God, deity
沈 [Shěn] A Chinese surname
慎 [shèn] Cautious
升 [shēng] Ascend, arise, raise, promote
生 [shēng] Life, Live, produce, born, grow
声 [shēng] Noise
昇 [shēng] Rise up
省 [shěng] Province
胜 [shèng] Victory, Win
圣 [shèng] Sage, holy, spiritual, sacred, saint
甥 [shēng] 外甥 [wàishēng] Nephew (sister's son), 外甥女 [wàishēngnǚ] Niece (sister's daughter)
昇 [shēng] Rise up
诗 [shī] Poetry, poetic
狮 [shī] Lion
师 [shī] Teacher
尸 [shī] Corps
尸 (尸字头) [shīzìtóu] 'Corps' radical
施 [shī] Grant, bestow, A Chinese surname
实 [shí] Solid, substantial, true, real, solid; honest
石 [shí] Rock, bouldcr
石 (石字旁) [shízìpáng] 'Stone' radical
十 [shí] Ten
食 [shí] Eat, food
饣 (食字旁) [shízìpáng] 'Food' radical
史 [shǐ] History
始 [shǐ] Begin
市 [shì] City
士 [shì] Person, soldier

457

士 (士字头) [shìzìtóu] 'Scholar' radical

世 [shì] World, era; life, generation

事 [shì] Matter, affair

视 [shì] Look

是 [shì] To be

寺 [sì] Temple

手 [shǒu] Hand

式 [shì] Style

寿 [shòu] Long life

书 [shū] Book

叔 [shū] Father's younger brother

鼠 [shǔ] Rat

竖 [shù] Vertical

丨 (竖部) [shùbù] 'Vertical stroke' radical

忄 (竖心旁) [shùxīnpáng] 'Upright heart' radical

树 [shù] Trees

淑 [shū] Kind and gentle

帅 [shuài] Marshall

双 [shuāng] Pair, both

彳 (双人旁) [shuāngrénpáng] 'Double persons' radical

水 [shuǐ] Water

顺 [shùn] Going along with

说 [shuō] Speak

思 [sī] Think, ponder

私 [sī] Private

厶 [sī] Private

厶 (私字部) [sīzìbù] 'Private' radical

司 [sī] Take charge of

丝 [sī] Silk, thread, trace

死 [sǐ] Death

巳 [sì] The sixth 'Terrestrial branch' element

四 [sì] Four

灬 (四点火) [sìdiǎnhuǒ] 'Four dotted fire' radical

寺 [sì] Temple

司马 [Sīmǎ] A military official, A Chinese surname

司徒 [Sītú] An official of ritual ceremony, A Chinese surname

松 [sōng] (M) Pine

宋 [sòng] A Chinese dynasty, A Chinese surname

讼 [sòng] Praise

颂 [sòng] Praise, song

苏 [sū]: Chinese surname; 江苏 [Jiāngsū] name of a province in China, 苏醒 [sūxǐng]: regain consciousness

肃 [sù] Solemn, serious

素 [sù] Vegetarian, simple, plain

算 [suàn] Calculate

遂 [suì] Satisfy

岁 [suì] Age

孙 [sūn] Grand child, descendent, A Chinese surname

T

它 [tā] It

台 [tái] Platform

太 [tài] Excessive

泰 [tài] Peace

谭 [tán] A Chinese surname

谈 [tán] Talk

汤 [tāng] Soup, A Chinese surname

唐 [táng] A Chinese dynasty, A Chinese surname

堂 [táng] Hall, cousins (father' side)

涛 [tāo] Big waves

逃 [táo] Escape
陶 [táo] Ceramics, A Chinese surname
疼 [téng] Hurt, ache
提 [tí] Lift
扌 提手旁 [tíshǒupáng] 'Hand' radical
体 [tǐ] Body
天 [tiān] Sky, heaven, day
添 [tiān] Add on, replenish, increase
田 [tián] Field, cultivated land, A Chinese surname
甜 [tián] Sweet
调 [tiáo] Adjust
铁 [tiě] Iron
厅 [tīng] Hall, Ministry
廷 [tíng] Imperial court
婷 [tíng] Graceful, pretty
通 [tōng] Unimpeded, connect, communicate, through
同 [tóng] Same, similar
冂 (同字筐) [tóngzìkuāng] 'Frame of the character 同' radical
童 [tóng] Child, A Chinese surname
桐 [tóng] Tung tree, Paulownia tree
统 [tǒng] Unify, unite, rule
偷 [tōu] Steal
头 [tóu] Head
土 [tǔ] Earth
土 (土字部) [tǔzìbù] 'Earth' radical
兔 [tù] Rabbit
团 [tuán] Group, unite
推 [tuī] Push
吞 [tūn] Swallow

W

歪 [wāi] Crooked
外 [wài] Outer, external
湾 [wān] Bay (sea, river)
完 [wán] Finish
丸 [wán] Pills
婉 [wǎn] Gracious, tactful
晚 [wǎn] Night, late
万 [wàn] Ten thousand, myriad; Chinese surname
汪 [wāng] A body of water, A Chinese surname
王 [wáng] Ruler, king, A Chinese surname
王 (王字旁) [wángzìpáng] 'King' radical
往 [wǎng] Towards
网 [wǎng] Net
望 [wàng] Look at
危 [wēi] Danger
为 [wéi] For, as
伟 [wěi] Great
玮 [wěi] Name of a jade, rare, precious
尾 [wěi] Tail
未 [wèi] The eight dizhi
魏 [wèi] An ancient Chinese kingdom, A Chinese surname
卂 [wéi] Chinese surname
卫 [wei] Health
温 [wēn] Warm, A Chinese surname
文 [wén] Culture, language, writing, A Chinese surname
文 (文字部) [wénzìbù] 'Script' radical
闻 [wén] Listen
问 [wèn] Ask, enquire
翁 [wēng] Elderly man, A Chinese surname
我 [wǒ] I, me

459

卧 [wò] Sleep
巫 [wū] Wizard, witch, A
  Chinese surname
屋 [wū] House
武 [wǔ] Martial art, fighting, A
  Chinese surname
无 [wú] Without
吴 [wú] Ancient Chinese
  kingdom, A Chinese surname
五 [wǔ] Five
五行 [wǔxíng] Five determinant
  elements
武 [wǔ] Martial art
午 [wǔ] The seventh dizhi, noon
务 [wǔ] Affair, business, matters
戊 [wù] The fifth tiangan
悟 [wǔ] Awakening, realisation,
  aware

X

西 [xī] West, occidental
夕 [xī] Sunset
夕 (夕字头) [xīzìtóu] 'Sunset'
  radical
希 [xī] Hope, wish; Rare,
  uncommon
茜 [xī] A feminine name
溪 [xī] Brook
熹 [xī] Bright, dawn
细 [xì] Fine, meticulous
媳 [xí] Daughter-in-law
惜 [xī] Cherish, value, treasure
霞 [xiá] Morning / evening glow
夏 [xià] Summer, a Chinese
  dynasty
下 [xià] Below
先 [xiān] Earlier, in advance
娴 [xián] Refined, gentle
贤 [xián] Virtuous, noble
闲 [xián] Free time, unoccupied

县 [xiàn] County
显 [xiǎn] Prominent,
  conspicuous
现 [xiàn] Present
香 [xiāng] Fragrance, scented;
  savoury; popular
相 [xiāng] Mutual
湘 [xiāng] A dialect group
乡 [xiāng] Village
翔 [xiáng] Soar, hover in the air
享 [xiǎng] Enjoy
详 [xiáng] Auspicious,
  propitious
想 [xiǎng] Think, imagine
象 [xiàng] Like, resemble
萧 [xiāo] Dreary, desolate
晓 [xiǎo] Dawn, know
小 [xiǎo] Little, small; young
小 (小字部) [xiǎozìbù] 'Small'
  radical
笑 [xiào] Laugh
邪 [xié] Evil
写 [xiě] Write
谢 [xiè] Thank, decline, a
  Chinese surname
辛 [xīn The eighth 'Celestial
  stem'
新 [xīn] New
心 [xīn] Heart; mind
心 (心字底) [xīnzìdǐ] 'Heart'
  radical
欣 [xīn] Happy, joyous
信 [xìn] Trustworthy, reliable
星 [xīng] Star
行 [xíng] Walk
形 [xíng] Shape
姓 [xìng] Surname
兴, 興 [xìng] Prosper, flourish
兄 [xiōng] Elder brother

兄弟 [xiōngdì] Brother; 兄弟爻 [xiōngdìyáo] – a hexagram line relationship

熊 [xióng] Bear (animal)

雄 [xióng] Masculine

凶 [xiōng] Fierce

休 [xiū] Rest

修 [xiū] Cultivate, study

秀 [xiù] Elegant

须 [xū] Need to

戌 [xū] The eleventh 'Terrestrial branch'

徐 [xú] Slowly, gently, A Chinese surname

许 [xǔ] Permit, allow, A Chinese surname

婿 [xù] 女婿 [nǚxù] Son-in-law

绪 [xù] thread, clues

旭 [xù] Rising sun, dawn

宣 [xuān] Declare, announce

璇 [xuán] Beautiful jade

玄 [xuán] Mysterious

薛 [xuē] A Chinese surname

学 [xué] Learn, study, knowledge

雪 [xuě] Snow

血 [xuě] Blood

寻 [xún] Search

迅 [xùn] Rapid

训 [xùn] Teach, lecture, coach, instruct

巽 [xùn] Joy, a trigram / hexagram

驯 [xùn] Tame

Y

压 [yā] Press

亚 [yà] Asia

雅 [yǎ] elegant

烟 [yān] Cigarette, smoke

严 [yán] Strict, severe, A Chinese surname

言 [yán] Speech

讠 (言字旁) [yánzìpáng] 'Speech' radical

延 [yán] Prolong

颜 [yán] Colour, A Chinese surname

阎 [yán] King of Hell

炎 [yán] Heat, flame

盐 [yán] Salt

言 [yán] Speech

艳 [yàn] Colourful, gorgeous, glamorous

妍 [yán] Beautiful

岩 [yán] Boulder

燕 [yàn] Swallow

羊 [yáng] Goat

阳 [yáng] of yīnyáng, Masculine

洋 [yáng] Ocean

杨 [yáng] A Chinese surname

杨, 楊 [yáng] (M) Poplar tree

扬, 揚 [yáng] Raise up, propagate

幺 [yāo] One

幺 (幺字旁) [yāozìpáng] 'One' radical

尧 [yáo] Name of ancient emperor

姚 [yáo] A Chinese surname

耀 [yào] Brilliance, glorious

要 [yào] Want

叶 [yè] Leaf, a Chinese surname

晔 [yè] Bright, light

一 [yī] One

衣 [yī] Clothing

衤 (衣字旁) [yīzìpáng] 'Clothing' radical

依 [yī] Depend on

医 [yī] Medical

义 [yì] Righteousness

弋 (弋字旁) [yìzìpáng]
  'Dagger-axe' radical
仪 [yí] External appearance
姨 [yí] Mother's sister
怡 [yí] Composed, pleasant
宜 [yí] Suit, convenient
易 [yì] Ease, change
乙 [yǐ] The second Tiangan
意 [yì] Meaning
忆 [yì] Recollect, remember
艺 [yì] Artistic
益 [yì] Benefits
逸 [yì] Peace, tranquillity, leisure
亿 [yì] One hundred millions
异 [yì] Different
音 [yīn] Music
阴 [yīn] yīn of yīnyáng
茵 [yīn] Carpet
寅 [yín] The third dizhi
尹 [yǐn] Ancient official title
饮 [yǐn] Drink
引 [yǐn] Draw in
印 [yìn] Press, print
瑛 [yīng] Pretty jade, lustre of
  jade
樱 [yīng] Cherry
应 [yīng] Respond, Should
鹰 [yīng] Hawk, eagle, falcon
英 [yīng] Illustrious, heroic
颖 [yíng] Clever, gifted
盈 [yíng] Surplus, Profit, filled
永 [yǒng] Forever, eternal,
  perpetual
勇 [yǒng] Courageous, brave
用 [yòng] Use
邮 [yóu] Postal
优 [yōu] Merit, strong point,
  excel, outstanding
忧 [yōu] Worry
尤 [yóu] Particularly, Especially

尤 (尤字旁) [yóuzìpáng]
  'Particularly' radical
由 [yóu] From
酉 [yǒu] The tenth dizhi
友 [yǒu] Friend
有 [yǒu] Have, possess, own
又 [yòu] Again
又 (又字部) [yòuzìbù] 'Again'
  radical
幼 [yòu] Young, tender
右 [yòu] Right
阝 (右耳旁) [yòu 'ěrpáng]
  'Right ear' radical
鱼 [yú] Fish
于 [yú] At, A Chinese surname
余 [yú] Surplus, A Chinese
  surname
禺 [yú] A type of monkey
语 [yǔ] Language
裕 [yù] Plentiful, affluent,
  abundant
玉 [yù] Jade
豫 [yù] Joy – a hexagram
袁 [yuán] A Chinese surname
源 [yuán] Source, origin, roots
元 [yuán] Beginning, primary,
  dollar
远 [yuǎn] Far
月 [yuè] Month
月 月字旁 [yuèzìpáng] 'Moon'
  radical
粤 [yuè] Guangdong
岳 [yuè] Wife's parent
越 [yuè] Jump across
云 [yún] Cloud
运 [yùn] Cycle, age, period
允 [yǔn] Permit

Z

灾 [zāi] Disaster

462

在 [zài] At
藏 [zàng] Tibet
早 [zǎo] Early
泽 [zé] Wetland
曾 [zēng] Great grand child or parent, A Chinese surname
增 [zēng] Increase
翟 [zhái] A Chinese surname
詹 [zhēn] A Chinese surname
展 [zhǎn] Exhibit
湛 [zhàn] Deep
张 [zhāng] Open, extend, A Chinese surname
章 [zhāng] Article
长 [zhǎng] Chief, Head
丈 [zhàng] Elder male relative
帐 [zhàng] Tent
赵 [zhào] A Chinese surname
肇 [zhào] Beginning
找 [zhǎo] Search
折 [zhé] Bend
哲 [zhé] Learned, philosophy
这 [zhè] This
贞 [zhēn] Faithful, loyal, chaste
珍 [zhēn] Treasure, precious
浈 [zhēn] Part of the name of 浈江[Zhēnjiāng]
圳 [zhèn] Farm drainage
震 [zhèn] Vibrate, shock, a trigram, hexagram
正 [zhēng] Proper, right, correct, principled
争 [zhēng] Fight for
征 [zhēng] Expedition, journey, conquer
蒸 [zhēng] Steaming
郑 [zhèng] A Chinese surname, 郑重 [zhèngzhòng]: serious, solemn
之 [zhī] Belong to
支 [zhī] Branch

知 [zhī] Know
指 [zhǐ] Finger, point
止 [zhǐ] End, Terminate
智 [zhì] Intelligence, intellect, wisdom
纸 [zhǐ] Paper
侄 - 侄儿 [zhí'ér] Nephew (brother's son); 侄女 [zhínǔ] Brother's daughter
治 [zhì] govern, rule, manage, control
致 [zhì] present, deliver
志 [zhì] Resolve, will, aspiration
忠 [zhōng] Loyal
中 [zhōng] Centre, central, middle
钟 [zhōng] Bell, clock, A Chinese surname
终 [zhōng] End, final
重 [zhòng] Heavy, emphasise, major, important
周 [zhōu] Week
州 [zhōu] A state, territory or area
宙 [zhòu] Universe, Cosmos
猪 [zhū] Pig
朱 [zhū] Scarlet, A Chinese surname
珠 [zhū] Pearl
竹 [zhú]
主 [zhǔ] Chief
助 [zhù] Help, aid
传 [zhuàn] Book
庄 [zhuāng] Village, A Chinese surname
壮 [zhuàng] Powerful
桌 [zhuō] Table
资 [zī] Resource, capital, qualification
子 [zǐ] Son, child

子 (子字部) [zǐzìbù] 'Child' radical

子孙 [zǐsūn] Descendent; 子孙 爻 [zǐsūnyáo] a hexagram line relationship

紫 [zǐ] Purple

自 [zì] Self

字 [zì] Words

宗 [zōng] Ancestor

总 [zǒng] Overall

邹 [zōu] A Chinese surname

走 [zǒu] Move, walk

辶 (走之部) [zǒuzhībù] 'Movement' radical

族 [zú] Race

足 [zú] Leg, sufficient

足 (足字部) [zúzìbù] 'Leg' radical

祖 [zǔ] Ancestors

阻 [zǔ] Impede

最 [zuì] The most

左 [zuǒ] Left

阝 (左耳旁) [zuǒ'ěrpáng] 'Left ear' radical

坐 [zuò] Sit

座 [zuò] Seat

作 [zuò] Make, compose

About the Author

DR. YOW YIT SENG 饶逸生 (Yit-Seng Yow in Western countries) comes from a family of Chinese school educationists in Malaysia. His father, 饶君良 alias Yow Soo 饶恕 alias Yow Chin Ping 饶劍萍, had set up Chinese schools for several decades since the early thirties, notably in the states of Johore, Pahang and Kuala Lumpur. His mother Tan Boon Kwang 陈坤光 was also a Chinese school teacher. Dr. Yow was educated in a Chinese language primary school; he then continued his high school in English. He graduated from the faculty of agriculture, University of Malaya in 1973. In 1980 he obtained the degree of *Docteur Ingénieur* from the University of Montpellier, France, majoring in food engineering and technology. He speaks and writes English, Mandarin, French as well as Bahasa Malaysia. He has served as a full-time/part-time lecturer to several universities in Malaysia.

In addition to his technical and professional expertise, he has strong interests in various aspects of Chinese culture. In Australia he has been involved in numerous social and cultural activities. He was active in Chung Wah Association 中华会馆, the major ethnic Chinese association in Western Australia. He was the editor of *Chung Wah News*, a bilingual newsletter, when he began writing articles about the ethnic Chinese. He was also the chairperson of the Chung Wah Chinese community language schools run by the Association during weekends.

He has served in the 'Western Australian Ethnic Community Council' which collectively represents various ethnic groups in Western Australia.

Dr. Yow was also the chairman of the 'Perth-Nanjing Friendship City' committee set up by the city of Perth to foster the two friendship cities.

He was also the Vice President of the Australia China Business Council (Western Australia), and had served as a member of the Governing Council of Central TAFE, a government owned technical college, when the College was expanding into China.

He was the author of the 'Chinese people' for the 'living in harmony' seminars, run by the Western Australian Chinese Chamber of Commerce to promote community understanding.

Dr. Yow currently provides consultancy services. He could be contacted at *yitseng@gmail.com*

Index